MW01253131

Ways of Living

Ways of Living

Work, Community and Lifestyle Choice

Edited By

Paul Blyton
Professor of Industrial Relations and Industrial Sociology, Cardiff Business School, Cardiff University, UK

Betsy Blunsdon
Senior Lecturer, School of Management, Deakin University, Australia

Ken Reed
Associate Professor, School of Management, Deakin University, Australia

Ali Dastmalchian
Dean, Faculty of Business, University of Victoria, Canada

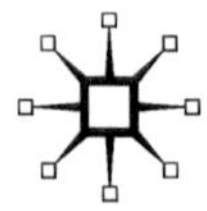

First published 2010 by
PALGRAVE MACMILLAN

Palgrave Macmillan in the UK is an imprint of Macmillan Publishers Limited, registered in England, company number 785998, of Houndmills, Basingstoke, Hampshire RG21 6XS.

Palgrave Macmillan in the US is a division of St Martin's Press LLC, 175 Fifth Avenue, New York, NY 10010.

Palgrave Macmillan is the global academic imprint of the above companies and has companies and representatives throughout the world.

Palgrave® and Macmillan® are registered trademarks in the United States, the United Kingdom, Europe and other countries.

ISBN: 978–0–230–20228–3 hardback

This book is printed on paper suitable for recycling and made from fully managed and sustained forest sources. Logging, pulping and manufacturing processes are expected to conform to the environmental regulations of the country of origin.

A catalogue record for this book is available from the British Library.

A catalogue record for this book is available from the Library of Congress.

10 9 8 7 6 5 4 3 2 1
19 18 17 16 15 14 13 12 11 10

Printed and bound in Great Britain by
CPI Antony Rowe, Chippenham and Eastbourne

Contents

List of Tables vii

List of Figures viii

Preface ix

Contributors x

1 Social Change and Ways of Living: An Introduction 1
Betsy Blunsdon, Ken Reed, Paul Blyton and Ali Dastmalchian

Part I Lifestyle and Identity

2 An Analysis of Time Use to Reveal National Differences in Lifestyle Patterns 17
Ken Reed and Guy Cucumel

3 Households, Work, Time Use and Energy Consumption 33
Steven McEachern

4 Longer to Launch: Demographic Changes in Life-Course Transitions 75
Rosemary A. Venne

5 Fortunate Lives: Professional Careers, Social Position and Life Choices 99
Tanya Castleman and Rosslyn Reed

6 'Live to Work or Work to Live?' The Search for Work-life Balance in Twenty-first Century Japan 120
Tim Craig

Part II Community

7 Personal Communities and Lifestyle: The Role of Family, Friends and Neighbours 147
Betsy Blunsdon and Nicola McNeil

8 To Downshift or Not to Downshift? Why People Make and don't Make Decisions to Change their Lives 175
Carmel Goulding and Ken Reed

9 Ways of Life after Redundancy: Anatomy of a Community Following Factory Closure 202
Paul Blyton and Jean Jenkins

Part III Work and Organisations

10 What Do (And Don't) We Know About Part-Time Professional Work? 223
Vivien Corwin

11 Work Values Across Cultures: The Role of Affect and Job Outcomes among Young Executives in Canada, Iran and Turkey 241
Hayat Kabasakal, Pinar Imer and Ali Dastmalchian

12 Designing for Well-Being: The Role of the Physical Work Environment 267
Claudia Steinke, Rei Kurosawa and Ali Dastmalchian

13 Shifting Responsibility for Health and Healthy Lifestyles: Exploring Canadian Trends 288
Angela Downey, Ali Dastmalchian, Helen M. Kelley, David Sharp and Kristene D'Agnone

Index 311

Tables

2.1	Sample sizes and numbers within each socio-demographic group, by country	24
2.2	List of activities	25
2.3	Socio-demographic differences in activity, by country	31
3.1	Descriptive statistics for data used in analysis	46
3.2	Linear regression of time spent on other activities, by household type	51
3.3	Linear regression of log (gross household income) on time use activities, by household type	52
4.1	Education enrolment (full and part-time) of 20–29 year olds (as a per cent of 20–29 year olds)	84
4.2	Percentage of population aged 25–34 with post-secondary education	84
4.3	Per cent of young adults living at home: Canada, U.S., and U.K.	86
4.4	Mean or median age at first marriage	88
4.5	Total fertility rate	89
4.6	Key population statistics – Canada, U.S., U.K. and Sweden, 2008	89
6.1	Workers' compensation claims, 2002–06[32]	131
7.1	Coding schema for content analysis of interviews	157
8.1	Demographic details of study sample	183
11.1	Loadings from factor analysis of items assessing work values	250
11.2	Means, standard deviations, Cronbach alphas and intercorrelations among study variables* (n=20)	253
11.3	Regression analyses results for job satisfaction as the dependent variable	254
11.4	Regression analyses results for performance as the dependent variable	256
11.5	Means comparisons (analysis of variance) and multiple comparisons (Scheffé tests) between Turkey, Iran and Canada	257
12.1	Results of the principal components analysis (n=180)	281
12.2	Descriptive statistics (aggregated measures; n=180)	283
13.1	The incidence of workplace health activities, 1996 and 2006	303

Figures

2.1	All four countries – dimensions 1 X 2	27
2.2	All four countries – dimensions 1 X 3	28
2.3	Age and gender differences in activity – Canada	29
2.4	Age and gender differences in activity – U.K.	29
2.5	Age and gender differences in activity – Australia	30
2.6	Age and gender differences in activity – France	30
3.1	A model of time use, income and energy consumption	34
3.2	Proportion of time spent in different locations in an average day by Australians	36
3.3	Proportion of time spent with particular groups in different locations in an average day by Australians	38
3.4	Household expenditure on electricity per annum by gross household income level	50
3.5	Relationships between time use, income and electricity expenditure – all households	55
3.6	Relationship between time use, income and electricity expenditure – by household type	56–57
3.7	Relationship between time use, income and expenditure on motor vehicle fuel – by household type	58–59
4.1	Median age of first marriage in the U.S. 1950–2006	87
6.1	Generic model of the influences and outcomes of individuals' work-life choices	122
6.2	Applied model: the influences and outcomes of individuals' work-life choices in Japan	125
8.1	Key influences on lifestyle change	191
8.2	The life trajectory of a lifestyle changer – common themes and patterns	194

Preface

The chapters in this volume were presented at an international colloquium held in Melbourne in December 2008. Four years earlier the same editorial team organised a similar event which resulted in the publication of *Work-Life Integration: International Perspectives on the Balancing of Multiple Roles* (Palgrave Macmillan, 2006). We found the experience of bringing the chapter authors together for discussion and reflection prior to chapter finalisation to be both productive and meaningful, and therefore wanted to utilise this approach again. However, unlike the earlier publication, which was squarely focused on the issue of work-life balance, what we became increasingly aware of in the intervening period was the greater need to situate continuing work-life discussions within a broader context.

We have sought to do this by inviting contributors to write chapters on a series of issues which help shape the contexts within which people develop and experience the relationship between their paid work lives and their lives outside work. These include chapters that explore values, identity and community, ones that examine how people use their time, and ones that consider the role that work organisations – their policies, practices and physical design – play in individual well-being. Overall we hope that this combination stimulates further interest in exploring the broader contexts within which the relationship between work and non-work lives are located.

Paul Blyton
Betsy Blunsdon
Ken Reed
Ali Dastmalchian
Cardiff, Melbourne and Victoria, May 2009

Contributors

Betsy Blunsdon is a Senior Lecturer in Management at Deakin University, Victoria, Australia and Co-director of Deakin's Computer Assisted Research Facility. Her main research interests include understanding how significant others (family, friends, neighbours) influence lifestyle decisions; issues around sustainability and lifestyle; understanding social and workplace trust and institutional level confidence; and the impact of organisational change on the individual experience of work, family and community. Her publications include work on organisational flexibility, work-family integration, and employee-management trust.

Paul Blyton is Professor of Industrial Relations and Industrial Sociology at Cardiff Business School, and a Research Associate in the ESRC Centre for Business Relationships, Accountability, Sustainability and Society (BRASS) at Cardiff University. His main research interests include workers' experience of working time schedules, and the relationship between working time and non-work life. Recent and forthcoming publications include *The Sage Handbook of Industrial Relations* (co-edited with N. Bacon, J. Fiorito and E. Heery, 2008) and *The Realities of Work* (with M. Noon, 4th Edition, 2010).

Tanya Castleman is Professor of Information Systems at Deakin University, Australia and is Head of the Deakin Business School. Her background in organisational sociology has underpinned her research on diversity and gender management issues and incorporation of technology, in particular eBusiness technologies, in the workplace. She has conducted research projects for business organisations, unions and government agencies.

Vivien Corwin is Assistant Professor of Organizational Behavior and Service Management at the University of Victoria, British Columbia, Canada. Her main research interests include work-life balance, meaning in work, and work and identity. Her research has been published in *Harvard Business Review, Journal of Organizational Behavior,* and *American Behavioral Scientist.*

Tim Craig is a Professor at Doshisha University's Institute for Language and Culture, Japan and guitarist and lead vocalist for the Zen Brothers band. Until 2008 he was Associate Professor of International Business and MBA Program Director at Canada's University of Victoria. His research, writing, and teaching cover a wide range of areas, including management, Japan, popular culture, and language learning.

Guy Cucumel is Professor of Quantitative Methods and Accounting at the École des sciences de la gestion of Université du Québec à Montréal (ESG UQAM), Canada and a member of the Centre de recherche sur les innovations sociales (CRISES) of UQAM. He presently serves as Associate Dean of Research at ESG UQAM. His main research interests include time use data analysis and consensus in cluster analysis. Recent publications include *Selected Contributions in Data Analysis and Classification* (co-edited with P. Brito, P. Bertrand and F. De Carvalho, 2007 Springer, Berlin).

Kristene D'Agnone received an MSc in Management from the University of Lethbridge. Her research interests have focussed on the integration of health care services, health promotion and organisational change.

Ali Dastmalchian is Professor of Organizational Analysis and Dean, Faculty of Business, University of Victoria, Canada. His recent research interests include organisational change, organisational design in health care, and healthy organisations. His work has appeared in journals such as the *British Journal of Industrial Relations, Industrial and Labor Relations Review* and *Human Relations*.

Angela Downey is an Associate Professor of Accounting at the Faculty of Business, University of Victoria, Canada. Her research interests are centred in the health environment with a special focus on measurement and design of meaningful metrics for evaluation. Her latest research in this area investigates the steps taken by successful firms to build a "wellness culture". She has published extensively on the role of measurement in health promotion and prevention as well as management's motivation to undertake worksite wellness programming.

Carmel Goulding is a PhD student at Deakin University, Australia. Her main research interests include the role of values in lifestyle choice and alternative lifestyle patterns. Previously she worked as a tourism economist and project manager with organisations in industry and government.

Pinar Imer is a PhD Candidate and Research Assistant in the Department of Management, Bogaziçi University, Istanbul, Turkey. Her research interests include the relationships between individual attitudes and both individual and interpersonal behaviours in work life as well as their potential causes.

Jean Jenkins is Lecturer in Human Resource Management at Cardiff University. Her research interests centre on employment relations in the manufacturing sector, particularly in the clothing industry, and employees' experiences in the increasingly internationalised market for labour. Her recent publications include *Key Concepts in Work* (with Paul Blyton), Sage 2007.

Hayat Kabasakal is Professor of Organisation Studies at the Management Department of Bogaziçi University, Istanbul, Turkey. Her research interests centre on organisational behavior, with a focus on leadership, culture, attitudes, and gender in organisations. She has published widely in journals such as the *Journal of Strategic Management*, *Journal of Applied Psychology*, *Journal of World Business*, and *International Journal of Human Resource Management*. She is the co-editor of *Human Side of Disasters* (Bogaziçi University Press).

Helen M. Kelley is an Associate Professor of Information Systems in the Faculty of Management and Director of the Master of Science in Management Program at the University of Lethbridge. Her research focuses on the individual user of information, enterprise resource planning, and eHealth technologies, viewed from social cognitive and attributional perspectives, within medical, governmental, and entrepreneurial settings.

Rei Kurosawa is a Research Assistant for Cohos Evamy Integratedesign and a student in Urban Studies with the Faculty of Social Sciences at the University of Calgary, Canada.

Steven McEachern is a Lecturer in Management in the Graduate School of Business at Curtin University of Technology. His research interests include industrial relations, work-life balance and household time use and decision-making.

Nicola McNeil is a Lecturer in Management at Latrobe University, Australia. Her main research interests include the impact of institutional forces on organisational practices. Her PhD thesis investigates the development of organisational strategies in pluralistic contexts. Other broad areas of research interests include organisation theory and the integration of work with other facets of life.

Ken Reed is Associate Professor and the director of an academic survey research centre at Deakin University. He is also currently Chair of the Australian Consortium of Social and Political Research Inc (ACSPRI) a consortium of universities and government agencies whose objective is to advance social science methodology in Australia. His main areas of research are in organisational theory and the sociology of work. His current research focuses on the issue of how people make choices about lifestyle, and the roles that societal institutions and social networks play in shaping those choices.

Rosslyn Reed is an Honorary Research Associate of the Faculty of Arts and Social Sciences at the University of Technology Sydney (UTS). She is a sociologist with a long-standing interest in researching work, employment and organisations with particular reference to gender and equal employment opportunities.

David Sharp is Associate Professor in the managerial accounting and control group at the Richard Ivey School of Business at the University of western Ontario. Apart from his interest in the role of workplace wellness programmes in reducing health care costs, his recent research includes cross-cultural ethics in the accounting profession, published (with Jeffrey Cohen and Laurie Pant) in *Contemporary Accounting Research, Journal of Business Ethics* and other publications.

Claudia Steinke is the Research Lead for Cohos Evamy's research initiatives in Calgary, Canada, with specialisation in Health Care. Her main research and teaching interests are in the areas of organisational design, organisational climate, service management, and health services research. She has a degree in nursing from the University of British Columbia, an MSc in management from the University of Lethbridge, and a PhD in business and public administration from the University of Victoria. Claudia specializes in applying a service industry perspective to the design of health care services with emphasis on physical design and service climate.

Rosemary A. Venne is an Associate Professor in the Department of Human Resources and Organizational Behaviour at the Edwards School of Business at the University of Saskatchewan. Her research interests include demography as it relates to human resource issues, including labour supply, aging of the labour force, and changing career patterns. Research interests also include hours of work, and alternative work-time arrangements, especially as these relate to an aging labour force.

1

Social Change and Ways of Living: An Introduction

Betsy Blunsdon, Ken Reed, Paul Blyton and Ali Dastmalchian

An important theme to emerge from our earlier collection, *Work-Life Integration* (Blyton et al., 2006), was the importance of understanding the experience and impact of work within a broader context than has often been the case hitherto. We were also very aware of a key issue in the work-life debate: the degree to which lifestyles, or ways of living, reflect choices motivated by personal values and preferences rather than economic, social, or cultural constraints. We aim to extend these themes and issues in the present volume and more explicitly to consider the factors that influence individual lifestyles. We do this by exploring aspects of lifestyle and identity before examining societal influences on ways of living, the relevance of social networks and geographic communities for lifestyle choices, and the significance of organisational policies and practices (in conjunction with other institutional actors such as government) for lifestyle outcomes.

Lifestyle, preferences and choice

Catherine Hakim's argument, known as preference theory, has been the focus of an 'agency versus structure' debate in recent research in the work-life area. She argues that women's participation in employment primarily reflects differences in preferences for involvement in work, home, or a combination of the two, rather than the economic and social constraints that women face (though she recognises that economic and social structures still impose a degree of constraint on employment choices, and that women's choices are more constrained than men's) (Hakim 2000, 2002). This contrasts with the view of others, however (for example, Crompton and Harris, 1998a, 1998b; McRae, 2003; Probert, 2002, 2005; Probert and Murphy, 2001) that choice remains highly constrained for some social groups, notably mothers of young children, whose options are limited by the provision of jobs, access to transport and the provision of affordable childcare. McRae (2003) also suggests that women are subject to normative constraints, in that social expectations of gender roles are internalised to form part of women's identities and, through the attitudes of those around them, are a persistent component of the social environment. A study by Reed and Blunsdon (2006) reported in our earlier volume, provides support for this. An analysis of survey data from over 40,000 people in 34 countries showed that normative constraints, as exemplified by the influence of religious affiliation on gender identities, affects choice in two ways: shaping evaluations of the desirability of certain courses of action (e.g. whether mothers of pre-school children should work); and influencing assessments of the feasibility of particular courses of action that depend on the approval of those with the power to provide or restrict opportunities. The debate over preference theory focuses on what roles choice and constraint play in women's employment patterns. However, we can consider this question more broadly by asking: what roles do individual choice and structural constraints play in shaping lifestyle? What factors shape lifestyle today? How free are we to choose? Have traditional structures and institutions shaping choices eroded? And if so, what are replacing those structures?

At the individual level, lifestyles reflect, on the one hand, habits and routines and on the other, choices. Sociological definitions of lifestyle focus on the 'patterns of unconstrained daily choice individuals make in leisure, shopping, recreation and so on' (Binkley 2007: 111). Time use and consumption patterns are important aspects of 'lifestyle' and reflect underlying sets of choices that people make. These choices are an indication of what individuals value, what they deem desirable, and the beliefs they have about the courses of action that are available. There is a widespread presumption that more choice leads to increased happiness because people best know what they want: increasing the options available to people is seen to improve the chances they will get what they want, and getting what one wants is more likely to make one happy. These are the principles that underlie economic models of individual choice-making where choice is seen as having high utility. Choice also connotes freedom and so is considered to be moral. As examples, this is a core principle in the abortion debate, and has been central to the legitimising of diversity of sexual orientation (and the rhetoric often associated with 'lifestyle choice' and the freedom to choose). Choice is therefore valued because it encompasses both moral and utilitarian values.

People, however, do seem to make 'wrong' lifestyle choices in that they find themselves in situations that make them unhappy. Dysfunctionality seems to be related to some choices (stress, drug abuse, and so on), and so-called 'lifestyle diseases' (such as atherosclerosis, heart disease, stroke, obesity and type 2 diabetes) are major issues for contemporary medicine. These outcomes may be the result of error – miscalculation or character flaws – on the part of those making choices and decisions, or it may be the result of the social context, or the environment, in which people find themselves and the habits that have been instilled in that environment.

To understand how people live their lives – their ways of living – we must understand both the values that motivate people, the beliefs that frame the way they interpret their worlds, and the social and institutional structures that constrain and provide opportunities for them to act on those desires and beliefs. In considering these, three societal changes that potentially shape modern lifestyles are particularly significant: changes in social structure; an increase in commodification and marketisation; and greater rationalisation through scientific knowledge and expertise. We will examine each of these briefly.

Structural change

Lifestyle construction is, on the one hand, an individual journey as argued by Bauman (2001). On the other hand, individuals are not isolated from others or their environments. As Jackson (2005: 20) observes: 'Modern society celebrates choice and personal opportunity, and at the same time we often find ourselves locked into rather predictable patterns of living, work and consuming'. Therefore, lifestyles may result as much from habits and routines as from choice. Structures in various forms hold people to traditions, habits and routines. Yet recent history is characterised by the re-structuring of a number of aspects of society. Constraints and opportunities that frame both habits and choices are embedded in social structure; and change in those societal structures alters the opportunities and constraints that individuals face. Elder-Vass (2008), drawing on Lopez and Scott (2000) identifies three dimensions of social structure – embodied structure, relational structure, and institutional structure.

Habits and routines are embodied structure, defined as,

> patterns of institutions and relations result[ing] from the actions of individuals who are endowed with the capacities or competencies that enable them to produce them by acting in organized ways. These capacities are behavioural dispositions, and so social structure has to be seen as an embodied structure. Embodied structures are found in the habits and skills that are inscribed in human bodies and minds and that allow them to produce, reproduce, and transform institutional structures and relational structures. (Lopez and Scott, 2000: 4)

One issue to understand lifestyle outcomes is in understanding the impact of norms and socialisation. So, for example, we know that lifestyle patterns are influenced by societal cultures and institutions which establish acceptable and preferable ways of acting that can last a lifetime (see, Reed and Cucumel, in this volume). Understanding habit is therefore important in understanding lifestyle (Jackson, 2005). Relying on established routines is efficient because it does not require complex decision making. However, habit can lead to inertia, which could explain the 'unhealthy or unsustainable lifestyle choices', noted earlier. These could be as much a result of habit (of which addiction is an extreme form) as choice. Yet, relational and institutional structural change can impact on the norms, routines and habits that form embodied structure.

Society is a relational structure – that is, a web of social networks and personal communities or interactions of individuals (Lopez & Scott, 2000; Elder-Vass, 2008). Beliefs and values are communicated through this web and norms are promulgated and enacted. Recent developments in empirical research demonstrate the importance and influence of these factors for understanding lifestyle. For example, obesity and smoking have recently been shown to be strongly influenced by the norms and expectations that arise from social networks (Christakis and Fowler, 2007, 2008).

Evidence is now also strong that social and environmental context have important implications for physical health outcomes (Reidpath et al., 2002; Warr, Tacitos, Kelaher and Klein, 2006) and psychological well-being (Ross et al., 2000; Sampson & Raudenbush, 2004). Embodied structure relies on an individual's commitment to norms of behaviour which, in turn, is linked to the effectiveness of sanctions for transgression or rewards for adherence. This depends on the strength of relationships within societies, social groups and communities. In social groups with dense social ties the consensus and support for norms are stronger and values are more homogeneous. The power of normative constraints lies in the individual's identification with the values of a group and the relative power of that group to exert influence on decision-making.

Changes in societal structures have meant that the decision-making demands on individuals have increased dramatically since the 1960s reflecting what Giddens (1991, 1994) refers to as the 'post-traditional' order. The social structures that dominated early modernity were based on a relatively clear and consensual understanding of cultural categories such as the nuclear family, defined gender roles, clear distinctions between family and others, and a clear division between 'work' and 'home life.' Institutions (e.g. , the state, welfare system, family, Fordist production and the industrial relations system) provided a normative structure that guided and framed life decisions. As the influence of these institutions has blurred and declined (on which, more below) individuals face less prescription about what is expected and acceptable in terms of life choices. It follows that with the erosion of rules comes the need to chart one's own course and construct one's own lifestyle and social network.

Post-traditional social order thus implies a greater choice of lifestyle and in the selection of significant social relationships. Where identity is changeable (because institution boundaries are fluid and ill defined) individuals must construct their own biographies in their own way and so may develop stronger commitments to those who affirm their identity than to families of origin (blood relations) (Giddens, 1994). This has been referred to as a shift from identifying with 'families of fate' to 'families of choice.' Families of choice are kin-like networks of relationships that are not based on blood-ties but on friendship and self-chosen commitment (Weeks, Heaphy and Donavan, 2001; Pahl and Pevalin, 2005). The empirical evidence to date finds that personal communities in the twenty-first century tend to comprise a mix of family and friends (Pahl and Pevalin, 2005; Spencer and Pahl, 2006; Blunsdon and McNeil, in this volume).

Personal communities are distinguished from social networks primarily because the former are defined by relations to a focal individual. One's work colleagues and school friends may form part of one's personal community but have no other connection to each other (Spencer and Pahl, 2006). The important point in understanding lifestyle is to consider the role that personal communities play in affecting both choice and habit. Personal communities, in differing degrees due to the strength of ties, reinforce common values, provide esteem and status, filter information that form the basis of beliefs, and provide models and cognitive scripts for decision-making (Cialdini, Kallgren and Reno, 1991; Goulding and Reed, in this volume). Adaptive choices – those choices that tend to respond to circumstantial change – will conform to the expectations imputed to one's personal community, cause a reconfiguration of relations, or lead to the construction of new social ties. Thus, personal communities provide both the support and normative constraints that encourage choice, based on routine and habit (embodied structure as discussed above). By the same token, personal communities are also a significant component of one's life situation; and so change within the community itself may provoke new choices and the emergence of differing interpretations, values and beliefs. Therefore understanding relational structure, as found in personal communities, is important in the study of lifestyle and lifestyle change (and is reflected in Blunsdon and McNeil, Goulding and Reed, and Blyton and Jenkins, in this volume).

Institutional structure

An important societal level change is represented in institutional structure. Institutional structure comprises the 'cultural or normative patterns that define the expectations that agents hold about each other's behavior and that organize their enduring relations with each other' (Lopez and Scott, 2000: 3). The period from the mid-nineteenth century to the 1960s was shaped by the development of a set of highly integrated institutions, with the growing dominance of the nation state. Stability was promoted through the legitimation of particular forms of social life (the nuclear family); knowledge (scientific); work (standard forms of employment based on the male breadwinner model); and statehood (nation state, welfare regimes) (Beck and Lau, 2005: 535). The 'post-traditional' order (Giddens, 1994) has transformed these institutions while the material and economic bases of modernity continue to expand (as through the rise in consumer culture.) The transformation of these institutions has altered the social landscape which is now comprised of a range of lifestyle configurations with different requirements for decision making, choice and for the legitimisation of different ways of living (Beck and Lau, 2005). Beck, Bonss and Lau (2003: 16) describe reflexive modernity as 'a vast field of social experiment, where under the pressure of globalization, various types of post-traditional social bonds and post-national imagined communities are being tried out in competition with each other.' It is thus timely, early in the twenty-first century, to explore this social landscape further to seek a greater understanding of the factors shaping and framing individual lifestyles today.

Marketisation and consumer culture

Since the Second World War, and especially since the 1960s, there has been a dramatic rise in the influence of the market and in consumer culture (Giddens, 1991, 1994) and a rise in affluence enabling people to purchase consumer goods and services. The shift in focus from production to consumption has created the notion of 'lifestyle goods'; as a result, there is not only choice in identity construction reflecting the decline in the influence of traditional structures, there is choice arising from the ability to 'buy an identity and the lifestyle that accompanies it' through consumer choice. Binkley (2007: 112) argues that 'lifestyles are seen as increasingly prominent in modern societies where the domain of unconstrained choice is seen as expanding – an effect partly attributable to erosion of the old culture of "mass" consumption, defined by uniformity and mass production, and the growing influence of a more personalized culture of consumption'. Consumer culture, with the seductive representations of 'imagined or ideal lifestyles', has also created a new type of constraint for reflexive individuals. Bauman (2001: 147) summarises this and its impact on individuals: 'the quandary tormenting men and woman at the turn of the [21st] century is not so much how to obtain the identities of their choice and how to have them recognized by people around – but which identity to choose and how to keep alert and vigilant so that another choice can be made in case the previously chosen identity is withdrawn from the market or stripped of its seductive powers.'

A characteristic feature of a consumer society is that it is based on high turnover and rapid replacement rather than durability (Bauman, 2007) giving rise to calls to curb the excesses of overproduction and overconsumption (see Schor, 2005). However, the consumer culture answer to this is rapidly-changing fashion trends so that one can, and must, constantly change and redefine one's identify and self (see Bauman, 2007). This is especially true in marketing to young people as they acquiesce to seductive representations of identity through the purchase of constantly changing lifestyle brands and modeling through the media (Schor, 2004).

In this way, consumer culture provides those with the economic resources the ability to purchase, manipulate and change their lifestyle and lifestyle 'image'. But consumer culture also 'sets the rules of the game' in terms of what is desirable and acceptable. Where once traditional authority structures in western society dictated many of the societal rules and norms, now the market has taken over this role by setting the standards of fashion, fad and acceptance. We can question whether consumer culture, as enacted through the market, provides opportunities for individuals to be whoever they wish to be, or constrains individuals through economic, social, cultural and political rules and norms.

Rationalisation of knowledge and the rise of experts

As well as consumer culture and the market, authorities and experts exert a strong influence on the establishment of norms and in shaping what is considered to be rational and acceptable as individuals go about writing their own biographies. There has been an increasing trend to look to experts and authority based on scientific evidence since the 1950s and 60s. Rationalisation brings new specialist knowledge which, in turn, generates new occupations such as personal trainers, counselors, colour consultants, relationship advisors, personal shoppers, life coaches, and de-clutterers. Here marketisation (the commodification of experts' advice) and rationalisation reinforce each other in the lifestyle choice domain.

The role of authority and experts in health and lifestyle decision-making became institutionalised in western societies after a committee of experts in the U.S. reviewed the scientific literature on the effects of smoking on health. The 1964 report, *Smoking and Health: Report of the Advisory Committee to the Surgeon General,* provided unequivocal evidence that smoking was damaging to one's health, especially in relation to the risks associated with lung cancer. This report was pivotal in terms of public understanding, debate and policy regarding the role of scientific experts and governments in shaping individual behaviour towards matters of health. It is now, in the twenty-first century, expected that the public has a right to know and be kept abreast of the scientific discoveries that relate to health, well-being and lifestyle choices.

This holds true more broadly in terms of making choices that will affect longevity, vitality, fitness and overall health (this extends to many choices and risks including the risk of contracting sexually transmitted diseases and AIDS, the risk of exposing oneself to many types of cancers and the risks associated with what types of food one eats). And so we see an increase in the range of choices available to individuals and an increase in the information (based on experts and scientific evidence) about the consequences of these choices. This then shifts the responsibility for the decision, and its outcomes, more clearly to the individual.

Expertise and authority are now part of a more contested sphere. Employing organisations play a role in influencing individual lifestyle choices and opportunities. The role of organisations in individual ways of living and lifestyle has increased in recent years and has extended beyond work-life balance issues to include health, well-being, stress management, relaxation and other areas of 'health promotion' (see Downey et al., in this volume). These developments not only influence the employee's experience of work, but potentially impact on social networks and personal communities. Organisations may encourage balanced and sustainable lifestyles among their employees if they produce beneficial organisational outcomes in the form, for example, of reduced absenteeism and turnover and greater commitment to work. There is a trend towards discourses of 'healthy organisations' and 'workplace wellness'; many organisations now attempt to influence the lifestyle behaviour of their employees at an individual level in a number of areas including the social, physical and psychological aspects of health and health promotion and in creating workplace environments that enhance health and well-being (see, Stienke et al. and Kabasakal et al., in this volume).

And as we indicated earlier, from these changes and developments a number of questions arise. To what extent are individuals free to construct their own identities based on their own desires and preferences? What opportunities and constraints do individuals face in translating their preferences into desired ways of living? It is evident that the institutional structures that dictated the norms and rules of behaviour and shaped lifestyle decision making in previous decades have eroded for many in western twenty-first century societies. However, what are the new constraints and opportunities that shape our ways of life? Is the influence of traditional institutions, such as one's blood family or the church, being replaced by other types of influences such as one's geographic community, friendship group, or workplace? Does the market and the strength of consumer culture aid or limit individuals as they seek to form and reform their identities? What about the whims of the market and the pressures that organisations face in a global environment? How do these impact on individual choice and the ability to realise individual dreams and aspirations? And what roles do contemporary work organisations play in lifestyle decision-making? Are organisations the new 'Big Brother' in disseminating information about health, well-being and ways of living? Or, are organisations playing a key role in assisting individuals achieve the ways they wish to live through policies, practices and workplace design that inculcate well-being and enhance choice and freedom in identity construction and lifestyle formation?

Plan of the book

In the different contributions, we explore these issues by first investigating aspects of the question of what factors shape lifestyle and identity. In the following chapter, Ken Reed and Guy Cucumel show how national time-use (diary) data can be used to reveal differences in lifestyle patterns. This is a macro view of lifestyle through the lens of 'national differences', and helps gain greater understanding of how embodied structure manifests itself at the societal level and influences patterns of daily living. In Chapter 3, Steven McEachern also draws on time-use data to study the relationship between time spent on activities and household energy consumption. He builds on the argument that time devoted to employment outside the home influences domestic patterns and leisure in the home, which in turn affects energy use.

Rosemary Venne's chapter (Chapter 4) also provides a societal-level account, using a demographic approach to examine the changing pattern of family life in general, and the tendency for offspring to make the transitions into work, independent living and parenthood much later than in the past. Venne explores the different factors accounting for this trend, and draws on cross-national comparisons to explore the role of different welfare systems in facilitating or hindering these transitions. The focus of Tanya Castleman and Rosslyn Reed's chapter (Chapter 5) is also on younger age groups, in particular considering the lives of young professionals in the early stages of their careers. By drawing on longitudinal data, the authors examine the implications of professional life, its demands and rewards, and the implications of these for decisions about other aspects of their respondents' lives. The chapter underlines the significance of work for this group and the perceived importance to them of building their lives around this work successfully to achieve their desired professional positions.

In the final chapter in Part One (Chapter 6), Tim Craig examines the issue of work-life balance in Japan. The author traces the economic, social and cultural factors that have hindered a work-life balance debate in the past and encouraged a strong 'presenteeism' work culture among many Japanese employees. He also points to the important changes taking place in Japanese society, and the way that factors are beginning to coincide to give a greater sense of legitimacy to a work-life balance discourse.

The authors of chapters in Part Two explore the influences of community, family, friends and significant others on individual lifestyle decision-making. In Chapter 7, Betsy Blunsdon and Nicola McNeil analyse types of personal community and interrogate the role that family, friends and neighbours play in lifestyle choices and outcomes. By drawing on detailed personal accounts, the authors highlight in particular the continuing importance of family ties in shaping people's lives. In Chapter 8, Carmel Goulding and Ken Reed also consider the role of personal communities in lifestyle outcomes. However, their particular focus is on the triggers and factors that lead to major lifestyle change, in particular the decision to 'downshift'. Goulding and Reed's investigation also considers the constraints on making a major lifestyle change even in situations where individuals are leading unsatisfying lives. Constraint is also an important theme in Paul Blyton and Jean Jenkins' discussion (in Chapter 9) of the impact that redundancy and changes to patterns of work have had on individuals, their families and community after the closure of a clothing manufacturing plant in Wales. Like the previous chapter, these authors also highlight the interdependencies between individual lifestyle, social networks and the wider community.

One of the issues underlined by Blyton and Jenkins' account is the important place that paid work (and its absence) has in shaping how people are able to live their lives. In Part Three, a number of contributors consider other aspects of the role that workplaces and organisations play in framing the choices and constraints individuals experience in creating and maintaining their ways of life. In Chapter 10, Vivien Corwin reviews the subject of part-time professional work. Given the continued relevance for many of part-time work as a vehicle for achieving a more satisfying relationship between paid work and other activities, this examination, among other things, highlights the as yet unresolved issues for organisations to change their value systems to accommodate more successfully part-time professional workers into organisational practice.

In Chapter 11, Hayat Kabasakal, Pinar Imer and Ali Dastmalchian examine the influence of work values in different countries, and the relationships between the values people hold and other aspects of their work and non-work lives. In their comparison of young executives in Turkey, Canada and Iran, the authors highlight both significant differences evident between the different cultural contexts, but also certain general influences, such as the widespread significance a positive outlook has for other aspects of their respondents' work and non-work lives. In Chapter 12, Claudia Steinke, Rei Korosawa and Ali Dastmalchian consider the role that physical workplace design has for the experience of work. The authors explore this important, but in the past often neglected, topic by focusing on the design of health care facilities, and the potential for design solutions to improve employees' experiences of work. They argue that while increasing attention has been given to the significance of design for improving patient recovery, similar attention is required to address employee experiences. The theme of employee well-being is also addressed in the final chapter (Chapter 13) by Angela Downey and her colleagues. The authors point to the increasing role that work organisations are playing in health promotion activities (such as by providing advice on diet and fitness, counseling services to reduce smoking or stress, and monitoring facilities for blood pressure and cholesterol) and thereby exert a broader influence on their employees' ways of living.

Overall, the contributions point to the diverse areas that need to be incorporated into a broader understanding of the influences – the choices and constraints – that people face in patterning their lives. By examining how people spend their time, how families and communities influence the way people shape daily life, and the various roles that work organisations play in this regard, we gain a fuller picture of the constellation of factors that impact on lifestyle formation. Yet, we are aware too that this exploration remains incomplete. In this respect, the collection poses further questions to be answered; we hope that the discussions contained in the following chapters will inspire further research to better understand the factors shaping the ways in which we live our lives.

References

Bauman, Z. (2001) *The Individualized Society*. Cambridge: Polity.
Bauman, Z. (2000) *Liquid Modernity*. Cambridge: Polity.
Bauman, Z. (2007) *Consuming Life*. Cambridge: Polity.
Beck, U. and Lau, C. (2005) 'Second modernity as a research agenda: theoretical and empirical explorations in the "meta-change" of modern society', *British Journal of Sociology*, 56: 525–57.

Beck, U., Bonss, W. and Lau, C. (2003) 'The theory of reflexive modernization, problematic, hypotheses and research programme', *Theory, Culture and Society*, 20: 1–33.

Beck, U., Giddens, A. and Lash, S. (1994) (Eds.) *Reflexive Modernization, Politics, Tradition and Aesthetics in the Modern Social Order.* Stanford, CA: Stanford University Press.

Binkley, S. (2007) 'Governmentality and lifestyle studies', *Sociology Compass*, 1: 111–26.

Blyton, P., Blunsdon, B., Reed, K. and Dastmalchian, A. (Eds.) (2006) *Work-Life Integration.* Basingstoke: Palgrave Macmillan.

Christakis, N. and Fowler, J. (2007) 'The spread of obesity in a large social network over 32 years', *New England Journal of Medicine*, 357: 370–9.

Christakis, N. and Fowler, J. (2008) 'The collective dynamics of smoking in a large social network', *New England Journal of Medicine*, 358: 2249–58.

Cialdini R, Kallgren, C. and Reno, R. (1991) 'A focus theory of normative conduct: a theoretical refinement and re-evaluation of the role of norms in human behaviour', *Advances in Experimental Social Psychology*, 24, 201–34.

Crompton, R. and Harris, F. (1998a) 'A reply to Hakim',*British Journal of Sociology*, 49 (1): 144–50.

Crompton, R. and Harris, F. (1998b) 'Explaining women's employment patterns, orientations to work revisited', *British Journal of Sociology*, 49 (1): 118–37.

Elder-Vass, D. (2008) 'Integrating institutional, relational and embodied structure: an emergentist perspective', *The British Journal of Sociology*, 59: 281–99.

Giddens, A. (1991) *Modernity and Self-Identity: Self and Society in the Late Modern Age.* Oxford: Polity Press.

Giddens, A. (1994) 'Living in a post-traditional society', in U. Beck, A. Giddens and S. Lash, *Reflexive Modernization, Politics, Tradition and Aesthetics in the Modern Social Order.* Stanford, CA: Stanford University Press: 56–109.

Hakim, C. (2000) *Work-Lifestyle Choices in the 21st Century: Preference Theory.* Oxford: Oxford University Press.

Hakim, C. (2002) 'Lifestyle preferences as determinants of women's differentiated labor market careers,' *Work and Occupations*, 29 (4): 428–59.

Jackson, T. (2005) *Lifestyle Change and Market Transformation: A Briefing Paper for DEFRA's Market Transformation Programme'.* Guildford: University of Surrey Centre for Environmental Strategy.

Lopez, J. and Scott, J. (2000) *Social Structure.* Glasgow: Harper Collins.

McRae, S. (2003) 'Constraints and choices in mothers' employment careers: a consideration of Hakim's Preference Theory', *British Journal of Sociology*, 54: 317–38.

Probert, B. (2005) ' "Just couldn't fit it in": gender and unequal outcomes in academic careers', *Gender, Work and Organization*, 12: 50–72.

Pahl, R. and Spencer, L. (2004) 'Personal communities: not simply families of "fate" or "choice" ', *Current Sociology*, 52 (2): 199–221.

Pahl, R. and Pevalin, D.J. (2005) 'Between family and friends: a longitudinal study of friendship choice', *British Journal of Sociology*, 56 (3): 433–50.

Probert, B. (2002) ' "Grateful slaves" or "self-made women": a matter of choice or policy?' *Australian Feminist Studies*, 17: 7–17.

Probert, B. and Murphy, J. (2001) 'Majority opinion or divided selves? Research, work and family experiences', *People & Place*, 9: 25–33.

Reed, K. and Blunsdon, B. (2006) 'Should mothers work? An international comparison of the effect of religion on women's work and family roles,' in, Blyton, P., Blunsdon, B., Reed, K. and Dastmalchian, A. *Work-Life Integration, International Perspectives on the Balancing of Multiple Roles*. Basingstoke: Palgrave Macmillan: 135–49.

Reidpath, D., Burns, C., Garrard, J., Mahoney, M. and Townsend, M. (2002) 'An ecological study of the relationship between social and environmental determinants of obesity,' *Health & Place*, 8: 141–45.

Ross, C.E., Reynolds, J.R. and Geis, K.J. (2000) 'The contingent meaning of neighborhood stability for residents' psychological well-being', *American Sociological Review*, 63: 581–97.

Sampson, R.J. and Raudenbush, S.W. (2004) 'Seeing disorder: neighborhood stigma and the social construction of broken windows', *Social Psychology Quarterly*, 67: 319–42.

Schor, J.B. (2004) *Born to Buy: The Commercialized Child and the New Consumer.* New York: Scribner.

Schor, J.B. (2005) 'Sustainable consumption and worktime reduction', *Review of Industrial Ecology*, 9: 37–50.

Spencer, L. and Pahl, R. (2006) *Rethinking Friendship, Hidden Solidarities Today.* Princeton, NJ: Princeton University Press.

U.S. National Institute for Health and Safety. (http://www.cdc.gov/niosh/worklife/ cited April 1 2009).

Warr, D.J., Tacticos, T., Kelaher, M. and Klein, H. (2007) 'Money, stress, jobs: residents' perceptions of health-impairing factors in "poor" neighbourhoods', *Health & Place*, 13: 743–56.

Weeks, J., Heaphy, B. and Donovan, C. (2001) *Same Sex Intimacies: Families of Choice and Other Life Experiments.* London: Routledge.

Part I

Lifestyle and Identity

2

An Analysis of Time Use to Reveal National Differences in Lifestyle Patterns

Ken Reed and Guy Cucumel

Aims of the chapter

This chapter examines lifestyles as patterns of daily life, and explores how differences between societies shape these patterns. We use time-use data to compare people from four countries – Australia, Canada, France and the U.K. – with respect to the consumption activities that characterise daily life.

The sociological literature on lifestyles is dominated by analysing the consequences of increasing choice in society, focusing particularly on the way in which we make consumption choices, the link between such choices and identity, and how consumption expresses who we are and what we want to be. Ways of living in contemporary society are characterised in terms of 'consumer lifestyles' constructed by choices within the markets, media and models encompassed by consumer culture. This is in contrast to earlier times, where more clearly defined social roles, hierarchies and status groups largely determined identity and its expression through consumption and lifestyle.

The focus on consumer culture and choice draws attention to the dynamic and variable aspects of lifestyle. But consumption forms part of everyday life, which is more routine, mundane, and stable than accounts of contemporary consumer culture and lifestyles imply. Also, lifestyles develop in national contexts, in countries that have distinctive traditions of taste, preferences, style and conduct and which themselves contribute to identity formation and expression. So the aim of this chapter is to examine ways of living from the perspective of the activities in which people engage as part of their everyday routines and to compare these across four countries. Giddens has been a key figure in the analysis of lifestyles in post-traditional society, and says:

> A lifestyle involves a cluster of habits and orientations, and hence has a certain unity – ... – that connects options in a more or less ordered pattern. (...) [T]he selection or creation of lifestyles is influenced by group pressures and the visibility of role models, as well as by socioeconomic circumstances. (Giddens, 1991: 82)

This emphasises the routine, habitual, and stable as compared to the extraordinary, exotic, and ephemeral, and focuses on the importance of the social milieu in influencing styles of life. This reminds us that lifestyles are also formed by family relationships, educational experiences, community involvement, and work patterns.

Background

There are two distinct literatures on lifestyle. One is based in the fields of health and social medicine and is concerned with the effects of behaviours such as exercise, diet, and smoking and drinking on health. This literature is of limited relevance to the concerns of this chapter, and is not reviewed here. The second, which is more central to this chapter, focuses primarily on cultural consumption – activities that reflect taste and preferences – and, in particular, what these reveal about class structure and social stratification.

Theories proposed independently by Beck and by Giddens suggest a de-coupling of the association between class and lifestyle. As the institutions of modernity began to decline in influence, bases for lifestyle no longer simply reflect class position, as other aspects of social location (such as age, gender, ethnicity, and sexuality) create a wider range of possibilities for identification and thus identity (Beck, 1992; Giddens, 1991). A greater realm of possible characteristics become salient bases of identity as traditional institutions exert less influence over the choices people make and constrain those choices less. People find new ways to identify who they are.

A major source of this is the market for lifestyle components. As the authority of traditional institutions and communities have eroded, people are constrained both to define themselves 'reflexively' or performatively, and to make unconstrained choices in leisure, dress, recreation, diet and so on, in order to express individuality of taste and style (Beck, 1992; Giddens, 1991). A postmodern extension of this argument is that there is no longer any structural connection, or inherent unity, between social location and lifestyle. In this view, society previously offered a set of types of lifestyle that people selected on the basis of choices determined by socialisation into class cultures. Post-modern society offers an enormous range of possible lifestyle choices from which 'consumers' construct lifestyles. Individuals now have to choose from these possibilities, as consumption choices and as displays of taste (e.g. Bauman, 1988, 2002).

Early writers, such as Weber (1946) and Veblen (1924) emphasise the link between status hierarchies and social power, whereby consumption and expressions of taste serve as displays of social differentiation that indicate prestige. This theme is extended by Bourdieu (1984), who begins with a rejection of Weber's distinction between class and status. Weber sees class and status as different, but often empirically linked forms of stratification, with class defined by economic relations and status dependent on the capacity to evoke social deference. Instead, Bourdieu argues these are two dimensions – economic and symbolic – of a single hierarchy of class positions. Taste, and its expression, marks out distinctions between classes and symbolically represents social rankings. Thus Bourdieu's analysis links lifestyle to social structure – lifestyles reflect and affirm people's social location which, in turn, reproduces the structures that define social positions.

Bourdieu's empirical evidence was based on surveys undertaken in the 1960s in Paris. This raises the question that the links between lifestyle and class is a peculiarity of French society or the 1960s (or French society in the 1960s). Peterson and Simkus (1992) undertook a comparative study of upper-middle class respondents in Paris and New York as well as a U.S. and a French provincial city to see if elites in different societies chose friends on the same basis. They found that only in Paris did cultural taste predominate as the basis for friendship networks. In New York, for example, friends tended to be chosen on the basis of economic capital, independently of taste. This suggests that the link between taste and class established by Bourdieu's research are not characteristic of modern society in general, but are particular to French society.

More recently, in a U.K. study Gayo-Cal, Savage and Warde (2006) used correspondence analysis to analyse preferences for a range of cultural activities such as types of television programme, movies, books, music, art, eating out and sport. Their method is very similar to that used by Bourdieu and has a similar goal, namely to map the lifestyle space of the U.K. They found that class differences were nested within age differences – among older age groups, the main distinction was between highbrow and popular culture. But among young people, the main distinction was between those tending to express likes versus those who express dislikes. Gayo-Cal et al. caution that this may be because respondents can only rate the activities included in the survey and so the 'dislikes' may occur because they have tastes and participate in cultural forms not included in the survey. While they do find that specific clusters of taste are associated with social position, there are also signs that this reflects a historical pattern that may not be a useful guide to the future – it may be that the link between social location and taste is becoming weaker.

Evidence of this erosion of the link between social location and taste is found in the work of Peterson and associates. Peterson and Simkus (1992) found that in the U.S. those in high status occupations exhibited a wide variety of cultural tastes, including popular and folk cultural activities. In contrast, those in lower status occupations reported a narrower range of cultural consumption. They coined the term 'omnivorousness' to signify the tendency for an association between location in the status hierarchy and the tendency to participate in, or consume, a wide range of cultural activity. They contrasted 'univores' and 'omnivores', and comparative studies in many (Western) countries subsequently provide good evidence that class location does not map neatly to the content of cultural consumption, i.e. an association between class and high- or low-brow taste. While high-brow activities are most associated with high status, a more important difference is the broadness or narrowness of the range of activities consumed. Later work by Peterson and Kern (1996) uses a survey instrument that replicates that of the original Peterson and Simkus study, thus allowing them to test whether tastes are changing. Their findings show that between 1982 and 1992 those displaying 'high-brow' taste had become more omnivorous. In a study of musical tastes in England, Chan and Goldthorpe (2007) found similar evidence, although the main pattern was more strikingly one of univorosness, especially at the lower levels of the stratification of contemporary English society, but also in the higher categories of social status.

Overall, the evidence suggests that the relationship between social status and lifestyle has become weaker in the post World War II period. One reason for this is that the class structure itself has changed, with the growth of the middle classes. While high- or low-brow taste may still characterise high and low social status categories, the growing middle-class is characterised by more heterogeneity and a wider range of taste. A second factor is a change in the production side of culture, independent of its consumption. The period covered by these various studies coincides with the growth of pop culture. The univore/omnivore distinction can be explained by the pervasive impact of pop culture on taste. Among higher status people, pop culture becomes part of a range of preferred genres, and so manifests as eclectic tastes, while among those of lower status, today's popular music, movies and novels replace those of yesterday.

Taken together, this body of work suggests that Bourdieu's original findings reflect a relationship between social structure and consumption that no longer holds for contemporary lifestyle practices. However, there are signs that the resources available to people – as evidenced by the relationship between status measures and consumption patterns – do influence lifestyle choices. The Chan and Goldthorpe study found that music consumption was strongly related to education and status, and omnivorousness is related to preferences for music, art and other cultural goods.

This may be explained by indirect connections between class and taste. Ganzeboom (1982), for example, argues that participation in highbrow cultural activities requires the cognitive capacity for processing complex information, and that such capacity is developed or enhanced through education. Chan and Goldthorpe note that

> the higher individuals' information processing capacity, the greater must be the information content of the cultural forms in which they participate if they are to derive satisfaction from them. Thus, the association between 'high' culture and educational attainment is due to the facts (a) that 'high' culture has, on average, a higher level of information content than 'low' culture and (b) that education is crucially involved in, and is thus a good proxy for, the information processing capacity of individuals. (Chan and Goldthorpe, 2007: 16)

Participation in high culture is also expensive. The financial cost of participation in activities such as opera, symphony orchestra performances, the purchase of fine art and live theatre discourage participation from all but the affluent. For these reasons, the relation between status and cultural consumption may better reflect consumer behaviour in markets than taste distinctions that mark out class boundaries.

Lifestyle as patterns of activities

The view of lifestyle discussed above emphasises aspects of consumption patterns that signal individual identity, self-expression and cultural style. In terms of the definition of lifestyle we employ (how one spends one time and who with, what one consumes, and what these mean to one) the emphasis is on consumption and what this means to the individual, particularly in terms of the ability of consumption to represent identity. Giddens describes 'lifestyle' as:

> a more or less integrated set of practices which an individual embraces, not only because such practices fulfil utilitarian needs, but because they give material form to a particular narrative of self-identity ... Lifestyles are routinised practices, the routines are incorporated into habits of dress, eating, modes of acting and favoured milieux for encountering others; but the routines followed are reflexively open to change in the light of the mobile nature of self-identity. (Giddens, 1991: 81)

Similarly, Featherstone (1987: 55) emphasises the way that consumption choices 'are to be regarded as indicators of the individuality of taste and sense of style of the owner/consumer'. However, time use is a fundamental, if neglected, aspect of describing lifestyle and the differences between lifestyles. How people spend their time reflects the activities in which they engage, and we want to describe lifestyle in terms of what people do and do not do. This captures 'practices' better than do expressions of preferences, likes, and dislikes. Second, time is probably the most fundamental resource available to people. It is finite and equally distributed – everyone, rich and poor, young and old, male and female, has the same amount: 168 hours per week.

These features mean that patterns of time use measure the lived experience of everyday life better than surveys that elicit preferences or tastes. Time use data is collected through diaries where people record how they actually spent time (see below), and is much less susceptible to measurement error due to errors of recall, or due to bias towards reporting socially desirable behaviours. But apart from the measurement issues, time use reflects what people actually do in their day, rather than what they might wish to do or think they ought to do. In that way, time use captures the fundamental nature of lifestyle.

Time use data

Surveys to collect time use data began in the 1920s and 30s, but their growth stems from an international comparative survey involving

12 countries in the 1960s (Andorka, 1987). Time use surveys required people to keep time diaries recording how time is spent over a period of one or two days. The variables are minutes spent in each activity per day, recorded either in fixed periods (e.g. ten minute blocks) or by recording the start and finish times. Diarists' entries are then coded to a standard classification scheme. Schemes vary from country to country, although now most are modifications of the Australian classification scheme.

The sample design is crucial for time use surveys. Respondents are usually asked to record their activities for one or two twenty-four hour periods. The unit of analysis is the 'person day', and the aim of the sample design is to collect data for a represent sample from the population of person-days in a year. This population is the number of eligible individuals in the country multiplied by 365. Eligibility varies from country to country – in some cases restricted to 'working age' (e.g. 20–64), but others are more extensive. The U.K. data, for example, includes a survey of children aged eight years and older. The French sample used in this chapter included one individual aged 103 years old.

In addition to collecting data on activities, it is common to seek additional information on the context of that activity, particularly the purpose of the activity, other activities performed at the same time, who else was present and the location. This information is helpful in interpreting how codes are to be employed, but also for understanding apparent change that actually reflects the meaning of the activity to the respondent. For example, an increase in the time devoted to child care in Australia has been partly attributed to how people think about the activity – for example, a change from attending a football match accompanied by the children ('watching sport') to looking after the children at a football match ('child care').

Production, investment, and consumption activities

There is some variation by country in coding frameworks for activities. This results from differences in the particular purpose of the studies, and reflects the specific conditions of the society. However, the 12-country international study, mentioned above, designed a coding framework comprising 37 categories that enabled almost all the country-specific activities to be aggregated to this more general set of categories. In the 1980s, the general coding framework was revised to 41 categories (including an 'uncodable' category), and a simpler 20-category framework was also developed. The original country coding frameworks use much more detailed categories. The Australian 1992 Time Use Survey, for example, used 281 categories, while the Netherlands surveys use 354.

Our analysis draws on a framework proposed by Ironmonger (e.g. Ironmonger, 2006) to develop a system of time accounts that complements the System of National Accounts. The framework employs the basic macroeconomic categories of production, investment and consumption. In terms of time use, production includes both market work and household work; investment – the largest time use component – includes education, self-care and study; consumption, the focus of the analysis presented here, includes leisure and activities, as well as socialising, eating and drinking and so on.

Data

Country samples

The data comprise large sample surveys from Australia (in 1997), Canada (1998), France (1998), and the U.K. (2000). We classify respondents by age group and gender, to enable valid comparisons between countries, and to identify age and gender differences in activity patterns. Sample sizes and the sizes of each socio-demographic group are shown in Table 2.1

Table 2.1 Sample sizes and numbers within each socio-demographic group, by country

	Canada 98	France 98	UK 00	Australia 97
Male 17–25	361	975	740	1,132
Male 26–37	985	1,455	1,376	1,874
Male 38–50	1,029	1,824	1,420	1,224
Male 51–65	648	1,389	1,330	1,187
Male 66–75	261	746	552	808
Female 17–25	456	1,050	976	1,190
Female 26–37	1,117	1,610	1,739	2,157
Female 38–50	1,100	1,928	1,754	1,313
Female 51–65	655	1,465	1,362	1,307
Female 66–75	303	976	668	919
Total	6,915	13,418	11,917	13,111

Variables

The variables are categories of time use, recoded from the original surveys to make them comparable across samples. The activities that are production activities (market work, domestic work and related activities) and investment activities (study, sleep, self-care and related activities) are grouped into two broad categories (production and investment). The variables are listed in Table 2.2.

Method of analysis

We use correspondence analysis to analyse the data, in order to map the socio-demographic groups within the space of lifestyle activities. Correspondence analysis analyses the rows and columns of a table simultaneously. It is a data reduction technique that quantifies the difference between rows (or columns) with respect to their

Table 2.2 List of activities

Variable	Description
eating	Meals/snacks
otravel	Other travel – leisure travel, excursions and trips
socialising	Visiting or entertaining friends, social clubs, pubs, restaurants
cinema	Movies, concerts, theatre, watching sport
religious	Religious activities
civic_duties	Civic duties and community participation
parties	Dances, parties
asports	Playing sport
walking	Walking for pleasure or exercise
radio	Listening to radio
tv	Watching TV or videos
cd	Listening to records/tapes/CDs
books	Reading books
papers_mag	Reading newspapers and magazines
relaxing	Relaxing
talking	Conversation
hobbies	Hobbies, games and pastimes
production	Market work and domestic work
investment	Study, sleep, self-care

profiles across the columns (or rows). The differences between the rows and the columns are decomposed into a set of dimensions that summarise the total variability in the table. A useful feature of the technique is that row and column points are scored on the dimensions, such that it is possible to display these points in a way that allows the distance between points to represent how different they are from each other (relative to an average for the table as a whole). These characteristics – the ability to analyse and visualise row and column points simultaneously – allow a set of complex relationships to be represented spatially.

For each country, a table is constructed consisting of the age/gender categories (as rows) and activity categories (as columns), with cells comprising the mean amount of time spent on each activity, by each group. In addition, we included variables to measure education and income but these show no clear patterns of association with the activities, and so were subsequently dropped from the analysis.

Five separate analyses are carried out. In the first analysis, all four country tables are stacked into a single supertable, which allows the direct comparison of the four countries. As indicated, it is common to summarise the main variation in the table as a two-dimensional map that translates the differences into distances. In this case, the differences in time use between socio-demographic groups in each country are displayed. We also look at the third dimension (in Figure 2.2) – these three dimensions account for 83 per cent of the total variation.

We then examine differences between the socio-demographic groups within countries, by analysing each country table separately. For these analyses we display maps of only the first two dimensions. Even with just two dimensions, the maps summarise more than 80 per cent of the variation in each country.

To simplify the displays, we show only those groups and variables that contribute significantly to the dimension, with those in bold contributing to the first dimension and those in italics contributing to the second. Activities are italicised to distinguish them from socio-demographic groups. Groups are labelled by country code, gender and age group. For example, aum17–15 means Australia, male aged 17–25 years.

Results

The first two dimensions account for 68 per cent of the variation in the table that includes all four countries (Figure 2.1), and both dimensions

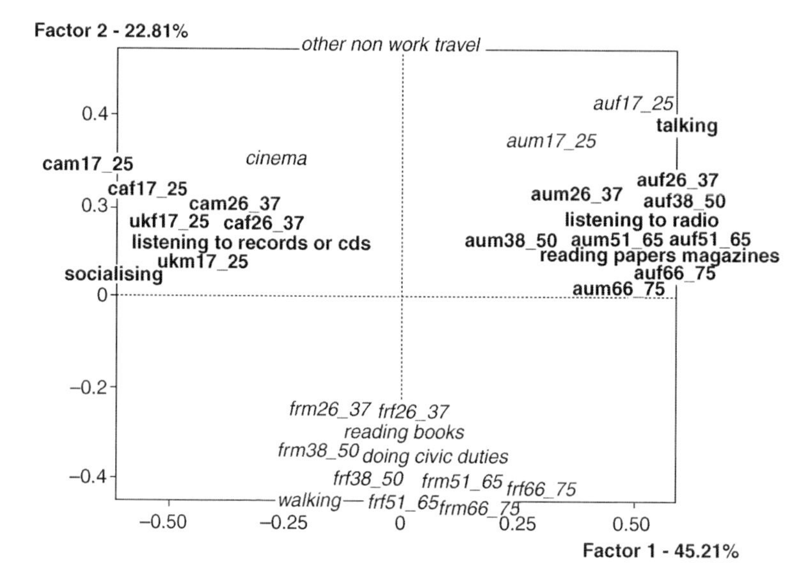

Figure 2.1 All four countries – dimensions 1 X 2

reflect differences between countries rather than socio-demographic characteristics. The overall pattern for the countries is the contrast on the first (horizontal) dimension between Canada and the U.K. on the left of the first axis, with Australia on the right. The second dimension shows that France differs from the other countries. The activities that distinguish national patterns are talking, reading magazines and newspapers, and listening to the radio (Australia); socialising and listening to music (Canada and the U.K.); and reading books, civic duties and community involvement, and walking (France), with the French spending relatively less time on leisure travel ('other non work travel'). The proximity of the points for Canada and U.K. show that these countries are the most similar with respect to lifestyle.

We also extract a third dimension which accounts for a further 15 per cent of the variability in the table. This third dimension (shown as the vertical axis in Figure 2.2) reflects age differences in activities. This is best exemplified by the contrast between older U.K. and Canada (relaxing and religious activities) contrasted with younger French (active sports and cinema). The third dimension is dominated by age differences though, and shows that reading papers and magazines, and

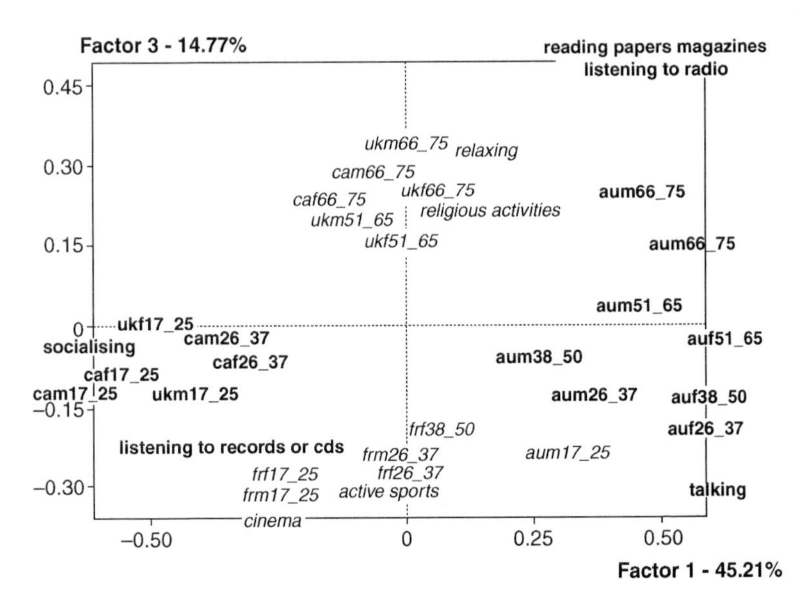

Figure 2.2 All four countries – dimensions 1 X 3

listening to radio are most associated with older people while younger people spend relatively more of their time talking.

Within-country differences

Figures 2.3 to 2.6 display the maps for each country. All four countries show a similar pattern, with the first dimension (horizontal axis) discriminating between the age groups and the second separating out the genders. Table 2.3 summarises the age and gender differences in time use for each country, identifying the activities most associated with each socio-demographic group (that is, the activities that are above average). This shows that age and gender are associated with quite similar patterns of activities in each country – older people engage in more passive activities than younger people; younger people are more likely to attend the cinema and, especially males, to spend time listening to music. Males appear to spend more time in solitary activities than do females, and females are more likely than males to be spend time on religious activities and civic duties than do males, except in France, where there is little gender difference in these activities among older people.

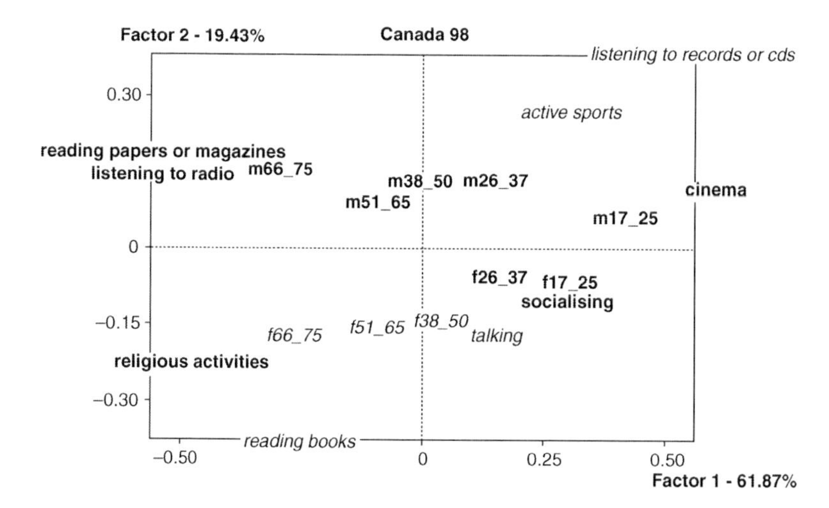

Figure 2.3 Age and gender differences in activity – Canada

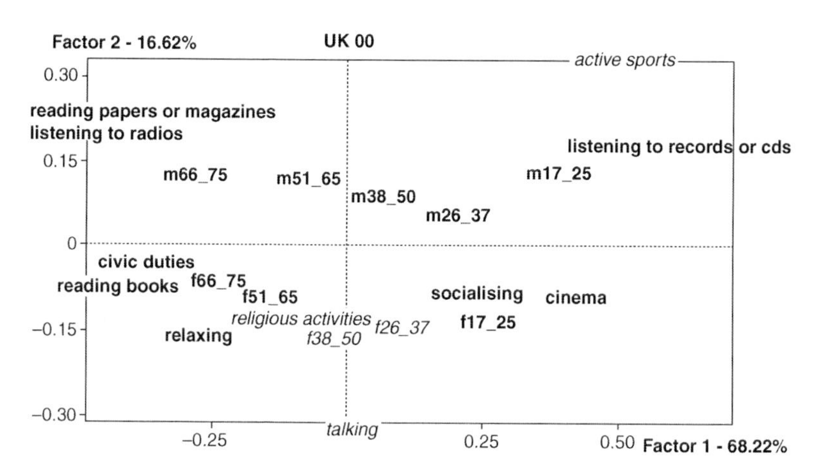

Figure 2.4 Age and gender differences in activity – U.K.

Generally, age explains more variation than gender. In France, age accounts for more than four times the variability than gender, and in Australia it explains about twice as much, implying that time use differs more markedly in France than it does in Australia.

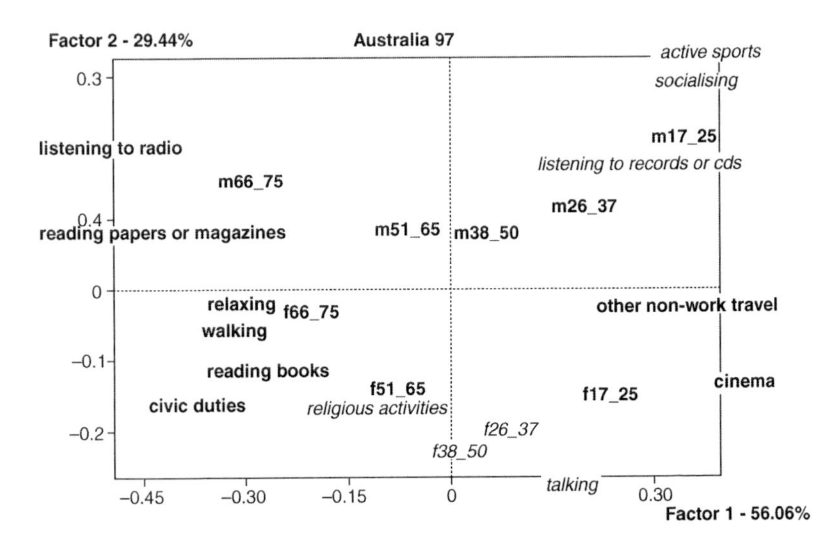

Figure 2.5 Age and gender differences in activity – Australia

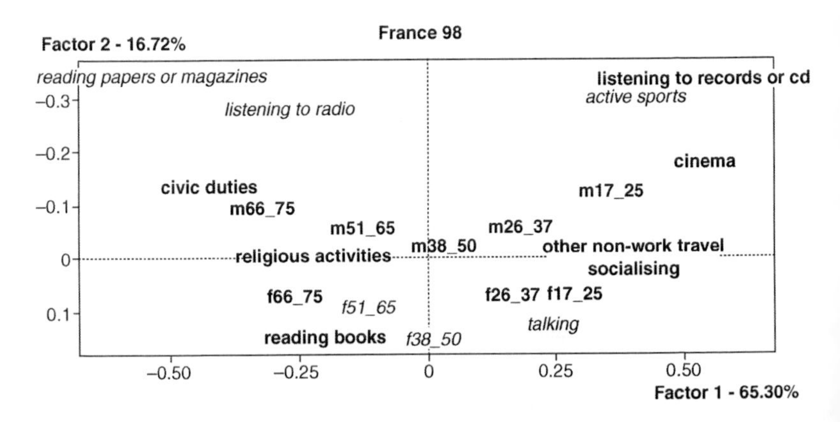

Figure 2.6 Age and gender differences in activity – France

Discussion and conclusion

The results of the analysis in which all four countries are combined show that country differences have more effect than age or gender. The time use patterns in each of the socio-demographic groups are similar to each other when examined on a country by country basis, but the

Table 2.3 Socio-demographic differences in activity, by country

	Canada	U.K.	Australia	France
Older males	Reading the paper and listening to the radio.	Reading the paper and listening to the radio.	Reading the paper and listening to the radio.	Reading the paper listening to the radio, civic duties, religious activities.
Older females	Religious activities.	Civic duties, reading books, relaxing, religious activities and talking	Civic duties, relaxing, walking, reading books, religious activities and talking	Reading books, religious activities.
Younger males	Cinema, active sports, listening to music.	Active sports, listening to music.	Active sports, socialising, listening to music.	Cinema, listening to music, socialising.
Younger females	Socialising and talking.	Socialising, cinema and talking.	Talking, leisure travel, cinema.	Socialising, leisure travel and talking.

first two dimensions of the analysis of pooled data discriminates mostly on country differences. Canada and the U.K. display similar patterns to each other, and are most different from Australia. There is a smaller difference, then, between France and the other three countries. People in Canada and the U.K. spend more time listening to music and, especially, socialising. In Australia, more time is spent in conversation, listening to the radio and reading newspapers and magazines. In France, more time is devoted to walking, reading books and community involvement.

Age differences dominate the within-country analyses in which the activity patterns of each of the age groups in different countries are quite similar to each other. This shows that lifestyle is structured by stage in the lifecourse, in a similar way in the four countries. Differences between males and females also show a similar pattern across the four countries.

Our aim in this chapter has been to examine lifestyles in terms of the activities that comprise people's everyday routines. The comparison across four modern, economically-developed countries shows that national differences produce distinctive ways of living. We also employed indicators of social status (education and income), but these did not show any pattern of association with the activities we examined, although previous studies have shown these to be related to taste and preferences in choices of cultural consumption.

Social and cultural change may well be leading to a post-traditional order, in which lifestyles reflect choices oriented to expressing identity and selfhood. Our data show that these choices are embedded in contexts that strongly shape their expression. Comparing societies shows how norms and values become actualised in the typical practices of daily life, while the stable patterns characterising age and gender differences show how the fundamental processes characterising development through the lifecourse shape patterns of daily life.

References

Andorka, R. (1987). 'Time budgets and their uses', *Annual Review of Sociology,* 13: 149–64.

Bauman, Z. (1988). *Freedom*. Milton Keynes: Open University Press.

Bauman, Z. (2002). *Society Under Siege*. Cambridge: Polity Press.

Beck, U. (1992). *Risk Society: Towards a New Modernity.* London: Sage.

Chan, T.W. and Goldthorpe, J.H. (2007). 'Social stratification and cultural consumption: music in England', *European Sociological Review,* 23: 1–19.

Featherstone, M. (1987). 'Lifestyle and consumer culture', *Theory, Culture and Society,* 4: 55–70.

Ganzeboom, H.B. (1982). 'Explaining differential participation in high-cultural activities: a confrontation of information-processing and status seeking theories', in Raub, W. (ed.), *Theoretical Models and Empirical Analyses: Contributions to the Explanation of Individual Actions and Collective Phenomena*. Utrecht: E.S.-Publications: 186–205.

Gayo-Cal, M., Savage, M. and Warde, A. (2006). 'A cultural map of the United Kingdom, 2003', *Cultural Trends,* 15: 213–37.

Giddens, A. (1991). *Modernity and Self-identity: Self and Society in the Late Modern Age*. Cambridge: Polity.

Ironmonger, D. (2006). 'A System of Time Accounts for Melbourne: a report commissioned by the Department of Infrastructure, Victoria, Australia', The University of Melbourne, Melbourne.

Peterson, R.A and Kern, R.M. (1996). 'Changing highbrow taste: from snob to omnivore', *American Sociological Review,* 61 (5): 900–07.

Peterson, R.A. and Simkus, A. (1992). 'How musical tastes mark occupational status groups', in Lamont, M. and Fournier, M. (eds), *Cultivating Differences.* Chicago: University of Chicago Press: 152–68.

Veblen, T. (1924). *The Theory of the Leisure Class,* New York: Viking Press.

Weber, M. (1946). 'Class, status and party', in Gerth, H. and Wright Mills, C. (eds) *From Max Webe.,* New York: Oxford University Press: 180–95.

3

Households, Work, Time Use and Energy Consumption

Steven McEachern

Introduction

This chapter explores the connection between two emergent phenomena within time use literature – the relationship between household time use activities and forms of household consumption, particularly energy consumption occurring within the dwelling and in travel. The premise of this chapter is that time spent in employment outside the household influences household lifestyle patterns, represented by time spent by household members in domestic work and leisure activities. This in turn influences the distribution of consumption activities within a household, and consequently the level and type of energy consumption.

The basis of this argument draws on two areas of research. In studies of household energy consumption, there has been a growing recognition of the impact of differences in householder behaviour on household energy consumption, an important contributor to climate change. While demographic, geographic, and housing characteristics have been shown as important determinants of household energy consumption, they typically explain only around 55 to 60 per cent of the variation in energy use between Australian households (Oliphant, 2003). This has lead some authors to suggest that the patterns of consumption within the residence itself (Lutzenheiser, 1993; Duchin, 1997) form a major source of variation in household energy use, a source that is not well understood in current research.

At the same time, time use researchers have identified an increasing divergence in the patterns of time spent at work between households, occurring both in Australia and overseas (Jacobs and Gerson, 2001; Bittman and Rice, 2002). This has also lead some to examine the consequences of these shifts in working hours for variations in patterns of consumption, particularly among 'income-rich, time-poor' households – those households with two employed adults generating high incomes through long working hours, but with little opportunity to realise the benefits of that income through extended periods of leisure (Sullivan and Gershuny, 2008).

One question which arises in examining the relationship between these two phenomena is the role of income in each. For Sullivan (2008) the effect of the time required to generate higher levels of income on consumption is a dilemma for capitalism. Those with higher incomes have higher resources available to consume (in the form of disposable income), but lower capacity to spend, due to limited time available to engage in the leisure time required for the process of consumption. The converse pattern however appears in the energy consumption literature. Those with higher incomes are more likely to invest in more 'energy-saving' devices (Brohmann, Heinzle et al., 2009), but also have a higher per-capita level of consumption.[1]

How then might the relationship between these elements be understood? Figure 3.1 presents a basic model of the relationship between time use, income and energy consumption. It is this model which is explored further in the body of the chapter, focussing on two elements of energy

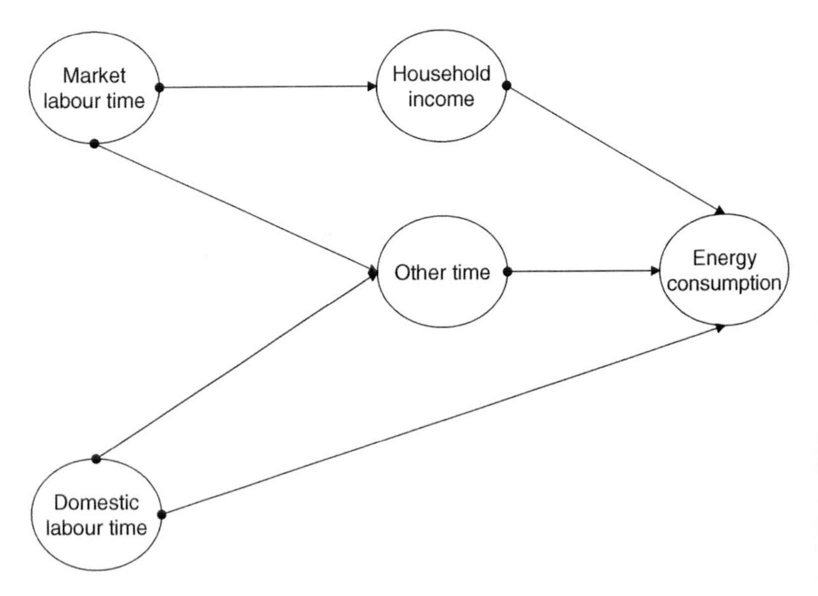

Figure 3.1 A model of time use, income and energy consumption

consumption: electricity and motor vehicle fuel (with both being forms of demand derived from lifestyle choices). The chapter uses household level data from the Household Income and Labour Dynamics in Australia survey to examine the relationship between working hours, other forms of time use, income and energy consumption. In doing so, the chapter explores the implications of ways of living for the consumption and management of environmental resources. In this way, it expands the possibilities for time use research beyond social policy applications into areas such as climate change and environmental policy.

Working hours and different patterns of household consumption

The relationship between consumption and time use is one that has a long history in the time use literature, going back to the work by Becker (1965) in his theory of the allocation of time. The core premise of Becker's theory and that of others in the same tradition (e.g. Gershuny, 2000) is that there is a fundamental constraint on the time use of individuals. For everyone this is 24 hours in a day, and for everyone there is no way of changing this constraint – unlike, for example, the income constraint, which can be altered by changing the conditions of employment and earnings. Becker examines the implications of this time constraint for working hours and consumption decisions, by considering the trade-offs made between allocations of time to each of the two.

This chapter seeks to examine this trade-off in a slightly different way. One aspect of the decision to work or consume in an industrialised society is that the two generally occur in different geographical locations or spaces. In simple terms, consumption occurs either in the home (private space) or in other locations (public spaces), while production (work) occurs in the workplace (which may be a public or a private space). This is an important distinction because it has implications for both the patterns of energy consumption that occur, and the extent to which the costs of energy consumption (being a derived demand) fall on the household or on the employer. This then provides the rationale for the chapter: how do differences in ways of living, as reflected by allocations of time, affect the incidence of energy consumption on households in Australia?

To answer this question, a more fine-grained distinction in the forms of time use is required, distinguishing both different forms of work and of leisure. For this we draw on the framework developed by Robinson (1988). In terms of working hours, Robinson makes a distinction in two areas of work in terms of remuneration. Here we use the term 'market labour' to comprise those time use activities funded by an employer or self-employment (i.e. paid employment). By comparison, 'domestic labour' comprises activities required for the operation of the household, but outside the paid employment sector, such as working for a family business, household care and childcare (i.e. unpaid employment). Robinson also distinguishes leisure activities between personal care and leisure. Personal care involves those activities required for personal maintenance and care, and may include sleep (depending on the author). By comparison, we use the term 'leisure' to denote what has been variously described as leisure, free time or uncommitted time. Leisure is the residual category after the other required activities of the day have been accounted for within the 24-hour daily time constraint.

Closer examination of the nature of domestic labour provides insight into the relationship between specific forms of time use and geographic space. Figure 3.2 shows the proportion of time spent in different types

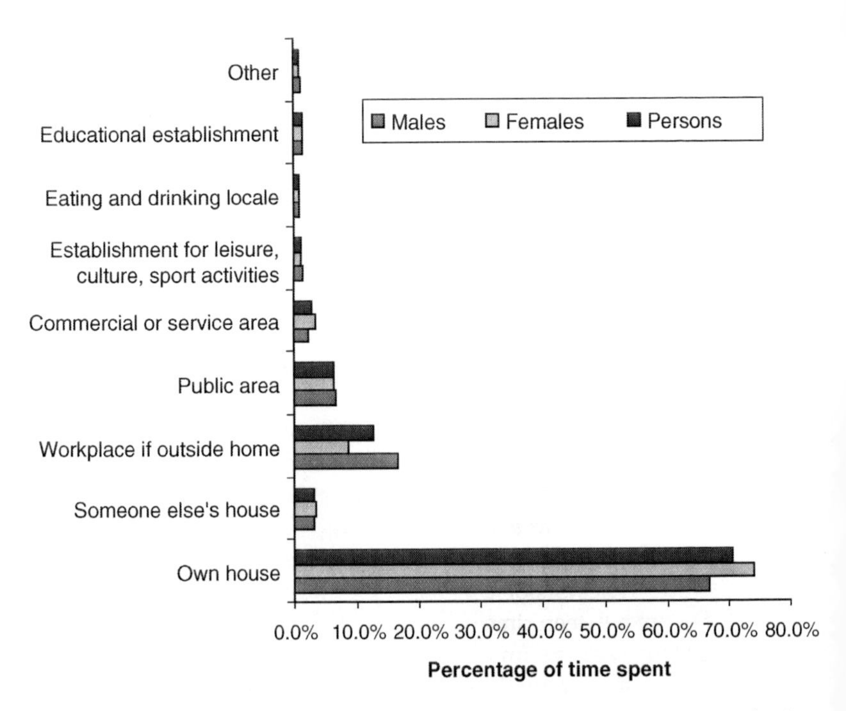

Figure 3.2 Proportion of time spent in different locations in an average day by Australians

Source: Derived from Australian Bureau of Statistics 2008, Cat. No. 4153.0 DO001 Table 18.

of locations in an average week by Australians in 2006, based on diary data from the Australian Time Use Survey. As can be seen, by far the greatest amount of time is spent in an individual's own home, approximately 112 hours per week for males and 124 hours per week for females. Beyond this however, the next largest amount of time is spent in the workplace (if it is outside the home). It is here that variation between genders begins to emerge, with an average of 28 hours per week for males and 14 hours for females.

The discrepancy between males and females is largely the result of the estimation, including those both employed and outside the labour force, where females have a much lower level of employment than males. This does signify, however, the extent to which market work or paid employment – as one aspect of time use – is a determinant of the forms of discretionary consumption by limiting the amount of time available to be spent on alternative pursuits. The difference is further illustrated in the proportion of time spent in commercial or service areas, where females average 7 hours per week compared to 5 hours and 19 minutes per week for males.

A similar pattern emerges if the nature of who time is spent with is considered. The Australian Time Use Survey also includes descriptions of who time is spent with during each activity throughout the day. Figure 3.3 shows who people spent their time with, broken down by the different locations in which they spend their time (again using the 2006 time use data). The pattern of relationships here is again informative, in that it illustrates the extent to which different types of personal relationships occur in different geographical spaces. For example, two types of relationships are largely occurring in a single place – the majority of time spent with direct family is spent in the home, and time with colleagues is in the workplace (as might be expected). By comparison, time spent with friends is distributed across a much wider range of locations, including home, friends' houses and various leisure and consumption establishments. This therefore begins to paint a picture of the extent to which different forms of consumption are dependent on the allocations of time to the other usage categories.

These broad indicators of 'average days' are crude representations of the relationship between time use and consumption patterns. However, they do encapsulate the underlying issue which this chapter is seeking to explore – that certain consumption choices (whether direct consumption or foregone consumption in the case of employment) are associated with particular geographic spaces, or what might be termed 'living spaces'.

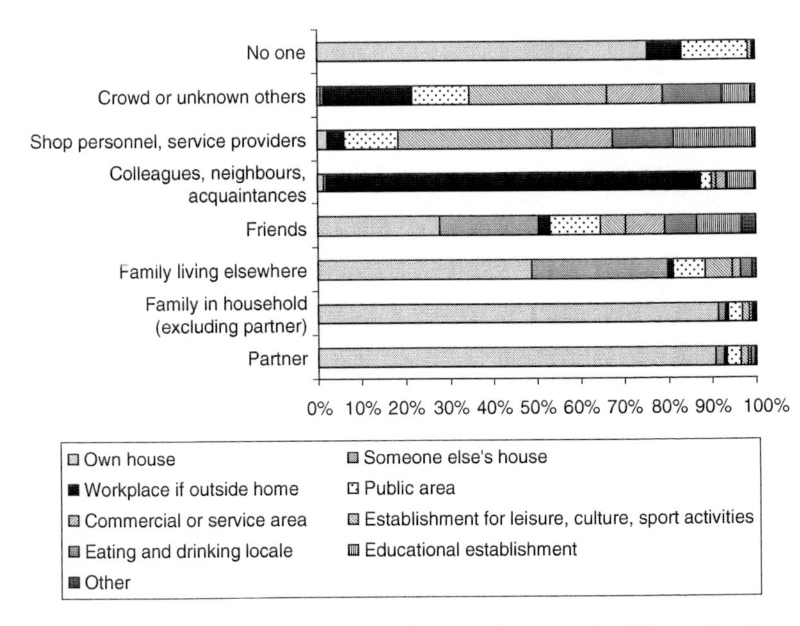

Figure 3.3 Proportion of time spent with particular groups in different locations in an average day by Australians

Source: Derived from Australian Bureau of Statistics 2008, Cat. No. 4153.0 DO001 Table 18.

Taking this further, the spatial patterns of consumption will also have associated with them patterns of travel and costs, and these patterns will also be interdependent. For example, time spent at work involves fewer variable costs for the household than time spent in home-based leisure. It is this pattern which also has implications for household expenditure. To focus on the issue considered here, energy use is a derived demand, based on the need for an underlying service such as cooked food or transportation to an event. Changes in patterns of daily time use will therefore be associated with different patterns of energy consumption, and the incidence of costs for that consumption will also vary, particularly depending on whether the individual is at work (where the costs are borne instead by the employer).

Connecting consumption, time use and energy use

The idea that time use patterns (as reflections of discretionary consumption) might be a potential explanation for variations in household energy demand was first explored by Schipper et al. (1989), who extend understanding of energy demand beyond basic demographic influences.

They note in their work that there are often wide variations in the level of household energy consumption, even at similar levels of household income, and similar household demographic profiles. Further, they find that changes in price could also not fully explain such variation, noting that:

> As long as energy prices do not rise abruptly, consumers' decisions about what kinds of houses they live in, how far they travel to work, and what they do in their free time will also remain relatively free from energy-price considerations. (Schipper et al., 1989: 275)

Given these limitations in the prevailing literature at the time, Schipper et al. (1989) posit the following in terms of the relationship between consumption patterns and energy use:

> changes in the patterns of consumers' activities, which we call their life-styles, can lead to substantial changes in energy use, particularly in the very long run, even with little change in energy prices or incomes. (Schipper, et al., 1989: 275)

Schipper et al. (1989) also consider the relationship between lifestyles and energy use, using time use as the means through which to connect behaviours (which are allocated a particular energy intensity based on engineering estimates) with energy consumption. They find that the largest expansion in energy consumption is likely to occur with growth in time spent travelling – that is, in the derived demand for activities that occur outside of the household.

Hours in employment and energy demand

One challenge in understanding the relationship between time use and consumption is in the consideration of the consequences of longer working hours. The debate in this area revolves around the relationship between working hours and leisure, given the overall time constraint of 24 hours in a day, or as Sullivan and Gershuny put it, 'the interdependence of the processes of production and consumption' (Sullivan and Gershuny, 2004: 80). On the one hand, longer working hours are generally associated with higher levels of income, which is in turn associated with greater consumption and subsequently higher environmental impact. Schor (2005) thus argues that there is need for reducing working hours to avoid the continued expansion of consumption.

By comparison, the expansion of working hours also will result in the reduced availability of time to consume, all other things being equal.

Sullivan in particular has noted that there is an emerging distinction occurring in patterns of consumption, related to the number of hours of work (Sullivan and Gershuny, 2004; Sullivan, 2008). Sullivan and Gershuny note that among high-income households where the employed work long hours (what they call income-rich, time-poor households), there are two forms of consumption likely to emerge – 'voracious consumption' of a larger number of short, intense events, and 'inconspicuous consumption', primarily the purchase of high-quality durable goods which do not require immediate consumption. These forms of consumption will entail different forms of household energy demand. Voracious consumption involves higher emphasis on fuel inputs for travel to the location of consumption and conduct of activities. By comparison, the energy demands of inconspicuous consumption are contained largely in the production process for the durable goods.[2]

Even the impact of this shift is unclear. Some of these durable purchases are also likely to change the level of direct energy consumption, although the direction of this change may vary. Take for example the effects of an increase in the number of appliances. The expansion in the number of new appliances has lead to an increase in daily energy use in Australian households overall (*Energy Efficient Strategies*, 2008). However, the purchase of more efficient appliances will result in lower levels of consumption per unit. For example, a new refrigerator now consumes approximately 40 per cent less energy than the same size unit built 20 years earlier.

The related effects of habitual consumption are also hidden within the impact of patterns of employment. Sociologists such as Lutzenheiser and Wilhite (Lutzenheiser, 1993; Wilhite and Lutzenheiser, 1999) have noted the social dimensions of the occupation of space and the implications for energy use. They also draw attention to the changes in behaviour that may result from dual employment within the household, also drawing on the example of the use of refrigeration:

> Families with two working parents may want to shop only once a week and to store a week's worth of food. They may want refrigerators to hold a number of 1-litre soda bottles so that children and their friends can be readily provisioned. One of the defining elements of being a good parent might include never running out of soda, hence the large storage unit. (Wilhite and Lutzenheiser, 1999: 283)

Although Wilhite and Lutzenheiser do not discuss it, the likely contrast here with a household choice for a parent to work at home, is notable.

In that situation, the direct energy demands are likely to be much higher, as lighting and appliance use increase, but travel decreases. Thus differences in employment patterns (a reflection of the time allocation decision) may generate highly differentiated energy demand patterns. The competing effects of the impact of income and employment patterns are, however, unclear.

Determinants of household demand for energy

At this point, it is useful to consider the existing literature on the determinants of household energy demand, to understand the likely contribution of a time use perspective. Research into household energy demand and behaviour change has a long history, having a particular peak in the 1970s around the era of the oil crisis, and experiencing a more recent upswing in activity with the growth in interest in issues of climate change and global warming related to the burning of fossil fuels (Lutzenheiser, 1993). In general, the prevailing research has focussed on three major types of influence on household energy use: housing and structural characteristics, family characteristics, and energy use behaviour (such as use of lighting, heating and appliances). Work in these areas is often tied to a particular field of science. Meta-analysis of the determinants of household energy demand is relatively common in the energy literature, and this chapter is not intended to recapitulate work previously completed in this area.[3] Rather, what follows is a summary of the relevant work in this area.

The area of housing and structural characteristics has largely been concentrated in science and engineering. Studies have looked at characteristics of the house such as type of house (whether it is a house, flat or apartment), the structural characteristics of the house (e.g. brick or timber), the physical condition of the house, and the presence of high-demand appliances and structures, such as air conditioners and space heaters. Policies designed to improve energy efficiency are often focussed on structural interventions, such as weatherising doors and windows, insulation, and subsidies for new technologies.

By comparison, economic approaches have been more likely to consider householder characteristics, such as demographics, employment, income and expenditure patterns, and family structures or household composition. Higher income households have generally been shown to demonstrate higher levels of energy consumption, explained usually as a higher capacity to pay as a result of greater disposable income (O'Neill and Chen, 2002). Number of residents in the household is also a significant determinant (Gatersleben, Steg et al., 2002). Larger numbers of individuals in a household increase overall demand, although the proportion of energy used per individual declines as numbers increase, due to the multiple users of a single source of energy such as lighting (O'Neill and Chen, 2002) and the lower energy demands of children. O'Neill and Chen also present evidence to suggest that a cohort effect is evident in the different patterns of consumption at different ages, although this may also be partly a function of the different lifestyle demands at different ages (another time use issue).

While economists give regard to the potential effects of employment status on energy consumption, employment more often is encapsulated in studies of demographic influences. However, the range of changes resulting from employment considered previously suggests that there is also a strong overlap with the third category of determinants, that is differences in energy-use behaviour. Studies in this domain have largely come from the psychology and sociology literature, particularly those that examine the determinants of behavioural change (Wilson and Dowlatabadi, 2007). Oliphant (2003) suggests that up to half of the variation in household energy consumption may be related to behavioural differences in the use of lighting, appliances and heating. As she notes in her study of variations in energy use among individual South Australian households, models focussing on demographics and household characteristics can only explain slightly over half of the variation in household demand between households. She suggests that a better understanding of energy use behaviour patterns might be the key to further research in household energy consumption. Influential behaviours here could include such things as thermostat settings, turning on lights and appliances, and household occupation patterns, which are a common focus for behaviourally-based policy interventions (Abrahamse et al., 2005).

One reason for the differences in energy use behaviours between households may be the differences in perceptions of impact. Gatersleben, Steg and Vlek (2002), drawing on Stern's (2000) conceptualisation of impact versus interest behaviours, examine the impact of several high-impact (i.e. high energy demand) behaviours, such as thermostat settings, driving cars, showering and holiday activities. In two studies of the impact of such household behaviours, they found that respondents were able to identify likely environmental impacts of major activities such as holidays and driving cars, but had little recognition of the impacts of high-demand but mundane behaviours such as showering and cooking.

Along related lines, studies of adopters of new technologies have often demonstrated rebound effects in energy consumption (Greening et al., 2000). This occurs where a reduction in energy demand of less than the energy saving expected from the installation of a new energy-efficient technology, due to shifts to less efficient behaviours. Such a result makes clear sense from a time allocation perspective, where a householder may for example, purchase an energy efficient dishwasher. Here, there may be less water and energy used due to improvements relative to washing by hand, but the householder makes greater utilisation of it due to ease of use.

Studies of energy demand and time use

At this point, it is worthwhile to consider the empirical evidence on time use and energy consumption. While there has not been a large number of studies looking at time use and energy consumption in conjunction, the work of two groups in this area is notable. The studies conducted by the Lawrence Berkeley Laboratory in California, of which the work by Schipper et al. (1989) discussed earlier is the most prominent, examine macro-level shifts in patterns of American consumption and note the potential impact of changing travel behaviour for overall household energy demand in the American economy.

The other work occurring in this area is that of Jalas (2005), a Swedish economist whose work also has its origins in the arguments presented by Schipper et al. (1989). Jalas explores the relationship between aggregate household consumption and aggregate time use patterns, matching behaviours to expenditure surveys to estimate aggregate levels of consumption and demand for the Swedish economy.

The notable aspect of this work is the focus on the aggregate level of demand. For both groups, the focus is on understanding overall household end-use consumption at an economy-wide level. While this is important for forecasting aggregate demand, it does not say very much about what might influence the behaviours of individual households, nor about the relationship between particular ways of living and their environmental impacts (in the form of energy consumption). This chapter therefore addresses this problem, studying fundamentally the same issue addressed by both Schipper et al. (1989) and Jalas (2005), but at a different level of analysis – focussing on household-level rather than economy-level variations in lifestyle and energy consumption.

Explaining household consumption – a time use approach

As identified earlier, the focus of this chapter is on the relationship between time use and household energy consumption, in particular:

> How are differences in ways of living, in the form of household allocations of time, related to the incidence of energy consumption in households in Australia?

To study this question, it is necessary to draw on data that incorporates the four areas of literature previously discussed, those of housing characteristics, householder characteristics, time use behaviours and energy consumption.

There is unfortunately no single data set available which incorporates all of these elements, particularly at a household level. The particular concern here is the availability of energy consumption data, which is generally either highly controlled or available only with a limited number of additional variables, making analysis problematic. As a next-best alternative, data from the Household Income and Labour Dynamics in Australia (HILDA) survey has been adopted for this study (Melbourne Institute of Applied Economic and Social Research, 2005).

HILDA is a nationally representative panel survey of 7,682 Australian households and 13,969 individuals, conducted annually since 2001. A face to face interview averaging around 25–35 minutes in length is conducted with individuals within the household aged 15 years or older, asking about 10 broad areas including demographics, family background, education, current employment, labour market participation, income, children, partnering, life satisfaction and mobility. A second questionnaire is also left for them to self-complete, asking about health, lifestyle, financial situation, values and attitudes, time use and expenditure. Finally, there is also a household-level survey collecting information on child care, housing, household expenditure and household relationships and structures. Thus across the household and individual data captured in the HILDA survey, there is sufficient data at a household and individual level to enable the different sources of variation to be considered – particularly time use, energy consumption (in the form of expenditure), demographics and employment, and housing and household structures.

Dependent variables

The analysis is first conducted using electricity expenditure as the outcome variable of interest (as an indicator of private energy consumption), and then replicated with expenditure on motor fuel, to examine the impact of consumption in different public and private spaces.

The unit of analysis here is the household, with the modelling assessing the determinants of the level of household level expenditure on (a) electricity and (b) motor vehicle fuel. It should be noted here that the use of energy expenditure is only a proxy estimator for the actual level of household consumption and may be influenced by other factors such as competitive arrangements in the electricity market of the household.

There is however an additional complication with using household level data – that of aggregation. In the words of Duchin (1997: 64), 'a household's lifestyle refers to the jointly determined work and consumption practices of its members'. As such, there is a need to find a measure which is comparable across households. For this reason, a number of the measures used in this analysis are standardised by the number of persons in the household. In the case of electricity and fuel expenditure, the measure is the dollar amount expended over the last 12 month period per adult in the household, while for time-based variables the measure is the number of hours per adult.

Predictor variables

Consistent with the material discussed so far, three broad sets of predictors are included in the analysis here. Because the level of analysis is the household level, data collected at the individual level has been aggregated where required from the individual to the household level. For most variables this is unproblematic, such as the number of individuals within the household within a particular category (e.g. children, holding a university degree, currently employed). A summary of the variables incorporated under the three areas is included in Table 3.1, and discussed further below.

Time use characteristics

Characteristics of household time use allocations were captured by two sets of variables. The primary measures are the number of hours and minutes per adult household member spent on particular activities by all members of the household. Activities included were of three types:

- Market labour: paid employment, travel to work:
- Domestic labour: caring activities, household errands, housework and outdoor tasks:
- Other time: playing with your own children, playing with other children, volunteering and charity work.

Table 3.1 Descriptive statistics for data used in analysis

Variable	Mean	Std. Deviation
Dependent variables		
Electricity bill per adult	497.2994	412.507
Gas bill per adult	153.3514	296.724
Motor vehicle fuel bill per adult	1023.9363	1202.119
Other heating fuel bill per adult	19.1073	79.485
Housing characteristics		
House type (base category – detached house)		
Semi-detached house	.0756	
Flat-apartment	.1170	
Housing condition (base: very good/excellent condition)		
Good condition	.3210	
Average condition	.2362	
Poor condition	.0452	
Very poor condition	.0038	
Unknown condition	.0217	
Housing location (base: Western Australia)		
NSW	.2973	
Victoria	.2402	
Queensland	.2103	
South Aust	.0946	
Tasmania	.0340	
Northern Territory	.0054	
Aust Capital Territory	.0186	
Remoteness index (base: metropolitan)		
Inner regional	.2581	
Outer regional	.1161	
Remote	.0163	
Very remote	.0029	
Householder characteristics		
Number of residents in household		
0–4 year olds	.17	.488
5–9 year olds	.19	.506
10–14 year olds	.21	.531
Adults 15+	1.95	.843

Continued

Table 3.1 Continued

Variable	Mean	Std. Deviation
Income and consumption characteristics		
Income (log) per adult	10.7935	1.11838
Expenditure on groceries per adult	143.8572	75.30440
Home ownership		
Rent	.2764	
Rent-buy scheme	.0014	
Rent-free	.0268	
Home loan paid off	.1809	
Time use characteristics		
Number of self-employed	.2026	.48216
Number of home duties (primary task)	.0935	.29241
FT Students for gt 1 month – Number	.2263	.53258
Working from home – hours	8.6576	64.18382
Employment – hrs/min	2.2052	2.74504
Travel to employment – hrs/min	21.6808	17.62023
Caring activities – hrs/min	1.0294	5.49243
Playing with children – hrs/min	5.7611	11.67229
Household errands – hrs/min	3.8976	3.91884
Housework – hrs/min	10.9036	8.18604
Playing with other children – hrs/min	.7238	2.84394
Outdoor tasks	4.0962	5.17719
Volunteer and charity work – hrs/min	.9009	2.73711

Three indicators of home-based labour were also included. The number of self-employed persons, full-time students and persons involved in home duties as the primary labour market activity were included, along with the number of hours of paid work (market labour) per person completed at home.

Householder characteristics

Control variables for householder and household characteristics were also included along with the time use variables, to factor out known influences on household energy consumption. In terms of householder characteristics, control variables included the number of household residents (broken up by age group), and expenditure controls for groceries, other energy bills and home ownership.

Housing characteristics

Four variables are included as measures of housing characteristics. The housing type distinguishes between separate houses, semi-detached residences and flats and apartments. The condition of housing is used as a control for the state of the housing, with houses in very good or excellent condition used as the base category, and dummies included for households in poorer conditions (which can be expected to be less efficient and therefore requiring greater energy consumption). To account for differences in the location of the household, control dummies for the state or territory, and the level of remoteness (using the ABS Remoteness classification) were included, with Western Australia and residents of metropolitan centres as the base category in each case.[4]

Sample

To account for cases where housing might vary frequently or where energy consumption decisions may be outside the control of the household, those households based in non-permanent structures (such as caravans and tents) and those in non-private households (e.g. nursing homes) were excluded from the analysis. Additionally, only households with expenditure on motor vehicle fuel were included. After listwise deletion of cases with missing data, the final sample in the analysis included 5,588 households for the analysis of electricity use, and 5,529 households in the analysis of motor fuel use.

Analysis method

The analysis which follows uses ordinary least squares regression to predict three elements of the model presented in Figure 3.1 – household income, other time and energy consumption. The discussion of the results is structured as a series of energy consumption situations, examining the three elements of the literature considered above. These situations, which have some degree of interdependence, are as follows:

1. The relationship between income and energy expenditure;
2. The relationship between market work, domestic work and other time use;
3. The relationship between time use and income;
4. The relationship between time allocation and energy expenditure – controlling for income.

Bivariate regression is used to study the relationship between income and energy expenditure, while ordinary least squares regression is used here to examine the relationships with time use controlling for the housing and householder characteristics. In the ordinary least squares models, variables were entered in step-wise fashion, commencing with housing characteristics, and then adding in householder demographics and income and expenditure controls. Time use variables were then added in the form of home working characteristics, and then estimates of weekly time use.

Analysis was completed on pooled data for all households, and then broken down by four broad household types: lone-person households, couples without children, couples with children, and single parents with children. The results of the regression analyses of electricity and motor vehicle fuel expenditure, including the number of cases included in the regression analysis for the household type subsamples are included in the tables in Appendices 1 and 2.

Results

Income and energy expenditure

The first relationship in the model to be considered is that between household income and energy expenditure. Figure 3.4 presents the scatter plot showing the relationship between the gross household income and annual expenditure on electricity. As can be seen, there is a weak positive relationship.

A regression of electricity expenditure on the logarithm of gross household income indicates the approximately 9 per cent of the variance in household electricity expenditure is associated with differences in income levels between households (adjusted $R^2 = 0.09$). A similar relationship was found between household income and expenditure on motor vehicle fuel (not shown here), with around 8.4 per cent of the variance in fuel expenses explained by the level of income. This suggests that the level of income is an important control variable in any model of energy expenditure, but that the incorporation of a broader range of variables is necessary properly to explain the variation in energy consumption.

Market labour, domestic labour and other time

To estimate the effect of market and domestic labour time on the availability of other time, a cumulative measure of hours per adult for each

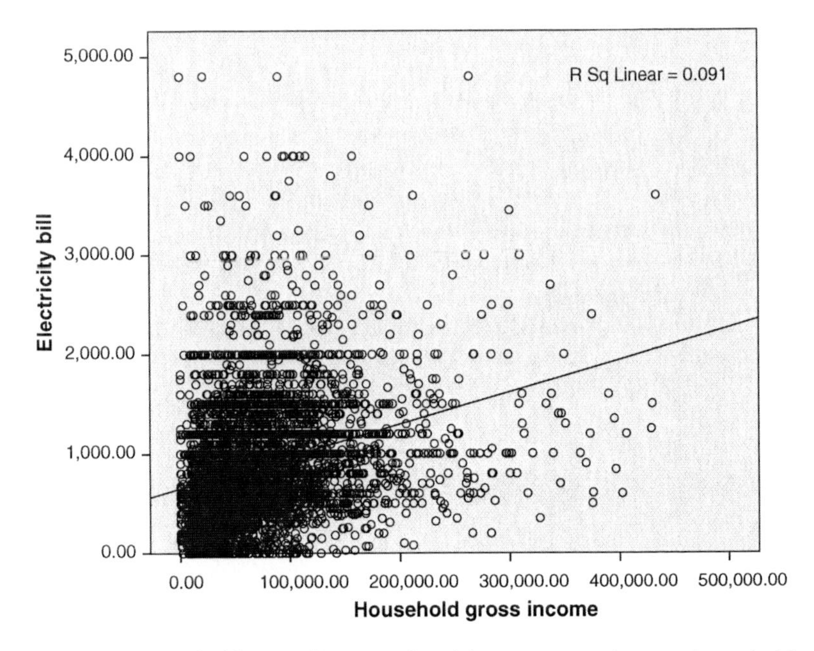

Figure 3.4 Household expenditure on electricity per annum by gross household income level

was calculated from the time use variables identified above. The 'other time' category (total other time per adult) was then used as the dependent variable regressed against market labour and domestic labour, first for all households, and then broken down by each of the four household types. The results of each of these are shown in Table 3.2.

The regression results indicate that the predominant time predictor of 'other time', or discretionary time available for leisure, is hours of domestic labour time. Counter-intuitively however, the relationship is generally a positive one, with more hours spent on domestic labour resulting in higher levels of time spent on other activities. The relationship is stronger in households with children. For example, in single parent households, an increase of one hour of domestic labour results in an average increase of 21 minutes (0.351 x 60) in 'other time' spent. This is partly a result of the time use categories making up the 'other time' measure, which is made up primarily of time spent with your own and other children, as well as volunteering and charity activities,[5] some of which might be perceived by a parent as domestic labour rather

Table 3.2 Linear regression of time spent on other activities, by household type

	All house-holds	Lone person	Couple - no children	Couple with children	Single parent with children
Intercept	2.581***	1.327***	2.127	10.409	11.274
(S.E.)	0.326	0.275	0.253	1.017	2.078
Market labour	0.05	0.008	−0.029	0.049	−0.03
(S.E.)	0.008	0.006	0.006	0.025	0.055
Domestic labour	0.166***	0.044***	0.029	0.3	0.351
(S.E.)	0.01	0.009	0.008	0.03	0.06
R2	0.04	0.014	0.034	0.065	0.087
Adj. R2	0.04	0.013	0.033	0.064	0.082

Note: *** P < .001

than leisure time. More notable is the absence of any effect of hours of market labour on other time. Regardless of whether the household has children, the number of hours per adult spent at work has virtually no effect on the number of hours of other time.

Time use and income

The third element of the time use-consumption model is the relationship between time use and income. The model in Figure 3.1 highlights that the effects of market labour time on household energy consumption may occur in two ways – a direct effect (discussed above) and an indirect effect, through the generation of income from paid employment, which provides the household capability to purchase electricity. While Table 3.2 above indicates that market labour does not have a significant effect on other time among the HILDA survey respondent households, it can be expected that market labour time will be a major determinant of income.

To assess the time use–income relationship, the logarithm of gross domestic income was regressed on the three aggregate time use variables (market labour, domestic labour and other time per adult) (see Table 3.3).

Time use, income and electricity expenditure

The final stage of the analysis, having assessed the relationships between different elements of time use, and between time use and income, is

Table 3.3 Linear regression of log (gross household income) on time use activities, by household type

	All households	Lone person	Couple - no children	Couple with children	Single parent with children
Intercept	9.731***	9.587***	9.829***	9.999***	9.793***
(S.E.)	0.018	0.034	0.038	0.038	0.052
Market labour	0.02***	0.02***	0.022***	0.016***	0.019***
(S.E.)	0	0	0	0.001	0.001
Domestic labour	-0.001	0.003***	-0.004***	-0.003*	0.003*
(S.E.)	0.001	0.001	0.001	0.001	0.002
Other time	0.007***	0.007***	0.003	0.005***	0.002
(S.E.)	0.001	0.001	0.003	0.001	0.001
R2	0.293	0.287	0.343	0.189	0.34
Adj. R2	0.293	0.285	0.342	0.187	0.335

Note: * P < .05; ** P < .01; *** P < .001

to examine the relationship between all of these and energy expenditure. The same approach to the regression models has been used in this analysis: firstly a pooled analysis of all households, and then separate regressions for each of the household types. The results of the regression for all households and the four household types are presented in Appendix 1.

The results of the model indicate that there is only a limited direct effect of measures of time use on electricity consumption. Across the four household types, addition of indicators of time use explained only around 1 per cent of the variation in the household's electricity expenditure. For single parent households, an additional 3 per cent of variance was explained; however this increase was not significant (F change = 1.333, p = 0.212).

The findings of the regression models also indicate that the effects of different types of time use varied depending on the type of household. The pooled analysis of all households indicated that hours working at home, hours of work-related travel and hours spent playing with other's children were the only time use factors that had an effect on electricity consumption. However, sub-sample analysis indicates that the pooled approach masks differences between households. For example, in single parent households an additional one hour of work per week per adult in the household was associated with a $25 decrease in the household's annual electricity bill ($p < 0.05$). By comparison, hours of work-related travel had a significant impact on the electricity bills of couple households, both with and without children.

The other finding of note from a lifestyle perspective is the effects of different forms of employment. Across most household types (other than single-parent households), the number of household members who were self-employed significantly increased household electricity bills. In lone person households, an increase in the number of hours spent working at home had a small negative effect on the electricity bill, with a decrease of around 40 cents for each additional hour worked at home (on average). By comparison, income levels had a significant positive effect in lone person and couple households with no children, but not in couple or single parent households with children.

Time use, employment and expenditure on motor vehicle fuel

The second stage of the energy use analysis focussed on expenditure on motor vehicle fuel. This was chosen as it provides insight into the impact of a different element of lifestyle patterns, namely the costs of moving between locations for different daily events. The same analysis procedure using the pooled household sample and then four subsamples of household types was used again, with annual expenditure on motor vehicle fuel as the dependent variable. The results of the ordinary least squares regression analysis are included in Appendix 1.

The explanatory power of time use variables was somewhat higher than for electricity expenditure. The increase in explained variance was between 1.7 and 3.7 per cent across different household types. This increase was significant for all types except single parent households. In general, the regression models explained between 13 and 17 per cent of the variation in household expenditure on motor vehicle fuel.

The pattern of variation between household types and the impact of different types of time use on expenditure was also present for motor vehicle fuel. In this case, there was a strong relationship with the number of hours of paid employment per adult (for couples either with or without children), and the number of hours of work-related travel (in lone person households). There were also significant relationships with different types of domestic labour, with hours spent on household errands and outdoor activities related to increasing fuel expenditure, but time spent on housework associated with decreasing expenditure.

There were also major differences between household types in the impact of income on fuel expenditure. For couple households, an increase in income of 10 per cent is associated with an increase in motor vehicle fuel expenditure of around 13 dollars per annum ($p < 0.001$), while for single parent households, the increase is close to 30 dollars per annum ($p = 0.051$). By comparison, the effects of income in households with either a lone person or a couple with children were not significant.

Discussion and conclusions

Having explored each of the paths present in the conceptual model presented in Figure 3.1, what conclusions can be drawn about the relationship between household lifestyles and energy consumption? In order to integrate the results of the various analyses, a summary of the significant results for the overall sample, and for the four subsamples of different household types are included in Figures 3.5 and 3.6 below. These figures draw together the results of all four sections of the results presented above, showing the nature of the relationships between each of the variables in the model.[6] The relationships shown in the model include control measures for the other householder and household variables discussed earlier – further details on these can be found in Appendix 1.

Figure 3.5 shows the regression coefficients (unstandardised beta coefficients) for each of the paths identified in the original conceptual model, for the pooled regressions of all households. The picture it suggests is that the there is a strong relationship of spending time on travel to work and of increasing income on expenditure on electricity, and very little effect of time spent on domestic activities (either domestic labour or other leisure activities).

This pooled approach, however, masks the differences that exist between different types of households in expenditure patterns. In order to identify these differences, the same summary of results has been developed for each of the four household types identified in the analysis – lone person households, couples without children, couples with children and single parent households. This summary, presented in Figure 3.6, shows a number of distinctions. In particular, caring activities increase expenditure for lone person households, while spending time with other children influences expenditure for couples with children. This suggests a difference in daily lifestyles among these groups – particular for parents where other children may come into the

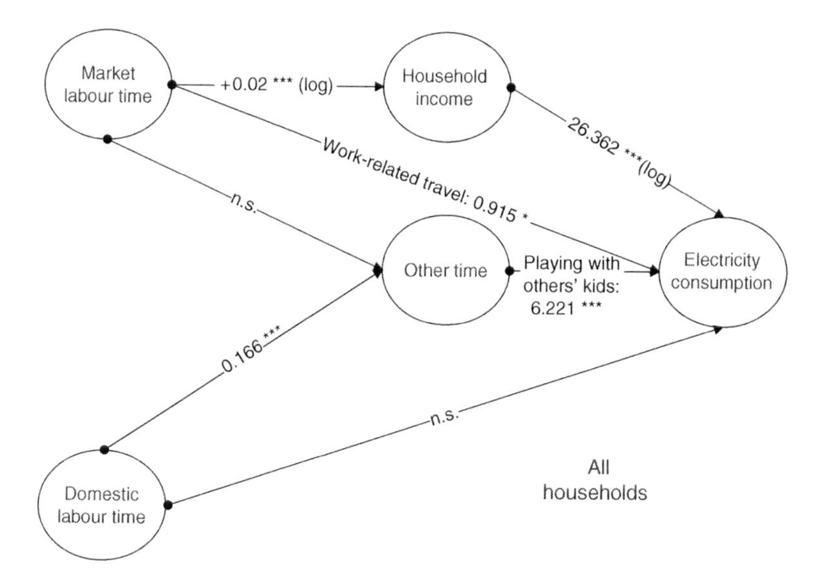

Figure 3.5 Relationships between time use, income and electricity expenditure – all households

house to visit the parent's own children, requiring activities such as entertainment and cooking, each of which consumes energy. Similarly persons living alone may be more likely to engage in care of others, such as grandparents looking after their grandchildren.

The other point of difference between households in electricity expenditure is in terms of the role of time spent in market labour. It was hypothesised that market labour may have an indirect effect on electricity consumption through the effect on income. While the hours spent in employment do have a clear effect on income levels, the indirect relationship with electricity expenditure was not apparent for either couples with children or single parent households.

A similar picture emerges when comparing household types in terms of expenditure on motor vehicle fuel. Figure 3.7 presents similar summary diagrams for each household type in relationship to fuel expenditure. Here the effects of income are even more marked, with income showing a strong relationship with fuel expenditure for couples without children, a strong but marginally significant relationship for single parent households, and no relationship for the other household types. The more consistent relationship with fuel expenditure was that of market labour time, either for work-related travel or hours of employment.

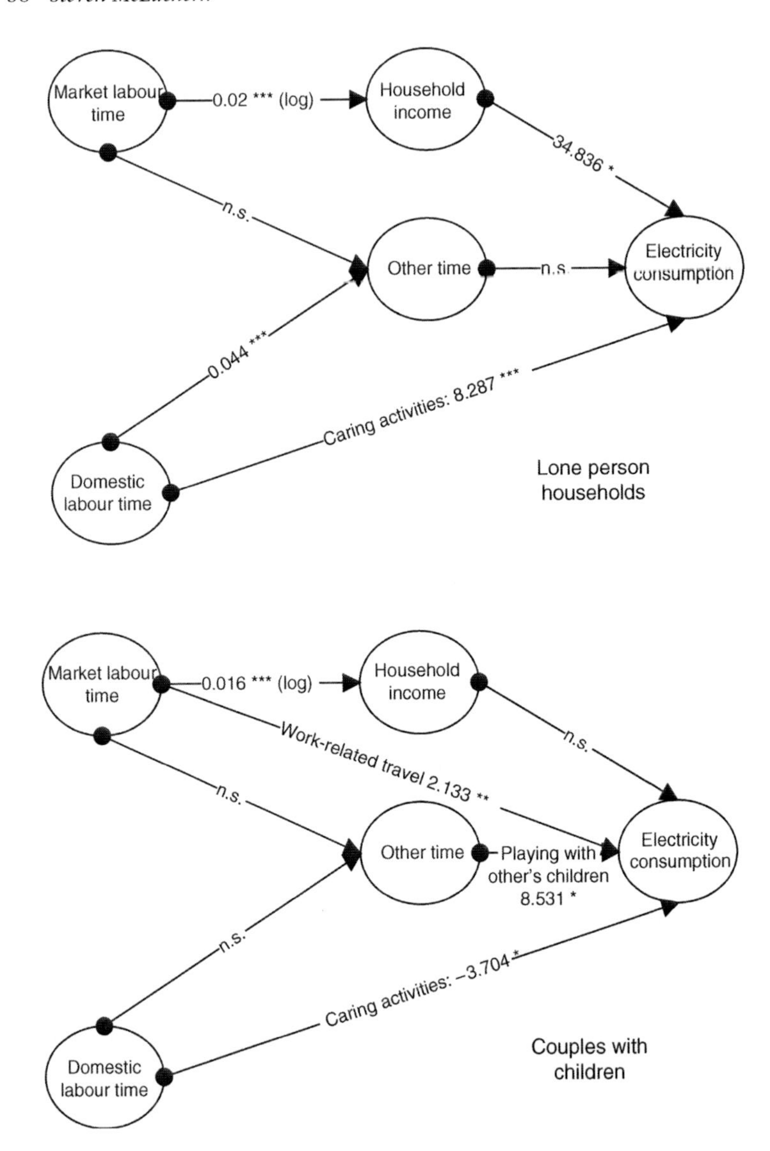

Figure 3.6 Continued

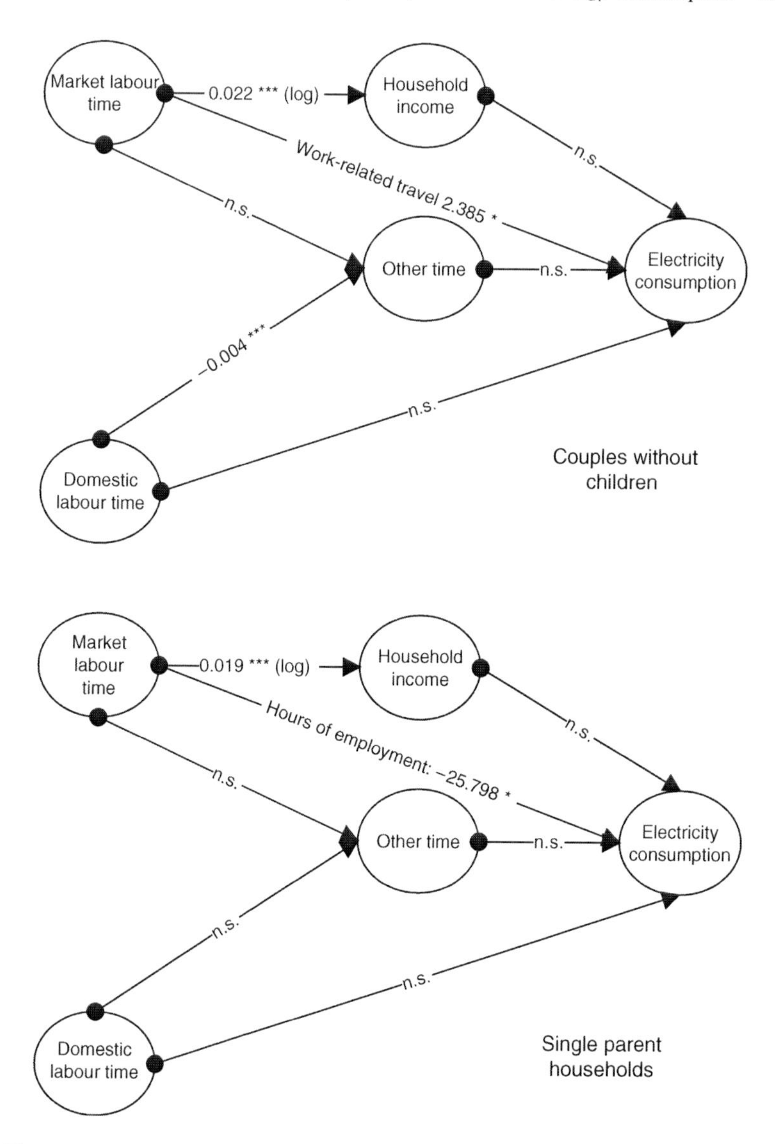

Figure 3.6 Relationship between time use, income and electricity expenditure – by household type

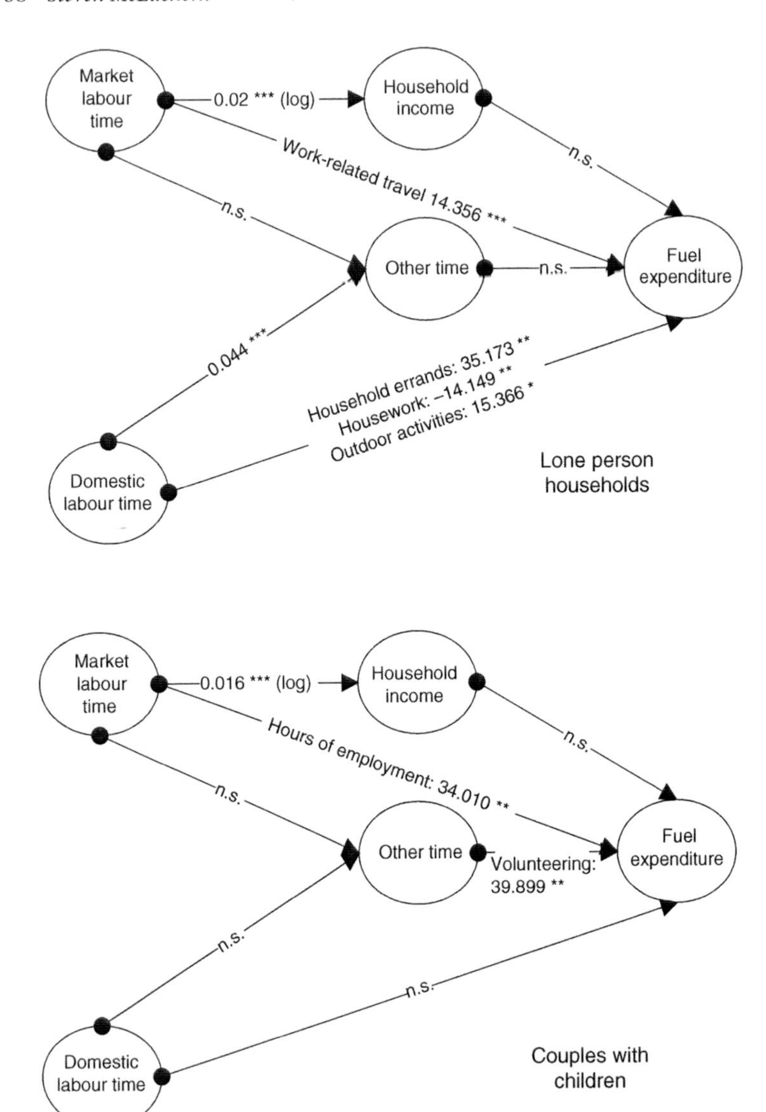

Figure 3.7 Continued

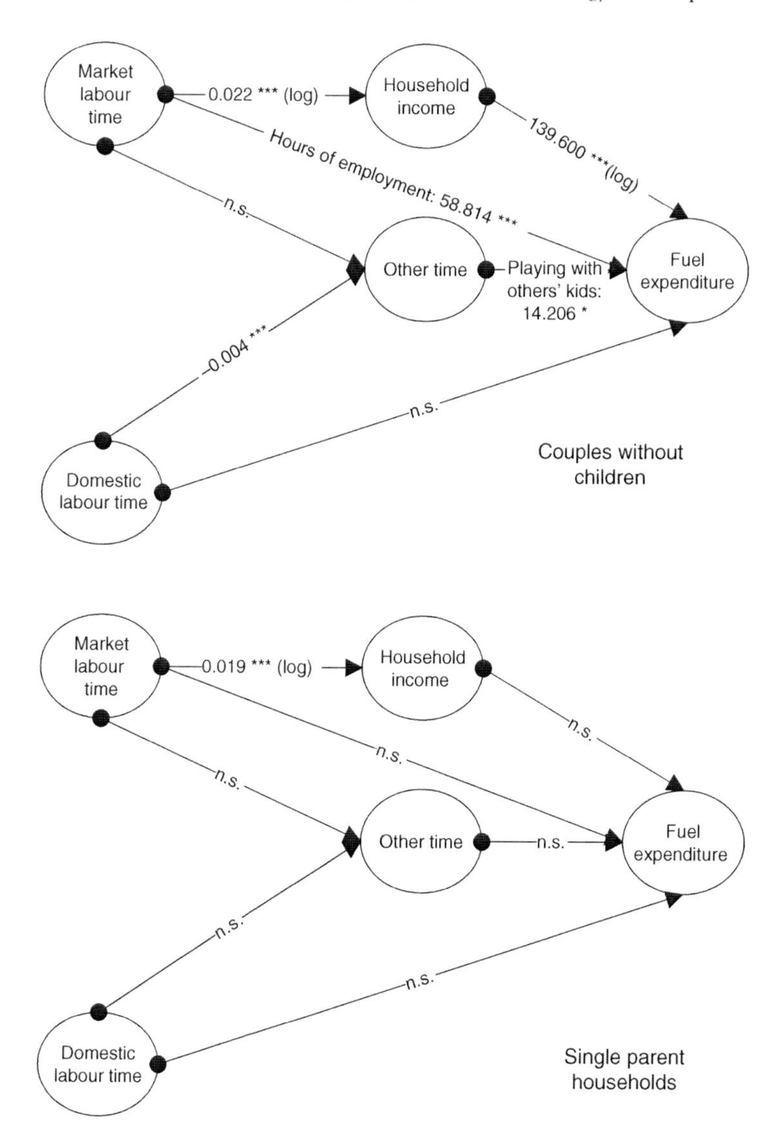

Figure 3.7 Relationship between time use, income and expenditure on motor vehicle fuel – by household type

The effects of living choices are, however, more apparent here. While there were few domestic labour or leisure activities which showed a significant relationship with fuel expenditure, there is a clear difference for those choosing to live alone. In this case, the choice of domestic labour activities has a strong effect on fuel consumption.

What conclusions then can be drawn from the results presented here for the implications of ways of living on consumption patterns? While the results from the HILDA data are somewhat mixed, the evidence does suggest that time use does matter for improving understanding of the patterns of energy expenditure associated with consumption.

It is clear from the results that one particular decision on how one lives has a significant consumption impact. The organisation of households, particularly whether one lives alone, has major implications for how individuals spend their time, and thus their capacity to 'efficiently' utilise time resources. Figure 3.7 highlights the notable demands living alone places on fuel consumption in order to maintain a household, while the time demands associated with market labour do require greater expenditure, but in different ways for different types of households.

Perhaps the more interesting implication of this study is the role of income for time-poor individuals. While the pooled results indicate a relationship between income and energy expenditure, this result largely disappears when the model is disaggregated into household types. The two exceptions here are couples with no children, where higher income is associated with higher fuel expenditure, and lone person households, where higher income is associated with higher electricity expenditure. This again, however, suggests a lifestyle influence – high income couples may use their income to go out, while high income single persons expend their funds on powering their residences.

The limited breadth of the HILDA data mean only tentative conclusions about the benefits of time use research for understanding energy consumption can be drawn. In particular, there are no data on the availability of appliances, either high-intensity or energy saving, and only condition reports to serve as proxies for more detailed data on household structures. These are both known and significant determinants of energy consumption, and such data would enable a better test of the links between time and energy discussed here. The availability of appliance usage data would also enable more detailed examination of Sullivan's (Sullivan and Gershuny, 2004; Sullivan, 2008) arguments about inconspicuous consumption. Similarly, the use of energy expenditure rather than direct energy consumption in the form of a measure of kilowatt hours leave this work open to considerations of the presence of measurement error, particularly given that households may be subject to different competition regimes and thus different capacities to influence their price paid for energy. This is less true for fuel consumption, but it does increase the need for more detailed data on both time use and energy use to get a better picture of their relationship.

Nonetheless, there is reasonable evidence from the results to suggest that further studies of the interaction of time, energy and consumption are warranted, to expand the understanding of the relationship between ways of living and the impacts of consumption. Such research would also enable improved policy making in the area of climate change policy. The comparison of the results for fuel and electricity expenditure do highlight that the incidence of the costs of energy consumption on households are partly a function of the lifestyle choices that households make, both how they set up their households, and how they choose to spend their time. This has implications for the equity of particular policies intended to mitigate the impact of climate change initiatives, particularly carbon taxes or emissions permit schemes. The evidence here suggests that persons living alone would be more prominently affected by petrol taxes incurred through maintaining their residence, whereas couples incur costs associated with their employment. Thus policy makers looking to understand the distributional and environmental effects of any climate change policies would be advised to look at the capacity of time use research to provide a more nuanced understanding of how differences in the way we live our daily lives might affect the world we live in.

Appendix 1

Table A3.1 Ordinary least squares regression of electricity expenditure on housing, householder and time use characteristics, by household type

	All households		Lone person household		Couple – no children		Couple with children		Single parent w/kids	
Variable	**B**	**Std Error**	**B**	**Std Error**	**B**	**Std Error**	**B**	**Std Error**	**B**	**Std Error**
(Constant)	3.594	83.154	–188.545	180.713	–242.044	152.342	44.707	196.963	460.048	654.003
Housing characteristics										
Semi-detached house	–12.413	18.350	–5.222	37.174	12.818	30.746	–91.880	44.275*	–108.669	91.760
Flat-apartment	10.312	16.390	–11.449	31.646	–17.551	27.180	–56.688	53.039	136.409	83.142
Good condition – house	–2.116	11.274	–9.308	29.933	–16.153	17.320	5.839	19.159	–51.640	65.324
Average condition – house	20.766	12.568	19.022	31.725	26.657	20.282	3.499	22.205	13.314	69.977
Poor condition – house	8.833	23.554	–4.613	52.956	–29.047	52.364	–39.240	46.180	–6.463	95.060
Very poor condition – house	–187.013	75.135*	–370.461	168.472*	–10.967	169.993	–161.767	120.955	–420.738	318.501
Unknown condition – house	–29.261	32.707	–157.437	76.024*	7.285	54.206	–19.863	59.277	179.676	172.653

NSW	81.595	17.095***	105.535	42.567*	53.391	26.205*	12.572	30.414	181.941	95.504
Victoria	17.846	17.587	57.185	43.814	74.907	27.066**	−18.829	30.992	99.383	100.202
Queensland	145.347	18.062***	202.473	45.006***	79.902	28.168**	46.562	32.170	198.905	98.763*
South Aust	112.662	21.103***	124.315	54.445*	110.389	32.019***	120.046	37.951**	191.402	109.296
Tasmania	266.158	29.983***	445.919	79.102***	141.593	47.651**	104.513	51.620*	688.875	149.391***
Northern Territory	269.397	65.422***	530.770	186.112**	368.491	134.471**	138.829	96.080	582.746	325.524
Aust Capital Territory	36.454	37.293	162.783	99.242	21.075	57.360	11.366	62.322	220.470	234.704
Inner regional	64.795	11.902***	74.892	31.032*	61.565	18.728**	49.244	20.485*	−8.997	58.947
Outer regional	119.625	15.993***	113.775	39.703**	109.369	24.475***	85.990	29.396**	138.333	83.448
Remote	78.811	37.455*	273.582	84.387**	27.033	61.772	24.322	63.217	−162.511	230.188
Very remote	137.543	86.814	28.890	254.342	80.924	121.917	−97.159	134.731	665.112	342.383
Householder characteristics										
No of 0–4 year olds	−0.065	12.626	–	–	–	–	15.598	14.590	54.914	51.862
No of 5–9 year olds	3.223	10.132	–	–	–	–	15.381	12.077	19.950	35.475
No of 10–14 year olds	12.519	9.729	–	–	–	–	23.482	13.364	15.052	45.662
No of adults	−89.192	7.562***	–	–	−2.795	42.713	−74.485	22.262***	−127.047	54.025*

Continued

Table A3.1 Continued

Variable	All households		Lone person household		Couple – no children		Couple with children		Single parent w/kids	
	B	Std Error	B	Std Error	B	Std Error	B	Std Error	B	Std Error
Income (log)	26.362	8.023***	34.836	17.602*	40.019	12.262**	33.825	17.708	–26.631	61.907
Expenditure on groceries	1.146	0.155***	0.789	0.337*	1.162	0.304***	0.799	0.282**	2.793	0.640***
Gas bills	0.633	0.017***	0.798	0.025***	0.166	0.050***	0.155	0.043***	0.293	0.092**
Motor vehicle fuel expenditure	0.029	0.004***	0.021	0.007**	0.044	0.008***	0.022	0.009*	0.004	0.023
Other heating fuel bill	0.421	0.060***	0.500	0.126***	0.289	0.107**	0.130	0.105	0.722	0.241**
Renting house	–13.694	12.413	–14.042	30.238	–20.777	22.258	–14.557	22.669	2.119	56.874
Rent-buy scheme	–246.206	120.777*	–87.658	250.182	–134.072	208.292	–250.174	212.285	–183.720	426.593
Living rent-free	–59.433	29.214*	–96.326	56.631	–48.063	48.161	21.758	68.690	–96.059	198.236
Home loan paid off	23.129	13.007	2.132	36.068	38.029	18.136*	8.893	26.553	53.301	114.820
Time use characteristics										
Number of self-employed	60.141	10.230***	152.758	47.536**	82.862	15.212***	51.669	14.517***	6.900	97.894

Number of home duties (primary task)	–1.807	16.687	–74.070	78.318	27.478	25.896	4.725	22.798	–73.779	88.618
Number of full-time students	27.831	10.851**	21.762	48.650	–9.012	26.811	17.331	22.563	41.643	57.049
Hours of work done at home per adult	–0.188	0.072**	–0.390	0.157*	0.075	3.442	–0.177	0.111	–0.057	0.848
Hours of employment per adult	–1.359	2.058	5.723	4.670	–0.105	0.602	–4.051	3.691	–25.798	10.878*
Hours of work-related travel per adult	0.915	0.374*	0.337	0.806	2.385	1.077*	2.133	0.783**	4.271	2.340
Hours of caring activities per adult	1.168	0.846	8.287	2.599**	–7.979	5.807	–3.704	1.720*	–2.475	11.266
Hours of playing with own children per adult	0.914	0.549	5.232	2.966	2.232	2.322	0.485	0.711	0.251	1.471
Hours of household errands per adult	–0.151	1.297	1.872	2.797	–1.379	1.189	–0.095	2.369	–3.019	4.595

Continued

Table A3.1 Continued

Variable	All households		Lone person household		Couple – no children		Couple with children		Single parent w/kids	
	B	Std Error	B	Std Error	B	Std Error	B	Std Error	B	Std Error
Hours of house-work per adult	0.438	0.670	1.008	1.420	–0.980	2.349	0.693	1.240	1.711	2.602
Hours of playing with others' children per adult	6.221	1.633***	7.298	4.132	2.061	1.500	8.531	4.056*	7.451	5.022
Hours of outdoor activities per adult	1.708	1.024	1.033	2.040	–1.363	2.525	0.928	2.556	–6.435	7.093
Hours of volunteering and charity work per adult Hour Outdoor tasks Hours of	–0.071	1.699	–0.269	3.301	–0.010	0.115	6.627	5.235	–9.407	7.998
N	5529		1386		1633		1363		326	
R^2	0.328		0.487		0.152		0.169		0.405	
Adjusted R^2	0.322		0.471		0.130		0.142		0.312	
R2 change	0.004		0.009		0.006		0.014		0.028	
F change	3.205		2.485		1.121		2.293		1.333	
df1	9		9		10		10		10	
df2	5484		1345		1591		1318		281	
Significance (F)	0.001		0.008		0.342		0.012		0.212	

Appendix 2

Table A3.2 Ordinary least squares regression of motor vehicle fuel expenditure on housing, householder and time use characteristics

	All households		Lone person household		Couple – no children		Couple with children		Single parent w/kids	
Variable	**B**	**Std Error**	**B**	**Std Error**	**B**	**Std Error**	**B**	**Std Error**	**B**	**Std Error**
(Constant)	–94.824	273.755	32.723	689.751	–632.055	455.447	588.726	581.723	–2333.830	1723.205
Housing characteristics										
Semi-detached house	–208.964	60.350***	–245.497	141.674	–221.851	91.738*	–217.806	130.890	53.767	242.931
Flat-apartment	–342.178	53.763***	–383.364	120.292***	–320.876	80.856***	–161.382	156.711	–275.575	220.024
Good condition – house	–26.127	37.113	–176.359	114.105	9.168	51.786	64.280	56.580	44.116	172.700
Average condition – house	–70.184	41.375	–118.980	121.013	–93.585	60.613	–78.416	65.571	–202.929	184.432
Poor condition – house	–48.763	77.543	–6.935	202.044	53.986	156.530	–161.325	136.407	–402.581	249.916
Very poor condition – house	49.743	247.495	150.706	643.910	813.817	507.711	135.006	357.589	–225.312	843.699

Continued

Table A3.2 Continued

Variable	All households		Lone person household		Couple – no children		Couple with children		Single parent w/kids	
	B	Std Error	B	Std Error	B	Std Error	B	Std Error	B	Std Error
Unknown condition – house	18.850	107.687	–290.276	290.408	–38.368	162.022	182.424	175.072	837.689	454.134
NSW	–119.120	56.374*	–265.345	162.616	–88.452	78.398	–78.939	89.838	–21.408	253.857
Victoria	23.896	57.905	85.352	167.254	–47.598	81.088	28.459	91.576	180.722	264.889
Queensland	–125.292	59.788*	–224.376	172.891	–74.386	84.388	–163.728	95.016	124.595	262.616
South Aust	–109.282	69.639	–226.154	208.034	–86.736	96.039	–98.277	112.521	26.017	290.230
Tasmania	–277.316	99.346**	–654.969	304.818*	–276.359	142.659	–133.727	152.705	–18.664	409.214
Northern Territory	–219.126	215.692	–79.429	712.212	–691.746	402.516	–320.443	283.961	–252.047	864.504
Aust Capital Territory	216.543	122.751	180.387	378.982	88.707	171.445	97.454	184.116	1808.894	611.403**
Inner regional	135.614	39.247***	329.769	118.310***	157.001	56.031**	42.473	60.644	31.859	155.680
Outer regional	114.880	52.897*	179.073	151.864	242.249	73.363***	–100.584	87.090	–105.491	221.381
Remote	62.991	123.357	0.970	323.217	–153.595	184.611	434.217	186.405*	–154.484	608.422
Very remote	38.834	285.872	1956.109	968.928*	–351.122	364.361	–892.794	397.387*	495.350	909.845

Householder characteristics										
No of 0–4 year olds	–1.407	41.565	–	–	–	–	32.901	43.115	–34.200	137.231
No of 5–9 year olds	15.853	33.355	–	–	–	–	28.516	35.697	–78.504	93.630
No of 10–14 year olds	–10.906	32.036	–	–	–	–	10.137	39.529	–116.399	120.422
No of adults	–155.346	25.122***			–125.030	127.634***	–105.350	65.989	–266.003	143.207
Income (log)	75.870	26.420**	34.591	67.248	139.600	36.607	32.491	52.385	318.520	162.449
Expenditure on groceries	2.701	0.513***	2.617	1.286*	1.413	0.912	2.909	0.832***	4.362	1.727*
Gas bills	–0.166	0.061**	–0.234	0.126	–0.093	0.149	–0.321	0.127*	0.178	0.248
Electricity bills	0.313	0.044***	0.304	0.104**	0.394	0.074***	0.191	0.081*	0.030	0.158
Other heating fuel bill	0.987	0.197***	2.029	0.479***	0.338	0.319	0.991	0.308***	–0.494	0.646
Renting house	46.325	40.865	79.605	115.354	78.018	66.519	–63.651	66.964	–37.972	150.194
Rent-buy scheme	–429.096	397.729	–460.426	954.479	–488.791	622.559	–366.042	627.456	245.760	1126.960
Living rent-free	95.068	96.206	176.518	216.243	48.310	143.995	–176.338	202.898	–667.352	522.268
Home loan paid off	23.900	42.832	–27.178	137.608	91.762	54.237	–10.385	78.455	–131.407	303.267

Continued

Table A3.2 Continued

	All households		Lone person household		Couple – no children		Couple with children		Single parent w/kids	
Variable	**B**	**Std Error**	**B**	**Std Error**	**B**	**Std Error**	**B**	**Std Error**	**B**	**Std Error**
Time use characteristics										
Number of self-employed	286.920	33.561***	1272.754	178.722***	236.859	45.505***	231.265	42.624	268.666	258.055
Number of home duties (primary task)	37.216	54.934	–142.876	298.879	10.044	77.430	–76.695	67.326	243.498	233.887
Number of full-time students	67.434	35.732	99.363	185.607	118.108	80.089	–87.774	66.634	232.911	150.173
Hours of work done at home per adult	0.517	0.237*	0.576	0.602	0.441	0.343	–0.107	0.327	1.277	2.240
Hours of employment per adult	44.965	6.747***	32.611	17.806	58.814	10.182***	34.010	10.871**	52.807	28.845
Hours of work-related travel per adult	7.054	1.229***	14.356	3.051***	–0.062	1.801	0.715	2.321	5.087	6.208
Hours of caring activities per adult	1.182	2.787	1.784	9.954	–3.439	3.222	–1.257	5.090	18.554	29.738

Hours of playing with own children per adult	2.677	1.806	–12.389	11.322	3.513	17.368	1.555	2.101	–1.594	3.884
Hours of household errands per adult	13.928	4.265***	35.173	10.628***	–3.811	6.942	9.579	6.993	–5.870	12.141
Hours of housework per adult	–8.227	2.204***	–14.149	5.404**	–2.900	3.554	–4.967	3.661	0.057	6.877
Hours of playing with others' children per adult	4.533	5.382	13.327	15.779	14.206	7.013*	–19.587	11.990	–3.366	13.315
Hours of outdoor activities per adult	10.730	3.370***	15.366	7.772*	5.154	4.484	11.126	7.547	13.971	18.743
Hours of volunteering and charity work per adult Hour Outdoor tasks Hours of	11.617	5.592*	11.375	12.590	4.878	7.546	39.899	15.439**	17.493	21.149

Continued

Table A3.2 Continued

Variable	All households		Lone person household		Couple – no children		Couple with children		Single parent w/kids	
	B	Std Error	B	Std Error	B	Std Error	B	Std Error	B	Std Error
N	5529		1386		1633		1363		326	
R^2	0.142		0.187		0.159		0.158		0.282	
Adjusted R^2	0.135		0.163		0.137		0.130		0.170	
R2 change	0.027		0.037		0.028		0.017		0.024	
F change	19.494		6.812		5.356		2.588		0.950	
df1	9		9		10		10		10	
df2	5484		1345		1591		1318		281	
Significance(F)										

Note: *P < .05; **P < .01; ***P < .001

Notes

1. Economists term this the income elasticity of demand.
2. This is usually termed indirect energy demand in the industrial ecology literature – Jalas, M. (2005) 'The Everyday Life Context of Increasing Energy Demands: Time Use Survey Data in a Decomposition Analysis', *Journal of Industrial Ecology*, 9(1–2): 129–45.
3. Suggested readings for those interested in this area are O'Neill and Chen O'Neill, B. and B. Chen (2002). 'Demographic Determinants of Household Energy Use in the United States.' Methods of Population-Environment Analysis, A Supplement to *Population and Development Review*, 28: 53–88, and Wilson, C. and H. Dowlatabadi (2007) 'Models of decision making and residential energy use', *Annual Review of Environment and Resources*, 32: 169–203.
4. Western Australia was chosen as the base category, as WA residents exhibited the lowest average household expenditure on electricity among the sample.
5. These are the only categories of 'other' or leisure time activities for which questions were asked in the HILDA survey.
6. Readers should note that the figure is not a structural equation model, but rather a summative representation of the beta coefficients for the three separate regression models included in the results (taken from Tables 3.2 and 3.3 and Appendix1.

References

Abrahamse, W., L. Steg, C. Vlek and T. Rothengatter (2005) 'A review of intervention studies aimed at household energy conservation, *Journal of Environmental Psychology*, 25: 273–91.

Australian Bureau of Statistics (2008) *How Australians Use Their Time, 2006*. Canberra: Australian Bureau of Statistics.

Becker, G.S. (1965) 'A theory of the allocation of time', *Economic Journal*, 75 (299): 493–517.

Bittman, M. and J.M. Rice (2002) 'The spectre of overwork: an analysis of trends between 1974 and 1997 using Australian time-use diaries', *Labour and Industry*, 12 (3): 5–25.

Brohmann, B., S. Heinzle, K. Rennings, J. Schleich and R. Wustenhagen (2009) 'What's Driving Sustainable Energy Consumption? A Survey of the Empirical Literature', Centre for European Economic Research. Discussion Paper No. 09–013: 1–30.

Duchin, F. (1997) 'Structural economics: A strategy for analyzing the implications of consumption', in P.C. Stern, T. Dietz, V.W. Ruttan, R.H. Socolow and J.L. Sweeney (eds) *Environmentally Significant Consumption: Research Directions*. Washington, DC: National Academy Press: 63–72.

Energy Efficient Strategies (2008) *Energy Use in the Australian Residential Sector 1986–2020*. Canberra.

Gatersleben, B., L. Steg and C. Vlek (2002) 'Measurement and determinants of environmentally significant consumer behavior', *Environment and Behaviour*, 34 (3): 335–62.

Gershuny, J. (2000) *Changing Times: Work and Leisure in Post-Industrial Society*. Oxford: Oxford University Press.

Greening, L., D. Greene and C. Difiglio (2000) 'Energy efficiency and consumption – the rebound effect – a survey', *Energy Policy,* 28: 389–401.
Jacobs, J.A. and K. Gerson (2001) 'Overworked individuals or overworked families? explaining trends in work, leisure, and family time', *Work and Occupations,* 28 (1): 40–63.
Jalas, M. (2005) 'The everyday life context of increasing energy demands: time use survey data in a decomposition analysis', *Journal of Industrial Ecology,* 9 (1–2): 129–45.
Lutzenheiser, L. (1993) 'Social and behavioural aspects of energy use', *Annual Review of Energy and Environment,* 18: 247–89.
Melbourne Institute of Applied Economic and Social Research (2005) Household, Income and Labour Dynamics in Australia (HILDA) Survey Wave 5. Melbourne, Melbourne Institute.
O'Neill, B. and B. Chen (2002) 'Demographic determinants of household energy use in the United States', *Methods of Population-Environment Analysis, A Supplement to Population and Development Review,* 28: 53–88.
Oliphant, M. (2003) *South Australian Residential Sector Baseline Study of Energy Consumption.* Mawson Lakes, Sustainable Energy Centre, University of South Australia.
Robinson, J. (1988) 'Who's doing the housework?' *American Demographics,* (December): 24–63.
Schipper, L., S. Bartlett, D. Hawk and E. Vine (1989) 'Linking life-styles and energy use: a matter of time?' *Annual Review of Energy,* 14 (1): 273–320.
Schor, J. (2005) 'Sustainable consumption and worktime reduction', *Journal of Industrial Ecology,* 9 (1–2): 37–50.
Stern, P.C. (2000) 'Toward a coherent theory of environmentally significant behavior', *Journal of Social Issues,* 56 (3): 407–24.
Sullivan, O. (2008) 'Busyness, status distinction and consumption strategies of the income rich, time poor', *Time and Society,* 17 (1): 5–26.
Sullivan, O. and J. Gershuny (2004) 'Inconspicuous consumption: work-rich, time-poor in the Liberal Market Economy', *Journal of Consumer Culture,* 4 (1): 79–100.
Wilhite, H. and L. Lutzenheiser (1999) 'Social loading and sustainable consumption', *Annals of Consumer Research,* 26: 281–7.
Wilson, C. and H. Dowlatabadi (2007) 'Models of decision making and residential energy use', *Annual Review of Environment and Resources,* 32: 169–203.

4

Longer to Launch: Demographic Changes in Life-Course Transitions

Rosemary A. Venne

Introduction

Since the late twentieth century, a new pattern has been witnessed in the life-course transitions of youth; it is one that is more prolonged and complex than it was a generation ago. Labelled as 'longer to launch.' the term refers to young people finishing their education, beginning their careers, and leaving their parents' homes later in life. Their transitions are not necessarily a one-step linear process. Rather, due to the increasing ages of home-leaving and the increasing percentage of youth who return to the parental home (after an initial departure), the phenomenon is one that is more complex as the literature on the cluttered nest (versus the empty nest) informs us (see Boyd and Norris, 2000 and Mitchell, 2006a).

Essentially, the story of longer to launch or delayed transitions begins with the related developments of rising life expectancy and rising postwar prosperity. These two developments have an enormous impact on our life course and our transitions within the life course. It is a story of an elongated front end of the life course and subsequent delayed transitions from youth to adulthood compared to the previous generation. The most relevant variable over the life course is increasing life expectancy. Life span at birth has increased by approximately two years per decade over the twentieth century in most industrialised countries, with greater increases earlier in the century and more modest increases in the latter part of the century (see Foot, 1998: 284). Several parts of the life course are being elongated, particularly youth and the end part, the post-retirement period. It is the former, youth to early adulthood, broadly defined as from mid-adolescence to the mid-30s, which is the focus of this chapter.

The most important transition in the youth stage of the life course is the education-to-work one, with the others (e.g. home leaving) being very related to this key transition. It has been said that delaying this first transition, the education-to-work transition (which is associated with greater educational attainment) delays all other transitions. In this analysis of the front end of the life course, the areas that will be addressed are: the expansion of youth and its place in the life course, the education-to-work transition, home-leaving, marriage and fertility patterns, followed by a conclusion and policy implications. The objective of this chapter is to analyse the factors related to delayed transitions by drawing comparisons between the benchmark post-war period and more recent changes. The lock-step and compressed patterns of the post-war era have given way to more complex and prolonged transitions with greater individual choice. Gaudet (2007: 7) for example, refers to the post-WWII period as one of the most standardised historic times in the twentieth century in that social norms in western countries required timetables for early adulthood based on the sequence of school, marriage and parenthood. She notes that there is consensus among researchers that beginning in the early 1970s, a change occurred in the standardisation of the ages associated with roles and the sequences of these roles. This chapter will discuss these changes and put them into context and show that while youth are taking longer to launch in the early twenty-first century, given the economic complexities and changing career patterns, it is certainly not a failure to launch.

Cross-national comparisons will mainly involve Canada and the U.S. Census data from Canada and the U.S. will be used to illustrate the changing life course transitions. Comparisons will also be drawn with two European countries, the U.K. and Sweden. Esping-Andersen (2006) provides a framework of various types of welfare state. Beaujot and Kerr (2007) discuss how these various welfare states can impact youth transitions as government assistance can affect the often-difficult entry into the labour force. The U.S., Canada and the U.K., being liberal democracies, are expected to have fairly similar patterns in youth transitions. In contrast, Sweden, being a social democracy with greater social transfers, is expected to be the most different from North America and the U.K.

Before delving into the analysis, it is necessary to first present definitions of the terms life course and transition. While life cycle refers to normative stages and an ordered sequencing of events (e.g. marriage followed by parenthood), the life course perspective is much broader and takes into account the connection between individual lives and the historical and socio-economic context in which these lives unfold (Mitchell, 2006a: 16). Within the life course, a transition is defined as a discrete life change. Mitchell (2006a: 2) points out that we cannot assume a fixed or normal life-cycle pattern of youth transitions, given the diversity and impermanence of many transitional behaviours. The title of her book, *The Boomerang Age*, refers to the popular expression 'boomerang kids,' describing youths returning to the parental home after an initial departure and also refers to the reversibility and impermanence of many of these youth transitions.

In explaining this perspective, Anisef and Axelrod (2001) state that within this life-course framework, education-to-work and other transitions are seen as constructed by individuals in the context of decisions that are beyond their control (e.g. state of the economy) and those which depend on personal choice (e.g. marriage). In this model the individual does her or his utmost in constructing a life script, while at the same time recognizing that there are social forces that might affect the available outcomes and options. One key point to note is that in terms of choices, there is an increased range of options available to contemporary youth compared to the life course of people a generation ago. The latter group mostly followed a compressed and somewhat constrained road map into adulthood.

The expansion of youth in the life course

The purpose of this section is to discuss the expansion of youth and its place in the life course. We tend to discuss rising life expectancy mostly in terms of the end stages of the life course or longer periods of retirement. Yet other parts of the life course have also been stretched out or elongated including adolescence, post-secondary education and the transition from education to work. Kaplan's (1997) theory of the life course proposes that later transitions can be linked to longer life spans. The period of emerging adulthood makes more sense with increased life expectancy as devoting years to exploration roles becomes more feasible and attractive when people can expect to live to be at least 70 or 80 rather than only 50 years old (Arnett, 2000). Arnett (2000) suggests that the prolonged period of emerging adulthood is possible only in industrialised societies that allow young people a period of independent role exploration. He views this as a culturally constructed period, typical in industrialised countries.

Instead of the typical three-stage life span model with first, a dependent childhood phase, second, a middle productive and reproductive adult stage and finally a retirement end stage, Beaujot (2004) refers to a five-stage model. At the front end, the childhood phase is subdivided into childhood and a youth/adolescence phase, while the retirement stage is subdivided into an early retirement stage and an elderly stage. Thus, his five-stage life-span includes the ages of childhood (0–14), adolescence and young adulthood (15–34), prime working adult ages (35–59), followed by retirement ages (60–79) and an elderly period (80 years and over).

Several terms have emerged to capture the phenomenon of prolonged youth including emerging adulthood, quarter-life crisis and 'fledgling' adults. The latter term was coined in a brief article entitled 'Adulthood Today' (2001), which appeared in a Canadian national newspaper. An American social psychologist stated that adulthood no longer arrives in the 20s, but instead arrives at age 35. He went on to note that the cost of housing, education, and delayed marriages are factors making twenty-somethings fledgling adults.

Ricard (1992: 76) discusses the prolongation of adolescence and the central position of youth in the post-war period as cataclysmic. Instead of a phase one quickly passed through, a new definition of youth emerged, occupying a central position in society, and lasting 10, 12, or even 15 years. Larson et al. (2002: 159) note that this adolescent stage is expanding in length in most parts of the world as a product of later age of marriage, longer schooling and more engagement in peer worlds. More recently, Arnett (2000) and Gaudet (2007) describe 'emerging' adulthood as a period of identity exploration that has emerged in the latter half of the twentieth century in industrialised countries due to sweeping demographic changes. This distinct life-course period occurring between adolescence and adulthood, defined as ages 18–25, is characterised by unpredictability and demographic uncertainty.

The term, 'quarter-life crisis.' after the term mid-life crisis, describes the period between graduation (high school or postsecondary education) and one's 30th birthday when young adults struggle to find their place in the world (Robbins and Wilner, 2001). The authors describe the disappearance of the road map that previous generations had in their smoother transition from education to work life. These late twentieth and early twenty-first century concerns about the education-to-work transition are exemplified by several popular as well as academic books (e.g. *Quarterlife Crisis: the Unique Challenges of Life in your Twenties,* (Robbins and Wilner, 2001), *The Turbulent Twenties Survival Guide* (Salazar, 2006), *Generation Me* (Twenge, 2006), *Adolescence and Emerging*

Adulthood (Arnett, 2007), *The Boomerang Age* (Mitchell, 2006a), and *Ready or Not, Here Life Comes* (Levine, 2005).

The book, *Quarterlife Crisis* (Robbins and Wilner, 2001) describes what Levine refers to as the start-up years and the problem of work-life unreadiness. Levine (2005: 3) notes that the start-up years, or the education-to-work transition period, can start in the mid teens, upon dropping out of high school, or as late as the late 20s, following a period of prolonged post-secondary education (e.g. a five-year medical residency following medical school). He acknowledges that the transition to adult work life is one of life's most daunting periods and he laments that we are in the midst of an epidemic of work-life unreadiness.

Levine (2005: 19) discusses 'persistent' adolescence and notes that we live in an era that inflates, celebrates and consecrates adolescence. Owram (1996: 124) also notes that as the school experience became more universal and prolonged, in the postwar period the sense of peer group was accentuated and daily contact with those of differing ages and experiences was postponed and one consequence has been shifting social norms. For example, in her examination of surveys over several decades, Twenge (2006) finds fundamental value changes in the generations from the late 1950s and early 1960s to the early twenty-first century including the loosening of social rules, decreasing respect for authority, and the increasing focus on the self in young adults. Other value shifts among young workers include increasingly vocal demands for work-life balance (see Lancaster and Stillman, 2002).

In short, the period of youth has become more central in our society as well as more elongated and challenging on an individual level with more choice than ever before. In the section that follows, the main transition of education to work will be examined. What emerges is that these concerns about quarter-life crisis and emerging adulthood began in the last decades of the twentieth century, during a time of significant change in career patterns (with an increasing demand for credentialism) and declining wage growth.

Education-to-work transition

Shanahan et al. (2002) posit that the education-to-work transition is a story about adolescents and their life histories, but it is also a story about how this age phase fits into the life course and society. Their main concern revolves around preparation of youth for adult work. The importance of this education-to-work stage in the life course cannot be emphasized enough as Larson et al. (2002: 159) point out: the future of societies depends on their success in providing stable pathways whereby youth develop and prepare themselves to be contributing adults in their communities.

In analysing this transition, a historical perspective will be presented to illustrate the nature of the post-war economy and its implications for career patterns over this period. The objective is to paint a picture of the demographic and work realities of this benchmark period to better illustrate how subsequent changes have led to delayed transitions in the life course of youth today.

It is generally acknowledged that the immediate post-war decades are anomalous as many demographic trends reversed themselves (see Coontz, 1992). Ricard (1992: 55) refers to this period in North America as the 30 glorious years of unparalleled prosperity marked by a steady rise in the standard of living, an acceleration of technological development and an expansion of consumerism.

It was a prosperity boosted by the interventionist role of the state. For example, the U.S. government provided education benefits, job training, guaranteed mortgages and loans (Mitchell, 2006a: 43). Coontz (1992) also points out that the upward mobility of the American suburban family was subsidised by government spending. Similarly, Owram (1996: 25) notes that in Canada, government aid for returning veterans also acted as a spur to the economy. The impact of such prosperity encouraged early home-leaving, early marriage and early childbearing as young people made an easy transition into the labour force. Thus, for the cohorts that came of age during the two postwar decades of the 1950s and 1960s, the transition to adulthood was compressed where transitions began to occur at increasingly younger ages (see Beaujot and Kerr, 2007: 30).

Betcherman and Lowe (1997: 16) question the use of the prosperous and anomalous post-war decades as the implicit benchmark for present-day life-course transitions. While explaining the post-war prosperity, they speculate that future historians will characterise the final decades of the twentieth century as a period when North America, and in fact all industrialized countries, struggled with the transition from a long and prosperous post-war period of industrialism to a new 'post-industrial' age. The economic slowdown of the last two decades of the twentieth century may be partly due to the fact that we have exhausted the growth potential of the post-war mass-production economy in North America (Betcherman and Lowe, 1997: 40). In contrast to the post-war boom, the economic slowdown since the late 1970s has been evidenced by slower wage growth, lessened job security, higher unemployment and increased credentialism (see also Mitchell, 2006a).

Mitchell (2006a: 58) goes on to note these late twentieth century economic deteriorations took place despite rising educational levels, increasing participation of women in the labour force and an increasing level of dual-earner households. Other economic forces included the growth of global trade, several severe recessions and the retrenchment of the welfare state. These cutbacks in state support are associated with later transitions with families having to shoulder the burden of their 'grown' children (Mitchell, 2006a: 130).

In analyses of the education-to-work transition there has been an emphasis on the appropriateness of interdisciplinary approaches. However, what is often missing from the current analysis of the school-to-work transition is any discussion of how career patterns are evolving. In terms of careers, Bardwick (1986: 31) points out that during the extraordinary period of post-war expansion, North America went through a period of very rapid organisational growth in which there was a disproportionate increase in white-collar and middle-management jobs. In her book, *The Death of the Organization Man*, Bennett (1990) points out that the one-company-for-life philosophy developed during a time of muted competition, when employees were hired at entry level, trained and groomed for lifetime employment at one particular workplace. Essentially, the organisation mattered greatly as it controlled an individual's career using internal career ladders. Leana (2002) discusses the transfer of risk from the organisation to the individual in terms of managing careers today. Organisations matter less now in that most employees will work for a greater number of employers for a shorter average duration over the course of their careers (Leana, 2002: 274).

The demographics of labour force supply in North America place another layer of complexity over this post-war growth period (see Foot and Venne, 1990). Bust, or small demographic groups, generally do well compared to boom groups, as the former groups face less generational crowding. During the post-war years, a small, mainly male, bust group (mostly born over the great depression and WWII) was entering the labour force. Driver (1985) notes that for the US, this bust generation enjoyed high job mobility and demand as they came of labour force age during the post-war expansion but the baby boom generation (born during the two immediate post-war decades) has faced a world of greater competition, lower demand and mobility.

Driver's (1985) key premise was that demographic boom and bust conditions can affect your career mobility. Cappelli (2003) however, points out that economic conditions are even more important. The large post-war baby boom in North America (comprising close to one-third of the population in Canada, slightly less in the U.S.) entered the labour force beginning in the late 1960s and into the early 1980s. Labour force growth also expanded during this time due to the significant entry of women into the workforce. To use a popular expression, the perfect storm, so to speak, occurred with the influx of the large post-war baby boom group, increased global competition and technological change. There was job growth in the expanding service sector over this time but technological change helped to eliminate many entry-level and support-type jobs as well as middle management jobs (see Bardwick, 1986 and Bennett, 1990). Cappelli (2003) notes that real wages fell sharply during this period of surplus labour.

Gaudet (2007) mentions that in North America, those born after the peak of the baby boom (after the late 1950s) began to encounter difficulty joining the labour market as globalisation, downsizing and saturation of the labour markets (due to the massive baby boom generation) intensified. Life-long stable career patterns of the early post-war decades have given way to less stable and more varied career patterns with organisational delayering and downsizing, creeping credentialism and life-long learning as issues.

One major point here is that the labour force entrants during the post-war economic expansion enjoyed an amazing interaction effect of being a bust group during a prolonged period of economic expansion. Their experiences were unusual and yet we frequently use them as a benchmark. Their experiences of early transitions are not likely to happen again, especially given that most researchers agree that credentialism or increased demand for education, discussed below, is here to stay (see Mitchell, 2006a).

With respect to credentialism Cote and Allahar (2007: 26) note that as more workers with university degrees flooded the job market (in North America this began with the large post-war baby boom generation) employers simply began to take those with the highest credentials. They point out that these university graduates may well be doing the same jobs as did workers of their parents' generation who were job-ready with a high school diploma.

It was mentioned earlier that the strong wage growth from the early post-war decades has slowed down dramatically beginning in the late 1970s/early 1980s. Cote and Allahar (2007: 173) give evidence that while inflation-adjusted average incomes of young Canadians and Americans have remained the same (Canadian) or increased by 5 per cent (U.S.) between 1980 and 2000, the incomes of high school graduates dropped by 10–15 per cent in Canada and by 20 per cent for the U.S. Those without some type of post-secondary education are dubbed the forgotten half. Little (1999) proposes that the 1990s will be described as the decade when the labour market divided into the educational haves and have-nots as most job growth over this decade went to those with post-secondary education. Gaudet (2007) notes that the now longer period of education among youth highlights the economic disparity between those with and those without post-secondary education.

In the book, *Improving School-to-work Transitions*, David Neumark and others assess the wide range of American educational policies aimed at easing young people's transitions (e.g. career academies, co-op programs). For example, Neumark (2007: 13) notes that the so-called forgotten half, the non-college bound students, have benefited from these programs, especially those males less likely to attend college. Though the transition to adulthood can take place in different order and over a wide age range, Jekeliuk and Brown (2005) note that in the U.S., a proportion of youth (defined as 18–24) experience mis-steps or set backs by entering parenthood too early, by dropping out of school, by failing to find work or by getting in trouble with the legal system. They point out that these mis-steps obviously make the transition more difficult and also have long lasting effects into adulthood.

Beaujot and Kerr (2007) explore important exceptions to the generalised data of delayed transitions. They discuss vulnerable youth populations, particularly immigrant and aboriginal youth in Canada. For example, aboriginal youth tend to engage in early home leaving which has often been linked with lower educational attainment and subsequent career problems. In contrast, immigrants in Canada delay home-leaving, making it possible to profit longer from parental transfers (Beaujot and Kerr, 2007: 22). In short, later transitions can enable youth to receive more transfers from parents and engage in greater educational attainment. Gaudet (2007: 16) makes the point that the flow of intergenerational assistance is an important factor in emerging adulthood, though it is obviously not available to all youth.

The importance of education and credentialism has been noted. Though the data comparison period in this chapter is more limited (i.e. over a 10- or 20-year period), it is worth mentioning the educational attainment comparison for North America from the mid-twentieth century historical benchmark which so many researchers use. For example in the U.S. in 1950, 8 per cent of 25–29 year olds had a college degree, compared to 16 per cent by 1970 and 38 per cent in 2006. From more recent data, it is noted that educational participation rates and educational attainment are still on the rise from 1995 to 2005 in all four countries under examination in this chapter, Canada, the U.S., Sweden and the U.K. (see Table 4.1). Percentages of those aged 25–34 with tertiary education are high, especially in North America and are rising from 1999 to 2005 levels (see Table 4.2). Canada is said to have one of the highest rates of post-secondary educational attainment among industrialised countries. Quintini et al. (2007), in a recent OECD report, note that educational attainment tends to be associated with higher rates of employment and this fact appears to be well known to those young adults who are increasing their education.

Quintini et al. (2007: 4) describe the education-to-work transition as an 'often prolonged and discontinuous process rather than a smooth and quick transition.' High turnover and job shopping are considered part of the natural dynamics of settling into the work world. In terms of the length of the education-to-work transition, their data indicate that it often takes a significant amount of time, 1–2 years, for young people

Table 4.1 Education enrolment (full and part-time) of 20–29 year olds (as a per cent of 20–29 year olds)

	1995	2000	2005
Canada	22	23	26
U.S.	20	21	23
U.K.	18	24	29
Sweden	22	33	36

Source: Derived from OECD (2008).

Table 4.2 Percentage of population aged 25–34 with post-secondary education

	1999	2005
Canada	47	54
U.S.	38	39
U.K.	27	35
Sweden	33	37

Source: Derived from OECD (2007).

to find their first job after finishing their education and even longer to find a permanent job. So the early years in the labour market after leaving school are characterised by high job turnover and temporary jobs. In fact even compared to the 1990s, the share of youth in temporary jobs has increased in most OECD countries during this first decade of the twenty-first century. So especially in Europe, temporary jobs after leaving school seem to be the rule (though these jobs can represent a stepping stone into the labour market for youth without work experience). Cote and Allahar (2007: 173) note a paradox in credentialism. That is, that credentialed skills may have little to do with the work that is eventually performed, but without the credentials, one's employability and earning power are seriously jeopardised.

Home-leaving and union-formation patterns

Given that it is well established that the acquisition of education affects the timing of transitional events, we know that young adults will delay leaving their parents' home as well as delay union formation (see Mitchell, 2006a: 177). Clark (2007) documents the transition of today's young adults compared to the early 1970s and notes that the transitions today are delayed because of taking longer to complete the first key transition and elongated because subsequent transitions take longer to complete. Or more simply put, staying in school delays all other transitions.

Again to return to the post-war benchmark era, Owram (1996) describes the 'cult of marriage' during these decades and notes that this was the last time where early marriage did not disrupt career plans since most youth were job ready at the end of high school. Jones (1980: 25) notes that the highest percentage of Americans ever were marrying during the early post-war years. Early marriage and home-leaving went together with marriage being the young adult's route to independence and respectability, with those not marrying labelled as deviant (Owram, 1996).

Boyd and Norris (2000: 268) describe the normative script of the transition to adulthood for young people in the recent past: leaving school, taking jobs, leaving the parental home and getting married. Decreasing proportions of young people lived with their parents, especially in the immediate post-war decades, following the twentieth century's general trend toward non-familial living arrangements among the young and the old. However, beginning in 1981, there was an increasing percentage of young Canadians aged 15–34 living with their parents, reversing the earlier pattern of decline (Boyd and Norris, 2000: 269).

The data for youth living at home reveal an increase in the average age over time (see Table 4.3). Though the comparison years and age groups vary, over the past few decades, Canada and the U.K. show a rise in the per cent living at home, while the U.S. rates seem more stable, with the U.K. rates being the lowest of the three countries. Beaujot and Kerr (2007: 31) attribute the earlier home-leaving and independence in the U.K. to fewer opportunities for higher education compared to North America and to fewer state transfers compared to some of the Nordic countries. These younger transitions in the U.K. are aided by lower youth unemployment rates compared to southern Europe. Mitchell (2006a: 66) notes that northern Europe, including Sweden, has some of the lowest rates of co-residence in Europe while Italy's is the highest. This point is related to other transitions for these two countries which will be discussed in the next section.

Mitchell (2006a: 89) documents the impermanence of these transitions when she notes that home-leaving is not a one-time event. Home-returning has become increasingly common in the late twentieth/early twenty-first century with the return explained by mostly economic reasons. So not only are youth delaying home-leaving but they are increasingly likely to return or 'boomerang' back. Home-return estimates

Table 4.3 Per cent of young adults living at home: Canada, U.S., and U.K.

Canada	**1986**	**2006**
20–24	49.3	60.3
25–29	15.6	26.0
U.S.*	**1986**	**2007**
18–24	52.6	50.2
25–34	11.1	11.6
U.K.**	**1991**	**2003**
Male 20–24	50	56
Male 25–29	19	21
Female 20–24	32	37
Female 25–29	9	10

Note: *unmarried college students living in dormitories are counted as living in their parents' home; **England only.
Sources: Canadian sources: Milan, et al. (2007); U.S. sources: U.S. Census Bureau (2008a); U.K. *sources:* Office for National Statistics (2004).

are highest for the U.S., followed by Canada and the U.K. with lower rates for Sweden (likely due to Sweden's more favourable economic conditions and housing policies conducive to independence, Mitchell, 2006a: 76).

Another indication of delayed transitions is the rise in the age of first marriage. For both Canada and the U.S., age of first marriage was dropping in the post-war period, reaching a low point in the early 1960s (see Figure 4.1 for U.S. rates). Since then, along with increased home-leaving ages, the age of marriage has been climbing (see Table 4.4 and Figure 4.1). Mean (or median) age at first marriage is strikingly similar between the countries with the exception of the U.S. Americans are marrying younger and have higher rates of marriage at all age groups compared to the other three countries. The U.K. rate is similar to Canada's. Sweden's ages of first marriage stand out as quite high. Mitchell (2006a) comments that the widespread popularity of cohabitation likely contributes to the late ages of first (legal) marriage in Sweden. So age of first marriage is now commonly occurring in the late 20s for women and early 30s for men with the Americans marrying at slightly younger ages and the Swedes at slightly older ages.

Gaudet (2007: 13) makes an important observation that the behaviour of today's twenty-something youth resembles that of their grandparents' who left the family home on average at about the same age.

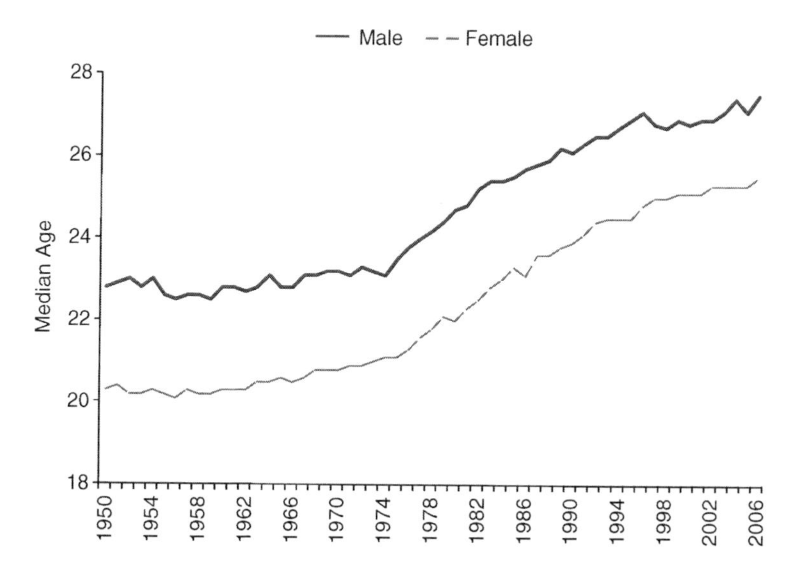

Figure 4.1 Median age of first marriage in the U.S. 1950–2006

Source: Derived from US Census Bureau (2008b).

Table 4.4 Mean or median age at first marriage

	1986	2006
Canada: Male	27	30.6*
Canada: Female	24.8	28.5*
U.S. male**	25.7	27.5
U.S. female**	23.1	25.5
U.K. male**	25.1	30.8
U.K. female**	23.1	28.6
Sweden male	29.9***	33.9
Sweden female	27.5***	31.3

Notes: *denotes year 2003. **denotes median age. ***denotes years 1990.
Sources: Statistics Canada (1999); Statistics Canada (2007). United States: United States Census Bureau (2008b). U.K.: Office for National Statistics (2008). Sweden: European Commission (2008).

Indeed union formation patterns also seem to be more similar to those of a century ago rather than the post-war patterns (see Mitchell, 2006b: 162). One important difference that defines young adults in recent years is their rates of home returning, which are unprecedented from a historical perspective and appear here to stay (see Mitchell, 2006a).

Instead of the post-war standardised life course in which people move through a series of predictable transitions, Coontz (2005: 277) describes how people now put together a highly individualised sequence of transitions. In her history of marriage she notes that this once-required gateway to adulthood and respectability has irrevocably changed and given way to lower rates of marriage, more solitary living, increased divorce and an increased rate of cohabitation.

Fertility patterns

In this section, the last transition, fertility will be examined, first using the census data, then using demographic theory. The cross-national data paint a picture of low rates of fertility and later childbearing which is typical in industrialised countries. All four countries with the exception of the U.S. have below-replacement-level fertility with Canada and the U.K. showing a slight decline and the U.S. and Sweden showing small increases over the 20-year period under review (see Table 4.5). Canada and the U.S. have remarkably similar demographic fertility profiles, with fertility rates showing some divergence during the last two decades. All countries, with the exception of the U.S., show a trend to older age-specific fertility, with declining numbers of women having children in their teens and 20s, and more women in their 30s having children.

A glance at the population statistics for most industrialised countries reveals declining percentages of youth and increasing percentages of elderly with low rates of natural increase. Among the four countries, the U.S. is the least elderly in terms of the percentage of the population over 65 years of age and the per cent under age 15 (see Table 4.6). Not surprisingly the U.S. also has the highest rate of natural increase,

Table 4.5 Total fertility rate

	1986	2007
Canada	1.76	1.57
U.S.	1.84	2.09
U.K.	1.73	1.66
Sweden	1.79	1.88

Source: Derived from US Census Bureau (2008c).

Table 4.6 Key population statistics – Canada, U.S., U.K. and Sweden, 2008

	Canada	U.S.	U.K.	Sweden
Population (in millions) 2008	33.3	304.5	60.9	9.2
Projected population (in millions) 2025	37.6	355.7	68.8	9.9
Per cent of population <15 years old	17	20	18	17
Per cent of population +65 years old	14	13	16	18
Per cent of population aged 16–64 years old	69	67	66	65
Natural increase (annual, per cent) 2008	0.3	0.6	0.3	0.2
Life expectancy 2008	80	78	78.7	80.6

Source: Derived from Population Reference Bureau (2008) World Population Data Sheet.

which is also evidenced by its projected population growth for 2025. The elderly or plus-65 percentages are most similar between Canada and the U.S. while Sweden and the U.K.'s rates are slightly higher. All four countries have shown at least a modest increase in life expectancy in recent years.

It is illustrative to use demography to explain fertility and population patterns. The demographic transition is a common model used to describe population patterns in industrialised countries over the twentieth century. It is defined as the historical shift of birth and death rates from high to low levels in a population (Haupt and Kane, 1991: 55). Simply put, industrialising countries first experience better life expectancy (decrease in mortality) followed by smaller family size (decrease in fertility). Put another way, as countries become more industrialised, urban and less agrarian, couples have smaller families. Canada, the U.S. and most industrialised countries in Europe have completed the demographic transition with slow rates of natural population increase (see McVey and Kalbach, 1995).

The unease regarding the increase in population aging in industrialised countries is being accentuated by a new phenomenon which some scholars have referred to as a second demographic transition (Haub, 2008). The term describes the situation where fertility has fallen below the two-child replacement level and population growth is negative (e.g. Japan). It has been linked to greater educational attainment, greater job opportunities for women, a shift away from formal marriage and the rise of individualism and consumerism (PRB, 2004: 6).

With respect to Europe, Haub (2008) suggests that a robust economy combined with family-friendly policies (both of which Sweden has) could well increase birth rates, though rates above replacement level are unlikely. The more conservative welfare states in southern Europe have fewer state transfers compared to Northern Europe (e.g. Sweden) with resulting delayed transitions evident in southern Europe relative to northern countries (Beaujot and Kerr, 2007). Not surprisingly, compared to Sweden, Italy's fertility rate is lower. Also, childbearing outside of formal marriage in Italy is not socially acceptable, and this fact combined with a tight job market results in delayed marriage and childbearing as well as later home leaving.

Though there is no magic bullet that would reverse fertility decline, there is evidence that government policies do make a difference (PRB, 2004: 28). Several governments in Europe and one province in Canada (Quebec) have or have had pro-natalist policies with family allowances for each child and currently Quebec has a family-friendly policy of highly subsidised daycare. These family-friendly policies try to ensure equal opportunities in the workplace in that they help women combine childrearing with employment (e.g. long parental leaves for both women and men, childcare assistance and flexible working arrangements, PRB, 2004: 29). For example, the higher level of government-provided family services and more open attitudes about marriage and childbearing in northern versus southern Europe is used to help explain why fertility is higher in Sweden and France compared to Italy and Spain.

Since fertility is higher in countries where gender norms encourage spousal support in childrearing and housework and where there is government-provided support, many governments are shifting towards a two-pronged policy approach of combining fiscal policies (allowances and tax breaks) with family-friendly policies (parental leave) that allow parents to combine work and family life (PRB, 2004: 31, 20).

Conclusions and policy implications

Though this chapter discusses the youth stage of the life course, all of the stages are interrelated. Beaujot (2004) for example, speaks of a delay in the early life-course transitions that cannot be separated from the rest of the life course. Other stages also merit brief mention. Sunter and Morisette (1994) note that the trends to more education and earlier retirement coupled with longer life expectancy have shortened the portion of the life cycle devoted to paid work quite noticeably in the last quarter of the twentieth century. By the late twentieth century, workers (e.g. males at age 16) spend 69 per cent of their remaining life expectancy in the labour force, compared to 90 per cent for workers (again males at age 16) earlier in the twentieth century. It is interesting to note that the one part of the life course that does not seem to be elongated is the time spent in the paid labour force. This shortened or compressed earning period has been accompanied by increasingly longer work weeks as workers recoup the higher cost of education and foregone wages (see Duxbury and Higgins 2001, and Thomas and Venne, 2002).

Given industrialised countries' concerns regarding the aging population and future labour-force supply and given the later labour-force entry of youth in the life course, many researchers have pointed out that our retirement age is early relative to our rising life expectancy (see OECD, 1996 and Judy and D'Amico, 1997). Myles (2005) advises that we need to take advantage of our increased longevity gains to offset our longer period of transition into adulthood with later retirement ages.

Thomas and Venne (2002: 215) point out that the main life-course transition points are changing where learning is now occurring over the life course, the so-called life-long learning trend. The boxes model of life, (education, work until 65 and then retirement) is recognized as outmoded but social policy seems not to have changed with this recognition. Given a longer education-to-work transition, career changes, and a less linear life-course model, they suggest that policies such as work sabbaticals, work-life leaves and tax incentives for mid-career education may be appropriate to support upgrading training, life-long learning and changing careers.

Beaujot and Kerr (2007: 33) note that many of the implications of a longer transition appear to be positive (e.g. by leaving home later youths receive more transfers from their parents). They point to one possible drawback at the individual level – that people may not have saved enough during a shorter working life. Yet with longer life expectancy people can work longer (indeed average retirement age has recently been slightly rising in Canada). The strongest negatives that they note for the societal level from delayed transitions are lower fertility and population aging. Gee (2000: 21) counters, however, that the consequences of population aging are being exaggerated, while Foot (1998: 277) concludes that the shift to an aging society is neither good nor bad. Rather he perceives it simply as a fact of life and the better we understand it, the better we can prepare for the changes it brings.

For those industrialised societies that experience an elongated period of youth and which encourage identity exploration, it is necessary that they develop policies that assist youth during the complex education-to-work transitions (Gaudet, 2007). One major policy proposal is intervention during the high school years with career-pathway programmes (Brisbois et al., 2008). In addition, Brisbois et al. (2008) suggest that career awareness and development activities be introduced in earlier grades. This is being implemented in the U.S. as Lobron (2007) in an article entitled, 'Hurry up, Grow Up' notes that seven states in the U.S. actually require all public high-school students to choose career paths, sometimes as early as their freshman year.

Levine (2005) also discusses career exploration assistance to help with work-life unreadiness as he notes that there are more work-life options now than have ever existed during any other historical period. Whereas in the past it was common for kids to do what their parents did, he asserts that today it is more complicated. Even if kids pursue the same career, he notes that the job descriptions likely have changed while the job title has remained unchanged. Feldman (2002) echoes

Levine in pointing out that youth in industrialized societies have more unparalleled independence than ever before in their career choice. Yet this very abundance produces confusion and a fear of making a poor career choice, especially given the rising cost of education. He adds that unlike youth who came of age during the great depression and chose a job for its high income and security, young Americans today place more value on careers that provide fulfillment. Perhaps the fulfillment criterion, which Twenge (2006) also discusses, makes the career choice even more challenging.

To reduce the fear and confusion which stem from the abundance of choices, Twenge (2006: 228) recommends more direction regarding career paths. She finds that the oft-repeated adage, 'you can be anything you want to be' is debilitating for young people for while they may have many options, not everyone will be capable or competent at what she/he would like to do. If too much choice does indeed make people unhappy (as Schwartz contends in his book, *The Paradox of Choice,* 2004) then the present abundance of choice in career areas might at the very least make for confusion.

Shanahan et al. (2002: 116) recommend that the roles of both public and private spheres in career exploration and search be enhanced so as to increase adolescents' awareness of occupational opportunities available. Morrison (2002) recommends that even college-level youths be provided with training on job search and career basics to help ensure a smooth education-to-work transition.

What has not been addressed in this discussion of the education-to-work transition is any mention of the role of employers. With predictions of a coming labour force shortage in the next decade (related to the retirement of the large post-war baby boom generation in North America) Morrison (2002) suggests strategies for employers to help attract and retain young employees. Among her suggestions are targeted orientation, use of a buddy system and mentoring. Williamson (2006) mentions the oft-cited fact that younger workers place a high importance on work-life balance. Lancaster and Stillman (2002) in their book *When Generations Collide* spend an entire chapter on work-life balance differences between the generations. While some studies do show that younger workers state a strong preference for work-life balance, Barbara Moses (2006) asserts that this fact has been distorted. Yes the younger workers want balance, but so do older workers. She points out that younger workers are more vocal in asking for work-life balance. Firms that don't provide some flexibility in terms of flexible work-time schedules and career pattern movement may encounter retention problems as young employees vote with their feet. One American accounting firm (Trunk, 2007) found that workplace flexibilities helped in retention of their young employees. Undoubtedly, the management of employee retention will most likely become a key workplace strategy.

Mitchell (2006a: 161) points out that, overall, policies need to reflect a non-linear model of development over the life course since the many transitions of young adults are less predictable and sometimes subject to reversibility. Given that the key markers of the transition to adulthood (especially the education-to-work transition) have been postponed, less orderly and more subject to individual choice she concludes that young people need multiple options and flexible policies (Mitchell, 2006a: 190, 192).

This chapter has documented the changes in the life course and the many transitions for youth today. The lock-step normative patterns of the post-war period have given way to more varied life-course patterns in that young people today take longer to launch. Given that the post-war decades are recognized as anomalous in many ways, perhaps the rapid transitions during these decades should not be held up as standards to which we should aspire to today, or against which contemporary youth are measured.

Yet Beaujot and Kerr (2007: 14) lament that increased educational attainment has pushed the end of this education-to-work transition period toward ages that historically have been associated with working, marriage and childbearing. The time span of such decisions has been enlarged during the late twentieth century in comparison to transitions in the recent past. But the fact that this standardisation of life-course transitions has broken down for subsequent cohorts during the past few decades is no surprise and should be expected as the immediate postwar decades are highly anomalous in many ways. Also, it was pointed out earlier that a prolonged period of youth makes sense given our increased life expectancy.

Damon (2008) also laments that young adults are shunning the roles that were former markers of adulthood. Yet the normative patterns of the post-war generation are no longer feasible. Career patterns, the economy and organisational hierarchies have all changed. Indeed given value changes, it is highly likely that today's generation would find the fixed career ladder of the 1950s stifling. I would argue that Damon's expression of alarm is misplaced. Yes the youth of today take longer to launch, but delayed transitions do not represent failure on the part of youth. In fact, Betcheman and Lowe (1997) point out that concerns about education-to-work transitions, living standards and technological change are historical themes. In short, historians and researchers have always worried and raised alarms about changes in these areas.

Gaudet (2007: 10) summarises it rather succinctly as follows: youth has become a complex life stage, a stage that is lengthening as well as diversifying as youths have more life choices to make with traditional roles being deferred. Taking longer to launch into adulthood is a reflection of the new realities of changing career patterns and longer life expectancy. Flexible policies that support this longer and less-than-linear emergence into adulthood are needed, especially for those youth who cannot rely on prolonged intergenerational transfers.

References

'Adulthood today,' (2001) *The Globe and Mail*, September 10, p. A16.

Anisef, P. and Axelrod, P. (2001) 'Baby boomers in transition: life-course experiences of the 'class of '73.' in V. Marshall, W. Heinz, H. Kruger and A. Verma (eds) *Restructuring Work and the Life Course*, Toronto: University of Toronto Press: 473–488.

Arnett, J.J. (2000) 'Emerging adulthood: a theory of development from the late teens through the twenties.' *American Psychologist*, 55 (5): 469–480.

Arnett, J.J. (2007) *Adolescence and Emerging Adulthood: a Cultural Approach* (3rd edn), New York: Prentice Hall.

Bardwick, J. (1986) *The Plateauing Trap*, New York: Amacom.

Beaujot, R. (2004) 'Delayed life transitions: trends and implications.' Accessed online at the Vanier Institute of the Family website (http://www.vifamily.ca/library/cft/delayed_life.html).

Beaujot, R. and Kerr, D. (2007) 'Emerging Youth Transition Patterns in Canada: Opportunities and Risks, Policy Research Initiatives.' Project discussion paper, December, Ottawa: Government of Canada. Accessed online: www.policyresearch.gc.ca/doclib/DP_YOUTH_Beaujot_200712_e.pdf

Bennett, A. (1990) *The Death of the Organization Man*, New York: William Morrow.

Betcherman, G. and Lowe, G. (1997) 'The future of work in Canada: a synthesis report.' Canadian Policy Research Networks. Ottawa: Renouf Publishing Co. Ltd. Online at www.cprn.org/documents/24985_EN.pdf

Boyd, M. and Norris, D. (2000) 'Demographic change and young adults living with parents, 1981–1996.' *Canadian Studies in Population*, 27 (2): 267–281.

Brisbois R., Orton, L. and Saunders, R. (2008) 'Connecting supply and demand in Canada's youth labour market.' Canadian Policy Research Networks, Pathways to labour market series no. 8, May. Ottawa: CPRN. Accessed online: www.cprn.org/documents/49679_EN.pdf

Cappelli, P. (2003) 'Will there *really* be a labour force shortage?' *Organizational Dynamics*, 32 (3): 221–233.

Clark, W. (2007) 'Delayed transitions of young adults.' *Canadian Social Trends*, Winter, 84: 31–21.

Coontz, S. (2005) *Marriage, a History*, New York: Viking.

Coontz, S. (1992) *The Way we Never Were: American Families and the Nostalgia Trap*, New York: Basic Books.

Cote, J. and Allahar, A. (2007) *Ivory Tower Blues: a University System in Crisis,* Toronto: University of Toronto Press.

Damon, W. (2008) *The Path to Purpose: Helping our Children Find their Calling in Life*, New York: Free Press.

Driver, M.J. (1985) 'Demographic and societal factors affecting the linear career crisis.' *Canadian Journal of Administrative Studies*, 2 (2): 245–263.

Duxbury, L. and Higgins, C. (2001) 'Work-life balance in the new millennium: where are we? Where do we need to go?' Canadian Policy Research Networks Discussion paper October. Ottawa: CPRN. Accessed online: www.cprn.org/documents/7314_en.pdf

Esping-Andersen, G. (2006) 'Three worlds of welfare capitalism.' in C. Pierson and F. Castles (eds) *The Welfare State Reader* (2nd edn), Cambridge: Polity Press: 160–174.

European Commission (2008) 'Eurostat: The life of women and men in Europe: A statistical portrait.' Online: http://epp.eurostat.ec.europa.eu

Feldman, D. (2002) 'When you come to a fork in the road, take it: career indecision and vocational choices of teenagers and young adults.' in D. Feldman (ed.) *Work Careers: A Developmental Perspective,* San Francisco: Jossey-Bass: 93–125.

Foot, D.K. with D. Stoffman (1998) *Boom, Bust & Echo 2000: Profiting from the Demographic Shift in the New Millennium*, Toronto: Macfarlane, Walter and Ross.

Foot D.K. and Venne, RA. (1990) 'Population, pyramids and promotional prospects.' *Canadian Public Policy*, 16 (4): 387–398.

Gaudet, S. (2007) 'Emerging adulthood: a new stage in the life course,' Policy Research Initiative, Ottawa: Government of Canada, accessed online: www.policyresearch.gc.ca/doclib/DP_YOUTH_Gaudet_200712_e.pdf

Gee, E. (2000) 'Population and politics.' in E. Gee and G. Gutman (eds) *The Overselling of Population Aging*, Oxford: University Press: 5–25.

Haub, C. (2008) 'Global aging and the demographic divide.' *Public Policy and Aging Report*, 17 (4). Accessed online www.prb.org/Articles/2008/globalaging.aspx

Haupt, A. and Kane, T. (1991) *Population Handbook: International Edition*. (3rd edn). Washington, DC: Population Reference Bureau, Inc.

Jekeliuk, S. and Brown, B. (2005) 'The transition to adulthood: characteristics of young adults ages 18 to 24 in America.' Population Reference Bureau, accessed online: www.prb.org/pdf05/TransitionToAdulthood.pdf

Jones, L. (1980) *Great Expectations: America and the Baby Boom Generation*, New York: Ballantine.

Judy, R. and D'Amico, C. (1997) *Workforce 2020: Work and Workers in the 21st Century*, Indiana: Hudson Institute.

Kaplan, H. (1997) 'The evolution of the life course.' in K. Wachter and C. Finch (eds) *Between Zeus and the Salmon: the Biodemography of Longevity*, Washington, DC: National Academy Press: 175–211.

Lancaster, L. and Stillman, D. (2002) *When Generations Collide,* New York: Harper Collins.

Larson, R., Wilson, S. and Mortimer, J. (2002) 'Conclusions: adolescents' preparation for the future.' in R. Larson, B. Brown and J. Mortimer (eds) *Adolescents' Preparation for the Future: Perils and Promise*, Ann Arbor, Michigan: The Society for Research on Adolescence: 159–166.

Leana, C. (2002) 'The changing organizational context of careers.' in D. Feldman (ed.) *Work Careers: A Developmental Perspective,* San Francisco: Jossey-Bass: 274–293.

Levine, M. (2005) *Ready or Not, Here Life Comes,* New York: Simon & Schuster.

Little, B. (1999) 'The importance of being educated.' *The Globe and Mail,* March 1, p. A2.

Lobron, A. (2008) 'Hurry up, grow up.' *The Boston Globe,* May 11, accessed online www.boston.com/bostonglobe/magazine/articles/2008/05/11/hurry_up_grow_up?

McVey, W.W. and Kalbach, W.E. (1995) *Canadian Population,* Toronto: Nelson.

Milan, A, Vezina, M. and Hall, C. (2007) 'Family Portrait: Continuity and change in Canadian families and households in 2006: National portrait, individuals (figure 15),' Census Analysis Series. Ottawa: Statistics Canada. Online: www.statcan.gc.ca.

Mitchell, B. (2006a) *The Boomerang Age: Transitions to Adulthood in Families,* New Brunswick, USA: Aldine Transaction.

Mitchell, B. (2006b) 'The boomerang age from childhood to adulthood: Emergent trends and issues for aging families.' *Canadian Studies in Population,* 33 (2): 155–178.

Morrison, E.W. (2002) 'The school-to-work transition.' in D. Feldman (ed.) *Work Careers: A Developmental Perspective,* San Francisco: Jossey-Bass: 126–158.

Moses, B. (2006) 'Gen Y-ers, boomers only sort of different.' *The Globe and Mail,* November 17, accessed online: www.bbmcareerdev.com/booksarticle_articles_detail.php?article=14

Myles, J. (2005) 'Postponed adulthood: dealing with the new economic inequality.' Canadian Council on Social Development, accessed online: www.ccsd.ca/pubs/2005/pa/pa.pdf

Neumark, D. (2007) 'Improving school-to-work transitions: Introduction.' in D. Neumark (ed.) *Improving School-to-Work Transitions,* New York: Russell Sage Foundation: 1–23.

Office for National Statistics (2004) 'Adults living with their parents by sex and age, Social Trends 34.' Online: www.statistics.gov.uk/statbase/expodata/spreadsheet/D7261.xls

Office for National Statistics (2008) 'First marriages: age and sex (England and Wales): Population Trends 133.' Online: www.statistics.gov.uk

Organisation for Economic Co-operation and Development (1996) *Ageing in OECD Countries: A Critical Policy Challenge.* Paris: Organisation for Economic Co-operation and Development. Social Policy Studies no. 20.

Organisation for Economic Co-operation and Development (2007) Centre for Educational Research and Innovation, Indicators of Education Systems 2007, *Education at a Glance,* Paris: Organisation for Economic Co-operation and Development. Online: http://www.oecd.org/edu/eag2007

Organisation for Economic Co-operation and Development (2008) Centre for Educational Research and Innovation, Indicators of Education Systems 2008, *Education at a Glance,* Paris: Organisation for Economic Co-operation and Development. Online: http://www.oecd.org/edu/eag2008

Owram, D. (1996) *Born at the Right Time: A History of the Baby-Boom Generation.* Toronto: University of Toronto Press.

Population Reference Bureau (2008) World Population Data Sheet, Washington, DC: PRB. Accessed online. www.prb.org.
Population Reference Bureau (2004) 'Transitions in world population.' *Population Bulletin* , 59 (1). Accessed online: www.prb.org.
Quintini, G., Martin, J. and Martin, S. (2007) 'The changing nature of the school-to-work transition process in OECD countries.' Discussion paper No.2582: OECD, accessed online: www.OECD.org
Ricard, F. (1992) *The Lyric Generation: The Life and Times of the Baby Boomers* (D. Winkler, trans.), Toronto: Stoddart Publishing Company.
Robbins, A. and Wilner, A. (2001) *Quarterlife Crisis: the Unique Challenges of Life in Your Twenties,* New York: Putman.
Salazar, M. (2006) *The Turbulent Twenties Survival Guide,* Oakland, CA: New Harbinger Publications.
Schwartz, B. (2004) *The Paradox of Choice: Why More is Less,* New York: HarperCollins Publishers.
Shanahan, M., Mortimer, J. and Kruger, H. (2002) 'Adolescence and work in the twenty-first century.' in R. Larson, B. Brown and J. Mortimer (eds) *Adolescents' Preparation for the Future: Perils and Promise,* Ann Arbor, Michigan: The Society for Research on Adolescence: 99–120.
Statistics Canada (1999) Vital Statistics Compendium. Accessed online www.statcan.ca
Statistics Canada (2007) *The Daily,* Marriages (January 17). Accessed online www.statcan.ca
Sunter, D. and Morissette, R. (1994) 'The hours people work.' *Perspectives on Labour and Income,* 6 (3): 8–12.
Thomas, M. and Venne, R.A. (2002) 'Work and leisure: a question of balance.' in D. Cheal (ed.) *Aging and Demographic Change in Canadian Context,* Toronto: University of Toronto Press, 190–222.
Trunk, P. (2007) 'What gen Y really wants.' *Time Magazine,* July 5, accessed online www.time.come/time/magazine.
Twenge, J. (2006) *Generation Me: Why Today's Young Americans are more Confident, Assertive, Entitled – and more Miserable than ever Before,* New York: Free Press.
United States Census Bureau (2008a) Current Population Survey Reports: Families and living arrangements, Table AD-1. Online at http://www.census.gov/population/www/socdemo/hh-fam/ad1.xls
United States Census Bureau (2008b) Current Population Survey Reports: Annual social and economic supplements: Median age of first marriage. Online: http://www.census.gov/population/socdemo/hh-fam/ms2.xls
United States Census Bureau (2008c) International data base: Population Division: fertility rates by country. Online at http://www.census.gov/ipc/www/idb/
Williamson, D. (2006) 'Young workers, new rhythms.' *Fusion Magazine,* summer, accessed online: www.naa.org/resources/publication/fusion.

5

Fortunate Lives: Professional Careers, Social Position and Life Choices

Tanya Castleman and Rosslyn Reed

Professions in an age of choice and opportunity

A professional career and its associated social position is well recognized as a key element of an individual's life chances. Being a professional confers privileges including income, status and esteem. Professional occupations are an important path to social mobility, rewarding a strategy of hard work rather than good luck or unique talent. Qualified professionals might be described as having made a choice and achieved success, as enjoying working lives free of the boredom, toil and occupational danger that characterise less exalted occupations and having skills that protect them in the labour market.

While professionals may enjoy these benefits, they nevertheless confront a range of choices and dilemmas about ways of living, some of which are particular to their occupation and status. A 'professional way of life' entails a number of constraints and challenges as well as widely coveted benefits. Professional life entails a certain discipline, especially in the demand for commitment. What is the nexus between pay-off and sacrifice for professionals and what do they see as the main costs and benefits of their chosen paths? Is this nexus different depending on the individual's social characteristics? If these dynamics are changing, how are professionals affected by those changes?

This chapter explores the ways in which a sample of university graduates enter their working lives and develop their careers, personal relationships and their sense of social location as professionals. It highlights the enabling and constraining aspects of professional occupations and the ways in which individuals grapple with the conflicting elements of their lives as young professionals. We begin by discussing the significance of professions as institutions and the changes that have emerged, largely in response to late modernity. After outlining how our longitudinal study was conducted, we report major themes in respondents' accounts of their lives as professionals and their careers, We discuss the importance of professionalism to their personal identity and aspirations as well as aspects of ambivalence about professional careers, highlighting the transitional character of their early careers as well as the transitional nature of professionalism in the early twenty-first century.

Professions as institutions of social location and identity

More than a century ago membership of a profession meant access to a community which more or less dictated a style of life. The German sociologist Max Weber saw professions as status groups rather than social classes premised on accumulated capital or location in labour markets. He argued that status groups as moral communities concerned with 'social honour' or prestige organised politically to restrict market-based competition and provided a shelter from the vicissitudes of the labour market (Weber in Gerth and Mills, 1948: 180–91). Status groups were stratified by consumption patterns such as membership of associations and styles of dressing as well as being bearers of conventions that gave rise to a specific professional identity (Weber in Gerth and Mills, 1948: 188–93). Being a professional involved not just a job but a vocation. Dedication to one's profession was accompanied by a strong social identification with that profession which became a central part of self identity. While leading to a privileged social position, professional commitment disciplined the actions and behaviour of their membership. Overwhelmingly male, traditional professionals were free from the concerns of day-to-day life to pursue their vocational interests. Their professional status secured entry to a career where life chances were largely determined by success in their chosen profession.

Law, medicine and the clergy were among the few traditional professions in early modernity. With industrialisation and the peak of Fordist institutions in the early post-World War II decades, the number of professions expanded to include new and transformed occupations such as engineering. These occupational groups sought status advantages through social closure, excluding less qualified competitors (Parkin, 1982). They achieved the attributes of professions with credentialing processes, codes of ethics and internal disciplinary practices. Now a large number of occupations claim to be professions (such as accounting and surveying) and more recently feminised occupations such as librarianship, nursing and social work have become recognised as professional.

Looking at professions through the lens of gender reveals much about the institution of the professions as well as the experiences of their members. Formerly, when women were largely confined to the domestic sphere, the professional was 'not woman/female, but ... man/male/masculine' (Dent and Whitehead, 2002: 6). As a consequence of the growth of women's employment and second-wave feminism, women gained access to professions such as medicine, law and engineering. Yet this has not been a straightforward process of gender integration despite formal equality of access to employment and life chances. Research (e.g. Cockburn, 1985; Wajcman, 1998; Pringle, 1998) shows that professional women encounter a special set of contradictions and

> in entering a masculine institution that sends conflicting signals, women are faced with the dilemma of embracing or denying conventional images of femininity in order to secure an identity. (Barrett, 2002: 160)

To achieve success, women professionals in organisations need to be able to adjust their subjectivities and embodied behaviours to do 'what "counts" as correct professional behaviour in any one time or place' (Kerfoot, 2002: 90–1). Disparate subjectivities and behaviours lead to them engaging in practices of negotiation and adjustment of personal professional identity as defined by others. Careers are, then, 'organic entities', products and producers of our work environments (Arthur et al., 1999: 5,7). Like much of life, careers are subject to 'chance or happenstance' and are largely 'enacted' (Arthur et al., 1999: 56). From this perspective,

> (t)he career is not defined by a series of occupational classifications, rules of professional practice, and progress, or company-based systems of human resource development or succession. These are relevant, ... but equally important, is the individual's own exertion of will in choice and activity. (Arthur et al., 1999: 41)

This is a process which both creates and modifies the structures of institutions and of individual lives (Arthur et al., 1999: 165). Women must still negotiate a professional identity according to the dictates of the predominantly male gatekeepers of professional conventions and cultures (see Kerfoot, 2002).

In the early twenty-first century, the term 'professional' carries a variety of connotations. It is frequently stated that in the postmodern age, we are all professional now. This view is usually accompanied by a blurring of the boundaries between professionalism and managerialism (Dent and Whitehead, 2002: 1). Professional status is associated with privilege but it is no longer associated purely with knowledge and has to be earned through performance appraisal processes which favour flexible, reflective, market-oriented individuals searching for an edge. This has become a discipline of management rather than of vocational commitment (Dent and Whitehead, 2002: 2–3). As well, there is a tendency for organisations to shape their own professional employees' identities (Casey, 1995; Dent and Whitehead, 2002). According to Casey (1995: 186),

> (p)ersons from expert professions along with those from trade and service occupations are being transformed into multi-faceted, pan-occupational team players in the new corporate organizations.

Nevertheless, as Dent and Whitehead (2000: 2–3) point out, professional privilege remains attractive. As the number of professional occupations and those claiming professional status increases, so the defining characteristics of professions (credentials, codes of ethics) are diminished in significance and the sense of belonging to a community of peers with a distinctive lifestyle to whom deference is owed, is eroded. Women increasingly occupy professional positions and domestic work, while still overwhelmingly the responsibility of women is no longer solely their sphere of activity. With the changes in the household composition, professionals cannot assume total freedom from unpaid work.

This chapter seeks to answer a number of questions about the perspectives of professionals, focussing on their early career experiences. What do they see as the attractions of professional occupations and how do these become part of their expectations of working lives? What influences their views of the range of choices and conflicts they encounter in their careers and personal lives? How do they navigate the competing demands and varied landscape of professional employment? Finally, what do their accounts suggest about the nature of professions and professionalism in the twenty-first century?

Longitudinal study of early career professionals

This chapter reports a longitudinal study of 86 Australian professionals who graduated with first degrees in four types of professional courses (engineering, business, social work and library studies) from four Australian universities in 1996. This sampling frame included traditionally male, traditionally female and gender balanced disciplines. All participants were 25 years or younger at the time of graduation.

The participant group was initially derived from those who responded to a mailed, questionnaire-based survey. Of the 993 questionnaires sent, 33 per cent (329) were returned. Of these, 36 per cent (120) agreed to an interview. Initial interviews were completed with 106 graduates (32 per cent) in 1997–8. A second round of interviews was conducted during 2001–02 for which 86 respondents (81 per cent of those who participated in the first round of interviews) were able to be located. This group was fairly evenly balanced between men (44 per cent) and women (56 per cent).

The interviews were semi-structured, eliciting descriptive accounts of their working lives and their reflections on their current and future plans. The interviews averaged a little over one hour and produced much rich information about the participants' early experiences of professional employment and the development of their working and domestic lives. The method of analysis included the identification of a number of themes through an iterative reading and meaning condensation process during which reliability of interpretation was addressed through multiple and independent analysis of the transcripts by the research team members (cf. Kvale, 1996). Quotations from 22 respondents are included here.

It is important to note that the interviews did not include direct questioning about the participants' professional identification or their reflections on their status as neophyte professionals. This chapter is based on an analysis of their responses to questions about related topics. This is a limitation of the chapter since specific questioning might have elicited more information and deeper insights, even as it might have brought out more self-conscious, conventional responses. A further limitation is the self-selection of the participants who are unlikely to be representative of young professionals. The contribution of this chapter lies in its exploration of ways of living shaped by professional occupations and the texture of the experiences of these articulate and varied participants.

Professional ways of life

In both rounds of interviews, most participants expressed a high level of commitment to their profession and expected to continue in and advance their careers over the long term.

Most made deliberate career choices and even the small minority who had deviated from a conventional career path, planned to pursue professional employment. Both male and female respondents indicated this perspective. In their descriptions of what would constitute a satisfying life, professional career figured prominently, though not always in terms of conventional success. Between the first and second interviews, participants had developed more specific ideas about their occupational goals and their longer term career plans. Most had settled into full-time employment.

Early workplace experiences, including among those with graduate positions, involved a degree of adjustment and some voiced concern about the discipline and constraint of long working hours and the impact on their social lives. But they expressed no significant re-evaluation of their chosen professional careers. Their expressed admiration for high levels of professionalism among their more senior work colleagues (and their disapproval of those who did not meet those standards) give an indication of their perceptions and values as well as their own aspirations about career.

Strategy vs. serendipity

The common view of professional careers assumes that professionals are highly organised and strategic. In fact, the majority of the participants did indicate a strategic orientation towards building their careers in that they made rational, informed choices about both career goals and the means to reach these. They often accessed expert advice on the best way to achieve their goals. That said, most were not single-minded in pursuing their career plans. While some were 'strategic careerists', others could best be described as 'career opportunists'. These respondents sought to develop their careers but left themselves open to unexpected opportunities. They were willing to alter their plans based on fortuitous events, not quite free and easy but clearly flexible. One man described his 'wait-and-see' approach, noting its benefits and downsides.

> I've got no idea how the next 12 months or two years are going to turn out, but I think when I get there I'm going to settle back and say 'Ah yeah, that's right.' I don't feel tied to a set path and I don't feel that there are any sort of relevant benchmarks which is good and bad. (Male engineer looking for development work internationally)

Such opportunistic approaches (cf. Devadason, 2008) were also linked to a willingness to learn from diverse experiences, even if they were not part of a clear career plan. This learning orientation, characteristic of graduates from all discipline areas, was well represented by an engineer working overseas in a new area of speciality. He saw the variety offered by a different position as being a benefit in itself.

> It's only a 3-month contract but it's certainly a good experience and the way I want to go. I believe I probably wasn't going to get much more experience from [my former company]...I don't see myself in this career, but it is all right, there are plenty of opportunities wherever I go. Maybe I'll be on more of a career path in a couple of years. I don't regret the experience so far; it's been great for me, but it could take some time to work out the direction I want to take. (Male engineer working overseas)

A few respondents can be seen as 'reluctant professionals'. They tended to describe themselves as 'not ambitious' but this was a way of expressing ambivalence about pursuing that profession. In the following passage a woman indicates neither devotion to the profession for which she trained nor interest in pursuing it further. She implies a lack of interest in professional employment as opposed to a more modest desire for job satisfaction.

> I really never did [have a clear idea of the future]...The way I was bought up, you get a job you work, that's what you do. I never really thought I want to be the CEO or whatever. That was one of the problems...I had with my previous boss because he expected me to be this ambitious and I'm not particularly ambitious. I want to do a good job and enjoy what I'm doing as opposed to climb the mountain, I guess. I guess I never really set out with a conscious path that I wanted to take. (Female accountant)

Reluctant professionals throw into relief the professional commitment of the majority of the respondents for whom mundane job satisfaction is not enough.

Rewards of professional occupations

The participants recognized the many advantages of being professional, able to support a comfortable life style and having valuable workplace skills. Yet the intrinsic satisfaction derived from professional work was a hallmark of their views of those occupations. They often expressed pleasure in their interesting jobs, but also voiced negative reactions when jobs were 'boring'.

> I suppose the best thing about this role is not one day's the same. That's what I love about it the most...I don't really have a typical week [because what] I do is normal troubleshooting. I try to find out what's going on around the place and who's having problems and look at them ... But I'm at a bit of a cross roads. I have to admit that I'm getting bit bored with this role. I feel that I've come to the point where I've done what I've wanted to do in this particular role. (Male accountant)

In discussing their job plans, a key element of decision-making was opportunity for development and learning which also indicates a high value placed on the stimulation and interest they wanted in their work. One woman was enticed back to work from maternity leave early, at least in part by the nature of the work.

> I went back part-time [after my son was born] ... I would have quite happily stayed home for another year [but] I did, *do*, enjoy working there, and I find the projects there very challenging and very interesting and stimulating, so I basically arranged to go back part-time to retain the position. (Female engineer)

Further study was usually mentioned in terms of advancement, especially moving into management, but the learning involved was also an attraction:

> I guess I found myself quite frustrated in my professional development because the job just wasn't [fulfilling] ... So I've actually gone back to uni to do my masters. And I found that really positive because...it's really helped me to feel like I'm actually growing professionally in my abilities and I've got something to compare myself to. (Female social worker)

Another woman referred to the challenges and variety in her engineering job and was scathing about the view that material advancement was the most important goal.

> I suppose there's certain things I want out of my work and I like to be challenged and have different experiences through it, and I need

> that more so than what my pay packet is. And my previous manager couldn't understand that. Like, how could you not want to be a level 10 manager by the age of 32 or whatever? Like, I don't even give a stuff, like I wouldn't have gone down the path of choosing engineering as a profession if I was driven by money! (Female engineer)

The specific job task is only one part of the stimulation of professional roles (albeit an important one). Another important source of stimulation, learning and interest is the collegiality of the professional workplace. Most take this for granted, but one respondent, temporarily working in a part-time job not in his professional area, lamented his lack of contact with fellow engineers.

> I do have interaction socially, but I don't have any *professional* interaction with other people within the building... I could not do this job full-time. There's not enough professional interaction with other people for my liking, you know, I do prefer that [but] it's actually a means to an end at the moment because I am studying full time. (Male engineer working temporarily in a non-engineering role)

Job stress was not a major theme of the accounts and when it was mentioned, it tended to be in terms of interpersonal issues with supervisors or colleagues or, less commonly, the challenges of developing a particular competence quickly enough. Whether this was because their relatively junior roles absolved them from higher levels of stressful responsibility or whether they were reluctant to recognise the stressful aspects of professional demands, is not clear.

Some spoke positively about the autonomy that their jobs afforded. When it was lacking, they resented it.

> I love this job a lot more [than my last one.] The main difference is probably because... the senior management were very much wanting to pull in the reins and not give anyone too much freedom, and they sort of wanted to say, 'Okay this is what you have to do' ... and it was almost like Big Brother was watching over your shoulder all the time. There wasn't really much freedom. (Male accountant)

Technical vs. managerial directions

At the early stages of their careers, most respondents saw their direction as being clearly aligned to the degrees they had studied and they concentrated on developing specific skills. By the second round of interviews, however, a number of people were planning or undertaking further study in order to move into management roles, mainly through MBA degrees. This was most common among the engineers for whom that is a common career progression. It was much less notable for the others and was not reported by any of the social workers whose career progression did not seem to incorporate a requirement for management study. They also seemed to be in fairly flat organisational structures with relatively few opportunities for advancement along defined career paths.

The move from technical to managerial roles did not seem to create difficulties for most respondents who saw their managerial careers as an extension of their professional careers. None had reached the stage where management roles would separate them from their technical involvement. More general management roles might come later. Where people did encounter this issue, it was discussed in terms of the interest in the work and the challenge of the position rather than in terms of career progression for its own sake.

One engineer articulated a common motive for seeking a management as opposed to a technical career, the desire for interesting and challenging work.

> I think I felt a bit constricted by [my role as an engineer] ... Certainly for the last year I haven't been very satisfied with the work, especially with the fact that it hasn't been technically satisfactory. I haven't been challenged... [F]or the past six months I've been given lots more responsibility and allowed to take on more of a management [role]...and that certainly picked things up a lot for me, like taking more control...I enjoyed...moving into a more organisational type role. (Female engineer)

Yet the technical vs. management path can be experienced as a dilemma and some found it problematic, as one woman described her difficulties in proceeding from a technical to a managerial role and her lack of knowledge about how to achieve this.

> I'm probably at that stage where I'm...too technical to move into management...My management experience isn't enough to move up, yet...you have to be really technical to move up. And I really don't want to be in a real technical role. I was given a good technical knowledge so that I could be a good technical manager and understand the technical people under me. That was my aim: to be

> in management in a technical area rather than just management. I understand technical but I don't actually like doing it. (Female engineer)

Most, however, did not perceive any contradictions between their technical professionalism and their managerial professionalism. Neither did they report being subject to strong managerial discipline in their workplaces (see Dent and Whitehead, 2002).

Recognition and respect

A recurring theme was the issue of recognition as a professional and the regard of others. It was important to them that their position and achievement were acknowledged, especially in the workplace. The satisfaction of such recognition was usually implied rather than explicit, but one man explained how he achieved respect both for technical and managerial skill and why this was valuable to him.

> I had the most success in progressing respect for myself and respect for my profession when I was able to…translate engineering and technical solutions into bottom line changes on a profit/loss statement.…Directors are concerned about risk because they are personally liable for safety and environmental damage…And that's how I felt I got the most respect as a professional engineer. The other aspect of it is primarily the people management aspect of it. It's being able to lead a group of people in addition to being able to manage them. (Male engineer)

Most of the discussion arose when recognition was seen as problematic. Interestingly, this was overwhelmingly raised by women. Some were in a traditionally male profession which may have made the issue more acute, even though they did not mention the gender issue directly.

Managers and colleagues were not the only important sources of recognition. An engineer reported how she worked to gain recognition from the (male) operators in the factory where she worked. Her sense of achievement was evident.

> [T]he guys on the floor [were wondering] 'Does she really know what she's talking about?' And once they knew that they were fine.…I think some of them were surprised that I knew so much, because I walked in, I knew how to make [the product] and I picked up pretty quickly how they used their computer system to do it and

> they were a bit surprised by that, because nobody else in the factory really knew. I mean they can fool management because management doesn't really understand what they do and I picked it up within a couple of weeks and so I knew when they were taking short cuts and when they weren't following procedures so picking them up on a couple of occasions like they thought 'Well, she *does* know'. (Female engineer)

Another female engineer attributed her struggle for respect and appropriate treatment to both gender and age.

> It's hard being a woman and young. If you say something that is questioned...they'll go, 'How did you know that? And how did you have that experience at the age of 26 or whatever you are?' Being female I find that some managers don't really take you seriously, which can be rather irritating. You get a bit of sexual harassment [from] some [external] people...some of the reason I left the project. I'd had enough of that kind of treatment – very annoying. (Female engineer)

For women in more traditional areas, issues of recognition were often linked both to gender and to the professional hierarchy. A female accountant reported her irritation at being mistaken for one of the non-professional employees because of her gender – and the steps she took to emphasise her professional status.

> When you meet new staff, some of them seeing you as a female they actually assume that you're admin sometimes, and even though you may dress professionally, and you've got the corporate suit on...I've had people say, 'Oh, you work in admin' [because] the majority of accountants there were men.... You just got to project yourself well, and do a good job. Like we've got a business casual policy here, but I tend to still wear a suit...if I wear a suit maybe it looks more professional and you get treated differently. (Female accountant)

These accounts describe both the contested nature of recognition and acceptance *as a professional* and the enormous importance it has for the respondents. These dimensions eclipse the material rewards in the imaginations of our respondents, in part perhaps because they take for granted that their professional skills can be relied on to provide good remuneration.

The right stuff: the requirements for professional careers

Participants' views were sought about what is necessary for professional success along with indications of their willingness to do so. While there is a strong acceptance of the professional role among some, others indicated a degree of ambivalence about the demands of life as a professional, even as they prepared for that life in the future.

The respondents often mentioned or alluded to the responsibility that comes with a professional position which was described positively, but sometimes with apprehension.

> I've got a team that's my responsibility. There's certainly a hell of a lot of autonomy and the fact that it really is a dynamic job, and the environment just changes so often. And I like to do that. It's an environment where I can put those skills to use. But it's ... also very unsettling, ... anything can happen which means that suddenly you're working until 10 o'clock or 11 o'clock because somebody in the States has decided to change their mind at the last minute, and ... while I manage good reactively, it'd be nice to be in a boring job ... occasionally. [*laughs*] (Male sales manager)

The positions they held sometimes entailed quite onerous demands on their time and impinged on other aspects of their lives. Some saw this as something of a badge of honour, indicating that they were successful and important to their organisations. One woman engineer described with relish the pressure of her job.

> When I got the job ... I was on the plane the next day. It was New Years Day. I came back to work and that afternoon I was told the job got approved and you can start tomorrow at 8 o'clock ... It wasn't even a question of going home – you'll come back when the job's finished. You're meant to be totally mobile, you walk in the door and you're handed the mobile phone and laptop ... you can work anywhere... I loved it. Sensational!

However, later in the interview she painted the job and its demands in less favourable terms.

> [Job demands make] life really difficult – long hours and working on weekends sometimes – really putting the strain on. If things aren't going well for me I'm falling to pieces. You haven't got time to build it back again. By the time you get the energy back you're exhausted

from work and then you don't have the energy to put back into the relationship. Yeah, so things are mixed. (Female engineer)

Others also noted the heavy requirements of their professional jobs and lamented the lack of time they had for other pursuits, including family and leisure. One man articulated the pros and cons of his demanding job.

I'm reasonably dissatisfied with [my job]. I mean it's interesting on occasions but ... you keep doing the same things day after day. It's not the same thing every day, but it's the same thing every three to six months. [I]t's good pay, but ... I'd like a life balance and all that sort of stuff. I'll still sit there and slog it out so I can live in this [city centre apartment]. I'd like to live in this place and earn less money. (Male investment banker)

The lack of challenge or interest in this man's job was as significant as its time demands and this was not compensated by his high salary.

Professional identity and confidence

The sense of professional identity was strong for most interviewees in every discipline area. Their accounts indicate the intersection between professional experience, their identification as professionals, and their self confidence.

[Interviewer: What effects have developments in your career had on your personal life?] I think also it's increased my confidence as a person and in my interactions with others. I think I have a lot more belief in what I can do. In fact I *can* handle difficult situations ... I've gone overseas a couple of times and done that independently whereas if I ... hadn't worked in this area I probably wouldn't have done that. (Female social worker)

There was evidence among many of the interviewees about how that confidence had grown over the years. In most cases this was implicit in the way they spoke about themselves, their jobs and their plans, but some of them articulated that development as did a librarian.

I'm much more confident in thinking of myself as a librarian now than I was when I last spoke to you. It was very difficult for me to do anything because of my lack of experience and I started to

> doubt whether I would actually ever get to be a librarian. But now I know that I can...and it's just a matter of thinking of yourself as what you want to be and then going out and getting it yourself. (Female librarian who had experienced difficulty in getting a professional job)

The growth in confidence from professional status affected personal life as well as working life. One of the women described the change in the dynamics of her relationship with her partner.

> I didn't really have a lot of confidence in my own abilities until I started this job. I didn't realise how important it was...I sort of got this job and it boosted my confidence, whereas my partner before was more like – I would even say a carer. Suddenly I was like, 'I feel more equal to you and I don't need to be cared for.' Position had changed. I don't think he liked it very much. (Female social work qualification now in a counselor position)

It is noteworthy that these are all accounts of women in feminised professions which may reflect the more problematic nature of professional identity for women. It may also indicate some interplay between the gender of the respondents and the gendered nature of their professions. Female engineers, like their male counterparts, seemed relatively confident about their professional identities, even if it was more difficult for them to establish their professional status than it was for their male colleagues.

Balancing acts: job, career, partners, family

The participants frequently mentioned their career aspirations and plans in connection with those of their partners. Notably, both men and women mentioned such considerations. This was not simply a matter of accommodating the other's wishes about where to live or need to find employment, but entailed a reflection on their own career values and the way that their career development was intertwined. They provided many examples of negotiation with partners about how they would manage their respective careers. These accounts also demonstrate the ways in which the respondents enacted their own careers and highlight their often opportunistic approach.

A common issue was where to live when the partners were both committed to their professional careers. One woman spoke at length about the calculations she and her partner made about their combined employment strategy. This calculation was underpinned by the assumption that both careers were important.

> [My boyfriend's] very sick of where he's working, but we've been really lucky in that way. I don't really want to compromise right now but I don't have to because we both want the same things... He said to me take a job wherever I find one because I have the specialist skills but he's got more general skills and could probably work in every major city. So he said to find work wherever I want then he'll find it around me. (Female engineer going to an overseas job)

Not every couple was so fortunate and several respondents reported (or anticipated) hard choices. This did not always cause angst and a number accommodated themselves to this, taking the longer view. One woman emphasised the positive aspects of locating to suit her partner's job.

> My partner's job is Melbourne based and there was talk at one stage of moving to Sydney, I had an offer, but I didn't really want to take it. I don't consider that a major obstacle, it's just a fact of life. If there was a dream job I might take it. The only thing I can think of is I've gained a little bit of maturity. (Female lawyer)

In contrast, another woman described the difficulties that she and her husband experienced in coordinating their life as a couple with the demands of their respective careers.

> I got offered a job [overseas], and I didn't end up taking it because of the wedding and because my husband-to-be at the time didn't want to go, didn't want to leave his job because he had just had a promotion into a supervisory role and he didn't want to give that up. There was no equivalent job over there that he could do with his company...Just recently he was offered a job in [Europe] which also has made a difference to what's going to happen. [My employer] can get me a job [there] possibly for a year, but it's for 2 years, so it would mean I would have to take off a year [which] sort of puts my career on hold. (Female engineer)

There were accounts from both men and women about delaying or disrupting their own careers in the interests of their partner's career.

Even when there were no issues about the priority of one career over the other, however, difficulties were reported in reconciling professional work with their family and relationships. The personal cost of meeting career demands was mentioned by a number of respondents. Despite their feelings of commitment to profession and engagement in the job, the personal costs were sometimes daunting. Their 'vocation' was tested by their dissatisfaction with their working routines, but they did not indicate loss of interest in the profession.

> My wife is not happy with the hours I'm working. I'm not happy with it. Obviously I do not think it's sustainable at all ... we just work absolutely crazy hours and I think that's a function of very interesting work we do, some amazingly interesting stuff ... I'm quite happy to travel but ... if I travel, I'd have less of a life than I already have, and I basically have no life except for work. (Male engineer)

These dilemmas suggest not so much a concern to balance competing but separate aspects of their lives but an effort to integrate these aspects to support a coherent personal identity as part of a broader view of a desirable life.

The big picture: a satisfying professional life

In the first round of interviews, we asked graduates what a successful life would be for them. The majority see career in terms of a broader perspective of work extending beyond the workplace and success as including aspects of work, relationships and family. While a few gave priority to family, most articulated the centrality of professional career and its advancement in their long-term plans.

> 'Successful' would be to have a good career, to be stimulated in my work life and to get a very nice salary. And to get into management. That'd be successful I think in terms of career. In terms of my personal life, just to have good friends, to keep in touch and to have a good relationship. To see my parents; not to lose touch with the important things in life too. (Female engineer)

The material benefits tended to be mentioned in passing, acknowledged but not a major factor. More central were the intrinsic satisfactions they anticipated from the variety, challenge and esteem associated with professional employment.

> Being challenged every day. Little challenges and big challenges as well so that I would have to keep pushing myself. I would hate to go

> to work and just do the same thing everyday and know that I could do it without a problem. I suppose respect from colleagues and know that I'm respected by other people of having knowledge and expertise in an area. (Female engineer)

Their focus was not solely on the profession as an end in itself but as a means to other social goals, a perspective akin to professions as vocations. Several respondents made this link explicitly as the two people quoted below illustrate.

> Something where I could see that I had made a difference…I would like to be able to say I had made a contribution to things in both my community and work…(Male investment banker)
>
> I've actually written it down different times in my life, trying to work it out. I think if I was thought of as honest and with integrity, I'd be successful. And if I'd achieved the goals which help…mankind…or improv(e) environmental situations…I wouldn't want to be a pillar of the community, but I'd like to be an assistant to a pillar of the community.…And children that came back to visit me when I was old, that would be good. (Male engineer)

The respondents' views of a satisfying life are conventional enough: a good career and interesting work, good family and personal relationships, a meaningful contribution to society. But their identity as professionals shapes this perspective in a fundamental way. Work satisfaction is a central component and entails both interesting work tasks and continuing personal development. Several explicitly differentiated the fabric of their lives from that of their non-professional parents. This was not a rejection of their parents' values but a sense that they occupied a different social status with a distinctive identity.

Commitment and ambivalence

The enthusiasm of most of the participants for the professions they had chosen was evident, even if they voiced irritation with aspects of their particular working situations. But it was also clear that there was some ambivalence about the professional path and its demands. As they became more experienced, they recognised that this tension would probably increase as they took on more responsibilities and more senior roles. There were several key areas in which this ambivalence was manifested.

The most commonly mentioned was the time pressure of professional work. Both men and women, but perhaps more of the women, recognise that life is more than work and as satisfying as a meaningful professional organisational career is, they also wish to develop friendships, pursue personal interests and start families. Achieving these goals requires more than a 'balancing of work and family' which has become something of a popular political mantra in recent years. This can be seen as ambitious in light of the demands of professional work. They talked about strategies they might employ to resolve the conflicts between work and personal life. Women were particularly likely to have considered strategies such as saving money so they could afford to take time off to have a family; reaching a sufficiently high level in their organisation before interrupting their career; seeking part-time employment in the early childrearing years (see Corwin, in this volume). But they did not evince a great deal of confidence that they would manage this conflict easily.

The second area of ambivalence revolved around the challenge of professional work and the onerous responsibility it entailed. While all their professional roles conferred high levels of responsibility, the issue seemed to be most acute for the engineers in the sample. Among this group there appeared to be the clearest polarisation between those for whom their professional background provided great confidence to deal with this responsibility and those who expressed apprehension about it.

A third area of ambivalence involved concerns about whether their particular choice of profession was the correct one for them. While professional status is clearly enabling, a particular professional path directs people narrowly and cuts off other choices. A few had made significant changes of direction, some were contemplating subsequent changes. These were weighty decisions and were recognised as having a fundamental impact on the person as well as their way of life. In a few cases, respondents voiced a sense of loss over changed directions or unfulfilled aspirations.

Professionalism in late modernity

Professions, as institutions of modernity, are under pressure in late modernity. Because these institutions are changed, graduates from the last decade of the twentieth century occupy a transitional territory between the traditional understandings of professions and the broader social trends that progressively affect professionalism. They have emerged from a credentialing process which allows entry to recognised professions. They find themselves negotiating a career path through a maze of requirements and implied demands including long working hours, the need for further study and globalised labour markets. Many planned to travel, 'to see the world' sometimes to work in low-status jobs, realising that this might disrupt their careers but also that travel and its experience could have other career enhancing benefits (see Arthur et al., 1999: 170). Interest in learning and stimulation motivated this willingness to take risks and openness to the opportunities that might result.

Gender continues to be a major factor shaping the responses of the interviewees. Superficially there were few differences between the perspectives of men and women. But a deeper reading suggests that professionalism continues to pose greater dilemmas for women. These are likely to intensify as respondents begin families and experience more acutely the conflicts between work and personal life. Increasingly, men are being drawn into these work-family considerations, both in their own right as husbands and fathers and as partners of professional women.

While the rise of new professions may have eroded some of the privileges of traditional professions, the respondents value this identity and the intrinsic rewards of professional work. The ethos of professionalism remains strong and there was no indication that its attractions were diminishing. They did not see work as detracting from their lives, though heavy job demands sometimes created stress and difficulties with relationships, especially if these included long hours or relocation. Their professional commitment did not diminish as they moved into management roles but rather informed those roles. No longer is the professional life limited to those in a few elite occupations or social categories. As a consequence, professionalism may be extending, both as an expectation of stimulating and fulfilling work and as a component of personal identity. With these changes, we see both the preservation of longstanding interpretations of professional identity and the transformation of its interpretation and practice.

References

Arthur, M.B., Inkson, K. and Pringle, J.K. (1999) *The New Careers: Individual Action and Economic Change*. London: Sage.

Barrett, F.J. (2002) 'Gender strategies of women professionals: the case of the U.S. Navy', in M. Dent and S. Whitehead (eds) *Managing Professional Identities: Knowledge, Performativity and the 'New' Professional*. London: Routledge: 157–73.

Casey, C. (1995) *Work, Self and Society: After Industrialism*. London: Routledge.
Cockburn, C. (1985) *Machinery of Male Dominance: Women, Men and Technical Know-how*. London: Pluto.
Dent, M. and Whitehead S. (2002) 'Introduction: configuring the "new professional",' in M. Dent and S. Whitehead (eds) *Managing Professional Identities: Knowledge, Performativity and the 'New' Professional*. London: Routledge: 1–16.
Devadason, R. (2008) 'To plan or not to plan? Young adult future orientations in two European cities', *Sociology*, 42 (6): 1127–45.
Kerfoot, D. (2002) 'Managing the "professional" man', in M. Dent and S. Whitehead (eds) *Managing Professional Identities: Knowledge, Performativity and the 'New' Professional*. London: Routledge: 81–95.
Kvale, S. (1996) *InterViews: An Introduction to Qualitative Research Interviewing*. Thousand Oaks: Sage.
Parkin, F. (1982) *Max Weber*. Chichester: Ellis Horwood.
Pringle, R. (1998) *Sex and Medicine: Gender, Power and Authority in the Medical Profession*. Cambridge: Cambridge University Press.
Wajcman, J. (1998) *Managing Like a Man: Women and Men in Corporate Management*. Sydney: Allen & Unwin.
Weber, M. (1948) 'Class, status, party', in H.H. Gerth and C. Wright Mills, *From Max Weber: Essays in Sociology*. London: Routledge & Kegan Paul: 180–95.

6

'Live to Work or Work to Live?' The Search for Work-life Balance in Twenty-first Century Japan

Tim Craig

Introduction

'Work-life balance' is trying to become a buzzword, and a reality, in Japan today. So far, it's not having much luck.

Statistics paint a grim picture. Working hours remain long by industrialised-country standards,[1] and are significantly underreported thanks to widespread unpaid overtime. On-the-job stress and suicide rates are up. Japan is one of just two countries – the other is South Korea – where *karoshi* (death from overwork) is a recognised phenomenon.[2] A 2007 study by IriS International Research Institutes found Japan to rank highest among 24 countries surveyed in the proportion of respondents reporting 'dissatisfaction with work-life balance.'[3]

This is not to say that efforts are not being made to address the issue. Pressures toward improved work-life balance (WLB) have been building steadily over the past two decades: from individuals seeking healthier, better-balanced lives; from companies that view WLB-friendly policies as a way to attract top recruits, including women, in a shrinking labour market; from the Japanese government, as a way to address the problem of population decline; and from academics and commentators who see connections between poor WLB and problems such as rising divorce rates, domestic violence, and low labour productivity.

Yet, gains are small and elusive. After falling steadily since the 1950s, reported work hours have recently began to rise.[4] Employee take-up of flexible and family-friendly work arrangements is low. And while growing numbers of 20-something Japanese are postponing or opting out of the corporate rat race for 'non-standard' jobs that allow them to pursue more fulfilling private lives, this is more often viewed as a problem than as a remedy.

Why the lack of progress? Are Japanese individuals and companies simply subject to the same forces that make the achievement of work-life balance a difficult task in any country, namely economic necessity in a globalised and increasingly competitive world where working less most often means earning less and settling for a lower standard of living? Or are there characteristics particular to Japan that make the debate over, and the challenges of achieving, WLB a different proposition from what it is in other countries? Is it possible that use of the word 'progress' itself, to describe a shift in the direction of greater focus on the 'non-work' side of life, imposes on the debate a Western framework that sits uneasily on a nation that drinks from a different cultural well?

This chapter examines the debate around and the reality of work-life balance in Japan in the first decade of the twenty-first century. Work-life arrangements and choices are compared across two distinct periods: Japan's 'strong growth' years, from around 1955 through the 1980s, and post-Bubble Japan, from around 1990 to today. It is seen that the context in which work-life choices are made has undergone significant change, driven by external forces, cultural change, and companies' responses to both of these. The picture that emerges is one of a nation caught in a complex web of conflicting pressures – demographic, economic, managerial, social, and cultural – that push and pull on organizations and individuals, some toward a 'healthier' work-life balance and some in the other direction.[5]

Understanding work-life choices: a model

Figure 6.1 presents a generic model of individuals' work-life choices, the factors that influence those choices, and their outcomes. This model is developed from the author's research of work-life balance in Japan and from paper presentations and discussions at the 'Ways of Living: Work, Organizations, Communities, and Lifestyle Choice' colloquium held in December 2008 in Melbourne, Australia.[6]

At the centre of the model lies 'work-life choices': the amount of time and energy that individuals devote to work, versus the time and energy they devote to other things such as family, individual pursuits (e.g. hobbies), and community activities. Time refers to measurable hours. Energy includes behaviour and attitudes; for example, how hard one works, or how much one invests emotionally in the workplace or the family.

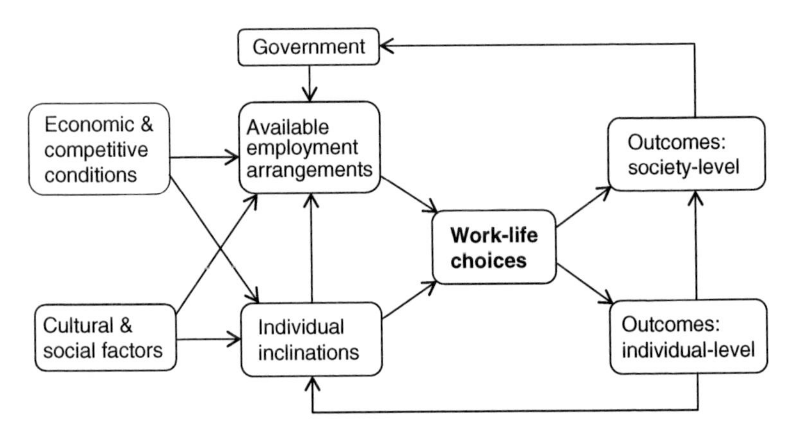

Figure 6.1 Generic model of the influences and outcomes of individuals' work-life choices

Individuals' actual work-life choices are a product of their individual inclinations and the employment arrangements that are available to them. Individual inclinations are the importance individuals place on, and their preferences for devoting themselves to, work vs. non-work pursuits. These are shaped by economic, social, and cultural factors, as well as by the level of satisfaction (or dissatisfaction) with current work-life arrangements. Available employment arrangements include employment options and the Human Resource policies and practices of employers. These are shaped by economic, social, and cultural factors, as well as by government.

There are two levels of outcomes from individuals' work-life choices. Individual-level outcomes include such things as economic well-being, mental and physical health, levels of happiness or stress, and the strength of relationships with family. Individual-level outcomes feed back into individuals' inclinations; for example, dissatisfaction with individual-level outcomes may influence a person's inclinations and thus trigger a change in work-life choice. Society-level outcomes include such things as national health levels, the birth rate, and social issues. When people's work-life choices are viewed as contributing to broader social problems, government may take action to influence work-life choices through its ability to shape employment arrangements, for example through labour law.

Let us now use this model to compare people's work-life choices across two distinct periods in post-war Japan.

'Pre-Bubble' work-life choices in Japan

Japan is well known for its post-war 'economic miracle' and for Japanese companies' success and leadership in automobiles, electronics, and other industries. The foundations of this success are many and complex, but counted among them are:

- social arrangements characterised by a clear division of responsibility between men (breadwinners) and women (homemakers);
- a strong work ethic, which gave higher priority to building the nation and gaining economic security for the family than to pursuit of outside-of-work fulfillment; and
- a set of particularly 'Japanese' human resource practices, including 'lifetime employment' and seniority-based pay and promotion.

These and other features made up a holistic system that can be said to have functioned successfully during the nation's strong-growth years, from around 1955 to the end of the 1980s. Males typically pursued the dream of 'lifetime employment' with a major corporation, studying hard to get into a top university from which the best companies recruited. Once hired, they devoted their lives to the company, working long hours (often coming home late and leaving for work early the next morning) and spending little time with their families by Western standards. In return they received long-term financial security and the social status that came with employment at a big-name company. Work also provided order and meaning to life, and an arena to satisfy their social needs.

Women also studied hard, went to the best schools they could get into, and joined companies after graduation. But few had long-term careers as a goal; the typical pattern was to work for a few years and then quit the company to get married and have children. After marriage women ran the household, controlled the family purse strings, were in charge of the children's education, and had a social world of their own: typically the neighborhood and other housewives in similar circumstances.

Under these arrangements, companies got a well-educated, hardworking, and highly committed workforce that they could invest in for the long term. Salary was structured to match the successive stages of life: low in the early years when employees were single; rising with the increasing financial demands of marriage, child-raising, and older children's education costs; and leveling off as retirement neared. The nation prospered, rising from the ashes of World War II to become the second largest economy in the world. And Japanese society was, on the whole, stable and peaceful, with a relatively even distribution of wealth and low crime rates that were the envy of most any other country. To be sure, there were problems: overwork, fathers with little presence at home, 'education mothers' pressuring their children to excel academically, and redundant workers kept on company payrolls. But overall, the system functioned well. There was little discussion of, and no term for what we now call, work-life balance.

New realities, new issues in 'Post-Bubble' Japan

Why has work-life balance become an issue in Japan today? Because economic, managerial, social, cultural, and demographic changes have occurred, and continue to occur, that have caused the pre-bubble system to work less well in terms of producing satisfactory outcomes for individuals, companies, and the nation. The year 1990 serves as a useful turning point for a 'before' and 'after' comparison of work-life balance in Japan. 1990 marks the end of Japan's 'bubble economy' and the beginning of the 'lost decade' of slow or negative economic growth, which had broad repercussions for Japan's workforce and their families. It is also a time when a number of social, cultural, and demographic trends that are related to work-life balance issues were becoming evident or more prominent.

Figure 6.2 applies the generic 'work-life choice' model (introduced above) to the specific case of Japan. The influencing variables, work-life choices, and outcomes included in the applied version of the model are those around which today's debate on work-life balance revolves. We now examine how these variables, choices, and outcomes have changed, and what this change has meant for work-life balance.

Economic and competitive conditions

The landmark event in post-1980 Japan is what is known as the 'bubble': a period of steep asset price inflation that occurred during the last half of the 1980s. Between 1986 and 1990, spurred by expansionary monetary policies designed to cushion Japan's export economy from the recessionary effects of a strengthened yen following the Plaza Accord,[7] huge amounts of Japanese savings – accumulated over 30-plus years of economic expansion – were poured into the country's property and stock markets, driving real estate and stock prices to extremely high levels.

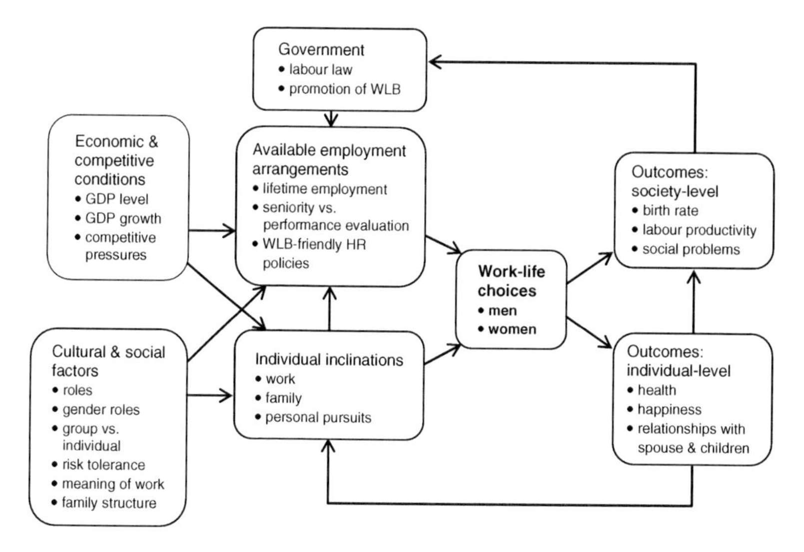

Figure 6.2 Applied model: the influences and outcomes of individuals' work-life choices in Japan

In 1992 the Bubble collapsed, sending stock and property prices crashing and ushering in Japan's 'lost decade' of low or negative growth. The extent and duration of the downturn can be seen in stock and real estate prices. The Nikkei stock index, which had peaked at 38,916 yen in December 1989, did not bottom out until April 2003 – at 7,608 yen, less than a fifth of its 1989 high. Japanese home prices reached their high mark in 1990, but dropped sharply in the early 1990s and continued to decline until in 2005 they had fallen by an average of 40 per cent overall, 65 per cent in major cities, and 80 per cent in Tokyo.[8] GDP growth resumed in the 2000s, but at much more modest levels than prior to 1990.

Even before the bubble collapsed, competitive pressures were increasing for Japanese companies, with rising labour costs, an appreciating yen, and the emergence of strong competitors in other (particularly Asian) countries. After 1992, with balance sheets damaged by the collapse of asset values and domestic demand down due to economic stagnation, the pressures on companies to reduce costs became very strong. This caused 'lifetime employment' and seniority-based pay and promotion systems to begin to erode. Widely adopted by major Japanese companies after 1960 to resolve the fierce labour-management conflict that marked the 1950s and to attract and keep workers in a rapidly expanding economy, 'lifetime employment' and seniority-based pay and promotion had significant merits for companies: they secured a committed labour force that tied its fortunes to that of the firm, worked hard, and could be invested in for the long run. However, there were costs as well. Companies were forced to keep even underperforming workers on their payrolls, and to continue to raise their wages as they built up seniority. Unable to lay off 'regular' employees, companies also had limited ability to downsize when demand dropped.

When the economy was growing and companies were prospering, the costs of 'lifetime employment' and seniority-based pay and promotion were bearable. But with the bursting of the bubble and the ensuing economic downturn, these costs became prohibitive. Thus the 1990s saw the beginning of permanent layoffs of regular full-time workers by major companies, a shift to more limited-term contracts, and increased use of part-time and temporary (*haken*) labour. Between 1992 and 2007, facilitated by changes in Japanese labour law, non-standard work contracts grew from 10 per cent to 30 per cent of the workforce.[9] Employee pay and promotion systems also began to change – toward less emphasis on seniority and greater emphasis on performance.[10] A 2004 survey by the Japan Management Association found that 83 per cent of 227 participating companies had introduced performance-based HR management systems in the post-bubble era.[11]

Social and cultural change

Gender roles

While gender roles in Japan remain quite clearly differentiated in comparison to those in many Western countries, they have gradually begun to blur, with women increasingly choosing (or desiring) to pursue careers rather than be full-time housewives, and men displaying more openness to being involved at home and with child-raising. This trend can be seen in popular culture – for instance in television dramas, which are recognised as reflecting and reconfirming existing social structures and also legitimising social change.[12] A study of Japanese TV dramas by Hilaria M. Gossmann found that 1960s and 1970s dramas portrayed the 'men work, women stay home' model positively; female characters were either happy 'reliable mothers' whose life centred on the home, or unhappy 'suffering women' who life lay outside the domestic sphere. In the late 1970s and 1980s, the traditional model began to show cracks; in a 1977 hit drama by famous script writer Taichi Yamada, for instance, a 40-year-old housewife has an extramarital affair because she cannot bear the isolation of life married to a husband who works all the time. By the 1990s, dramas centred on working women, and even men taking on household and child-care responsibilities, had become common, as they remain today.[13]

Marriage

Marriage views and practices have also changed. Marrying late or not marrying have become more common, and socially acceptable. In 1980, only 24 per cent of Japanese women in the 25–29 age range were unmarried; in 2008, 59 per cent were.[14] Derogatory terms for older unmarried women such as 'hai misu' (high miss) are heard less frequently than they once were, and single career women are portrayed positively (though not without challenges to face) in popular culture and the media.

The view that the foundation of a marriage should be a close personal relationship between husband and wife, where husband and wife do things together and enjoy each other's company, has gained favour in comparison to the past, when there was greater emphasis on finding (or being introduced to) a partner who met certain economic or social status criteria. There are fewer *omiai* (arranged meeting) marriages in Japan today, more 'love' marriages. Husbands' sharing of housework and child-raising, though still small by Western standards, is on the rise.[15] Incompatibility between spouses, once of secondary importance, is now widely viewed as legitimate grounds for divorce.[16]

Work ethic

During the 1980s the word *shinjinrui* ('new breed') came into popular usage to describe a new generation of young Japanese with a more lax attitude toward work than that held by previous generations. Born after 1960 and coming of age in the 1970s and afterwards, *shinjinrui* did not experience the economic hardship that their parents had in post-war Japan. The Japan they grew up in was a rich country, and they had enjoyed the fruits of that wealth, having their university education paid for by their parents, travelling abroad and seeing other lifestyles, and developing a taste for the good life.[17]

For this generation, the concepts of hard work and sacrifice for the company and the nation were alien – at least in comparison to previous generations. To their seniors at the company, *shinjinrui* were difficult to understand, and soft. Many preferred to go home at five o'clock rather than work overtime or go drinking with colleagues after work, and not a few quit their new full-time jobs after a few months, something quite rare in previous decades. The attitude gap between *shinjinrui* and management was much discussed, and managers struggled both to shape new recruits into hard-working employees and to adjust the way they themselves managed so as to not alienate and lose younger employees, who had been carefully recruited as the future of the company.

Impact on individuals and companies

These social and cultural changes – the shift away from traditional gender roles, changing views toward marriage, and a weakened work ethic – may seem mild by Western standards, for Japan remains a country in which men dominate the business world, marriage is an assumed goal for most people, and people work hard. But they are significant changes for Japan, and have affected both individual inclinations and available work arrangements. Men are less eager than before to devote their lives to the company at the expense of time and energy spent with family or in personal pursuits. Japanese still take their jobs seriously and work hard, but do not put in overtime as much, or as unquestioningly, as they once did. Fewer women now embrace the 'work for a few years, then quit to get married' model; more aspire to build careers, and are willing to delay marriage or even remain single if marriage means giving up meaningful work. And both men and women increasingly seek in marriage a relationship that includes more than simply playing the role of breadwinner or homemaker; this requires more time spent together, and therefore less time spent at work.

Companies have had to respond to these social and cultural changes, and to the shifting inclinations of their existing and future workforce, in order to successfully recruit and retain quality employees. One way that they have done this is to introduce 'work-life balance' friendly HR policies, such as reduced work hours, flextime, parental leave, and child-care support. The government website 'Change! Japan' provides a list of 160 major Japanese companies and their corporate policies and practices in the areas of child care leave, nursing care leave, flextime work options, maternity and paternity leave, financial assistance for child and nursing care, and work-from-home options.[18] The impression one gets reading through this data is that, though some firms have clearly done more than others, overall, Japan's name-brand companies have come a long way in making family- and personal life-friendly work arrangements available to their core employees. While a few companies began doing this in the 1980s, the vast majority of company WLB-friendly policies were introduced in the 1990s.[19]

Work-life choices and outcomes in today's Japan

Individual level

While Japanese individuals are increasingly inclined to (or would like to) spend more time and energy on family and individual pursuits and less on work, and while companies have introduced new HR policies that make this more possible than it once was, the evidence does not show that individuals' actual work-life choices have changed all that much. Work hours remain long. According to the *OECD Factbook*, Japanese work an average of 1784 hours per year in 2006, slightly above the average for OECD countries.[20] Actual work hours, however, are almost certainly significantly higher than this given the widespread practice of 'service overtime' (*saabisu zangyou*, or *'sabi-zan'*): unpaid and unreported overtime. A 2006 survey found that 30 per cent of male private-sector employees in Tokyo and Osaka work over 12 hours a day.[21] According to a 2007 Labour Ministry survey, full-time employees take only half their allotted paid holidays.[22]

And although WLB-friendly work options are increasingly available, few employees are choosing to take advantage of them. Only 0.5 per cent of working fathers take the parental leave that the law entitles them to, and only 30 per cent of working women return to work after having children.[23]

This is not to say that Japanese are satisfied with their current work-life options and choices; in fact, the evidence suggests that dissatisfaction has increased. A 2007 survey by IriS International Research Institutes found Japan to rank highest among 24 countries surveyed in the proportion of respondents reporting 'dissatisfaction with work-life balance.' And the fact that the term 'work-life balance' has entered the national vocabulary – a Google search for the Japanese pronunciation of the English term, *'waaku raifu baransu,'*[24] produces 930,000 hits – shows that it is on people's minds. Though not specifically about WLB satisfaction, longitudinal survey data collected by the Japanese government on 'degree of satisfaction with your life' shows satisfaction levels decreasing steadily since the early 1980s.[25] This is not due to falling living standards – Japan's per capita GNP has risen steadily during this period – but rather, most likely, to lifestyle issues such as WLB.

Dissatisfaction with the outcomes of their current work-life choices can lead individuals to reassess and potentially change those choices. To cut back on work in order to spend more time on family or personal interests, however, can have high economic costs, particularly in an economic environment where secure full-time jobs have become hard to find and permanent lay-offs (*risutora*, or being 'restructured') are common. And so, though many would like to 'downshift,' few actually do. The above-cited survey that reported Japanese to rank highest in dissatisfaction with work-life balance also found Japanese to be pessimistic about the prospects of WLB improvement and passive about pushing to achieve it. 'It can't be helped' (*shikata ga nai*) is a phrase commonly heard in Japan, and one that many use to express the resignation felt toward having to work long hours at the expense of non-work activities.

The pulls that many Japanese feel both toward and away from improved work-life balance are illustrated by the 'freeter' phenomenon. The term 'freeter,' a combination of 'free' or 'freelance' plus *arbeiter* (German for labourer), was coined in the late 1980s to describe the growing numbers of young Japanese adults who do not have a permanent full-time job but instead hold one or more part-time jobs or move from one short-term job to another. During the bubble economy, freeters had a positive image: as people opting out of the rat race to pursue their dreams. But when economic conditions worsened following the collapse of the bubble, more people became freeters out of necessity. Both the positive and negative reasons for becoming a freeter are shown in a 2001 survey by *Web Japan* that asked freeters why they chose this lifestyle. The responses, in order of frequency, were: 'to give priority to the things I myself want to do' (40 per cent); 'as a stopgap until I can find a job I want to do' (23 per cent); 'I wanted to get a regular position, but under present employment conditions that was impossible' (18 per cent); and 'Even with a job as a regular employee, I would change jobs anyway' (8 per cent).[26]

Society level

Public discussion of work-life balance in Japan typically focuses on its potential to help create a 'healthier' society in general and to address specific issues that are seen as nation-level problems. The Japanese government's 'Work-life Balance Charter' (see below) defines a society with good work-life balance as one in which 'Citizens find meaning and fulfillment in their work, and while carrying out their work responsibilities are able, in both family and community life, to choose and realize diverse ways of living that match each stage of their lives, such as child-raising, middle age, and old age.'[27] The annual white paper on labour economy released by the Health, Labour and Welfare Ministry in August 2006 stated that Japan needs 'to create an employment system in which (workers) can strive for a balance between work and life in order for our country and society to continue economic development amid depopulation.'[28]

Specific issues that are part of the WLB discussion – problems for which poor WLB is seen as a cause or for which improved WLB is seen as a part of the cure – include work-related health issues; population decline and a shrinking workforce; family breakdown; and low worker productivity.

Health issues

Health issues seen as related to poor WLB include death and disability from overwork, and stress. While it is difficult to show conclusively that work-related stress, disability, and death are on the rise, available data suggests that this is the case. The suicide rate for Japanese males doubled between 1992 and 2003, from 20 per 100,000 to around 40 per 100,000, and 65 per cent of companies report rising levels of mental illness among employees.[29] Ministry of Health, Labour, and Welfare data show that workers' compensation claims for both *karoshi* and work-related psychological problems have increased in recent years (see Table 6.1). Ministry officials attribute the increase in worker's compensation cases involving psychological problems to long working hours and the spread of performance-based pay scales.[30] A Mental Health Institute spokesperson cites increased emphasis on individual performance, which is at odds with the group orientation that is a deeply-held cultural value, as a cause of mental turmoil for Japanese workers: 'People tend to be individualized under the new working patterns. When people worked in teams they were happier.'[31]

As in many countries, in Japan there is a sense among workers that the sheer amount of work that has to be done has increased, due to the

Table 6.1 Workers' compensation claims, 2002–06[32]

Year	Number of workers' compensation claims for work-related death and disability	Number of workers' compensation claims for work-related psychological disorders & depression
2002	819	341
2003	742	447
2004	816	524
2005	869	656
2006	938	819

spread of information technology, reductions in staff, and an increasingly competitive environment for companies. In a 2007 government survey of regular employees at Japanese companies, 67 per cent reported that their workload and work responsibilities had increased compared to five years earlier.[33] A Japanese employee in his 40s observes:

> Thirty years ago, ordinary workers didn't need to worry about how much money their company was making – that was the job of the president and top management. Ordinary employees just had to do their job. My father was a bus driver. All he had to do was drive his bus. But now even ordinary employees have to think about their company's financial performance. A bus driver today can't simply drive the bus. He/she must also worry about company profit, and what might be done to increase revenues, reduce costs, or operate more efficiently.[34]

Population decline

Japan is an ageing society with one of the lowest birthrates in the world. While most other developed countries still have population growth, Japan's population has begun to shrink. The country's fertility rate – the number of children a woman is expected to give birth to in her lifetime – has steadily declined over the last two decades, from 1.57 in 1989 to 1.25 in 2005. (The average birthrate in developed countries is 1.6 children per woman, while the rate needed to prevent population decline is 2.1.)[35] The nation also faces a looming labour shortage, with 6.8 million baby boomers scheduled to retire in 2007–09, and immigration strictly limited. By one estimate, the Japanese workforce will shrink by 10 million, or 15 per cent, between the years 2003 and 2030.[36] These facts spell trouble in the form of a shrinking domestic market for companies and increased strain on the nation's finances, as taxes on a smaller workforce must support a larger non-working proportion of the population.

The Japanese government acknowledges that the falling birthrate is connected to job-related factors. Among those factors,

- Job security has declined with the erosion of lifetime employment and the increase in non-standard work contracts and performance-based evaluation. As a result, many young people don't feel financially stable enough to start families.
- Underdeveloped maternity leave and child care options (compared to Western countries), plus societal expectations (weakened but far

from extinct) that mothers be full-time mothers, make it difficult for women to have children and continue a career.
- With long work hours, husbands have little time to help out with child-raising. This places a heavy burden on the wife, particularly in an age of nuclear families where grandparents and other family members are not around to help.

In addition, procreation generally requires having sex. When husbands come home late and exhausted from overwork, and when spousal relationships suffer due to work stress and lack of time together, less sex takes place.[37] International surveys have shown that Japanese married couples have sex less frequently than couples of any other nation.[38]

Family breakdown

It would be problematic to argue, and I do not believe, that Japan is less 'healthy' than other nations in terms of family health and relationships among family members. But there are a number of recognised social problems in Japan that have developed or grown worse in recent years and that appear to be related in part to weakened relationships between spouses or between children and parents. These include:

- *hiki-komori*: people who withdraw from society, shunning other people and not venturing out of their home or room;
- *toko kyohi*: the phenomenon of children or young people refusing to go to school;
- domestic violence, in particular that between children and parents; and
- rising divorce rates, especially around retirement age.

It is argued that among the causes of these problems is the division-of-labour arrangement under which husbands and wives lead quite separate lives, with men focused on work – 'the company as family' is a common phrase – and women focused on home and children. This is often exacerbated by the practice of *tanshin funin*: husband and family living apart when the husband is transferred to a different city or country but the wife and children stay put because they don't want to move or interrupt the children's education.

Husbands/fathers thus often have low visibility and involvement at home, meaning that many children grow up without, or with a very distant, father figure. This makes it harder for healthy father-child relationships to develop, and in some cases may also negatively affect social and emotional growth. It also hinders the development of a strong bond between husband and wife, one that goes beyond the roles of breadwinner and homemaker to encompass the development of common interests and friendship. This is clearly a contributing factor to the boom in middle-age or retirement-age divorce (*jukunen rikon*, or 'mature age divorce'); one hears and reads frequently of married couples who have led separate lives while the husband was working but find, upon the husband's retirement, that they have little in common, get on each others' nerves, and dislike spending time together.

Labour productivity

A final issue often tied to work-life balance is labour productivity. In 2006 Japan ranked 20th out of 30 OECD countries surveyed in overall per capita productivity, and was the least productive of any G7 nation.[39] The problem is not with blue-collar productivity – Japanese firms, known for excellence in manufacturing, have excelled in this area – but with white-collar productivity, which remains low despite the erosion of guaranteed employment and the shift toward more performance-based pay and promotion schemes. This is particularly problematic for Japanese firms: with the IT revolution and with much of Japanese manufacturing moving overseas to access cheaper labour, innovativeness and white-collar productivity have increased in importance for companies' international competitiveness.

Long meetings, meaningless reports, slow decision-making, doing things a certain way because 'that's how it's done' – these and other 'inefficiencies' are famously a part of working for a Japanese company. But with long hours and overtime an accepted, almost given, aspect of the 'salaryman' life, there is little pressure to raise efficiency. Why hurry if you have to stay late at the office anyway because that's the norm? Leaving the office at five o'clock while your colleagues are still working is considered selfish and invites disapproval. After-work socializing is also considered part of the job – valuable for relationship-building and discussion that, with alcohol as a cover, can be more open and frank than that conducted in the sober workplace. And so, in the absence of pressure to complete one's work in a limited amount of time, Japanese productivity continues to lag behind that of other nations.

Work-life balance as remedy

Improved work-life balance – which is to say less time and energy spent on work, and more spent on 'life' – is today increasingly being held out in Japan as a potential, if partial, remedy for the individual- and society-level issues described above. The keys to achieving this are to reduce work hours and to increase the availability and take-up of WLB-friendly HR policies such as flextime, on-site child care, and parental leave. The potential benefits, it is argued, include

- Reduced work hours would go a long way toward reducing stress and work-related illness. Workers would suffer less sleep deprivation, and would benefit mentally from the refreshment and change of pace of doing things other than work. Better rested and healthier physically, employees might also perform better at work, lessening some of the anxiety around performance-based evaluation.
- Reduced work hours and an increase in flextime schemes, on-site childcare, and maternity leave would make it easier for women to have children and pursue a career, instead of requiring them to choose one or the other. This would help increase the birthrate and also raise female participation in the workforce, thus helping address the coming labour shortage.
- Reduced work hours, flextime schemes, and parental leave would also allow husbands and fathers to spend more time with their wives and children, strengthening family relationships. Increased husband availability to help with child-raising would help raise the birthrate. And to the extent that weak or broken family relationships contribute *hiki-komori*, *toko kyohi*, domestic violence, and rising divorce rates, these problem areas would be positively affected.
- Finally, if work hours were reduced – by law or by company policy – employee productivity would rise because workers would need to finish their work in a limited amount of time and would therefore find ways to work more efficiently. The case of increased labour productivity in British companies resulting from reduced work hours and the adoption of WLB-promoting policies in the 1990s is cited as evidence in support of this argument, as is a study by Fujitsu Research that found Japanese firms ranking high on a set of WLB-related measures to significantly outperform firms ranking low on the same measures.[40]

In the 2000s, the Japanese government began to actively promote work-life balance as a way to help address the problems outlined above. In particular, several government agencies have embraced the idea that improved WLB can help halt population decline by changing the situation where women of childbearing age feel they must choose between motherhood and having a career. The centerpiece of government initiatives is Japan's 'Work-life Balance Charter,' signed in December 2007 by Chief Cabinet Secretary Nobutaka Machimura, head of a government task force including academics and representatives from management (Keidanren – the Japanese Business Federation) and labour (Rengo – the Japanese Trade Union Confederation). The charter stresses the importance of achieving a better balance between work and life in Japan, where many company employees 'are overworked to the point of exhaustion and are unable to spend enough time with their children or care for ailing parents.' Specifically, the charter calls for:

- increasing female (age 25–44) participation in the workforce from 64.9 per cent in 2007 to 69~72 per cent by 2017;
- increasing senior citizen (age 60–64) participation in the workforce from 52.6 per cent in 2007 to 60~61 per cent by 2017;
- cutting in half the number of people working 60 or more hours a week by 2017 (from 10.8 per cent of workers in 2007);
- increasing to 100 per cent workers' taking of entitled paid holidays by 2017 (from 46.6 per cent in 2007);
- increasing the ratio of women who continue to work after giving birth to their first child from 38 per cent in 2007 to 55 per cent by 2017;
- increasing take-up of maternity leave from 72.3 per cent in 2007 to 80 per cent in 2017;
- increasing take-up of paternity leave from 0.5 per cent in 2007 to 10 per cent in 2017; and
- increasing the average amount of time husbands spend on housework and childcare from an hour a day in 2007 to 2.5 hours a day by 2017.[41]

The government has also launched a 'Change! Japan' campaign and website to explain and promote WLB.[42] The site outlines the benefits of WLB, provides information on WLB-related events and survey data, and provides examples of WLB-promoting efforts and measures taken by regional organisations, Japanese companies, and foreign companies and organisations.

Is Japan different? The meaning of work, and other cultural factors

As elaborated above, increasing numbers of Japanese are dissatisfied with their current work-life balance and desire to improve it; many

Japanese companies have introduced WLB-friendly HR policies, such as flextime, parental leave, and child-care support; and the Japanese government and other organisations are actively promoting WLB as a means of addressing health issues, social problems, low productivity, and population decline. Yet it seems that little progress is being made in rebalancing the equation toward less work and more 'life,' and in ameliorating the problems that poor WLB creates or exacerbates. This raises two questions: 'Why?' and 'Is Japan different?' To what extent is Japan similar to other nations, in that improving work-life balance is a difficult undertaking anywhere? To what extent is Japan different, in that there are cultural or other factors at work that make achieving work-life balance more elusive than it is in other nations? The remainder of this chapter attempts to answer these questions.

Similarities among countries

Certainly, much of the difficulty of attaining better work-life balance, for individuals and for nations, is not unique to Japan. In her chapter in this volume, Vivien Corwin cites studies by Van Echtelt et al., Dick, and Callan that explore why Europeans work longer hours than they say they would like to and why the availability of family-friendly policies such as flex time does not always translate into high adoption by employees. Among the reasons highlighted by these studies are the 'time greediness' of project-centered ('post-Fordist') job design, which pressures (or lures) employees to stay late to finish a project rather than stop at a prescribed time, losing momentum and risking missing a deadline; fear of being seen as unmotivated or uncommitted by colleagues; and workplace cultures and managerial attitudes or imperatives that are less than fully supportive of shorter working hours or family-friendly work arrangements. There is little evidence to suggest these that these factors are less prevalent in Japan than in Europe.

Competitive pressures – at both the firm and the individual level – also help explain why improved WLB is hard to attain. For most Japanese companies, competitive conditions are fierce, both domestically and internationally. Increasingly, the competition is from less-developed nations, where people are happy to work long hours (as the Japanese once were) and the idea of work-life balance is a dream only richer nations can afford. Productivity gains could theoretically allow work hours to be shortened, but these are difficult to achieve and unlikely, most managers believe, to be of a scale that would permit significant work hour reduction without hurting firm financial performance. At the employee level, with job security and pay depending more heavily on individual performance than before, cutting back work hours is a risky business indeed. These pressures would seem to apply in both Japanese and non-Japanese work settings.

Differences

At the same time, however, as anyone familiar with Japan can attest, Japan is in some ways fundamentally different from other nations and cultures, and especially from Western nations and cultures. A survey conducted by the city of Tokyo on the topic of work-life balance reveals some of those cultural differences. Respondents who indicated they were unenthusiastic or pessimistic about the prospect of improving work-life balance were asked why. Their top three answers were:

1. The reality of the matter is that it would be very difficult to achieve.
2. When there is an increase in the number of people who work putting priority on their own convenience, this causes trouble for others in the workplace.
3. Housework and raising children should be women's work.[43]

The first answer reflects a Japanese tendency, seen in the often-heard phrase *shikata ga nai* ('It can't be helped' – mentioned above), to accept and endure things as they are ('reality') rather than to actively push for change. This makes it easy to say: Yes, better work-life balance would be nice, but it's unrealistic to think that it could actually be achieved. The same sentiment shows up in a 2006 Cabinet Office white paper which reported that 36 per cent of men surveyed said they would take parental leave if possible but that doing so was 'unrealistic.'[44]

The second answer reflects the well-known Japanese emphasis on the group (vs. the individual), and on harmony and team spirit. Japan scholar Edwin O. Reischauer writes: 'Cooperativeness, reasonableness, and understanding of others are the virtues most admired, not personal drive, forcefulness, and individual self-assertion.'[45] Thus Japanese, to a greater extent than Westerners, take into account the negative effect on colleagues and on workplace harmony of actions that would prioritise personal interest over work considerations.

The third answer, so politically incorrect in the West that few would dare utter it, shows that the traditional view of men as breadwinners and women as homemakers is alive and well in Japan, even if weakened compared to a generation or two ago. Bolstering the idea of fixed gender roles is the high value that Japanese place on specialisation itself; devoting oneself to a single pursuit or role is generally viewed quite positively, while spreading one's efforts over multiple pursuits is not.[46] These values continue to act as a brake on the efforts of women to pursue work careers (especially after having children) and of men to be more involved at home, and on the effectiveness of WLB policies designed to enable and support such efforts.

But perhaps the greatest cultural difference impacting work-life balance in Japan, versus that in other countries, has to do with the meaning of work itself. The term 'work-life balance' posits work and life as opposing forces that must be balanced off against each other. But what if work *is* life? Not just for workaholics, which make up some proportion of any population, but for a nation? To say that Japanese workers believe work is life overstates it, but it is clear that in Japan work occupies a higher, and different, place in the scheme of things than it does in the West. Work is how one earns a living, of course, but it is also more: it gives meaning to life and constitutes a central part of one's identity to a degree not often found in other countries. This can be seen, for example, in Japan's popular culture; countless *manga* (Japanese comics), *anime* (animated cartoons), and TV dramas revolve directly around work, with protagonists devoting their lives to becoming good office workers, bosses, sushi chefs, architects, tofu makers, shoe salesmen, bodyguards, money lenders – you name it. It is also reflected in work hours. To a greater extent than in other cultures, long hours spent on the job are not viewed as time taken away from one's personal life; they are a valuable and meaningful part of life. Work is not time taken away from self-actualization; it *is* self-actualization. This observation is supported by an eight-country investigation by the Meaning of Work International Research Team which found Japan to rank highest in individuals' ideas of the relative importance of work compared to that of leisure, community, religion, and family.[47] It also calls into question the appropriateness of using words like 'better' and 'improved' to describe increased time given to non-work activities.

For Japanese men in particular, the workplace also satisfies the human need for social life and membership in a group – of special importance in a group-oriented society like Japan's. To again quote Edwin O. Reischauer:

> A job in Japan is not merely a contractual arrangement for pay but means identification with a larger entity – in other words, a satisfying sense of being part of something big and significant.... There is little of the feeling, so common in the West, of being an insignificant and replaceable cog in a great machine. Both managers and

> workers suffer no loss of identity but rather gain pride through their company, particularly if it is large and famous. Company songs are sung with enthusiasm, and company pins are proudly displayed in buttonholes.[48]

A Japanese professor who has lived in the West makes these observations:

> In the West, a clear distinction is made between work and life. But in Japan, it's much more blurred. For many Japanese men in particular, work *is* life. And they *enjoy* work. For male company employees, the company is their home; their actual house is a sort of 'sub-home.' That's why they are in no special hurry to return home from work; they enjoy the camaraderie with colleagues, whether in the office or going for drinks after work.
>
> Japanese female employees are actually more like Westerners in this sense; for them the workplace is less like 'home,' and they prefer to return to their real homes early rather than lingering at the office or going for drinks at the end of the workday.[49]

The same professor describes a situation he experienced that illustrates the different approaches of Westerners and Japanese toward work. Thirty teaching staff at a Japanese university had one week scheduled for the marking of a large number of student exams. Around 20 of the exam markers were Japanese; the other 10 were North Americans and Europeans.

> All the Westerners arrived on time on the first morning, while the Japanese straggled in, many arriving 30 minutes late or more. The Westerners went right to work, working alone and with very little talking. The Japanese took a more leisurely approach, and spent a lot of time chatting as they worked. The Japanese also worked together more; if someone finished a batch early, he or she would help someone else finish theirs. As a result, by day three the Westerners had finished all their marking and didn't show up any more. The Japanese took the full five days to finish their marking. But one interesting thing was that the Westerners made many more mistakes in the marking; the Japanese took longer to finish but made very few mistakes.

Is Japan different, then, when it comes to work-life balance and efforts to 'improve' it? The answer is yes. Culture does matter. While the broader dimensions of Japan's work-life balance movement mirror those in Western countries, important differences are found in the actual work-life choices of Japanese men and women, and in the influencers and outcomes of those choices. The generic model (Figure 6.1) developed from this investigation has, I believe, broad applicability to nations and cultures other than Japan. But the specific economic, social, and cultural factors that shape individuals' work-life choices differ greatly from country to country, producing outcomes, both 'ideal' and 'actual,' that also differ across nations.

The Canadian Mental Health Association defines work-life balance in this way: 'Achieving work/life balance means having equilibrium among all the priorities in your life – this state of balance is different for every person.'[50] It may be different for every country as well.

Notes

1. OECD Factbook, 2008, http://titania.sourceoecd.org/vl=2116759/cl=16/nw=1/rpsv/factbook/060302-g1.htm (accessed 23 December 2008).
2. Scott North and Charles Weathers, 'All work and no pay in Japan', *Asian Times Online*, 6 January 2007, http://www.atimes.com/atimes/Japan/IA06Dh01.html (accessed 2 December 2008).
3. Yuko Yoshida, '"Waaku-raifu baransu ni fuman" Nihon ga ichii, shoshika ni mo han'ei ka', ITmedia Biz.ID, 16 January 2007, http://www.itmedia.co.jp/bizid/articles/0701/16/news068.html (accessed 2 December 2008).
4. *Japan Working Life Profile, 2007/2008 – Labour Statistics*, The Japan Institute for Labour Policy and Training, p. 56, http://www.jil.go.jp/english/labourinfo/library/documents/workinglifeprofile07_08.pdf (accessed 25 November 2008).
5. The author is grateful to the University of Kitakyushu for support which made this research possible.
6. Colloquium sponsored by Faculty of Business and Law and Deakin Business School, Deakin University BRASS, University of Cardiff, 11–13 December 2008.
7. The Plaza Accord was an agreement reached in September 1985 by the Finance Ministers of France, Germany, Japan, the U.K., and the United States at New York City's Plaza Hotel. The five nations, at the time the world's five largest economies, agreed to (among other things) intervene in currency markets to allow the Japanese yen rise against the U.S. dollar, to help address the problem of Japan's large trade surpluses. The yen rose 51 percent against the dollar in the two years following the agreement. Appreciation peaked at 85 yen per dollar in 1995, compared to 240 a decade earlier.
8. 'The dangerous disconnect between home prices and fundamentals', *eFinance Directory*, 9 July 2007, http://efinancedirectory.com/articles/The_Dangerous_Disconnect_Between_Home_Prices_and_Fundamentals.html (accessed 7 December 2008).
9. M. Osawa, Abstract of 'Labour Law Change, Female Employment Patterns, and Work Life Balance in Japan', Paper presented at the annual meeting of

the The Law and Society Association, TBA, Berlin,Germany <Not Available>, http://www.allacademic.com/meta/p177717_index.html (accessed 20 May 2008).

10. Markus Pudelko, 'The seniority principle in Japanese companies: A relic of the past?' *Asia Pacific Journal of Human Resources,* 44, 3 (2006), pp. 276–94.
11. Hideaki Tsukuda, 'From seniority to seika-shugi or how HR management is evolving in Japan', *Egon Zehnder International,* http://www.egonzehnder.com/global/thoughtleadership/knowledge/humanresources/article/id/11900274 (accessed 11 January 2009).
12. Elizabeth Lozano and Arvind Singhal, 'Melodramatic television serials: Mythical narratives for education', *Communication: The European Journal for Communication*, 18 (1993), pp. 117–18.
13. Hilaria M. Gossmann, 'New role models for men and women? Gender in Japanese TV dramas', in *Japan Pop! Inside the World of Japanese Popular Culture,* ed. T. Craig (New York: M.E. Sharpe, 2000), pp. 207–19.
14. Ohayo Nippon news program, NHK, 9 December 2008.
15. Noted Japan scholar Edwin O. Reischauer vividly describes this shift: 'I can remember very well that in the 1920s a wife was likely to follow differentially a pace behind her husband on the street, encumbered with whatever babies or bundles needed to be carried, while he strode ahead in lordly grandeur. Over the years I have seen the wife catch up with her husband, until they now walk side by side, and the babies and bundles are often in his arms. If the family has a car, the wife is likely to drive it as much as the husband. Whereas once no husband would stoop to doing any housework, increasing numbers now help out with the evening dishes. And many a wife has made it clear that she will not tolerate bar hopping or other dalliances on the part of her husband.' (*The Japanese Today,* p. 180)
16. NHK Kokusai Hosokyoku, 'One wife out of three is dissatisfied with her husband', in *Japan Datalogue* (Tokyo: Kodansha, 2003), pp. 17–19.
17. See, e.g., Paul A. Herbig and Pat Borstorff 'Japan's Shinjinrui: the new breed', *International Journal of Social Economics*, 22, 12 (1995), pp. 49–65.
18. To provide an idea of the calibre of firms listed, the first 15 on the list are: NEC, Mazda, Chiba Co-op, Roland, Kyushu Electric Power, Konica Minolta Holdings, Seiko-Epson, Tobu Utsunomiya Department Stores, Wacoal, Hankyu Department Stores, Osaka Gas, Kao, Hiroshima Cooperative, Nikko Securities, and Hitachi.
19. Office for Work-Life Balance, Cabinet Office, Government Of Japan, 'Shigoto to seikatsu no chowa (waaku raifu baransu) no jitsugen ni mukete', http://www8.cao.go.jp/wlb/company/index.html (accessed 4 July 2008).
20. OECD Factbook 2008: Economic, Environmental and Social Statistics, http://puck.sourceoecd.org/vl=665112/cl=13/nw=1/rpsv/factbook/060302-g1.htm (accessed 11 January 2009).
21. '30 percent male Japanese work over 12 hours', CSR Asia, http://www.csr-asia.com/index.php?page=3&cat=58 (accessed 3 February 2009).
22. Tomoko Otake, 'What's the right work-life balance?' The Japan Times Online, 22 April 2008, http://search.japantimes.co.jp/cgi-bin/fs20080422a3.html (accessed 20 May 2008).
23. Setsuko Kamiya, 'Office weighs less in the work-life balance', Japan Times Online, 29 June 2007, http://www.accessmylibrary.com/coms2/summary_0286-31763865_ITM (accessed 3 February 2009).

24. The purely Japanese equivalent, 'shigoto to seikatsu no chowa' (harmony between work and life), is used less frequently.
25. Kokumin Seikatsu Jisho (Tokyo: The Cabinet Office, 2007), p. 3.
26. 'What do you think of freeters?' Trends in Japan online survey, Web Japan, 4 February 2002, http://web-japan.org/trends01/article/020204fea_r.html (accessed 7 December 2008).
27. Office for Work-Life Balance, Cabinet Office, Government Of Japan, 'Shigoto to seikatsu no chowa (waaku raifu baransu) kensho' oyobi 'shigoto to seikatsu no chowa suishin no tame no kodo shishin' no sakutei', http://www8.cao.go.jp/wlb/government/top/k_2/pdf/s1.pdf (accessed 4 July 2008, translation by Tim Craig).
28. Masami Ito, 'Work-life balance starts at home: Rengo chief', *The Japan Times,* 9 January 2007, http://search.japantimes.co.jp/cgi-bin/nn20080109f2.html (accessed 17 June 2008).
29. Leo Lewis, 'Western values "are causing mental illness"', *Times Online,* 10 August 2006, http://www.timesonline.co.uk/tol/news/world/asia/article604588.ece (accessed 6 October 2008).
30. 'Stress related compensation hit record', *CSR Asia,* http://www.csr-asia.com/index.php?cat=67&page=4 (accessed 3 February 2009).
31. Leo Lewis, op. cit.
32. 'Kyuzo suru karoshi, seishin shikkan ni yoru rosai shinsei', *TORI Kenkyusho,* 25 May 2007, http://tori-s.at.webry.info/200705/article_16.html (accessed 28 January 2009).
33. *Kokumin Seikatsu Jisho,* p. 172.
34. *Conversation with Ken-ichi Ito,* 5 December 2008.
35. 'Japan fertility hits record low', *BBC News,*1 June 2006, http://news.bbc.co.uk/2/hi/asia-pacific/5036672.stm (accessed 3 February 2009).
36. Katsuhiko Fujimori, 'Nihon de wa naze waaku raifu baransu no kakuritsu ga muzukashii no ka', *Mizuho Joho Soken,*19 July 2005, http://www.mizuho-ir.co.jp/column/shakai050719.html (accessed 21 October 2008).
37. E.g., Genda and Kawakami, 'Divided employment and sexual behaviour', http://www.jil.go.jp/english/ejournal/documents/200611.pdf; or 'We're not in the mood', http://www.nomarriage.com/articlesexless.html (accessed 2 December 2008).
38. E.g., Sheri and Bob Stritof, 'Marital sex statistics: who's doing it and how often?' About.com, http://marriage.about.com/cs/sexualstatistics/a/sexstatistics.htm; or 'One in four Japanese not having sex: survey', *AFP,* 18 March 2008, http://afp.google.com/article/ALeqM5izYhjwaTOFfaPiaUAhn1IXoDyOTA (accessed 2 December 2008).
39. 'Historical income and productivity levels', *OECD Factbook 2008: Economic, Environmental, and Social Statistics,* http://oberon.sourceoecd.org/vl=6194697/cl=38/nw=1/rpsv/factbook/120202-g1.htm (accessed 3 February 2009).
40. 'Senryaku to shite no waaku raifu baransu', WLB – Kabushikigaisha Work-Life Balance, http://www.work-life-b.com/modules/g4/ (accessed 4 February 2009).
41. Office for Work-Life Balance, Cabinet Office, Government Of Japan, 'Shigoto to seikatsu no chowa (waaku raifu baransu) kensho' oyobi 'shigoto to seikatsu no chowa suishin no tame no kodo shishin' no sakutei', op. cit. (accessed 4 July 2008).
42. 'Change! Japan' website URL: www8.cao.go.jp/wlb/index.html

43. Emi Kanno, 'Waaku raifu baransu no genkai wa rodo jikan 12 jikan ika – rodosha no honne to wa', *Maikomi Journal,* 19 June 2008, http://journal.mycom.co.jp/news/2008/06/19/007/ (accessed 20 May 2008).
44. Setsuko Kamiya, op. cit.
45. Edwin O. Reischauer, *The Japanese Today,* 1988, p. 136.
46. For example, athletes in middle school, high school, and university play one sport only, not rotating sports with the seasons as is common in other countries. Baseball players are baseball players, and soccer players are soccer players. And Japanese typically have a single hobby, often pursued with fanatical dedication. ('Work/Life Balance – Coming Never to Japan', *NEOMARXISME a post-blog,* 6 March 2007, http://www.pliink.com/mt/marxy/archives/2007/03/worklife-balanc.html) (accessed 20 May 2008).
47. Meaning of Work International Research Team, *The Meaning of Work: An International Perspective* (New York: Academic Press, 1985). *In Helen Deresky, International Management: Managing Across Borders and Cultures,* 6th edition (Upper Saddle River, NJ: Pearson Prentice Hall, 2008), pp. 400–01.
48. Edwin O. Reischauer, *The Japanese Today,* 1988, p. 133.
49. Conversation with Ken-ichi Kihara, 5 December 2008.
50. http://www.cmha.ca/BINS/content_page.asp?cid=2-1841 (accessed 25 November 2008).

Part II
Community

7

Personal Communities and Lifestyle: The Role of Family, Friends and Neighbours

Betsy Blunsdon and Nicola McNeil

Sociologists argue that changes in society's institutional and traditional structures, since the 1960s, have resulted in a more 'individualised' society (Giddens, 1994; Beck, 1994; Beck and Lau, 2005). Proponents of this view suggest that individualisation diminishes the importance of blood family, often called 'families of fate', (Beck and Lau, 1995; Beck and Beck-Gernsheim, 1995) while increasing the importance of chosen relationships, such as friends and families of choice (Weeks, Heaphy and Donovan, 2001; Goss, 1997). This chapter examines the influence that families, friends and neighbours have on individuals' lives and lifestyle in the midst of this perceived propensity towards individualisation. A qualitative study, consisting of semi-structured interviews with 40 participants (20 telephone and 20 face-to-face interviews), was conducted in early 2008. In these interviews, individuals were asked to elaborate on the nature of their relationships with friends, family and neighbours, and discuss the meaning and significance of these relationships in their lives. The purpose of the study is to ascertain the nature of these relationships, and their influence on lifestyle decisions and outcomes. This chapter presents the results of an analysis of the twenty telephone interviews.

Post-traditional society

A central feature of 'post-traditional society'[1] is the decline in influence of institutions (Giddens, 1994). This has produced a marked shift from a society where individual identity and lifestyle are mainly determined by 'social location', (especially gender and class), to one in which lifestyle and identity are based on individual choice in 'constructing identity'.

Early modernity, from the mid-nineteenth century through the 1950s, was dominated by a set of integrated institutions within the framework of the nation-state. Certainty and stability were promoted through the legitimation of specific forms of social life (such as the nuclear family, blood relationships and clear, acknowledged gender roles), knowledge (based on scientific principles), work (standard employment, based on the male breadwinner model), and moral authority (through established community norms and the influence of religion and the church). Identity was largely determined within institutional boundaries and by one's social position. As Bauman argues, 'class and gender looked uncannily like "facts of nature" and the task left to most self-assertive individuals was to "fit in" into the allocated niche through behaving as its established residents did.' (2001: 144). However, from the 1960s there has been a weakening of these dominant influences, compelling people to construct their working lives, families, friendships, leisure and civic selves amidst a wider range of legitimate, acceptable life choices (Weeks et al., 2001).

Individualisation

Modern society is characterised by heterogeneity of individual lifestyles. Rather than 'fitting in', the challenge for an individual lies in deciding 'what to be' and 'with whom to be associated' (Bauman, 2001; Beck, 1994; Giddens, 1994). Individualisation is a process in which lifestyle results from producing one's own story or biography, in contrast to identity and lifestyle being tied to social location (Beck, Giddens and Lash, 1994: 13). Giddens (1994: 75) argues that 'in post traditional contexts, we have no choice but to choose how to be and how to act'. According to Bauman the issue for individuals today is not the choice itself but the need for the choices to be 'liquid' or changeable 'in case the previously chosen identity is withdrawn from the market or stripped of its seductive powers' (2001: 147). It follows that there is heightened pressure on individuals to make decisions about how to live their life, including how time is apportioned to various activities. For individuals, this means an increase in the choices available and, by corollary, the volume and complexity of decisions that have to be made (Beck and Lau, 2005: 536).

There are also marked consequences of increasing individualisation at the societal level. The resultant social and cultural pluralism has resulted in diversity of lifestyles, personal relationships and communities that are constructed through choice and freedom, rather than obligation and fate. These new forms of social bonds vie for legitimacy and popularity in post-traditional societies (Beck, Bonss and Lau, 2003: 536). Giddens (1994) notes that within this new social order, social ties are consciously constructed, rather than merely adopted due to prevailing norms and legitimacy. Giddens considers the fragility of such novel social structures, suggesting that 'where social bonds have effectively to be made, rather than inherited from the past – on the personal and more collective levels this is a fraught and difficult enterprise, but one which also holds out the promise of great rewards' (1994: 107). A focus of this study is gaining an insight into the nature of personal relationships in contemporary society. This involves consideration of the influence of blood family, personal communities and types of friendship on lifestyle choices.

Influence of blood family

A consequence of the individualisation of society is an erosion of importance of 'families of fate' in two ways. First, individualisation provides more choice about involvement with blood family than in the past, when norms were much stronger regarding social roles and obligations (e.g. family roles like spouse, daughter, son, brother or sister). Second, the influence of the nuclear family as a societal institution has diminished as different types of family arrangements have become prevalent and social roles have blurred (Beck and Lau, 2005). Giddens (1992) provides an explanation for this phenomenon, arguing that some types of interpersonal relationships are becoming 'democratised' – that is, intimate bonds are increasingly founded upon a private understanding between partners, rather than being shaped by laws or societal expectations.

The decline of the influence of family is also linked to a lack of practical assistance and personal attachment, which were previously considered to be the hallmark of the family unit. More geographic mobility for employment and personal reasons causes an erosion of family ties because of physical separation. Thus, individualisation brings a new importance to friendship due to demands of the labour market, job insecurity and more geographic mobility leading to a tendency to be more reliant on chosen relationships and discerning of social networks (Beck and Beck-Gernsheim, 1995).

The decline in importance of blood family and kinship networks is debatable and requires further empirical research. Putnam (1995a) suggests that the changing character and patterns of family life is an important consideration in understanding the declining levels of social capital in the United States. Social capital is defined as the degree of shared values, trust and norms of reciprocity that facilitate cooperation for mutual benefit (Putnam, 1995a; 1995b). Putnam (1995b: 73) states that 'the most fundamental form of social capital is the family, and the massive evidence of the loosening bonds within the family (both extended and nuclear) is well known. This trend, of course, is quite consistent with – and may help to explain – our theme of social decapitalisation'.

Pahl and Spencer's work in the United Kingdom reveals that family and kinship networks are still important for some of us, at least some of the time (Pahl and Spencer, 2004; Spencer and Pahl, 2006; Finch, 1996). Finch (1996), in a study of the quality of relationships in families, finds that kin relationships remain important to most people at some level in their lives. This examination also finds variability in the responsibilities associated with kin relationships. This results from a lack of clear, well understood rules 'about who should do what for whom' (Finch, 1996: 127). A consequence of individualisation is diversity in the types and nature of relationships with family. Another outcome cited is an increase in the importance of personal communities based on choice, rather than fate based relationships (Weeks et al., 2000; Goss, 1997). In this study, we investigate the salience of blood family to people's lives and whether or not proximity to family has an important role to play.

Personal communities

Personal communities can be broadly defined as 'significant others who inhabit our micro-social worlds' (Spencer and Pahl, 2006: 2). The concept draws our attention to how people bring 'together in their day-to-day lives a range of given and chosen relationships representing different forms and styles of suffusion.' (Pahl and Spencer, 2004: 2003). Personal communities are different from social networks because the members of a social network are connected to each other, in some way. By contrast, personal communities are defined by relations to a central individual. Members of one's personal community may not be connected to one another – for example, one's work colleagues and school friends may form a part of one's personal community, but they may have no connection to each other except through the focal individual. The idea of personal communities challenges conventional ideas of community, which are typically characterised as a collection of individuals within a geographic space who share a 'commitment to the common good' (Spencer and Pahl, 2006: 11). The rise of personal, rather than place-based or geographic, communities is said to be the result of individualisation, geography and social mobility. The development of these personal communities is facilitated by the development of new technologies, which enable people to develop and maintain interpersonal relationships across both space and time (Giddens, 1994; Spencer and Pahl, 2006). Such technologies include email, instant messaging and social networking sites such as Facebook or MySpace.

An important feature of personal communities, in contrast to geographic communities and families of 'fate', are that they are the result of individual choice. Therefore, personal communities are one aspect of writing one's own 'biography' and reflect the development of strong commitments to those who affirm one's identity. They represent one's significant personal relationships and, as described by Spencer and Pahl, contain people that contribute to our sense of belonging, comprise a shared history or 'biographical anchor', and include those for whom we feel responsible (a 'moral' aspect) and those we feel we *should* include (a 'normative' feature) (2006: 56). Work in the United Kingdom finds that personal communities tend to include a mixture of family (blood ties) and friends (Pahl and Spencer, 2004; Pahl and Pevalin, 2005; Spencer and Pahl, 2006). Others argue that the decline of community is accompanied by the decline in the importance of families of fate (Putnam, 2000). Our study investigates the nature of individual personal communities and whether or not they are dominated by family, friends or a combination of family and friends. We also consider the impact this has on aspects of individual 'lifestyle.'

The nature of friendship

It is well accepted that 'friends' comprise an important element of personal communities and, as such, are often very important to understanding how individuals live their lives. However, 'friend' is a vague concept and is used to denote a variety of qualitatively different relationships. Borrowing from Spencer and Pahl (2006), the following characterise 'friend' relationships (although not all have to be present): chosen not given, sharing of something in common (or many things), informal ties, mutual enjoyment, mutual 'liking', practical support, trust or confidence, and a narrative (a shared history or 'being through things together') (Spencer and Pahl, 2006: 59). Spencer and Pahl (2006) distinguish between types of friendships, forms of friendship trajectory ('friendship career'), development and types of 'friendship repertoires' and different friendship modes meaning the way they are formed, maintained or lost. These are important to this study because they provide insight into the patterns of individual lives and the nature of personal communities.

Friendship types

Spencer and Pahl (2006) identify friendship types from 'simple' to 'complex.' Simple friendships include categories such as 'fun friends', 'useful contacts', and 'favour friends'. Simple friendships involve one main way of relating. By contrast, complex friendships are multi-faceted and involve numerous ways of relating. Spencer and Pahl position complex friendships on a continuum with 'helpmates' providing mutual support and 'soul mates' the most complex involving high degrees of commitment and strong emotional bonds (2006: 60–70). The presence of different types of friendship has an impact on the nature of one's personal community and on the influence friends have over how one lives. Clearly, more complex friendships, in the form of 'confidants' and 'soul mates' are likely to have more influence on one's life decisions than simple, superficial friendships.

Friendship careers

Another aspect of friendship important to understanding individual life outcomes is what Spencer and Pahl call the 'friendship career'. This refers to the history of the relationship, how it originated and whether it has evolved or been relatively stable over time (Spencer and Pahl, 2006: 72). Fixed friendships change little over the course of one's life while progressive friendships become more intimate as time passes. Variable friendship careers ebb and flow depending on circumstances and life events.

Friendship repertoires

Important to our study is an understanding of the various types of 'friendship repertoires' or the role that friendships play in one's personal community. Spencer and Pahl (2006: 77–82) identify four basic repertoires in their study: basic, intense, focal and broad. Basic friendships are limited and specialised, usually involve shared interests but rarely involve emotional support. By contrast, intense friendship repertoires are characterised by intimate bonds where a distinction is made between 'true friends' and others. Spencer and Pahl (2006) call repertoires which include both simple and complex friends 'focal' friendship groups. These are comprised of a small group of soul mates and confidants and a larger group of simple friendships. Broad repertoires are those which contain a variety of types of friends playing different roles.

Friendship mode

The last aspect of friendship which is important to consider is 'friendship mode' or the ways in which friends are made, maintained, fostered or 'lost'. Spencer and Pahl (2006) identify bounded, serial, evolving and ruptured as the main mode types. Bounded are characterised by friends made at a point in time. Serial modes are likely to replace friends at different stages of life and rarely carry friends from one stage of life to another. Evolving modes make friends at all different stages of life but add them to their personal communities as they make them (rather than replacing them). Ruptured modes are characterised by a total replacement of friends usually due to a dramatic change in circumstances or major life event. This usually means a total change in one's friends and personal community.

Configurations of personal communities

The relative importance of friends, as 'chosen' and families, as 'given', in personal communities is one way to understand the configuration of the community. Some personal communities are family-focussed, where the dominance of relationships is based on blood ties and families of 'fate'. Friendships, if present, are likely to be simple friendships where emotional bounds are limited with social and emotional support likely to be drawn from blood ties. In these cases, individuals are more likely to speak of 'family as friends'. By corollary, friendship-focussed personal communities are likely to be based on chosen relationships. In this case, blood ties are less salient and friendships are likely to be characterised by more complex relationships where friends are categorised as confidants and soul-mates. If relationships with blood family remain they are likely to be less emotionally intense and based on roles and obligation (or 'duty'). In friendship-focussed personal communities, often there have been ruptures with blood family or isolation due to perceived social differences. Some personal communities are a hybrid containing a mixture of different types of friends and different types of familial relationships. The importance of this hybrid form is that both family and friends play different roles in one's micro-social world.

Post-traditional society is argued to be largely characterised by personal communities of choice rather than fate. Therefore, one would expect that personal communities will now be comprised of friends or a mixture of family and friends rather than blood family ties. In addition, the argument follows that friends and chosen relationships will be more influential than family in lifestyle decisions.

Understanding lifestyle

'Lifestyle' has been conceived of in a variety of ways depending on one's area of interest. The medical model of 'lifestyle' generally focuses on various risk factors related to 'health' and well being including nutrition, exercise and smoking. The marketing conception of 'lifestyle' focuses on psychographic differences for market segmentation according to consumption and leisure preferences. In this chapter, we conceive of 'lifestyle' as patterns of daily life or 'the orientation of the individual towards shaping its life' (Camstra, 1996: 285). Lifestyle patterns are characterised by three elements: the activities individuals spend time on; who people spend their time with and what one consumes in these activities and relationships; and, the meaning, values and importance placed on the activities, people ('relationships') and objects of consumption. The way in which people spend their time frames other aspects of their lives because increasing time spent on one activity decreases the time available for other activities.

Understanding and conceptualising 'lifestyle' is a multi-level problem in that it involves understanding the desires and preferences of individuals and the contexts in which individuals find themselves. Important aspects of context include the household (who they live with and how this impacts on patterns of daily life), the neighbourhood, blood family and friend relationships, and the physical, cultural and economic context of their daily lives. Personal communities may affect choice by reinforcing common values, providing esteem and status, filtering the information that forms the basis of beliefs, and providing models and cognitive scripts for appropriate choices (Cialdini, Kallgren and Reno, 1991). Personal communities can also shape peoples' desires, and influence beliefs about the structure of opportunities and constraints in life situations. Adaptive choices – those choices that respond to changes in circumstances – will either conform to the expectations imputed to one's personal community, cause a re-configuration of relations or, for significant life events, lead to the construction of new personal communities. Thus, personal communities potentially support, and impose the normative constraints that encourage choices based on routine and habit. By the same token, personal communities are also a significant component of one's life situation, and so change within the community may itself provoke new choices as new interpretations, values and beliefs emerge.

Individuals often respond to choice situations passively, by relying on routines and habits, rather than by evaluating actively what they can feasibly do to meet their needs (Aarts and Dijksterhuis, 2000; Bargh,

1994; Bourdieu, 1990). Personal communities can reinforce routine and habit because they entail a set of commitments – to other people, to relationships and to common values. Members of one's personal community often have an orientation to life that is similar to one's own. Whether personal communities reflect one's background, or form around new interests developed through one's biography, is explored in this chapter. First, the methodology employed to investigate the role of personal communities on individual lives is detailed.

Methodology

The sample for this study was drawn from a systematic random sample generated for a community survey of residents in the state of Victoria, Australia conducted in late 2006. The focus of this survey was on understanding individual perceptions of one's community and personal values and aspirations. In this questionnaire, respondents were asked if they would be willing to participate in future research at a later date. Potential participants were told that this future research would involve an in depth discussion about other aspects of community and individual lifestyle. Approximately 700 respondents from the original sample agreed to participate further. We purposly selected 10 per cent (70) of this group and sent them a letter inviting them to participate in this study. Our sampling was intended to obtain a mix of gender, age and geographic location (urban, rural, various socio-economic areas).

One week after sending the letter of invitation, we telephoned participants to seek their cooperation and to set up an interview time. Out of the initial 70 interested participants, we gained cooperation from 50. Forty interviews were completed during the study period. Twenty of these interviews were conducted through face-to-face interviews, typically at people's primary residence (there were a few exceptions including one conducted at a workplace and two at cafes). The other 20 interviews were conducted through computer-assisted telephone interviewing (CATI).

This chapter presents the results of the analysis of the 20 telephone interviews (later analysis will be conducted on the face-to-face interviews separately and then we will pool the data and also, consider mode effects). Participants included seven males and 13 females that ranged in age from 20 to 87 years of age. The living arrangements of respondents were mixed: some lived alone, with a partner, with a partner and children, alone with children, alone with grandchildren, with a partner and other relative, or with a partner and unrelated housemate.

Neighbourhoods included inner urban, suburban, regional and country areas of Victoria.

The interviews were semi-structured and lasted between 45 and 90 minutes. The interview protocol included a series of questions about their neighbourhood, neighbours, family, and friends with the second half of the interview focusing on how they spent their time and with whom. Finally, we asked respondents to reflect on how they spent their time, and what factors influenced their choice of activities.

All interviews were digitally recorded and later transcribed for analysis. NVIVO software was used to code the text into themes or categories (called nodes), and to create hierarchical node structures. The coding framework can be established *a priori* or can be created through the analysis process (*in vivo*). In this case the coding frame was established *a priori* although additional nodes were added as 'free nodes' during the analysis.

Transcripts were coded according to the coding scheme below and then further refined to ascertain the dominant themes emerging from the data. These themes are summarised in Table 7.1, and the results of the analysis are discussed in the following section.

Results

The results of the analysis of interview data are presented as detail of relationships with family, friends, neighbours and time use. In terms of understanding the role of family in shaping life decisions, the focus is on answering the following questions:

- What is the nature of blood family ties for participants?
- How important is given family to individuals?
- Does geographic proximity influence the intimacy of family ties?
- How are family ties maintained?
  -What is the role of family occasions and holidays?
  -How do holidays shape familial relationships?
  -What role does travel play?
- What is the role of blood family in providing social support?

On family

Our data reveals strong blood ties and family bonds for the majority of individuals interviewed. Most participants cited blood family (sister, brother, mother, son, daughter) as the person, outside of their household, to whom they were closest. Explaining the closeness she

Table 7.1 Coding Schema for content analysis of interviews

Key theme	Sub-themes
Family	Conflict Involvement with Importance of Influence of Traditions Holidays Family as friends
Friends	Proximity to Origins of Importance/salience Interactions with Breakdowns of
Neighbours	Stability of Interactions with Quality of Friends as
Time balance	Satisfaction with time use Desire for change
Time use	Personal care Domestic Education Employment Purchasing goods and services Recreation and leisure Social and community interaction Voluntary work Caring (for others)
Holidays	When Where How often Satisfaction with
Housemates	
Major events	
Pets	

felt with her sister one participant explained *'I think the blood ties are there and I think possibly because we share a background the same. We know where each other is coming from, although she has had a totally different life than mine.'* Another described the relationship with her sister, *'We have a really good relationship. We don't have to do anything we just enjoy being together.'* On family closeness generally, one female respondent said *'We are very close, we do see a lot of each other.'* One participant explained the relationship with her mother as her closest relationship even though they are often in conflict *'...we clash like hell but that's because we are very close.'* In response to a question about how often she speaks to her mother she continues *'too often, she drives me crazy (laughing)...I am a sucker for punishment, I call her.'* And one interviewee summed it up by saying that her brother and sister *'are like close friends.'*

Participants were also very forthcoming in expressing the importance of immediate, and at times extended, family. 'I've done it, I've lived my life. I have had my fun, different type of fun. It's fun now, it's certainly better now with my family. My focus is getting amongst my kid and my child now and hopefully another if we are lucky.' But, this young family man goes on to say that part of this is that it is 'important to carry on generations.' Another participant said that they now 'want to focus all of my time on my family.' Some individuals spoke of their focus on family as a lack of focus outside of the family, 'We tend to stay with one another. We are not very social people. I don't know why we are just not.' Even those that didn't see family very much explained that they found it difficult to catch up due to limited time off 'but we do try because it is important.' This suggests that family relationships endure over the life course, whilst other types of bonds are more transient.

Being geographically close to family was not a prerequisite to remaining emotionally close and tied to blood family. A number of respondents had blood family, such as brother, sisters or grown children, living overseas but they maintained very close emotional ties in their daily lives by using the telephone and email to maintain regular contact and through travel. One participant explained *'The phone keeps us in touch with family, we see each other at least twice a year.'* Others said that email was a way to keep in touch with family overseas and keep abreast of their day to day lives. Thus, family ties persist across both time and space.

Maintaining relationships across time and space

Travel is an important way to stay involved with family that live interstate or overseas. One participant said that her sister lives interstate but she talks to her on the phone everyday and they catch up a half a dozen times per year. Others travel to visit family overseas, especially for family occasions such as special birthdays, the birth of grandchildren, family weddings and important holidays, such as Christmas.

Family occasions were cited as an important means to maintain blood family ties. Interviewees noted that 'Family "commitments" like birthdays bring people together' and 'We always make a fuss of occasions, we make them family occasions', and 'Holidays are family times. We usually get together at birthdays, Christmas and Easter... really like Christmas and birthdays because there are enough family members that would probably be once a month or once every six weeks or so.' Further, the impact of a large family was explained 'it's such a large family there is a lot of family events, a few of those family Christenings or whatever.'

The tradition of the Sunday 'family lunch' seems to be one which lingers but may not be as strong as in the past. Many still cite Sunday as a day to visit family. Respondents said that 'We see family on the weekend and just chat and have a meal together' and 'Sunday tends to be a day when I catch up with family and have lunch or dinner and just basically nothing just catch up and chat.' One participant explained that when he was growing up the expectation was that you would go every week to the extended family lunch on Sundays. He said the older generation still does this religiously. However, he stopped going to this each week when he bought his house and had his own child: 'There was too much to do. We couldn't afford not to get things done every Sunday, it's a full day. You get there at 12 to 1 pm and we don't leave until 6 pm.' So now, he explained, they try to go about once a month.

Holiday traditions, for this group, are dominated by family tradition. Some explained that some of this does change at different stages of life – for example, once your children are grown there tends to be a focus on having 'your own Christmas with your own immediate family.' However, it is clear that for many, holiday time and Christmas in particular, is a time to share with family (even for those from non-Christian backgrounds as Christmas in Australia is 'summer holiday season'). Respondents note 'we all get together as a family for Christmas' and 'we normally do a large family party at Christmas which we attend religiously because they are like good fun, lots of food, lots of drink, that sort of thing' and 'We all get together as a family for Christmas'. Others said 'We get together and do all the traditional stuff and everything that you think of that goes with it. We have a lovely time and then we play games till all hours' and 'We are pretty much devoted to family stuff through Christmas and the New Year.' Many indicated that the biggest challenge at holiday time was the need to juggle both families, 'split up the time' or take turns. However, at least a couple of those interviewed solved this challenge with big multi-family gatherings. Hence, there is a strong suggestion that public institutions, such as national holidays or religious events, are typically used as a vehicle for family activities. Thus, societal norms are appropriated as family norms.

It is also clear that blood family remain an important source of social support. Parents provide support for grown up children in a variety of ways, including checking on their houses, helping with repairs, watering gardens and caring for pets. Childcare and babysitting support comes from parents, in-laws and siblings while care for elderly parents or grandparents was also a commonly cited area of support. In some cases, grown children said they would not be able to hold down their jobs without the support of their parents. One interviewee commented that she would have no time to herself to go to the hairdresser, without the childcare assistance she received from her parents. One sister said that she cares for her nieces and nephews 'All the time. She [her sister] has more of a social life than I do.' A grandmother explained that she currently had her granddaughter living with her as a way to help her out. One male respondent explained that he provided support for his family by managing the family superannuation and trust fund. Even those with family overseas extended their support at important life events and transitions, as evidenced by those that travel overseas to help with the birth of grandchildren and to attend family weddings and other important family events. These are all examples of families pooling resources, such as time, money and knowledge, to negotiate social and economic challenges.

On friendship

The analysis of friends focused on understanding friendship types, trajectories ('careers'), repertoires and modes (refer to Spencer and Pahl's (2006) model of variation in friendship).

The participants in our study identified both simple and complex types of friendships. Simple friendships tended to be described as 'activity friends' or 'interest friends' such as those you play golf with, learn French with, with whom you play sport or engage in crafts (Spencer and Pahl, 2006). These friendships are based on an interest or activity and tend to continue as long as the activity continues. One person said that they have grown apart and changed friends due to changing interests. Simple friendships were also those that are described as *'social friends, where we do things like eating out.'* For a number of people, males in particular, there was discussion of 'footy friends', those that you attend the football with or friends and sport, those that you go to watch the sport with. In addition, there are 'work friends' *'who I socialise with occasionally.'* Often these relationships tend not to continue after the work relationship has ended. But, as this respondent notes, in some cases they become long term friendships: *'I made quite a few friends, my teaching friends, and I have kept them.'*

More complex friendships evolve over time and those in this study tended to describe their complex, more intimate friendships as those that were 'older' and often these originated at School. Examples include: *'We first became friends when we were about 13. We were in high school together so we have been friends for about 30 years'*; *'School friends are core'*; *'School friends are different than casual friends made through interests'*; *'School friends are the closest friends.'* On the nature of real friendship, one participant described it thus *'from the moment we are together we laugh and have a good time. Friends talk, do things, have a good time.'* Complex friends were also described as 'help mates', people to turn to, people to rely on for both physical and emotional support. No one described any of their friends as 'soul mates', this was reserved for partners or family members.

There is some evidence of differences in the trajectories of the friendships of our respondents. In most cases, those friendships that continue seem to be more likely to be quite fixed or variable (they ebb and flow), rather than becoming 'more intimate and complex.' Some individuals talked about losing touch with friends when their children were small, but reconnecting later or drifting apart and back together as interests or circumstances change. The stability of friendship was described by one as *'we have always been really close friends, we always pull together, we used to have cheap holidays and chatting and sleeping under a tarpaulin.'*

There is also evidence of variation in friendship repertoires with some clearly distinguishing between 'close friends' (intense) and 'social friends' (basic). Close friends, as the discussion of school friends as core illuminates, are more like 'family' and often they attend family events such as weddings and birthdays – *'I call these "occasion friends" friends that come to weddings and family occasions.'* Some individuals cite a broad array of friends but they do put them in different categories such as 'casual friends', 'school friends', 'old friends', 'footy friends', 'social friends' and core or focal friends.

Our discussions of friendship provided some insight into modes, or the ways in which friends are made, maintained, fostered or lost. There was very little evidence of 'bounded' friendship modes, those that were made at a point in time and remained stable. Most people described changing aspects of friendship similar to serial or evolving modes. One person said that *'My friends are spread out everywhere due to moving'* implying an evolving mode. While others described changes that seem to characterise serial modes. For example, respondents note that *'Over time I didn't have much in common with original friends'*, or *'I have grown apart from many friends due to changed interests'* and *'Over time people have their own lives so it is harder to maintain friends.'* Another said she lost touch with original friends whose children grew up together because later they had very little in common. In this particular group, there was no evidence of ruptured modes. Even those that had gone through major life events such as divorce described some stability in friendships.

On neighbours

We considered a series of questions to understand the importance of relationships with 'neighbours' in people's lives. Respondents were asked questions about the difference between neighbours and friends and family; the hallmarks of a 'good neighbour', the type and level of interactions with neighbours and the key features of 'neighbourliness'.

The nature of neighbourly relations was quite consistent for this group of informants. Only one participant described their 'neighbours as friends'. It was very common to describe ones relationship with neighbours as something very different to 'friendship' or to family relationships. Relationships with neighbours also tended to be polarised, meaning that either people described them as 'really nice people' or as people they had nothing to do with. There was rarely a middle category. Those that described their neighbours in positive terms said things like: *'I have nice neighbours'* or *'People are fantastic'* or *'They are the same, they are just beautiful people. I don't know what else to say really.'* One participant said that their whole neighbourhood was friendly *'...people in the street would walk past and wave hello.'* Another said *'We have very good neighbours. We get on very well together.'*

Even though the majority of people described at least some of their neighbours in positive terms, people qualified their relationships with neighbours as distinct and separate from their own lives (in a way that people did not speak of either blood family or friends). For example, *'The neighbourhood is fairly friendly... we don't necessarily know the names of other neighbours but everyone is quite friendly. Everyone has their own space, everyone has animals, so they are all considerate of other peoples needs.'* Another noted *'We do have a good relationship with our neighbours, we don't intrude on them and they don't intrude on us but we know that they are there if we need them.'* Several respondents identified respecting one's privacy and being there to help if needed as important features of being a 'good neighbour'. For example, one respondents noted *'everyone basically keeps to themselves but I think if they needed help they will get it from any of us'* and *'we meet so often when we are outside doing our bit [in the body corporate garden]...but we don't live in each others pockets'*, and *'We are not in each others pockets or anything like that. If she rang me for help I would be straight around there to help her. It is sort of like that around here. You are not in each others pocket but you would help out if they needed help.'* Another said: *'we have got very good neighbours. We get on very well together. We have even got a gate at our side of the fence to one another. We have keys to one another's houses if either of us are away the other one looks after the others home. Yet, we don't live in each others pocket.'* These comments suggest that, for these participants, relationships with neighbours are based on mutual trust and norms of reciprocity.

Being friendly and having a chat seems to be the dominant theme in terms of interactions with neighbours. One respondent said *'I say hello to everyone but I don't know them by name.'* Another noted that *'we have always found them to be quite good people, not that we have a very close relationship with our neighbours. Just a bit of a "hi" and a bit of a conversation now and again. Not that we party with them or anything like that.'* Others said: *'we chat pretty well every time we are at the back, really if we are out, then we say hello and vice versa. We don't actually have coffee and that sort of thing, we are very friendly, we have long chats and what have you been up to but not in and out of one's houses, if that makes sense'* and *'well, I know them to speak to them. If they're not there I would bring their dust bin in or something like that. I speak to them but I don't have any social contact'.* Others said *'everyone is quite friendly. We don't have any street parties are anything like that, we don't sort of visit each others place but everyone is pleasant'* and *'I know the neighbours quite well. We stop and have a chat but we don't really ever socialise together.'*

If socialising does occur, it tends to be casual or around an occasion, such as the holidays. One respondent stated *'we get along really well and know fairly well the neighbours on both sides and behind us and across the road and down the street sort of thing. Always wave and smile and chat over the fence and on the weekend sometimes a bit of a drink.'* Another noted that *'we don't see the neighbours much but we are there for them ... We have a get together every Christmas ... get to meet some of the other neighbours so we do see them but we are not hanging over* the *back fence.'*

Some interviewees stated they do not interact with their neighbours. One respondent said: *'We don't see them a great deal. We don't socialise'* and *'I don't have much to do with them. I keep to myself. If I need them they would be there to help me. I am pretty sure about that.'* Similarly, another noted that *'we are not the best neighbours. From a neighbourly point of view I guess we are not necessarily the best neighbours, we don't live in neighbour's pockets. Never have done. That's been more an attitude of my wife than my own. That's how it's worked out.'* Another said: *'[Don't really know neighbour.] I know them by their faces but not personally.'*

For most participants the key elements of 'neighbourliness' emerge as friendliness, respect of privacy and being helpful when needed with the most cited phrase *'we don't live in each others pockets'* or *'we don't hang over the back fence.'*

On lifestyle

Blood family seems to have more influence on 'lifestyle' and patterns of daily life than either friends or neighbours. Those people you live with, as in those in your household, have a major impact on time use and who you spend time with. For example, those participants with school age children in their household cite their children's activities and school involvement as dominating the time available after paid employment and household duties. One respondent explained that her work day was framed by her children's schedule. *'Yes and [two days a week] I don't actually finish until 4:30 pm. I go back to the school, pick the kids up and then they come back to my work.'* Another noted, *'I usually do my shopping when the kids are at school, that would be my big shop.'* Another participant who runs a business with her husband said she does all the bookwork for the business after the children are in bed. Respondents with teenage children in the house said their allocation of time to tasks was largely determined by their teenager's activities – for example, one respondent claimed to *'spend all my time in the car.'* A respondent who had fostered a number of children over the years explained *'Well, you have a certain amount of social life with it. You are involved with the school. I got all my social life out of the school.'*

There was also evidence of the role of parents on shaping the interests that their children undertake, as well as the role of children in shaping parents' interests and activities. One parent said: *'Basketball was a sport I played when I was young and then as my son grew it was something because I had some background in it and knowledge of the game, it was something that we could share together. They both still play, yes, so it stays through the kids.'* By corollary, one woman explained that she developed one of her hobbies (stamp collecting) through her children's interest in it when they were young. The children lost interest and she recommenced her passion for it after her children were grown. One man got involved in parent education activities when his children were at school but has continued with it after they left. Another participant explained how she got involved in aerobics with her daughter. She now describes herself as a total 'gym junkie' and participates in aerobics classes most days of the week and three times over the weekend. She explained *'I suppose the family might sort of say, can't you stop or have one less session of aerobics or whatever and you would have more time at home. And then I sort of think, then I would probably do more housework so I may just as well enjoy my aerobics.'*

Many described their lifestyle and time use patterns as a dynamic with the others in their household. For example, one respondent said that she lived by the beach because her partner was a surfer. Now, she explains, *'We now have teenage boys who adore the beach and wouldn't want to live anywhere else, we have tried.'* Other individuals with partners who work 'unsociable' hours describe how this frames their own lifestyle. A couple that worked in the entertainment industry have had to be mobile with the study participant having to be prepared to move interstate to be with his partner, depending on where her next job is located. This type of work also has an impact on the pattern of daily life. *'For me, for us, it's like we don't necessarily have a weekend because on a weekend she would do a lunch time show and a night time show on both Saturday and Sunday so it doesn't feel like a weekend for us.'* A participant with a partner who was a chef and restaurateur commented that she had to fit in with his schedule as best she could, or they wouldn't have any time together.

Others described paid employment as an important factor shaping their own lifestyle, and in some cases, that of their family. Shift workers had to fit 'life' around their work schedules and this was often unpredictable. One respondent discussed how he wants to start his own business so he has more time with his family. He said that in his current position the demands of making overseas phone calls in the evening takes time away from his family. *'I would love to spend more time with my family, the rest of the family…eventually I will hopefully change the way I do things. Starting my own business so my wife and kids can be home, or going part time, depending on the situation. And that will allow my wife to spend more time with my son and I will still want to do that.'* One man explained that there is a familial line to the business he was in. *'I have two sons in law and a nephew all [in the same business I was in.]'* At least two participants described how family members (particularly children and siblings) have followed each other into various jobs.

The role of family in social support activities was also a very important factor in shaping lifestyle. As mentioned earlier, grown children spoke of the role their parents played in childcare and more than one participant said that they would find it very difficult to manage their paid employment without the help of family members, especially parents and siblings. Some grandparents had 'regular' days where they cared for their grandchildren, while others were on call on a needs basis, either when grandchildren were sick or absent from School. One grandparent explained that she continues to go and see her grandchildren on given days even though her daughter-in-law has had another child and is home full time. *'I keep on going there because that's my time with the boys.'* One participant said that his parents provided after school care. Yet, caring and social support went beyond childcare. Grandparents providing a place for grandchildren to stay, and the care of the sick, infirm or elderly all fell within the blood family domain. One participant explained the impact this care giving had on his life *'We have my ninety-one year old [elderly relative] living with us…She needs a lot of assistance now a days and so it is very difficult to get out either for social things or for general things.'* Another participant was the main carer for her infirm spouse and described anything else she did in terms of the time she had 'left over' from her caring duties. Other types of social support cited include house repairs and maintenance for grown children and elderly relatives, helping 'emerging adults' with finances and looking after the family finances, trust and family history.

There is also evidence in this data that blood family has an impact on consumption decisions, such as what trips to take and how to spend money. A number of participants select holiday destinations based on visits to family and this included visits to grown children and grandchildren, extended family (such as siblings) and brother and sisters living both interstate and overseas. One grandmother said she chose to spend money on her grandchildren rather than herself. *'I like to buy for my grandchildren, so I come home and have my cup of coffee'* [rather than pay money for a coffee]. Another talked about the influence of her mother on her choice of food and the time she spent shopping and selecting food. *'I think I got that from my Mum. She has always been on us about eating fresh food and not tampered with, like organic stuff. We used to have a veggie garden growing up so I like organic foods so anything that is not canned or too pricey. I know I get that from Mum, she's always like "What's on special? We will try that but is it okay to eat?" So, I think it is from shopping with my mother. Yes, it's inbred; you can't get away from it.'*

Our data reveals that the role of friends on lifestyle is most salient when it comes to 'leisure activities'. However, some individuals noted they weren't very sociable and didn't have time to foster friendships. Most other individuals associated friendship with 'fun'. This was especially true for 'social friends' and 'footy' or 'sport friends'. Attending regular sporting events, like following a particular football team, was a means of meeting up with friends a routine. A number of people said that it was easy – '*we just routinely go to the football together.*' People mentioned '*it was no big deal*' if you can go you go and if you can't it is not an issue. One person talked about their '*circle of friends as the people you mix with.*' The mix was mainly around leisure and fun activities such as going to the movies or out for a meal or significant events like birthdays and weddings.

The role of neighbours on lifestyle is not as clear. However, there was evidence that neighbours had an impact on the nature of the 'neighbourhood' and on individual involvement in community activities. Most people were on speaking terms with at least some of their neighbours and this made a difference to the quality of their daily life. Individuals were positive about a '*friendly neighbourhood*' where people wave and have a chat. However, some also cited a good neighbourhood as a '*quiet neighbourhood*'. The nature of the neighbourhood, whether it was friendly and helpful, was also related to individual involvement in community activities. One participant got involved with the local council through a neighbour, another got involved with a community 'friendship group', another the Fire Brigade and another through involvement in local clean up days: '*[One of my neighbours is] into land care. She often rings me to maybe plant trees sometime or we do clean up Australia each year together*'.

If neighbours do not directly influence lifestyle, then the neighbourhood does have some impact. Physical space and environment impacts on activities related to personal care, leisure activities pursued and proximity to work. Those individuals that lived near the beach or in country or rural areas described being outside and walking as important 'self-care' and leisure activities. Many chose to live near the beach because they could walk on the beach for well-being or pursue interests such as surfing. Those that lived in regional or country areas spoke of wanting a 'quiet lifestyle'. One participant lived in the country because of her passion for horses and horse-riding while another had many animals, including alpacas. Those that lived in the city and suburbs described the advantages of their neighbourhoods as '*having everything you need close at hand*', being close to cafes and shops, and being close to public transportation. The disadvantages cited were noise, congestion and traffic. Clearly, physical environment plays a role in how one lives and experiences life and whether this is chosen or given depends on individual circumstances.

Discussion: the nature of personal communities

The analysis of these 20 interviews provides evidence of the existence of two types of personal communities – those that include a mixture of family (blood ties) and friends, and those that are dominated by family. None of our participants had personal communities that were totally 'chosen' and devoid of blood family relationships, although one participant had immediate family and a wider 'family' based on ethnic, not blood ties. Therefore, we do not find strong evidence that blood families are less important than chosen relationships for these respondents. In fact, these results demonstrate the significance and relevance of traditional family ties among respondents. Blood family usually form the focal core of the personal community, with non-blood family relationships serving more limited, less complex, and in many cases more transient roles in individual lives. It was more common for individuals in our study to describe family as friends (especially siblings) than it was to describe friends or neighbours as family.

The evidence from this study reveals that for many 'given' social bonds prevail and for others there is a mixture of given and chosen or constructed relationships. There are a number of participants that very clearly had family-focussed personal communities and some of these were immediate family-focussed (meaning those that live in one household) with extended family relationships being more role-based. Those that had 'hybrid' personal communities tended to have close ties with family and differing types of friendships from simple to complex. Thus, irrespective of the composition of the personal community – either given or constructed – it is clear that a personal community shapes one's way of living. The evidence presented in this study indicates that in many cases, given ties are still very strong. Thus, family-centred personal communities appear to have the greatest influence on lifestyle choices.

The importance of families of fate

Our data shows that blood family relationships are very important to people in many different circumstances — young partnered couples who find it difficult to see family often but still try because 'it is important', to retirees who make decisions to spend fixed income on visits to family overseas and interstate, to dual working couples with young children who rely on their family for social support, to people who live alone of various ages who rely on family occasions to stay connected, to the recently arrived refugees who have their immediate family and a wider ethnic based community family. Individuals at all different stages of the life course (between the ages of 20 and 87) expressed the importance of family and family ties. Even those that had ruptures with some family members (more typically a sibling) still maintained positive relationships with others.

There is evidence, in wider society and in this study, of a decline in the prevalence of a traditional 'nuclear family', comprised of a mother, father and children. Within this study, family arrangements were dynamic and varied. De-facto relationships were not discernibly different from legal marriage, and family structures were complex, often involving step-parents and step-siblings. However, this increased complexity does not diminish the importance of family and blood relationships. These social changes and the breakdown of acceptable norms in relationships increased the demands on individuals in terms of fulfilling family roles but there is little evidence in this study of a decline in the importance of family. In fact, the increasing complexity and uncertainty of these new types of family structures may actually make family ties more important, requiring more investment in fostering these relationships.

Finch (1996: 123) posits that 'the decline of both practical assistance and personal attachment is integral to that belief [that family is in decline], the two acting as twin signals that families no longer matter to us in a way that they did to their grandparents'. Finch's results do not support this claim, and nor do ours. Finch (1996: 126) found great variability in family relationships but 'despite these variations, almost all interviewees were at pains to emphasize that they do belong to a wider family group which has meaning in their own lives well beyond any list of names on a Christmas card list'. The findings here are consistent with this and do not support the view that individuals do not and cannot rely on blood family for practical assistance and social support. In fact, this data demonstrates that our respondents first look to blood family for support and look to others, such as friends, neighbours or institutional support, as backup.

There is evidence in the data that there is variability of roles as families change and evolve. This is especially true for families where there are breakdowns in relationships, such as divorce, and new relationships have formed over time. Siblings discuss assuming parental-like roles as their parents go through difficulties and grandparents talk about looking after their grandchildren as extensions of their own childrearing. Even in those families that have had serious breakdowns and problems individuals still express the importance of family. Our data supports Finch's findings that 'high value is placed on "belonging to a family which works", even if that never gets tested, and perhaps even if it is tested and found wanting' (1996: 127). The interviewees in this study were realistic about the problems which face families and the shortcomings of family relationships. However, this did not diminish their expressions of the significance of family to their lives.

Geographic mobility and proximity to personal communities

There was clear evidence that there is a lot of variation in geographic proximity to both family and friends. Some participants lived close to family and saw them often and others had to travel long distances to see new grandchildren and to have family get-togethers. In terms of family, there was little evidence that proximity was an important element to intimacy and closeness. Individuals had a variety of strategies to keep in touch and maintain close contact which, not surprisingly, has been made much easier with cheaper phone costs (and VOIP services), email, instant messaging and digital technologies (such as digital photos). A number of participants also discussed the importance of travel to remaining close and being there at important occasions and many commented that the relative speed of long distance travel made even this easier.

The story was not as consistent for friendships. Many participants talked about the difficulty of maintaining friendships when one party or the other moved away. However, others kept up long distance friendships through letters, email and phone calls while getting together in person infrequently. The evidence here is that friendships are more prone to change due to changed circumstances such as moving, changes in the life course or different interests. Relationships with blood family appear to be more enduring, as these are typically characterised by stronger, more intimate ties.

The situation with neighbours was different again. Very few respondents reported keeping up with their neighbours after they moved. This is not surprising given the overall theme to emerge of 'neighbour' as friendly, helpful but 'remote' with a high value on the maintenance of privacy.

Personal communities: background or interest-based?

Most of the individuals interviewed had personal communities that were dominated and shaped by blood family and friends with 'shared backgrounds' rather than independent, personal choice. The importance of 'school friends', or childhood friends as close friends (or complex friends), as distinct from social and interest-based friends, illustrate this pattern. Individuals did have interest-, activity- and social-based relationships in their personal communities, but they tended to be simple, less intimate friendships. Often 'school friends' and childhood friends were more like given, blood family, relationships than chosen relationships because they had come about through family ties or circumstances dictated by others when very young. Many respondents talked about 'old friends', school friends and childhood friends in terms that were similar to family relationships such as knowing them forever, having a shared history, understanding where the other was coming from. Often these friends shared in family occasions and important events. However, there does not seem to be the pressure or obligation around intimate friendships, as there does with blood family, to provide social support and 'to be there for them'.

These findings suggest a high level of trust and reciprocity underpin familial relationships. Family-centred personal communities appear to be more able to build and maintain social capital, compared to other types of collectives. Personal communities based around strong family ties are able to develop and mobilise social capital, because they are built on intimate relationships based on mutual trust and respect.

Personal communities and lifestyle

There was strong evidence here that lifestyle, defined as a constellation of how you spend your time, your money and with whom and the value you place on these, is related to one's personal community. Our data supports the idea that social bonds and relationships provide individuals with social support and esteem, help shape and reinforce one's interests, create a framework for the development of desires and aspirations, and influence the pattern of everyday life through obligations, commitments and interactions with others. The relationship between one's personal community, whether family- or friend-focussed or a 'hybrid', on individual lifestyle can perhaps best be understood as a dynamic interaction between individual needs, desires and aspirations and the reactions of those in one's personal communities.

Our data suggests that family focussed personal communities are very 'tight knit', with norms of behaviour that are well understood, and lifestyle choices based on 'tradition', routine and habit. There was some evidence of generational change and a loosening of some traditions due to changes in the economic and social environment, such as needing two incomes to purchase a home and the pressure on available time for traditional events. Other personal communities experienced profound change, such as losing focal family members or family separations such as divorce. This creates a need for new normative structures and routines to develop and a renegotiation of roles and expectations.

Individual choice plays the major role in areas such as the structuring of partnership relationships, choice of career, and where one lived geographically, although there was ample evidence of the influence of personal communities on these choices. But, this process of individualisation does not appear to be accompanied by a weakening of given ties. In fact, the ability to exercise choice over one's individual lifestyle and biography was generally supported by 'creative ways' to maintain strong bonds (such as travel, using technology, family occasions, relying on holidays). Personal communities also influence lifestyle decisions in quite concrete, practical ways, such as where to spend holidays, what trips to take, where and when, purchasing the 'tools' to communicate remotely and decisions about where to purchase homes.

Limitations and conclusions

A qualitative study, such as this, is limited in its generalisability. However, it is indicative of what is going on in the lives of the group studied and this group is quite diverse comprised of varying ages, backgrounds, geographic communities and different household and partnership arrangements. Social change generally and how this impacts on individuals in particular must be studied in a variety of ways in order to understand social change and the reasons for the changes that are occurring.

Our aim was to better understand the impact of family, friends and neighbours on configurations of personal communities and to then explore the relationship between personal communities and individual lifestyle. We began with the argument that society is becoming more 'individualised' and that the ways that people live vary greatly and are less structured by rules and roles. This study supports the argument that contemporary society is characterised by diverse family and living arrangements and also, great variation in paid employment. Certainly, in this sample there was a variety of family and household arrangements and none of these was modelled on the male breadwinner model of the family. It also shows diversity and complexity of family structures. However, the results do not point to a situation where change in the nature or composition of family means that family is less important. Putnam (1995a) argues that communities of place are eroding, resulting in a decline in connectedness and social capital. Family, like community, might be changing and evolving, as social changes occur. However, it appears that blood ties may remain strong, or even be strengthened, by renegotiating and re-evaluating these relationships. It seems premature to predict a demise of the strong ties that bind blood families when evidence in the United Kingdom and now in Australia point to the fact that personal communities are most likely to be comprised of blood family and chosen friends; and, personal communities do influence lifestyle outcomes in both quite diffuse and specific ways.

Note

1. Also referred to as 'reflexive modernity' by Beck (1994) or 'second modernity' by Beck and Lau (2005).

References

Aarts, H. and Dijksterhuis, A. (2000) 'The automatic activation of goal-directed behaviour: the case of travel habits'. *Journal of Environmental Psychology*, 20: 75–82.

Bargh, J. (1994) 'The four horsemen of automaticity: awareness, intention, efficiency and control in social cognition' in Wyer, R. and T. Skrull (eds) *Handbook of Social Cognition*, 2nd edition, Vol. 1: Basic Processes. Hillside, NJ: Lawrence Erlbaum: 1–40.

Bauman, Z. (2001) *The Individualized Society*. Cambridge: Polity.

Beck, U. and Beck-Gernsheim, E. (2001) *Individualization*. London: Sage.

Beck-Gernsheim, E. and Beck, U. (1995) *The Normal Chaos of Love*. Cambridge: Polity.

Beck, U. (1994) 'The reinvention of politics: towards a theory of reflexive modernization' in, Beck, U., A. Giddens and S. Lash (eds) *Reflexive Modernization, Politics, Tradition and Aesthetics in the Modern Social Order*. Stanford, CA: Stanford University Press: 1–55.

Beck, U., Bonss, W. and Lau, C. (2003) 'The theory of reflexive modernization, problematic, hypotheses and research programme'. *Theory, Culture and Society*, 20: 1–33.

Beck, U. and Lau, C. (2005) 'Second modernity as a research agenda: theoretical and empirical explorations in the 'meta-change' of modern society', *British Journal of Sociology*, 56: 525–57.

Bourdieu, P. (1990) *The Logic of Practice*. Cambridge: Polity.

Camstra, R. (1996) 'Commuting and gender in a lifestyle perspective', *Urban Studies* 33: 283–300.

Cialdini R, Kallgren, C. and Reno, R. (1991) 'A focus theory of normative conduct: A theoretical refinement and re-evaluation of the role of norms in human behaviour', *Advances in Experimental Social Psychology*, 24: 201–34.

Finch, J. (1996) 'Responsibilities and the quality of relationships in families' in Offer, A. (ed.) *In Pursuit of the Quality of Life*. Oxford: Oxford University Press.
Giddens, A. (1992) *The Transformation of Intimacy: Sexuality, Love and Eroticism in Modern Societies*. Cambridge: Polity.
Giddens, A. (1994) 'Living in a post-traditional society' in, Beck, U., A. Giddens and S. Lash (eds) *Reflexive Modernization, Politics, Tradition and Aesthetics in the Modern Social Order*. Stanford, California: Stanford University Press: 56–109.
Goss, R. (1997) 'Queering procreative privilege: Coming out as families', in R.E. Goss and A. Squire Strongheart (eds) *Our Families, Our Values*, New York: Haworth Press: 3–27.
Pahl, R. and L. Spencer (2004) 'Personal communities: not simply families of "fate" or "choice"', *Current Sociology*, 52: 199–221.
Pahl, R. and Pevalin, D.J. (2005) 'Between family and friends: a longitudinal study of friendship choice', *British Journal of Sociology*, 56: 433–50.
Putnam, R. (1995a) *Bowling Alone: The Collapse and Revival of American Community*. New York: Simon & Schuster.
Putnam, R. (1995b) 'Bowling alone: America's declining social capital', *Journal of Democracy*, 6: 65–78.
Spencer, L. and Pahl, R. (2006) *Rethinking Friendship, Hidden Solidarities Today*. Princeton, New Jersey: Princeton University Press.
Weeks, J., Heaphy, B. and Donovan, C. (2001) *Same Sex Intimacies: Families of Choice and Other Life Experiments*. London: Routledge.

8

To Downshift or Not to Downshift? Why People Make and don't Make Decisions to Change their Lives

Carmel Goulding and Ken Reed

Introduction

A fundamental assumption about choice is that greater choice leads to greater happiness. Modern societies offer more choice than in the past, and are increasingly characterised by elastic and fluid social bonds – we are no longer defined by a clear sets of social ties which bind us to our life situation. We can choose our friends, geographic locality, and employment and, perhaps, our gender and that of our children, the shapes of our bodies, religious beliefs and lifestyles. We can, if we choose, radically alter the way we live, and might be expected to do so if our current life situation makes us unhappy. But many people do not, 'choosing', apparently, to remain in unsatisfying jobs with time stressed lives. However, some people do radically alter their way of living through a voluntary reduction in working time and income, in return for a slower pace of life and increased free time – a phenomenon popularly known as 'downshifting'. We suggest that this phenomenon – the choices involved in radical lifestyle change – can tell us something about why people 'choose' not to change, even when their present lifestyle makes them unhappy.

Australian research suggests that 23 per cent of adults aged 30–59 have made a voluntarily, long-term change in their lifestyle, other than planned retirement, which resulted in them earning less money (Hamilton and Mail, 2003). A U.K. study of downshifting shows similar results, with an estimated 25 per cent of British adults having downshifted over the last 10 years (Hamilton, 2003). The focus of this chapter is the question of why some people adopt simpler lifestyles in societies in which consumption is central to identity and to definitions of success.

The chapter draws on a series of in-depth interviews conducted in Australia and the U.K. to examine how personal values, commitments and social networks influence the choices they make about how they live. The interviews cover respondents' life histories, particularly the situation that led to the decision to change. A particular focus is the respondents' significant social relationships, and the analysis of the data emphasises how these influence their choices.

The concept of personal communities

Roles, relationships and identities are much less clearly defined now than in the past. These are negotiable and identity, in particular, is something that must be constructed, rather than being given by one's social location, class, gender or ethnicity. Although people need to construct their own biographies in their own way they will develop stronger commitments to those who affirm their identity than to families of origin or kin relations. For example, Roseneil and Budgeon's (2004) study of non-partnered relationships in the U.K. suggests that personal and social life in modern society occurs largely outside the family, with most of the caring and intimate relationships occurring between partners who are not living together as 'family' and within networks of friends. This has been referred to as a trend from families of fate to families of choice. Families of fate are those into which we are born, and families of choice are kin-like networks of relationships not based on blood-ties but on friendship and self-chosen commitment (Pahl and Spencer, 2004; Pahl and Pevalin, 2005).

Pahl and Spencer (2006) conceptualise community in terms of the 'social relationships of belonging', arguing that the dichotomy between family of fate and family of choice is less clear-cut than previously conceived. According to their qualitative study of sixty U.K. residents, personal communities contain multiple social networks, many of which do not overlap, with people embedded in highly complex sets of relationships in which they invest different levels of commitment. They distinguish personal communities from social networks, with the former defined by relations to a focal individual – for example, work colleagues and school friends may be part of personal community but have no connection to each other.

Pahl and Spencer's research builds on Wellman's substantial work on personal networks (see, for example, Wellman, 1979, 1982). Wellman proposes that people operate in 'liberated communities' not binding solidarities, which can and do change in response to opportunities, difficulties and changes in personal and household circumstances (Wellman, 1997). Personal networks are a form of social capital which makes resources available through interpersonal ties, and confirm identity, influence behaviours and reinforce integrative links between individuals, households and groups.

Allan (1998) also argues that the contextual circumstances of friendships are a significant factor in modern day relationships, with friendship ties fashioned by social and economic situations. This becomes increasingly evident when people change their social location. For example, life course transitions such as divorce significantly alter informal social networks. But not only do networks alter – emergent ties help create and establish a new identity such as 'a divorced mother' or 'a single father'. In general, informal networks are increasingly important in fostering self as a personally and socially constructed life-style choice.

In sum, there is growing support in the literature for the view that personal networks strongly influence one's sense of self, status and identity, and they affect choice by reinforcing common values and providing scripts for appropriate choices. They shape views about what is desirable and influence beliefs about the structure of opportunities and constraints in an actor's life situation.

Commitment to personal communities

Commitment results from the investments people make in social relationships. Personal communities elicit and sustain commitment in a variety of ways. First, personal communities depend fundamentally on a degree of commonality of values. Social relationships, unlike purely economic relationships, depend on people agreeing to some extent about what is important. Second, there must be a degree of commonality of belief, both factual (that is, shared interpretations of what the world is like) and moral (that is, agreement about right and wrong, good and bad). Third, values and beliefs are experienced through judgements of, and views about, appropriate (or inappropriate) behaviour, and the persistence of such judgements establishes norms within a personal community. Information exchange, communication and interaction within a personal community tend to re-affirm and reinforce shared values, norms and beliefs; so as relationship ties are loosened (or strengthened) so, too, commitment declines (or increases). These cognitive or cultural aspects of relationships within personal communities bind members together through what Durkheim referred to as 'the likeness of consciences' (Durkheim, 1933: 226).

Personal communities are also a source of resources. Relationships in personal communities are diffuse, and entail expectations of support and reciprocity. This builds up commitments through the process Becker compares with placing side-bets, where

> the committed person has acted in such a way as to involve other interests, originally extraneous to the action he is engaged in, directly in that action. By his actions he has staked something of value, something unrelated to his present line of action. (1960: 35)

As Blunsdon and McNeil (in this volume) show, commitment in family life is underpinned by a series of side-bets – choosing housing to be close to relatives, giving advice, child-care, intimacy and the various forms of support all involve the expectation and obligation of reciprocity that are diffuse, rather than specific to a particular action or exchange. These diffuse investments into relationships within personal communities foster commitment to membership, which in turn provides motivation to conform to norms and to concur with common beliefs and values. Similarly, Rusbult et al. (1998) show that 'investment size' – the quantum of resources attached to relationships – is a significant factor in their persistence. Invested resources, such as mutual friends, children and financial and material possessions, enhance commitment because the act of investment increases the costs of ending a relationship.

Thus, social attachments and relationships will tend to shape lifestyle choices – in part, because of their influence on how the desirability and feasibility of possible lifestyle choices are evaluated, and in part because investment in social relations and resources creates the risk of loss. By corollary, radical lifestyle change is more likely to occur in circumstances where attachments to others are weak, or where a crisis loosens existing social investments and attachments. Low levels of social commitments and low levels of life satisfaction together provide conditions that motivate substantial lifestyle change. These conditions for lifestyle change are discussed in the following section.

Downshifting as lifestyle choice

Lifestyle choices are increasingly the outcomes of individual aspirations, preferences and personal values rather than traditions and customs. For example, Giddens (1991: 81) understands lifestyle to mean: 'a more or less integrated set of practices which an individual embraces, not only because such practices fulfil utilitarian needs, but because they give material form to a particular narrative of self-identity'. In this sense, modern economies offer a 'supermarket' of lifestyle preferences – selecting which one suits is as much about aspirations and values, as it is about daily behaviours. However, our understanding of what influences the selection of one lifestyle preference over another is limited.

Behavioural change and the impact it has on daily living can range from minor purchasing decisions to extreme lifestyle change such as deciding to live a simpler, less consumerist life. However, it is notoriously difficult to change attitudes and behaviours, as the consumer behaviour literature shows. For example, Jackson (2005a) in a comprehensive review of sustainable consumption practices and approaches, indicates that persuasive communication has little impact in attempting to make consumers alter their consumption patterns. In fact, consumers show a high level of reluctance to change their daily behaviours even after extensive media campaigns (Jackson, 2005b). Given this, what does influence people to modify or radically alter consumptive lifestyles practices? And what assists or hinders the decision making process?

Low consumption lifestyles, such as voluntary simplicity, offer important insights into these questions. As a lifestyle choice, voluntary simplicity is conceived both as a belief system and practice of conscious living. However, its defining characteristic is the conscious reduction of consumption and the pursuit of satisfaction through non material aspects of life. According to Eztioni (2004), the central tenets of voluntary simplicity lifestyles are firstly, the removal of time stress; secondly, the balance of the inner and outer self; and finally, the expression of values through outward living.

Voluntary simplifiers can be broadly classified into several distinct typologies. For example, Eztioni's classification of voluntarily simplifiers includes downshifters, strong simplifiers and holistic simplifiers (Etzioni, 1998). According to this classification, downshifters make a lifestyle change to achieve greater work-life balance and are not necessarily driven by ethical considerations. They are also more likely to have the necessary financial resources to make such a lifestyle change and for many the downshift may take the form of early retirement. Strong simplifiers, on the other hand, give up high levels of income and status to reduce stress and a reduction in consumption is a consequence of their changed economic status. The holistic simplifier includes those who simplify their entire life according to an ethos of voluntary simplification.

Eztioni's classification has been well explored and the literature clearly identifies several distinct motivations for living simply, ranging from self-centred responses – such as a change from a hurried lifestyle in order to increase well being – to more altruistic motives including moral and ethical concerns with the environment, spirituality and community (see for example, Craig-Lees and Hill, 2002; Shaw and Newholm, 2002). The literature shows that improving quality of life is the most significant reported outcome of the lifestyle change (Gribsy, 2004; Huneke, 2005). However, downshifters and voluntary simplifiers only account for a small proportion of the population in advanced economies, and most people who have the option of maintaining a consumerist lifestyle choose to do so. But many people choose to pursue lifestyles that provide or lead to less than optimal happiness. For example, in the study of Australian downshifters Hamilton (2004) identified another distinct lifestyle typology, namely the 'deferred happiness' classification. This classification includes people who are willing to suffer now (e.g. long working hours, a pressured job, and a chaotic home life) in the expectation of future happiness. According to Hamilton, an estimated 30 per cent of the Australian full-time working population are characterised by deferred happiness syndrome. For many, the primary factor behind their less than optimal life satisfaction is the time stress associated with working long hours and trying to manage family responsibilities.

In summary, the empirical evidence suggests that the struggle over meaning in a consumer society is both psychological and cultural. The stakes in this struggle involve a host of adverse consequences or costs, required to maintain a certain lifestyle. These include social and psychological harmful effects that arise from the pursuit of a consumer lifestyle and which are a corollary to the 'freedoms' of consumer society. The costs of exercising market freedom may exceed the benefits and contribute more to the degradation of quality of life rather than enhancement.

Viewed in this light, at the heart of the search for meaning in modern societies is the relationship between quality of life, the availability of resources and opportunity, and the search for identity and alternative life situations. On the basis of this critical relationship, we argue that there are several pre-conditions which enable an actor to make substantial lifestyle change. The first condition is an already low level of life satisfaction or uneasiness with an existing life situation. The second condition is an image of 'something better' – a conception of a lifestyle that is more desirable. These create the conditions which enable 'the search for alternatives life situations' to begin. The level of attachment an actor has to their existing life situation (including career ties, relationships and personal networks) influences these conditions – by providing reference groups by which we assess life satisfaction, by influencing our views of what alternatives are desirable and available to us, and by increasing the costs of change because of existing investments and commitments.

In this way, the framework in this chapter builds on rational choice theory from the starting point that individuals make choices based on the knowledge and information available to them. However, our account of rational action focuses on the subjectivity of information in the decision making process, emphasising what supports and sustains the decision filtering information. We refer to this as subjectively rational action (see Goulding and Reed, 2006). We propose that information and beliefs are constructed through the complex sets of social networks that influence an individual's life, and that inputs to the decision making choice (such as information, beliefs, judgments) are sustained within the personal communities that comprise one's social world.

Research procedures

The study reported here focuses on how people make decisions that lead to a substantial change in their life, and how commitments within personal networks affect those decisions. The study is based on a series of personal interviews in Australia and in the United Kingdom with people who had made substantial lifestyle change. In total 55 interviews were conducted during the period 2006 to 2007. Typically, interviews ran between 45 and 60 minutes.

Recruitment

Respondents were recruited through a number of mechanisms. In the first instance, a website was established to describe the project and identified what was expected from people who may be interested in volunteering for the study. The website included a registration page for interested volunteers. A list of relevant organisations was identified through searches of the Internet and other media. These organisations were approached to promote the study via electronic newsletters and the establishment of a direct link to the project website. Targeted organisations included those that promote ethical behaviour, downshifters and lifestyle specific sites, as well as health and wellbeing sites. In addition, a review of secondary data identified geographic areas which have attracted alternative and downshifter communities. These areas were targeted for promotion in local newspapers and other local media including local government newsletters and websites. Following response to the recruitment campaign, a database of potential respondents was established and an interview schedule developed.

The recruitment strategy also targeted individuals living in intentional communities both in the U.K. and Australia. Intentional communities include co-housing communities, residential land trusts, eco-villages, communes, survivalist retreats, kibbutzim, ashrams and housing cooperatives. Potential communities were identified through a review of the literature and other electronic sources including the Internet. Communities were subsequently selected on the basis of length of establishment, community purpose, number of members, and economic and social structure. Selected communities were approached via written correspondence requesting promotion of the study to community members. In total, five communities responded positively and information on the study was distributed to individual community members. The researcher travelled to these communities and stayed in each community for approximately one week. An overview of the key demographic features of the study sample is shown in Table 8.1.

Personal interviews

Interviews were conducted in the respondent's normal place of residence either in person or via the telephone. The interviews were recorded on a digital video camera or in the case of telephone interviews via digital recording. Given considerations of travel and cost, telephone interviews were also conducted with U.K. residents, while all the Australian interviews were conducted in person. The personal interviews took the form of an ethnographic interview in which the respondent's life history, key events and motives for lifestyle change were explored, aiming to contextualise the choice within key situations in the lifecourse. Questions were asked on life change events, relationships with family, friends and work colleagues, the biographical context of relationships, and the levels of personal well being and life satisfaction. The focus of the interview was to understand the choice process and the extent of relationship change as substantial lifestyle decisions were made. In addition, a short questionnaire was completed prior to the open ended interviews and this captured data on life satisfaction, work commitment and general values, as well as demographic information.

Table 8.1 Demographic details of study sample

	Number	**%**
Gender		
Male	23	42
Female	32	58
Residence / Location		
Australian	32	42
U.K.	23	58
Household Type		
Residential Household	37	67
Community	18	33
Age		
Median	51	
Range	33–71	
Education Levels*		
Not completed	2	4.3
Secondary	9	19.6
Certificate / Diploma	9	19.6
Tertiary Degree	18	39.1
Tertiary Higher Degree	8	17.4

Notes: *Excludes missing cases (n 9).

Analysis of the interview transcripts was broadly based on the Framework approach (Spencer, Ritchie and O'Connor, 2003). Framework is a matrix based method which uses a thematic framework to classify and organise data according to key concepts and categories. Essentially, it involves the process of content analysis in which themes are identified and categories or indexes developed. Two main forms of analysis were employed for the case study data, namely with-in case analysis and cross-case analysis. The with-in case analysis focused on reducing each individual account of the respondent's life situation and history to a manageable set of themes and events. The cross-case analysis looked across each of the cases and sought out differences and similarities across the cases. Using both approaches enabled the data to be organised and reduced in a way that allowed for patterns within the data to be identified (Miles and Huberman, 1994). This approach also facilitated three key levels of analysis, namely, the development of thematic categories and patterns across cases; associations between phenomena within each case; and associations in phenomena between the cases. The central themes and nodes which emerged from the data are shown in Appendix 1.

Key findings

The following sections provide a descriptive account of lifestyle change and identify the key life events which lead to and precipitate change. Three broad factors were covered in the research design including the extent of lifestyle change, connection to personal networks and personal values and beliefs. While not the focus of this paper, it is important to note that in terms of demographics, behaviours and general values our case study sample is not dramatically different from a random sample of the population. The case study sample was compared with a random sample of the Australian population (n = 1,947) who participated in a survey run in parallel with the study reported here. The comparison indicates that there is little difference in the basic profile of lifestyle changers – they tend to be quite representative of the population in their behaviours and values. They also differ little in terms of their demographic profile other than they tend to have slightly higher education levels.

Given the apparent 'normality' of the case study sample, our qualitative study sought to understand why people did make decisions to change their lives. The key finding of the study is that lifestyle change is not necessarily a one-off occurrence; change occurs over a period of time and it often reflects the cumulative effect of a series of significant, often traumatic life events. However, a significant aspect of our findings is that the 'journey of change' varies across the spectrum of cases. Significant commonalities are evident, for example, the three most common triggers for change are health, work and search for meaning (or happiness) in life. But the process of undertaking change is complex and the searching for alternative life situations – or alternative realities – varies vastly across the cases. For many, the search for an alternative 'desirable' life situation has taken place over years, often commencing with minor changes to diet and other daily habits and this develops over time into a major lifestyle change. For example, a shift to vegetarianism, a change in job, a search for more happier, alternative life situations, experimentation with alternatives, and then an ultimate change. However, for others there appears to be what we could call a 'critical moment' – a point in time when what it is that will make for a better life situation crystallises very quickly and results in a more dramatic and immediate lifestyle change. This change spectrum is an interesting and significant finding of our study as it suggests that while the triggers for change may be similar across the cases, the process of change is diverse and complex. With this in mind, the following sections describe the triggers for change and illustrate the broad spectrum of change as identified across the cases.

The influence of health

The strong causal relationship between health and happiness is well documented in the literature (see for example, Borghesi and Vercelli, 2008 for a thorough overview of the empirical evidence). The perceived happiness of individuals deeply affects their health status – people who feel happy enjoy better health, while unhappiness may lead to deterioration in objective health status.

In respect to the study findings, it is not surprising that health features as one of several significant triggers for lifestyle change. Respondents reported both minor and major changes to lifestyle as a means of improving health and consequently life satisfaction. For some respondents, minor dietary and daily lifestyle changes were a small part of a more radical lifestyle transition. For example a shift to vegetarianism is described in the following:

> It was actually a conscious decision to really change our diet quite considerably and to search out new and interesting things to eat and to cook and so on. And I almost immediately started to feel better, both physically and sort of mentally in terms of my feeling a little bit more at peace with myself from dropping meat out of the diet.

However, much of the health events reported by case study respondents related to psychosomatic diseases, with just under half of respondents (26) describing mental or stress-related illness and personal injury and trauma as a significant life event. For many, their stress-related illness required medical intervention mainly in the form of therapy or counselling. Often the intervention came at a crisis point, as is illustrated by the case of a self-employed builder with a long history of substance and alcohol use:

> I fell off the wagon a couple of times and then I wrote the family car off which is about the ninth time I'd smashed a car and I should've died and walked away from it. I just went to the doctor in tears and said 'listen this has got to stop, if I don't kill myself I'm going to kill someone else.'

However, for many a deterioration in health was not sufficient in itself to trigger substantial lifestyle change and in many ways, this reflects the strong causal relationship between objective health status and subjective wellbeing. Put another way, poor health is both a consequence and a cause of life dissatisfaction. Take for example, a 37-year-old single female, who made the shift from being a highly paid marketing manager of a major national corporation to a full-time yoga teacher over a period of several years. She described years of being dissatisfied with her marketing career, leading to heavy alcohol use and a low level of life satisfaction. However, as she describes in the following, it was a knee injury resulting in change to recreational habits that lead to substantial changes in daily behaviours and eventually a substantial change in employment. She also described a great sense of loss associated with 'giving up hockey' and the friendships associated with the sport.

> I started drinking a lot started missing work um, because I was too hung over and really just hated everything I was doing. Um, my life was just falling apart, um my relationship was deteriorating um, and everything was just falling apart around me. I think one of the most significant things was I had to give up hockey um, about 10 years ago cause the doctor said if I continued to play I'd probably end up in a wheel chair because at one point I couldn't walk after a game um, so that was after twenty one years of playing hockey so I'd lost something really quite significant so I felt really lost.

This case shows the cumulative effect of health events on lifestyle and similar stories unfold in many of the respondents' life histories. As another illustration, after a series of workplace traumas including the death of a work colleague and period of workplace bullying, Kerry went from a stable, employed, married 42-year-old female to a geographically isolated, divorced, work insurance recipient.

> I guess the biggest change for me if you're interested in change was being...going from a full-time working person, married in a stable home life to finding myself by myself...not knowing anyone without a job. And fairly mentally unstable, depression and the like.

As suggested by the above case, stress-related illness and work issues feature strongly in the case study findings.

The influence of work

Dissatisfaction with work is a key theme to emerge from the case study findings, with just under half of study respondents (27) describing substantial dissatisfaction with work as a factor in their life history. In particular, the effect of long working hours on work life balance features significantly in a number of the cases. For example, Ken a 41-year-old male executive who left a mining company to start his own consultancy, recounts the effect of long working hours on his family and daily life.

> You know, 60 hours a week plus. I would leave before 6:00 am in the morning. I'd get back after 6:00 pm at night and which meant the kids were asleep when I left and they'd go to bed ... these kids were only two, she was only a newborn, a year old when we left and the other ones were four and five or something like that so they would be in bed by 7:00 pm/7:30 pm, so I'd barely see them. I'd come home tired and grumpy and stressed, very high stress levels because there was always too much to do and on the weekends, you're struggling to unwind and by the time you had, it's back to work again.

For other respondents, work dissatisfaction and ill health appear to be closely linked. For example, the case of Julie a 49-year-old married female demonstrates the cumulative effect of work dissatisfaction on objective health. For Julie, the combined effect of work dissatisfaction and a major illness lead to both a substantial geographic relocation and a major shift to self employment.

> I just wasn't particularly happy in the job and there was all sorts of dramas and issues and things and I just thought no, this is not me. I did have a reservation when I did start and after the first week, I felt that it wasn't right for me anyway and then I developed very severe shingles and became bedridden and couldn't continue working, so I handed my notice in.

For other respondents, the central theme in regards to dissatisfaction with employment as a trigger for change was the intrinsic satisfaction of work or more pointedly the dissatisfaction of working in a way that is not meaningful. This is illustrated by Richard:

> Oh, yeah. I hated it when I was doing it for the money. Who else works in advertising apart from you do it for the money.

> Well, I think deep down I've always been very dissatisfied with working in that way, a means to an end. I've always gone and followed the herd, if you like, followed everyone else in thinking that this is okay to do that but I've never felt very satisfied with it.

However, it is important to note that work commitment among the respondents was high, with 29 indicating they would continue to work even if they had the financial capacity not to. So it is not the case that respondents are work-averse, but quite the contrary. For example, take the case of Liz who after 15 years of stable employment in an administrative role in a major education institution decided to shift to more 'fulfilling work'.

> Yes I love not working but it's not the work I don't want to avoid work it's not that it's going and sitting in an office for 8 hours a day where the environment of air conditioned fluorescent lights its really unhealthy its people around you who are really unhealthy and whinging and toxic about everything. And the company values you know don't match with mine so it's the whole combination of things that makes working in an office really unpleasant.

The participants often display similarities in early experiences of work. The findings suggest that the capacity to adapt and change employment, or to be open to change, is often reflected in early adult life employment experiences. In the majority of cases (31), early adult life was characterised by several diverse career paths and substantial change in employment. As illustration, in the case of a 38-year-old U.K. male his career trajectory of 20 years included travel consultant, business manager, IT consultant and student. In this context, a recurrent theme in our study was the idea that searching for 'something more in life' is a critical part of achieving personal happiness and often work in itself is not sufficient to provide for high levels of personal well being.

> And just suddenly reached a point where I thought, you know what? I can't just keep sitting at work, bored, doing stuff I don't believe in, 'cause I was freelancing at a multinational drinks company producing websites for Alco pops in fact. There's got to be more to my life than this. And so yeah, the whole light bulb kind of pinged one day when I was at work. It's like I can't do this. And I was quite lucky. I found a couple of universities that were doing degrees that I wanted to do,

> applied to them both and got offered placements with them both. So it was like okay, this is what I should be doing then.

Search for meaningfulness and happiness

The data suggest that lifestyle change is often driven by the need to find greater personal happiness and meaning in life. Such change commonly occurs after long periods of questioning and general dissatisfaction with a life situation. For example, comments from a 42-year-old female living in an intentional community illustrate the frustrations associated with search for meaning:

> I really, really envied people at school who kind of knew they wanted to be a nurse or a lawyer or you know anything because at least they knew which direction they were going in and it's funny, because I'm 42 and I'm still wondering what I should be doing, you know.

For some this search for meaning revolved around simplifying their life, with the current pressures of modern life reducing life satisfaction rather than enriching it. As with Hamilton's (2003) study of downshifters, a major focus was on reducing complexity and achieving greater balance between work and lifestyle needs.

> I wanted less stress. I wanted more time to be able to just enjoy life. I wanted to be able to spend time in nature and be able to live life rather than wait 'til whenever, when you retire to be able to go for a nice walk or whatever, and I suppose I had that slightly idyllic dream of nice cottage in the middle of nowhere. ... I just wanted a simpler life.
>
> You can't live the life and spend as you do or did when you're in full-time employment. So there is a balance to be made and I think that's a crucial thing to think about.

In line with lifestyle simplification, others described the desire to live a more self-sufficient lifestyle revolving around engendering a greater connection to the land and community.

> Whereas now, I just feel completely different. I want to do meaningful work involving design and building natural homes from natural building materials basically. That's what I really want to do and to set up communities like the kind of housing at Star communities in order to live a natural, simple life.

Identity change also featured for large number of case study participants particularly in regard to establishing new networks of friends whom reinforced the 'new' reality of their life situation. For example, significant lifestyle transitions such as a change in sexuality or a divorce are reinforced by the emergent ties that help create and establish a new identity such as 'a homosexual' or 'a single father'.

> It was a fairly major shift to re-jig my identity I think because I think I'd internalised a lot of homophobia from my family who are very strong Catholics and I think I'm still having to deal with some of that.

For others in the study, the concept of whether they had a 'choice' in making change was questioned and this was particularly evident among respondents who were living in intentional communities. For these respondents, their change was either realised or confirmed through cathartic moments.

> I thought it was like the pits of hippydom and at the end of the second week, I had a total eureka moment, absolutely you know road to Damascus thing. I'm sitting in my camp chair outside the caravan and this thought just flooded through me and it said this is your home, this is where you're meant to be. My jaw dropped and I couldn't believe that I was getting this sort of message but it really did happen here. And so that was my first thought was this is where I'm meant to be. I'm home and my next thought was oh my God, how am I ever going to talk the family into this and I just couldn't see how the two were going to reconcile.
>
> ... and all of a sudden, I looked out the window and there was a western person dressed like this. Shaved head, a mala, a male and I wasn't at all attracted to the physical male and something happened and I knew that I had something different to do. It happened almost immediately and then two months later, I'd finished everything, the relationship and everything and ... I went off to India.

More commonly, the change of lifestyle developed as a deliberate and conscious choice often reflecting a re-assessment of values.

> It was a bit of a journey. It certainly wasn't a quick thing but it started with some of the development, sort of personal development work

> that the company was doing for all the leadership in the company, which started to make me more aware of my own values.

Often the decision process is both based on, and driven by, the availability of resources, particularly financial resources. This is illustrated by the case of a 51-year-old female who planned her change, including travel to the U.S. to investigate alternative lifestyles, over several years. She describes her experience of change in the following.

> But generally speaking, apart from a few little bits along the way, we're extremely happy with the decisions that we've made. We've been very lucky and when we did earn a lot of money and we did make provision for private pensions and that sort of thing but instead of keeping those going, we've realised the money from those savings and we've been able to pay off most of our mortgage. Otherwise, we wouldn't be able to live here, not at the level of work that we do. So that's been good in one way. We're sort of living for the now though, rather than the future. ... The practical choices that we make on limited resources but our lives are much richer and diverse than they were before.

Figure 8.1 summarises the key influences on lifestyle change to provide an overview of the themes that emerged from the interviews. The figure illustrates the relational nature of change demonstrating that change is not necessarily just a point in time decision. The calculation

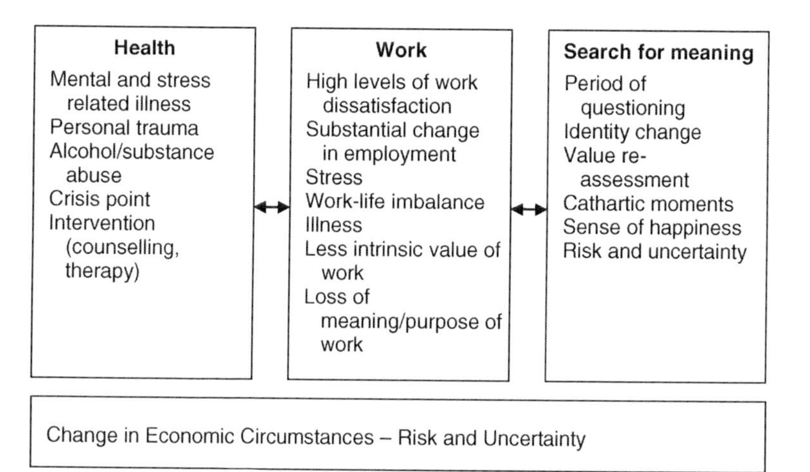

Figure 8.1 Key influences on lifestyle change

of change takes place over a period of time – often years – and is weighed against the risk and costs (both economic and social). In this way, our study findings suggest that risk and uncertainty and the weighting of options in the decision making process includes both rationally calculated and normative aspects.

Risk and uncertainty are key themes in the decision to make lifestyle change for the majority of respondents. The issue of investment in relationships, in employment and other social situations emerged across a significant number of cases. For many, the normative sanctions and opinions of friends and families were closely linked to the risk and uncertainty of change. For other respondents, fear of failure and a sense of loss were key themes in the process of making a decision to change:

> It was interesting. There are a couple that just didn't get it. They thought it was really dumb but most of them were supportive, envious. You know, comments like oh, it's really brave. I wish I could do that, you know and it was stressful, hey. It was a really hard thing to walk away from the business card, the status, the role, the position especially in that industry where the whole town is involved in it and your position and social was really determined by your status in the company hierarchy. Mm, very stressful. Yeah, it was a real sense of loss and of becoming a nobody. You know, you're really defined by where you sit in a social order and so it was really tough. Once I made it, I was fine. In fact, now I love it. I don't think I'd ever go back.

Personal communities exert an important normative influence on sense of self, status and identity and so affect choice by reinforcing common values and providing scripts for appropriate choices. In this respect, personal communities shape views about what is desirable, and influence beliefs about the structure of opportunities and constraints in an actor's life situation.

> It sometimes can be quite daunting to make that step into the unknown, although I have no fear of it at all really. I have no fear of that change whatsoever but it's more the reaction of other people, particularly my close friends and family that might think that I'm making a big mistake or they just can't understand it. They can't understand where I'm at whereas I'm pretty clear as to where I'm at, if you know what I mean.

The study findings suggest that an actor's personal community mediates major life transition and critical life events, such as a substantial change in employment:

> I was really scared of telling people I'd gone back to nursing because I felt within myself that was a failure because I felt I'd failed that I had to go back to something I didn't like without recognising it as a step forward and its a means to end – its not my career – its actually just helping me get through the next couple of years so I can go back and restudy and be a little more flexible in what I do.

As this shows, even in the face of fear and uncertainty, and strong normative sanctions, respondents were prepared to make substantial lifestyle changes. But the study shows that people's life histories reveal or support a disposition toward being able to make difficult and risky decisions. This is described in the following section.

The influence of life history

Our data suggest that life history matters in respect to the making of a lifestyle changer. Early exposure to change, including major geographic relocation, death and separation from family are significant factors across cases. For example, all respondents had experienced a major relocation in their early childhood – not just a shift from one suburb to another but a major geographic relocation either overseas or between states. Further, a common theme across a number of cases was early experiences of separation from significant family members, either through sudden death of a sibling or parent, or separation through boarding school or divorce. For some, their early exposure to death of a significant other shaped their early adult life.

> When I was in my final year at school, my brother was killed suddenly in a car accident which has definitely had a big impact on my life choices I think. He was 20. It was a month before my 18th birthday and probably three or four months before his 21st birthday. So that was a significant, like a major life event that is undeniably threaded through my life.
>
> Because I had ... I'm very philosophical about it. Because I had a misspent childhood in other words I had some significant events such as my sister dying and um, so forth. I also had my mother stabbed when I was in year 11 ...

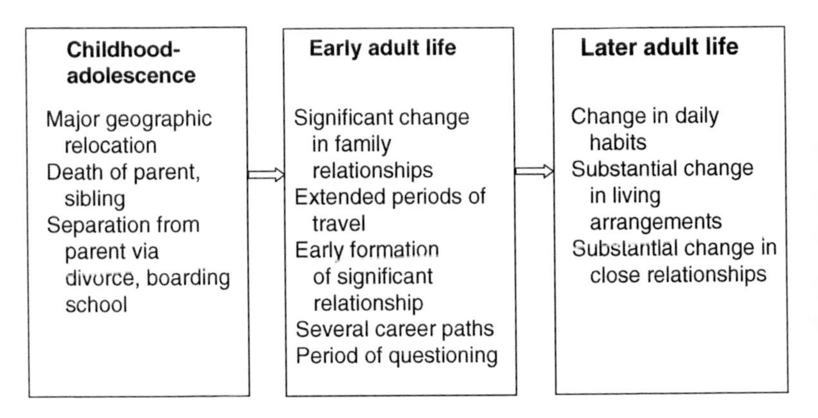

Figure 8.2 The Life trajectory of a lifestyle changer – common themes and patterns

Another significant similarity across cases was the substantial amount and extent of employment change in early adult life. This was generally coupled with exposure to international travel – that is, there was either continued change in employment to enable extended periods of travel, or travel to take up new employment opportunities. On the flip side of this apparent flexible and fluid life trajectory, was the early formation of significant relationships. Just under half of respondents had formed significant relationships in their early 20s many of which were still continuing or had lasted for several decades. Across the cases, periods of questioning particularly in early adulthood coloured perceptions of life satisfaction and this was often linked to changes in employment as well as major geographic shifts. For many, their later adult life was coloured by substantial change in living arrangements as well as significant change in personal relationships. As a way of illustrating the dispositional tendencies of lifestyle changers, and the impact of significant biographical events, Figure 8.2 summarises common themes and patterns that emerged across the cases.

Change in personal networks

For many case study respondents, their later adult life is coloured by shifting personal relationships. For example, divorce, children leaving home and also death of parents, siblings and close friends feature in personal network change. Change in networks, such as that resulting from divorce or death of close relative or partner, is often a trigger for lifestyle choice.

> I was 48 had no kids no commitments or attachments. While it was amazing in one sense it was a devastating lifestyle change it was also incredibly liberating it was the first time ... it was the first time I had my life to myself and I didn't need to be responsible to anyone I could make whatever decisions I wanted.
>
> So I knew very, very strongly that I needed to leave the marriage although it was difficult but I never regretted it. Once I'd done that, I was then a person on my own, still teaching at my old school but suddenly, it all seemed different and suddenly, it seemed a very small, narrow world ruled by bells and so on and yeah, I just needed, I knew I needed to do some exploring and pushing back horizons and so on, which I hadn't really done.
>
> So we went through the whole trauma and we sold that house which was a fabulous house but my mum had spent three days a week in it with us and we sold it in June and she died, they died in March ... And on reflection a year later, that's what I was doing. I just couldn't bear being there and picturing her standing there.

Change in personal networks opens up new ways of living and this is in part influenced by the strength of ties with personal networks. There tends to be the least amount of lifestyle change where given ties are strongest, whereas for cases where chosen ties feature more prominently, the extent of change is greater. That is, strong ties to given personal networks tend to be reflected in a more 'stable' life history. Conversely, the stronger the tie to chosen networks the greater the extent of lifestyle change.

Individual biographies greatly affect the strength of personal network ties. For example, early experiences of network change affect the development of network ties in later life. The extent to which someone tends to invest in social and economic relationships is strongly influenced by early life experiences.

Conclusions

In this chapter we have considered the question of why people make radical lifestyle change. Events of greatest significance in terms of lifestyle change are ill health, work dissatisfaction and the loss of significant network members either through death or separation. This is consistent with recent empirical evidence which shows that the events of greatest importance in terms of their impact on life satisfaction are death of spouse or child, and separation as well as deterioration in financial resources (Frijters et al., 2008). These findings indicate that while people are often able to adapt to separation and loss of financial resources typically after one year, adaptation or recovery from the death of close relative or partner is a much slower process.

Our findings indicate that lifestyle change is cumulative – often it is a result of a series of events over a period of time, i.e. physical illness, death of close relative/spouse, employment dissatisfaction, general sense of unwellness, discontentment, divorce etc. However, dissatisfaction with an existing situation does not in itself lead to change. Issues of the meaningfulness of life and personal identity lie at the core of lifestyle change, as one's role in the world is less clear and change provides a new clarity.

Our findings highlight the importance that the experience of work has for life satisfaction. Dissatisfaction with work and the struggle to find meaning and purpose in life seem to go hand in glove. Without meaningful work, life satisfaction diminishes and the consequences are great. The impact of stress-related illness is well demonstrated in the study's findings.

In analysing the role that personal communities play in lifestyle choice, we attempt to shed some light on the question of why people remain in less than satisfying situations, such as stressful jobs. We propose that personal communities provide inertial forces that tend to maintain people within the habits and routines of daily life. We identify two sources of this inertia: first, the normative and cognitive constraints whereby personal networks function to limit the range of options that people see as available to them in the micro-social worlds of daily life, and establish expectations of behaviour. Personal networks filter the information people receive about the world and how it operates and in this way, choice is normatively defined. This is particularly evident when change occurs in the personal network and such change tends to stimulate a redefinition of one's life situation.

Second, personal communities offer practical and emotional resources, on the assumption that the relationships which comprise them are enduring and open-ended. Consequently, people make investments – and create obligations – so that a radical lifestyle change can entail costs associated with those investments.

These features of social life work against change, and foster the maintenance of a status quo. Change involves risk, and the cognitive and resource aspects of personal communities shape calculations of the costs and benefits of change. However, while we have focused on the 'holding power' of personal communities, we have also noted that changes in relationships expose people to novel values and beliefs, and provide access to new resources. But we have restricted our analysis to the issue of why people pursue unsatisfying lifestyles, and the role that personal communities play in maintaining that pursuit. We have emphasised the tendency for people to do what others close to them do. But a shift of perspective might provide insight in the role that exposure to new personal communities play in generating alternative images of life, and the re-appraisal of the value of existing social and emotional investments.

Appendix 1 Thematic framework and key nodes

1.	**Change in economic circumstance**
1.1	Loss of income
1.2	Sense of loss fear, risk and uncertainty
2.	**Change in social networks (new groups, new friendships)**
2.1	Influence of counsellors
2.2	Influence of family on change
2.3	Influence of friends on lifestyle change
2.4	Normative sanctions on change
2.5	Reactions from friends to lifestyle change
3.	**Education**
3.1	Commenced training course
3.2	Finished training course
4.	**Family and close friends**
4.1	Death of family member
4.2	Death of partner
5.	**Health**
5.1	Change in daily habits
5.2	Commenced personal counselling
5.3	Drug / alcohol abuse
5.4	Mental breakdown or stress related illness
5.5	Personal illness / injury /trauma
6.	**Life History**
6.1	*Childhood to adolescence*
6.1.1	death of sibling, parent
6.1.2	difficulty at school

Continued

Appendix 1 Continued

6.1.3	early experience of religion
6.1.4	family turmoil difficult family relationships
6.1.5	major geographic relocation
6.1.6	separation from parent boarding school
6.1.7	separation from parent divorce
6.2	*Early adult life*
6.2.1	change in family relations
6.2.2	early formation of significant relationship
6.2.3	extended period of overseas travel
6.2.4	major geographic relocation
6.2.5	period of questioning
6.2.6	relationship breakdown
6.2.7	several career paths, substantial change in work
6.3	*Later Adult Life*
6.3.1	change in daily habits, eating sleeping recreation
6.3.2	change in health leading to professional help
6.3.3	change in social activities
6.3.4	substantial change in close personal relationships
6.3.5	substantial change in living arrangements
7.	**Personal network**
7.1	Children
7.2	Father
7.3	Friends
7.4	Geographic community
7.5	Husband
7.6	In laws
7.7	Mother
7.8	Neighbours
7.9	Old school friends
7.10	Partner boyfriend girlfriend
7.11	Siblings
7.12	Social groups
7.13	Sports groups friends
7.14	Wife
7.15	Work colleagues
8.	**Personal or social**
8.1	Legal disputes or difficulties
8.2	Major decision regarding immediate future

Continued

Appendix 1 Continued

8.3	Major personal achievement
8.4	Overseas travel
9.	**Personal relationships**
9.1	Began close personal relationship
9.2	Change in partners work
9.3	Change of friendship
9.4	Divorce or separation
10.	**Residence**
10.1	Change of residence in same town
10.2	Major geographic relocation
11.	**Search for meaning**
11.1	Religious experience
11.2	Cathartic moments
11.3	Emptiness of life
11.4	Esoteric courses
11.5	Identity change
11.6	Period of questioning
11.7	Self sufficiency
11.8	Sense of happiness
11.9	Social isolation
12.	**Work**
12.1	Change in work conditions
12.2	Difficulty at work
12.3	Difficulty finding work
12.4	dissatisfaction at work
12.5	Major change in type of work
12.6	Retirement
12.7	Retrenchment

References

Becker, H.S. (1960) 'Notes on the concept of commitment', *American Journal of Sociology*, 66: 32–40.

Borghesi, S. and Vercelli A. (2008) *Happiness and Health: Two Paradoxes*. DEPFID Working Paper, University of Siena.

Craig-Lees, M. and Hill, C. (2002) 'Understanding voluntary simplifiers', *Psychology and Marketing*, 19 (2): 187–210.

Durkheim, E. (1933) *The Division of Labor in Society,* Translated by George Simpson. New York: The Free Press.
Eztioni, J. (1998) 'Voluntary simplicity: characterization, select psychological implications and societal consequences', *Journal of Economic Psychology,* 19: 619–43.
Eztioni, J. (2004) 'The post affluent society', *Review of Social Economy,* 62 (3): 408–20.
Giddens, A. (1991) *Modernity and Self-Identity.* Cambridge: Polity Press.
Gribsy, M. (2004) *Buying Time and Getting By: The Voluntary Simplicity Movement.* Albany: State University of New York Press.
Goulding, C. and Reed, K. (2006) 'Commitment, community and happiness: a theoretical framework for understanding lifestyle and work', in Blyton, P., Blunsdon, B., Reed, K. and A. Dastmalchian (eds) *Work-Life Integration: International Perspectives on the Balancing of Multiple Roles.* Basingstoke: Palgrave MacMillan: 216–33.
Hamilton, C. (2003) *Downshifting in Britain: A sea-change in the pursuit of happiness,* Discussion Paper No. 58, Canberra: The Australia Institute.
Hamilton, C. (2004) *Carpe Diem? The Deferred Happiness Syndrome,* Web paper, May, Canberra: The Australia Institute.
Hamilton, C. and Mail, E. (2003) *Downshifting in Australia, A sea-change in the pursuit of happiness,* Discussion Paper No. 50, Canberra: The Australia Institute.
Huneke, M.E. (2005) 'The face of the un-consumer: an empirical examination of the practice of voluntary simplicity in the United States', *Psychology and Marketing,* 22 (7): 527–50.
Jackson, T. (2005) *Lifestyle Change and Market Transformation, A briefing paper prepared for DEFRA's Market Transformation Programme,* Guildford: Centre for Environmental Strategy, University of Surrey.
Miles, M.B. and Huberman, M.A. (1994) *Qualitative Data Analysis*, 2nd Edition. Thousand Oaks, CA: Sage.
Pahl, R. and Pevalin, D.J. (2005) 'Between family and friends: a longitudinal study of friendship choice', *British Journal of Sociology,* 56 (3): 433–50.
Pahl, R. and Spencer, L. (2004) 'Personal communities: not simply families of "fate" or "choice",' *Current Sociology,* 52 (2): 199–221.
Pahl, R. and Spencer, L. (2006) *Rethinking Friendship: Hidden Solidarities Today.* New Jersey: Princeton University Press.
Roseneil, S. and Budgeon, S. (2004) 'Cultures of intimacy and care beyond the "family": personal life and social change in the early 21st century', *Current Sociology,* 52 (2): 135–59.
Rusbult, C., Martz, J. and Agnew, C.R. (1998) 'The investment model scale: measuring commitment level, satisfaction level, quality of alternatives and investment size', *Personal Relationships,* 5: 357–91.
Spencer, L., Ritchie, J. and O'Connor, W. (2003) 'Carrying out qualitative analysis', in J. Ritchie and J. Lewis (eds) *Qualitative Research Practice: A guide for Social Science Students and Researchers.* London: Sage: 220–57.
Shaw, D. and Newholm, T. (2002) 'Voluntary simplicity and the ethics of consumption', *Psychology and Marketing,* 19 (2): 167–85.

Wellman, B. (1979) 'The community question: the intimate networks of East Yorkers', *American Journal of Sociology*, 84: 1201–31.
Wellman, B. (1982) 'Studying personal communities', in P. Marsden and N. Lin (eds) *Social Structure and Network Analysis*. California: Sage: 61–80.
Wellman, B. (1997) 'An electronic group is virtually a social network', in S. Keisler, N.J. Mahwah and L. Erlbaum (eds) *Culture of the Internet*. NJ: Lawrence Erlbaum Associates: 179–205.

9

Ways of Life after Redundancy: Anatomy of a Community Following Factory Closure

Paul Blyton and Jean Jenkins

Introduction

This chapter examines the fate of redundant workers and their community in the industrial region of South Wales, U.K., where redundancy has been a 'normal rather than exceptional feature' of life since the middle of the last century (Harris and Fevre, 1987: 49). It analyses the experiences of workers made redundant by the international clothing company Burberry, as it closed its manufacturing plant in the Rhondda Valleys and moved its production to China. The chapter begins by considering redundancy in the context of contemporary capitalism. It then briefly examines the particular experience of the South Wales valleys, followed by an evaluation of the impact of job loss on the lives of the individual employees, their families and their community. In terms of the themes being explored in this volume, we discuss the challenge that different groups face in achieving a satisfactory integration of their work and non-work lives in a context of redundancy, poor job prospects and low pay.

The wider academic canvas for this chapter is that much of the discussion on work-life balance in recent years has been restricted to an overly-narrow range of issues and contexts. In part this reflects the influence of two background factors: the increased participation of women in the labour force, and the fact that much of the attention on work-life issues is an outgrowth of 'family-friendly' practices and policies that have focused primarily on working mothers with child-care responsibilities. Attention has concentrated primarily on individuals and dual earners juggling work and non-work responsibilities so as to maintain (and advance) their careers whilst fulfilling care activities. Elsewhere, we have discussed the limitations of this pattern of response to work-life pressures – the emphasis it places on satisfying all the work and non-work role demands, rather than for example, seeking to modify those demands (see for example Blyton and Jenkins, 2007; Noon and Blyton, 2007). However, a further restriction of focus is the way the work-life issue, and related concerns with family and community, contains implicit assumptions regarding the status of the workers under discussion – assumptions about their security, relative affluence, available choices, and so on. Yet, as writers such as Warren (2004), Lautsch and Scully (2007) and Warren et al. (2009) have recognised, people on low incomes, in insecure work, and able to call on few resources within their locality, will have a distinct experience of work-life balance compared with higher earning dual-career couples. Achieving a balance between paid work and the rest of one's life depends in no small way on the opportunity to make a choice; for low paid workers that opportunity may be severely constrained.

Redundancy, risk and contemporary capitalism

A working life is built around needs and aspirations. At the most basic level, workers everywhere understand the need for a living wage, the aspiration to prosper, to build a better life for their children and to have some comfort in old age. A job can bring such modest ambitions within reach; job loss can potentially snatch them away. Redundancy involves the termination of employment on the grounds that a job previously being done is no longer required – possibly because of automation, changing skills, shifting business needs, corporate restructuring or falling demand – rather than any deficiency or fault on the part of the employee (see Blyton and Jenkins, 2007: 185–189). But job loss, blameless or not, carries enormous costs and risks for the individuals concerned. The end of one employment may indeed lead to better opportunity elsewhere for some, but much hinges on the state of the labour market and the personal circumstances of those affected.

Clearly, redundancy need not mean unemployment if suitable and acceptable alternative work is available, or if one has the means and desire to retire from work. But for the majority of people faced with job loss it will mean disruption, stress, and financial uncertainty (Warr, 1987). If one needs to continue to work and is part of a large pool of relatively low skilled and easily replaceable labour, as were the majority of redundant workers in our study, one is at a disadvantage in terms of job search. As a carer or someone with family responsibilities the capacity to embark on a 'new opportunity' may be seriously constrained by, for example, the inability to travel for work, or to find childcare to accommodate a different working pattern. Historical analysis of survey data from British workplaces has not supported the view that flexibility in working patterns has provided a more 'family friendly' environment for workers in the private sector (Cully et al., 1999: 144). Though a more recent survey suggests changes in employers' attitudes (possibly linked with new legislative provisions) there is still considerable disparity between the public and private sectors in this respect, with managers in private sector workplaces far less likely to be understanding about employees' non-work responsibilities (Kersley et al., 2006: 249–274). Essentially, flexible working in the U.K. has not generally been driven by employee needs (see Ackroyd and Procter, 1998: 163–183). This was the case even before the 2008–09 economic crisis, but such problems can only be compounded by a weak labour market and rising unemployment, where employers have greater scope to choose workers to be as 'flexible' as they demand.

At the end of the first decade of the twenty-first century, the context of recession and fears of deflation and depression, suggests that competition within the labour market will grow as employers become focused more on downsizing than recruitment. This is exemplified in the U.K. context by a joint guidance note published in February 2009 by the U.K.'s Advisory Conciliation and Arbitration Service (ACAS) and the Chartered Institute of Personnel and Development (CIPD), entitled *How to Manage your Workforce in a Recession*. While the declared intention of the document is to encourage employers not to opt for redundancy as a choice of first resort in challenging times, the document includes an entire section devoted to 'getting redundancy right' and is symptomatic of a time when opportunity is likely to be constrained. Similarly, it is instructive that at this time the Trades Unions Congress (TUC) has established a multi-disciplinary Commission to investigate 'vulnerable employment' in the U.K. This they define as 'precarious work that places people at risk of continuing poverty and injustice resulting from an imbalance of power in the employment relationship' (TUC, 2008: 3). For workers like those on the shop floor at Burberry, relatively precarious work may be all that is available to them to replace the jobs they have lost, and it is unlikely that their redundancy compensation will offer much of a financial 'cushion' to enable them to retrain for a totally new skill or to establish their optimum work-life balance.

For those facing redundancy in the U.K., statutory levels of financial compensation are low. Some decades ago, when the first Redundancy Payments Act was passed into British law (in 1965), the rationale for legislation on compensation for redundant workers was based on a measure of pluralist consensus. It was acknowledged that the 'general good' demanded a strong economy, that prosperity demanded efficient use of resources and modernisation of working practices, and that this meant that some workers would be put out of work to allow others to hold on to their (now more efficient) jobs. As redundancies were (perhaps paradoxically) reasoned to be for the general economic good of a prosperous society, it was accepted that 'the redundants' alone should not have to bear the costs of job loss (Daniel, 1972: 124). This might suggest that the British system of compensation for redundancy would have provided adequate financial protection for redundant workers, but statutory payments were (and remain) comparatively small. The statutory redundancy payment is based on a calculation of service times earnings, where the maximum length of service to be taken into account is capped at twenty years and earnings are also capped at a weekly maximum. In 2009, the statutory *maximum* that a redundant worker could receive on this multiplier would be £10,500.[1] This was the scale on which compensation for the Burberry workers would have been calculated had their campaign not been successful in applying pressure on the company to increase its payments. More generally, it is only in well organised trades where collective bargaining has won significant additional provision may workers expect any more than their statutory entitlements. It remains the case that Britain is far less rigorously regulated on redundancy and compensation than its continental European partners, with the costs to British employers of statutory severance having been described as 'paltry' (Turnbull and Wass, 2000: 69).

Thus we may conclude that to a great extent the economic risk of redundancy continues to fall on the workers involved. Furthermore, where employment does exist employers have progressively transferred economic risk to employees through increasingly precarious employment patterns (see Heery and Salmon, 2000: 1–24). In this context we see the casualisation of work, the distancing of the employment relationship by means of agency employment, unpredictable hours, low pay, and the commodification of labour. Such practices are particularly noticeable in certain sectors and occupations, and typify work in areas of the service sector like call centres, retail and low skill caring occupations. This type of work is associated with feminised employment and characterised the opportunities that were available for redundant

Burberry workers, most of whom were female. However, Cobble (2007: 2–3) makes the point that in the US, as a result of factors such as restructuring and blue collar unemployment, such work is now just as likely to be done by men as by women, and similar trends may be seen in the U.K.. The fact is that in the current context being *in* work is the prime objective, and as well as competition between workers for employment in their local labour markets, the increased influence of globalisation means that competition for work extends across geo-political boundaries.

In practice, the lives of workers around the world are 'becoming more integrated' as their futures are influenced by corporate decisions about how, what and where work is located (see Munck, 2002: 64–69). The complex inter-relationships of global financial institutions were highlighted by the banking crisis of 2008–09, and the absence of regulatory controls has been exposed in a way that has brought the role of the state to the fore once more. Time will tell whether this will be a lasting, changed phase in capitalism but for today's workers in both manufacturing and service sectors, the situation remains that being 'more integrated' means that increasingly they compete for work against one another within the boundaries of the same multi-national corporation, or as outsourced 'suppliers' of goods and services to larger corporate ventures. Thus it was that Burberry workers in Treorchy found themselves in direct competition for work with Chinese workers in what were for them distant, un-named destinations.

Around the globe, the increasing focus on the nature of supply chains and the fate of workers highlights pressures being placed on low cost producers to be cheaper still, and this is particularly pertinent in the clothing sector.[2] The nature of the British clothing industry is such that restructuring and relocation of operations characterised the activities of the giant clothing firms in recent decades, most of which now produce outside the U.K. (Winterton and Winterton, 1997: 26). This makes it all the more remarkable that for Burberry workers in Treorchy in 2006, the news of closure came as a complete shock; when Burberry announced it was to transfer production of their 'polo shirt' to China, it took the small Welsh community that had relied on the factory as its main employer completely by surprise. There were rational reasons for this surprise, related to the way the garment was marketed and the profitability of the plant, and these will be explored in the next section. But while previously Burberry workers had not worried about their futures, once notice of redundancy was given their 'certainties' about employment were forever shaken. The insecurity generated by the fear of job loss exerts an adverse influence on the quality of workers' lives, both inside and outside the workplace and may be a powerful instrument of managerial control (Blyton and Dastmalchian, 2006: 21–22; see also, Hudson, 2002: 46–50). It was, for example, instrumental in inhibiting solidarity action by workers within the same union in other U.K. Burberry plants at the time the closure of the Treorchy plant was announced. As for the redundant workers in South Wales, we will see that the majority entered other employment that will not allow them to ignore their vulnerability ever again, as on a weekly basis they cope with irregular work patterns and non-standard contractual arrangements which are designed to satisfy the employer's demands for flexibility with little account of employees' need for a balanced and secure life outside work. It is to a review of their experience in the context of their locality, that we now turn.

Local and global – the 'spirit of the Rhondda', redundancy and the Burberry workers' campaign

Industrial South Wales always had a close relationship with global capitalism. It became a major centre of iron production and the greatest coal exporting region in the world in the nineteenth century, as English businessmen invested heavily in its natural resources (Minchington, 1969: xvii). Some commentators have drawn historical parallels with the contemporary world, where countries with 'developing' economies are exploited for their labour forces (see Lovering, 1983: 53). The last greatest crisis of global capitalism in the 1930s resulted in severe social deprivation (see Fogarty, 1945: 87) and the end of coal mining in the region in the 1980s meant that industrial decline and unemployment has been an ongoing feature of Valleys life. Much has been written of the nature and characteristics of the history of this region, often focusing on, analysing and even mythologising the 'class consciousness' and 'community consciousness' that supposedly grew out of struggle and hardship (see Francis and Smith, 1980: 55).

We need to take care to employ a critical eye and should not 'romanticise' a community (see Berger, 2001: 26; Williams, 1973: 43), but nevertheless even today the people of these valleys refer to a particular 'pride and spirit of the Rhondda', which was possibly born of isolation and the shared experience of adversity. It was certainly commented on by the respondents in our study as having been a factor in their determination to campaign against Burberry's decision to close their plant which had first been established in 1937, when it was owned and run by a firm named Poliakoff and supplied Burberry, as well as other retailers. The age of the plant meant that generations of workers had moved in and out of employment at the factory and it had become an integral part of community life that they 'never thought would close', as one of the union stewards said when interviewed. Burberry took full ownership of the factory in 1990.

In 2005, Burberry took the decision to allocate its 'polo-shirt' manufacture exclusively to the South Wales plant, leaving the manufacture of its world famous 'iconic' raincoats to its other two plants in the North of England. With only one product going through its doors, the Treorchy plant made considerable improvements in productivity as it concentrated on polo shirt production, and it was a profitable factory. Based on information disclosed by Burberry, the union estimated that the factory yielded profits of around £24 million in the year 2005–06. Thus it was that despite trends of relocation elsewhere in South Wales manufacturing (see Munday, 2003: 5) and long established restructuring of the British clothing industry (Winterton and Winterton, 1997: 18–40), the workforce had confidence in their futures based on the longevity of the plant (it had survived previous industry restructurings); increased levels of productivity; profitability; and the Burberry brand image of being 'quintessentially British'. On these grounds, workers had felt that the company was being well served by the Treorchy plant, that it would not be likely to manufacture outside Britain, and had not foreseen that redundancy was something that posed a threat to *their* working lives.

But the plant was unable to 'buck the trend' of manufacturing moving to lower cost newly-industrialising countries. In September 2006 a senior Burberry manager visited the plant and gave 90 days' notice of the closure of the factory. There was no prior warning and no consultation with either workers or the union. The prospect of closure threatened an entire way of life for employees whose families had worked at the plant for several generations; many had known no other employment and foresaw little opportunity of alternative work in the locality. The sense of shock and outrage at the company's actions galvanised the workers, union and local politicians who formed a coalition determined to fight the plant closure. They embarked on a remarkable campaign which drew support from a range of media celebrities and elicited international union solidarity to expose Burberry's actions and highlight the contradictions and ethical issues raised by a luxury 'British' brand, retailing its goods for premium prices, shifting production to China in search of even higher profits at the expense of its customers around the world, and to the cost of its British workers.

Worker demonstrations outside Burberry's stores in London, as well as in France and the U.S., embarrassed the firm, which was called to account by the media, faced a legal challenge from the main trade union involved, and had to appear before a Select Committee of the House of Commons to explain its actions. Ultimately the campaign failed to keep the factory open but succeeded in securing from the company an extra three months' employment for its workers, a doubling of their statutory redundancy payments and also a commitment from Burberry to a 'community fund' of £1.5million over ten years, to be spent within the locality. On the last day of work at the factory, on 30th March 2007, the workers marched out of their plant, accompanied by a brass band and choir, to a barrage of press photographers and television crews. It was an emotional day; a triumph for the spirit of resistance of the ordinary worker against the overwhelming forces of capital, and one that those who took part say they will never forget.

But what came next? Where did these workers go when the television crews and reporters moved on to another story and their redundancy payments got eaten away by everyday living? What happened to their community when the work disappeared? Our study set out to shed light on these questions. Having followed the initial campaign in 2006–07, we returned in 2008 to examine the subsequent experience of these redundant workers. With the support of the trade union involved (the GMB) a questionnaire was sent to all its former members at the factory (191 shop-floor employees) plus six non-union workers that we had made contact with. Union density among shop floor workers at the plant had been high, at around 90 per cent. Eighty usable replies were received (we omitted several other returns from the analysis where employees had left the plant prior to the closure or had been on long-term sickness absence for a considerable period). The questionnaire surveyed opinion and experience in several areas. In this chapter we focus on the responses concerning the search for new employment and the nature of work secured, and the perceived changes in health, family life, friendships and community since the closure.

Work-life experience after redundancy

Our sample reflected the nature of a workforce that had been largely female (sewing machinists) and that, due to the lack of recruitment at the firm in recent years, the workforce had an older age profile, with long average years of service. Thus, in the sample of former Burberry workers, 71 (out of 80) were female, and over seven out of ten were

45 years or over. Three-quarters of the sample were married or living with a partner. The age of the sample is also reflected in the finding that a majority (72 per cent) had no children living at home.

Almost all of the respondents had been employed at Burberry for at least 5 years, and many had worked there for all the time the company had owned the factory; indeed many had also worked for the previous owner and, as a result, the average number of years that respondents had been employed at the factory was almost 16 years. The largest group in the sample were former machinists with smaller proportions in inspection, cutting and supervision. Almost all (all but two) had been employed full-time. A point worth making, and one which is instructive for understanding the impact of the plant on the lives of women, their families and the community, is that the average length of service of employees is likely to have been even higher if we could have identified the years of employment for each respondent, rather than their most recent period of continuous service at the point of plant closure. As female workers generally moved in and out of employment at the factory in line with patterns of child-bearing, many had contributed substantially more years of their working lives to the plant than was reflected in their period of continuous service when it actually closed down.

One year on from the factory closure, three-quarters of the respondents were in paid work with the remainder divided equally between those who had retired and those still seeking employment. Of those who had found a job, just over one-quarter had done so straight away, while for over two in five the job search had taken more than three months. The majority of those in work were in the same job that they found on leaving Burberry, while 15 respondents had had two or more jobs since their redundancy. Most commonly, the jobs found were in retail or care work, and to a lesser extent in manufacturing.

What is striking about the jobs secured is the high level of part-time working compared to the very low level of part-time working at Burberry. In the clothing factory, child care was accommodated by breaks in employment rather than part-time hours; return to work was relatively straightforward for women as their children reached school age (even if there was a waiting period for a vacancy). But after redundancy our survey showed that of those in work, just over half were in part-time jobs, with weekly hours ranging from 6 to 30 (and with a mean and mode of 20 hours); those in care work and retail jobs were especially likely to hold part-time contracts. From our discussions with former workers, it is evident that part-time contracts were generally not sought, but rather reflected the only vacancies available. The care contracts for example, typically began as (effectively) zero-hour contracts with no hours guaranteed until a training period was completed. After that, just 16 hours per week were commonly guaranteed, though workers could be asked to work as many as 30 hours in a week depending on demand. The same was true of retail work, with the proviso that attaining a 30-hour week was far less common in that sector. For many, this part-time status was a principal reason why their weekly earnings were lower than they had received at Burberry, rather than their hourly rate of pay. Effectively, Burberry sewing machinists had been on a rate roughly equivalent to Britain's National Minimum Wage (NMW). Thus their hourly rate of pay did not have far to fall, but almost three in five indicated that their weekly earnings were now lower, compared to less than a quarter who reported their earnings to have risen since leaving the clothing factory. Thus the predominance of part-time work was not the result of redundant workers choosing to engage in 'multi-activity'[3] as a new way of living (see Gardiner et al., 2007: 486). Rather, for the majority of former Burberry workers, part-time work was their only opportunity for paid employment. This has serious implications for work-life issues as these workers were relatively low paid for their entire working lives, and even with the cushion of redundancy payments they faced enormous challenges in terms of economic survival.

A large majority of the respondents (79 per cent) reported that overall they missed working at Burberry. By far the most common reason was missing 'friends' and 'workmates'. One respondent summed this up in referring to missing the 'family feeling among employees – everyone knew everyone'. The survey results suggested that this was a continuing source of regret for respondents, even for those who had found jobs they had settled in to well. For example, as another wrote, 'I love the job I'm doing now, and glad I have moved on, but miss my friends'. Secondary reasons for missing working at Burberry were the higher pay workers had received and the proximity of the workplace to their home. All the men in the sample missed working at the clothing factory. This may have been at least partially due to the fact that men typically occupy 'skilled' jobs in the clothing sector (see Phizachlea, 1990: 58) and prior to closure the majority of male employees at the Burberry plant were either engaged in maintenance, cutting or stores work. In particular, maintenance and cutting were jobs which carried higher rates of pay, some autonomy and a significant element of status within the factory. Local opportunities for male employment of a comparable nature were limited.

The broader impact of the closure

As well as exploring their experience in the labour market, we asked several broader questions about what had happened to respondents since being made redundant from Burberry: what changes had occurred in their health, family life, socialising and friendships, and community involvement, for example.

In terms of their reported health, while approaching half felt that their health had stayed the same, almost two in five reported their health to have deteriorated. This latter group were more likely to be older individuals, those working, and people who had lower earnings. As regards family life, a majority (54 per cent) reported no change since the redundancy; the remainder were equally divided between those who said their family life had improved and those reporting a deterioration (the latter more likely to be younger and female).

In relation to socialising and friendship patterns since the closure, the level of reported deterioration was particularly marked. Almost three in five (58 per cent) indicated that this area of their life had got worse (including 19 per cent who reported that this aspect had got 'much worse'), compared to 30 per cent saying it had stayed the same and less than one in five (18 per cent) indicating an improvement. Those noting a decline in friendships and socialising were most likely to be younger, those not in work and those on lower earnings than when they worked at Burberry.

To a less marked degree, a similar picture is evident in relation to community involvement. Over two in five (43 per cent) reported a decline in involvement since the factory closure, compared to one in seven (13 per cent) who reported an increase, with the remainder indicating that their level of community involvement had stayed the same. Again, those on lower earnings were disproportionately represented in the group who reported a decrease in community involvement.

Reviewing our findings it is evident first that for the large majority, life at the factory was something they missed. For most the loss was one of a community at work. References to friends and workmates as the main thing they missed were frequently made in the survey. During the campaign against closure one worker summed up his feelings, saying, 'I have two families, one at home and one here in this factory'; the survey confirmed these sentiments as widespread and there was clearly an ongoing and keen sense of loss of a workplace community. The long average length of service among those at the factory, both during the Burberry ownership and under the previous owners, coupled with a lack of recruitment in recent years and low turnover rates due to an absence of equivalent jobs in the area, acted to reinforce the community character of the workplace. Further, while a small proportion of the workforce travelled to the factory from outside the immediate community (a smaller clothing operation had been absorbed into the Treorchy factory some years earlier) the great majority of the workforce lived very locally. This bond between community and factory was long established and was maintained partly by the practice of employees introducing (and vouching for) other family members who sought employment at the factory. The geography of the region – narrow valleys running north to south, historically with poor road and transport connections between them – further reinforced the community base of the workforce.

Thus, it is not surprising to find a strong sense of missing friends and work colleagues. One factor in accounting for why three in five indicated that friendships and socialising had deteriorated is likely to be this removal of a key locus of interaction with other members of their community. Likewise, one reason why more than three times the number of people indicated that their community involvement had declined since the closure compared to those who said it had increased, probably relates to the rupture of an essential connection with other members of the community at the workplace. The closure campaign itself had contributed to a community involvement, with many employees travelling to London to voice their protest outside Burberry's principal retail outlets in Bond Street, and to attend the Law Courts where their case was put, as well as attending meetings locally. But by the time of our survey this campaign had finished, other than for a handful of people involved in a committee to determine how the community fund that had been established should be spent. Thus in this respect community involvement was bound to have declined alongside the end of campaigning.

For the workers an intense period of community-based activity and protest was followed by the anti-climax of redundancy and all its implications. Perhaps this begs the question of whether workers' sense of loss of community was actually intensified by having been part of the campaign. This is of course possible, but an event on the final day of the factory illuminates the attachment workers felt for their community at work which existed outside and beyond the campaign. An elderly lady, described as being 'in her eighties', presented herself at the factory gates on the morning of the plant's closure. She explained she had worked at the factory as a young girl and was distressed to think that a part of her history was actually ending that day. She had followed the story of the campaign in the press, and asked that she be allowed to walk through the factory on its final day. Workers helped her to do so and were moved by the event, which they recounted as an example of how long and how much the factory had meant to this community. In interviews, their descriptions of their feelings as they left the plant suggested that they felt not only their own immediate loss but also took with them the memories of mothers, sisters and aunts who had lived a common history.

Yet while some of the reported decline in friendship contacts, socialising and community involvement can be linked directly to the effects of closure and the disbanding of the work community, a second, related factor is also evident in the survey results and this relates to subsequent job experience. As we noted above, while for some former employees, life after Burberry meant retirement, unemployment or temporary work, for the majority it entailed another job, and for just over half of these part-time work, particularly in the care and retail sectors. Many have commented on the potential contribution of part-time work to broader work-life integration (see for example, Hakim, 2000) and in these, part-time working is typically portrayed as a means by which dual-earning couples achieve a balance between work and non-work domains: one (usually male) working full-time, while the other (usually female) undertakes paid work part-time while also fulfilling various other roles, notably childcare. Thus in this depiction, any former 'balance' created by the combination of a male breadwinner and a female homemaker is modified by female part-time working combined with (at least a partial adjustment) by both partners to fulfilling other, non-work roles.

Yet this depiction of part-time work as the solution for many people to work-life imbalance has been being challenged by a growing number of writers, notably Warren (2004) and Walsh (2007). One problem that these writers identify is the unsuitability of viewing all part-time jobs, and more specifically all part-time job holders, as equivalent. While for some dual earners, one member of the couple working part-time while the other continues in full-time work may indeed represent an ideal solution to securing both desired levels of income and job satisfaction, while leaving time to fulfil other non-work activities. For others, however, part-time working has very different outcomes: a source of inadequate income, accepted only in the absence of a full-time position, and for many involving working time patterns that can be both inconvenient and variable. For Warren (2004) the financial implications of part-time working – and the restrictions that limited finance places on leisure and other non-work activities – represent a key source of imbalance and a reason why those working part-time are unable to achieve other, non-work goals. As Walsh (2007: 173) comments, 'the practical realities of part-time work are rather more complicated and ambiguous than is commonly depicted in optimistic accounts of such arrangements'. For some, part-time work may indeed provide those involved with the 'best of both worlds' (ibid) of fulfilling work and family roles. For others, however, part-time work creates problems and pressures more than it solves them.

For many in the present sample, the gaining of a part-time job meant a sharp drop in earnings: over four out of five reported that their earnings were now lower than they had been at Burberry. As well as reference to the loss of friendships and socialising, respondents commonly referred to missing 'the money' as one of the factors they regretted about leaving the plant. Thus, here is a group of workers working fewer hours of paid employment, accruing fewer earnings but with potentially more time to devote to other activities. But for many this extra time did not translate into improvements in different aspects of their non-work life. Those working part-time for example, were considerably more likely (compared to their counterparts in full-time jobs) to indicate that their pattern of friendships and socialising had deteriorated in the time since the factory closure. Similarly, more of those in part-time jobs reported a decline in their community involvement since Burberry closed, compared to those in full-time jobs. Moreover, those in part-time jobs showed no greater improvement in family life compared to those in full-time jobs: in both cases equal numbers reported family life to have improved and to have got worse since the closure.

Partly these findings may reflect the fact that some part-time schedules involved fragmented working patterns. Retail workers are generally unable to dictate or predict the shifts they will be asked to work, and care workers are required to attend people in their homes at critical points of the day which may be hours apart. For example, care in the community may involve morning bathing and lunchtime supervision, and very possibly another period of attendance at bedtime. Many of these jobs have also involved additional travelling time: a number of part-time jobs were further afield than the work at Burberry had been (though this latter aspect was also true of the full-time jobs). But more significant appears to have been the lower income that the part-time jobs entailed, leaving less money available for socialising and other activities. While the redundancy payments created an important financial buffer in the short-term, nevertheless the lower weekly earnings from the part-time work translated into a level of income which undermined rather than facilitated a satisfactory non-work life. As Gardiner et al. (2007: 486) comment, a fulfilling range of interest and multiple sources of activity is 'only feasible in the context of financial security'; this did not exist for the majority of the former Burberry workers who were low paid prior to losing their full-time jobs, and many became lower paid still now that they worked part-time. Furthermore, irregular hours and the nature of the work itself further isolated workers in their new employment.

Conclusion

This has been a small-scale study, but its conclusions raise important issues for consideration in the scheme of working lives. Too often the debate on work-life balance risks neglecting the reality that for many of the globe's vulnerable workers who lack wealth and opportunity, whether they be factory workers in production units in developing economies, or contingent service sector workers in the U.K., there is no such thing as 'equilibrium' in their lives as they negotiate their economic survival. This is not simply the preserve of unregulated, overtly exploitative labour markets. Vulnerable workers who are unable to influence the terms and conditions under which they labour, are part of the equation whereby other workers become vulnerable. As capitalism restructures and workers are channelled into new forms of work, their working lives are fundamentally affected, as has been the case for the former Burberry employees. These never were the type of workers who could afford to pay to achieve work-life balance by off-loading domestic chores or child care. As many moved from manufacturing into service sectors which have to cater for flexible provision of a service to their customers, we see the effect of redundancy in a variety of ways: loss of friendships, socialising and community, but also loss of a working routine that gave them – perhaps by default – a better trade-off between their working life and leisure. As perceptions of job insecurity and precarious employment patterns persist, the work-life balance debate will neglect the experience of a significant proportion of the labour force if it fails to address the fate of the redundant, the low paid and the under-employed. Within a working life, balance must be paid for, and this study suggests that part-time work in the low-paid service sector simply does not foot the bill.

Notes

1. Source: Department for Business, Enterprise and Regulatory Reform, UK, 26.02.2009.
2. See for example the work of: Clean Clothes Campaign; Playfair2008; Home Workers Worldwide.
3. By multi-activity we refer to people adopting a range of activities, including part-time work, which yield a more fulfilling life style.

References

Ackroyd, S. and Procter, S. (1998) 'British manufacturing organisation and workplace industrial relations: some attributes of the new flexible firm', *British Journal of Industrial Relations*, 36 (2): 163–83.

ACAS/CIPD (2009) Joint Guidance Note: *How to Manage Your Workforce in a Recession*, www.cipd.co.uk

Berger, S. (2001) 'Working-class culture and the labour movement in the South Wales and Ruhr coalfields, 1850–2000: a comparison', *Llafur Journal of Welsh Labour History*, 8 (2): 5–40.

Blyton, P. and Dastmalchian, A. (2006) 'Work-life integration and the changing context of work', in P. Blyton, B. Blunsdon, K. Reed, and A. Dastmalchian (eds) *Work-Life Integration: International Perspectives on the Balancing of Multiple Roles*. Basingstoke: Palgrave Macmillan: 17–27.

Blyton, P. and Jenkins, J. (2007) *Work: Key Concepts*. London: Sage.

Cobble, D.S. (2007) 'Introduction' in Cobble, D.S. (ed.) *The Sex of Class – Women Transforming American Labor*. Ithaca: ILR Press: 1–12.

Cully, M., Woodland, S., O'Reilly, A. and Dix, G. (1999) *Britain at Work: As Depicted by the 1998 Workplace Employment Relations Survey*. London: Routledge.

Daniel, W.W. (1972) *Whatever Happened to the Workers in Woolwich? A Survey of Redundancy in S.E. London*. London: Political and Economic Planning.

Fogarty, M.P. (1945) *Prospects of the Industrial Areas of Great Britain*. London: Methuen & Co.

Francis, H. and Smith, D. (1980) *The Fed: A History of the South Wales Miners in the Twentieth Century*. London: Lawrence and Wishart.

Gardiner, J., Stuart, M., Forde, C., Greenwood, I., McKenzie, R. and Perrett, R. (2007) 'Work–life balance and older workers: employees' perspectives on retirement transitions following redundancy', *International Journal of Human Resource Management*, 18 (3): 476–89.

Hakim, C. (2000) *Work-lifestyle Choices in the Twenty-First Century*. Oxford: Oxford University Press.

Harris, C.C. and Fevre, R. (1987) 'The history of a labour market' in C.C. Harris (ed.) *Redundancy and Recession in South Wales*. Oxford: Basil Blackwell: 44–63.

Heery, E. and Salmon, J. (2000) 'The insecurity thesis', in E. Heery, and J. Salmon (eds) *The Insecure Workforce*. London: Routledge: 1–24.

Hudson, M. (2002) 'Flexibility and the reorganisation of work', in B. Burchell, D. Lapido, and F. Wilkinson, (eds) *Job Insecurity and Work Intensification*. London: Routledge: 39–60.

Kersley, B., Alpin, C., Forth, J., Bryson, A., Bewley, H., Dix, G. and Oxenbridge, S. (2006) *Inside the Workplace: Findings from the 2004 Workplace Employment Relations Survey*. Abingdon: Routledge.

Labour Behind the Label Report (2006) *Let's Clean Up Fashion: The State of Pay Behind the UK High Street, www.cleanupfashion.co.uk*

Lausch, B.A. and Scully, M.A. (2007) 'Restructuring time: implications of work-hours reduction for the working class', *Human Relations*, 60 (5): 719–43.

Lovering, J. (1983) 'Uneven development in Wales: the changing role of the British state', in G. Williams (ed.) *Crisis of Economy and Ideology: Essays on Welsh Society, 1840–1980*. Swansea: B.S.A. Sociology of Wales Study Group.

Minchington, W.E. (ed.) (1969) *Industrial South Wales 1750–1914: Essays in Welsh Economic History*. London: Frank Cass.

Morris, L.D. (1987) 'The household in the labour market', in C.C. Harris (ed.) *Redundancy and Recession in South Wales*. Oxford: Basil Blackwell: 127–40.

Munck, R. (2002) *Globalisation and Labour: The New 'Great Transformation'*. London: Zed Books.

Munday, M. (2003) 'Wales today', *Welsh Economic Review*, 15 (2): 5–6.

Noon, M. and Blyton, P. (2007) *The Realities of Work*, 3rd Edition. Basingstoke: Palgrave Macmillan.

Phizacklea, A. (1990) *Unpacking the Fashion Industry: Gender, Racism and Class in Production*. London: Routledge.

Trades Union Congress (TUC) (2008) *Hard Work, Hidden Lives: The Short Report of the Commission on Vulnerable Employment*. London: TUC.(www.vulnerableworkers.org.uk)

Turnbull, P. and Wass, V. (2000) 'Redundancy and the paradox of job insecurity' in E. Heery and J. Salmon (eds), *The Insecure Workforce*. London: Routledge: 57–77.

Walsh, J. (2007) 'Experiencing part-time work: temporal tensions, social relations and the work-family interface', *British Journal of Industrial Relations*, 45 (1): 155–77.

Warr, P. (1987) *Work, Unemployment and Mental Health*. Oxford: Oxford University Press.

Warren, T. (2004) 'Working part-time: achieving a successful "work-life" balance?', *British Journal of Sociology*, 55 (1): 99–122.

Warren, T., Fox, E. and Pascall, G. (2009) 'Innovative social policies: implications for work-life balance among low-waged women in England', *Gender, Work and Organization*, 16 (1): 126–50.

Wass, V.J. (1988) 'Redundancy and re-employment: effects and prospects following colliery closure,' *Coalfield Communities Campaign Working Papers*, 5: 3–23.

Williams, L.J. (1973) 'The road to Tonypandy,' *Llafur The Journal of the Society for the Study of Welsh Labour History*, Facsimile Edition (1983) 1 (1–4): 41–52.
Winterton, J. and. Winterton, R. (1997) 'Deregulation, division and decline: the UK clothing industry in transition' in I.M. Taplin and J. Winterton (eds) *Rethinking Global Production – A comparative analysis of restructuring in the clothing industry*, Aldershot: Ashgate: 18–40.

Part III

Work and Organisations

10

What Do (And Don't) We Know About Part-Time Professional Work?

Vivien Corwin

Introduction

As the chapters in this collection demonstrate, people are living and working in ways that are far richer and more varied than any single scholarly model can capture. And as organisations and employees alike tinker with (or in some cases recraft entirely) how, when, and where work is done, management scholars are realising that we need new frameworks for explaining and understanding the role and meaning of work (and our attachment to work organisations) (cf. Ashford et al., 2007). The focus of this particular chapter is *part-time work*, and more specifically still, managerial and professional part-time employees. As the literature review which follows will show, this is a group of employees with particular characteristics that differentiate them both from other nontraditional professional workers (such as contractors or teleworkers) and from other groups of part-time employees (classified in the literature as 'earners', rather than 'career workers'). The underlying argument is that the part-time professional employee is a socially constructed category, rather than a descriptively demographic one, and can be best understood with reference to both broad institutional logics and local organistional efforts to enact its meaning. What follows is an overview of the literature in this area, a discussion of some of the general themes or questions which continue to be raised about the meaning, enactment, and sustainability of a part-time professional working arrangement, and some discussion of future research directions to address these questions. Consistent with the broader thrust of this book – that individual decisions are shaped by social contexts and by patterns of paid work – an overview of the current research around this topic demonstrates that the 'choice' to work part-time can be positioned squarely within the broader contexts of identity (both professional and 'extra-professional'), symbolism and shared meaning, organisational culture, and local organisational politics. While managers and professionals would, on the face of it, appear to be in an ideal position to construct a lifestyle that reflects their preferences, the reality is that they face a variety of constraints which end up shaping their lifestyle choices.

What do we think we know about part-time professional work: a research overview

Part-time work

Part-time work has been around for long enough that it doesn't *seem*, on the face of it, to represent a particularly novel category of work, or to pose a distinctive challenge to conventional understandings about what work could (or should) look like. Researchers have been studying the topic for several decades (cf. Rotchford and Roberts, 1982; Feldman, 1990; Tilly, 1991, 1996; Kahne, 1985) and part-time workers are now well represented in the workforce. The European Union has taken the lead in promoting legislation around the rights of part-time workers to ensure that part-time workers are afforded the same rights and opportunities as full-time workers (Cousins and Tang, 2004). In the Netherlands, 71 per cent of female employees work part-time (Cousins and Tang, 2004), with female part-time employment estimated to be in the range of 37–44 per cent in the U.K. (Cousins and Tang, 2004; Bonney, 2005). In North America, roughly 20 per cent of the labour force works part-time (Caputo and Cianni, 2001; Nardone, 1995; Tilly, 1996), Nor is part-time work solely confined to hourly wage earners: in the U.K. in 2002, an estimated 13 per cent of employees in managerial, professional, and associated professional and technical roles worked part-time (Dick, 2004), while roughly 10 per cent of the professional labour force in the U.S. and Canada works a reduced schedule (Corwin et al., 2001). And organisations have made hay of implementing flexible work practices which demonstrate a willingness to accommodate work-family balance (cf. Hochschild, 1997; Fleetwood, 2007), to the point that the number of organisations with family-friendly policies has been interpreted as evidence that employees may increasingly consider it to be an implicit aspect of their psychological contract with their organisation (Dick, 2006).

All of that said, a review of the literature raises some interesting challenges to this notion that the meaning and implications of part-time work are shared and clearly understood by either academics or practitioners. Research in the area of part-time work has tended to distinguish between good and bad part-time jobs on the basis of whether the part-timer's status puts them at a disadvantage in comparison to their full-time counterparts (Broschak et al., 2008; Tilly, 1991; Kahne, 1985). Retention part-time workers (who tend to be part-time of their own volition) often expect that they will continue to have long-term employment with their organisation, along with continued benefits and promotion opportunities. Other part-time workers, who may not be part-time by choice, are more vulnerable to limited opportunities and precarious employment: a significant percentage of part-time work continues to be performed by workers with low skill, low educational qualifications, and little employment security (Cousins and Tang, 2004). Research into these 'bad' (or secondary) part-time jobs has approached the topic from different angles. A significant area of research has explored the broad question of whether the limited career prospects of part-time workers can be explained by their own preferences (cf. Hakim, 1991, 1998) or are better explained by structural inequities built into the design and use of a part-time workforce more generally (cf. Clinebell and Clinebell, 2007; Lane, 2004; Nadeem and Hendry, 2003; Walters, 2005). Cross-national studies have focused on the broader cultural context around part-time work, and the extent to which the presence or absence of child care provisions, parental leave measures, and employment protection at the legislative level can explain employment patterns and the choices (or lack of choices) available to part-time workers (cf. Cousins and Tang, 2004; Callan, 2007; McGinnity and McManus, 2007). Work is beginning to address the tension between the desire for organisational or personal flexibility (which can lead to an increased use of part-time workers) and the desire to engage employees at all levels and the demand for service and innovation from even part-time, hourly employees. Felstead and Gallie (2004), for example, have looked at the ways in which high involvement workplaces can mitigate the negative impact of part-time work on skills, training and job security. But as Fleetwood (2007) highlights, a close look at 'flexibility' indicates that organisations are still more likely to offer (and employees more likely to participate in) flexible work arrangements which accommodate the organisation's desire to manage workload, rather than those that meet the employee's demands for work-life balance. So, for example, despite the rise in flextime work (through which employees can balance work and family demands), we still see policies such as involuntary part-time work, unsocial hours, and 24–7 rotations dominating 'flexible' work practices for employees in 'earner' (as opposed to 'career') jobs (Fleetwood, 2007).

Part-time professionals

In comparison with those in 'bad' part-time jobs, part-time professionals and managers occupy a privileged position: these tend to be 'new concept' part-time work arrangements, crafted as a way of attracting and retaining valued employees who are unable or unwilling to work a full-time schedule (Kahne, 1985; Broschak et al., 2008). However, the fact that their job security is relatively guaranteed does not mean that part-time professionals and managers can shift naturally and easily from a full-time to a part-time work schedule without consequence. Research into the long term success or failure of part-time work arrangements for managers and professionals has been highly equivocal. For example, Lee and Kossek (2004) have argued that the part-time professionals in their longitudinal sample enjoyed good benefits, job security, opportunities for promotion, and pay comparable to that of their full-time coworkers. However, other research has found the opposite: that despite ambitious promises, part-time professional work arrangements enjoy little local management support, and are viewed by professionals themselves as being unworkable and career-limiting (cf. Dick, 2004).

These equivocal research findings can be explained in part by the level at which research focuses on the notion of part-time professional work, and by the way that they define 'professionals.' It is common for researchers to treat 'part-time managers and professionals' as one broad social category, without offering a clear rationale for why these groups are lumped together, or how inclusive the definition of either 'manager' or 'professional' is meant to be. On the one hand, this categorisation is a reasonable one: both managers and professionals tend to have significant autonomy and control over their work, allowing them a measure of power to ask for, and benefit from, part-time opportunities that would not be available to lower-level employees. On the other hand, however, the categorisation is very broad, and leaves open legitimate questions about the terms of membership. Are semi-professions such as school teachers included? Can (or should) all professionals be assumed to handle the notion of part-time professional work similarly? For example, researchers have discovered that certain professions – general medicine, for example, and teaching – are regarded as offering better opportunities for professionals wanting to enact and sustain a truly part-time schedule, and to do so in such a way as not to be seen as marginalising themselves within the profession (cf. Briscoe, 2006). Further research into this area could benefit from closer study of the literature on professionals, and particularly of the structuration of professional role identities (cf. Chreim et al., 2007) and professional fields (cf. Lawrence, 2004). A central idea here is that '[m]embership is a particularly critical issue in professional fields, where the importance of boundaries between members and non-members stems not only from their role as guides to action and identity, but also from their economic implications. The rules that demarcate membership in such fields as law, medicine and accounting are typically oriented around bodies of specialized knowledge that are often safeguarded formally by universities and professional associations and informally by culturally entrenched understandings of the meaning of professional work (Abbott, 1988)' (Lawrence, 2004: 116). Further research at the institutional level could shed useful light on the processes through which part-time professional identities have been enacted and rendered legitimate (or illegitimate) in specific professional and organisational contexts.

In their research into over-employment, Van Echtelt et al. (2006) attempted to answer the question of why most Europeans work more hours than they say they would like to. Their argument is that despite legislated efforts to allow workers more of an opportunity to achieve work-life balance by limiting their hours of work, features of 'post-Fordist' job designs make work particularly 'time-greedy,' and that these work designs are likely to be particularly disadvantageous to those employees who choose to limit the time they formally commit to their employer by shifting to a part-time schedule. Their central argument is that, asked directly, many professionals might state that they would prefer to work less and have more time available for leisure or family. Faced with small, daily decisions about how to spend their time and whether to continue working on a particular task, however, they are more likely to frame the issue as 'shall I stay late to finish this project, or risk being seen as uncommitted to my work and to my colleagues?' The result, argue Van Echtelt et al. (2006), is that the cumulative effect of small decisions works directly against the employee's desire for more time to spend at leisure. And this challenge is especially pronounced in job designs where 'responsibility for attaining production goals is further shifted to the worker... Organizing occupations in this way is characterized on the one hand by much autonomy for the employee and by interesting tasks. The job does not need to be performed at fixed hours and locations and the employee can decide where and when to work. On the other hand, job security depends more heavily on performance than before and predictable career paths give way to more uncertain and competitive promotion systems (Arthur and Rousseau, 1996)....We expect that this form of work organization shifts the focus of the employee from working a certain number of hours, to bringing a project to a good end or finishing a particular task before the deadline' (Van Echtelt et al., 2006: 496).

It is worth noting that the Van Echtelt et al. (2006) study was of the Dutch labour market, which has made particular efforts to allow employees more control over the amount of time they spend at work. That setting clear limits around one's availability for and time spent at work is a challenge for Dutch professionals suggests that the challenge is likely to be still greater in contexts such as the United States and Britain, where there is less broad cultural and institutional support for the legitimacy of part-time professional work.

The importance of the local work context

While acknowledging the broader institutional and cultural contexts within which part-time professionals are embedded, it's also important to address the primary significance of the local context. The practical implications of professionals working a reduced schedule are most easily observed at the work-group level, highlighting the salience of local organisational contexts in explaining the successful creation and maintenance of part-time work arrangements (cf. Lawrence and Corwin, 2003; Van Dyne et al., 2007). Broschak and Davis-Blake (2006) argue that 'employment arrangements (standard or nonstandard) are observable and salient characteristics of workers' (p.372), and suggest that the composition of heterogeneous work groups (mixing standard and nonstandard employees) highlights differences and potential conflicts around group or organisational status, mobility opportunities, and the allocation of tasks. Consistent with Rousseau et al.'s work on idiosyncratic employment arrangements (Rousseau, 2001, 2005; Rousseau et al., 2006), Broschak and Davis-Blake (2006) caution that the construction of nonstandard work arrangements to retain valued employees may lead to negative work group relations, perceptions of inequity, and job dissatisfaction.

In particular, by virtue of their absence from the organisation for chunks of the 'standard' work week, part-time professionals represent a challenge to 'normal' ways of working, to the cultural rhythms of the organisation, and to commonly shared understandings about what constitutes a 'professional' employee (Corwin et al., 2001; Lawrence and Corwin, 2003; Dick and Hyde, 2006; Van Dyne et al., 2007).

Research at this level has explored strategies through which successful part-time professionals and those they work with in their local context are able to create and manage a reduced work load (cf. Corwin et al., 2001; Lawrence and Corwin, 2003; Dick, 2004, 2006; Van Dyne et al., 2007). For example, Corwin et al. (2001) emphasise that successful part-time professionals need to manage how the work is done (either through more efficient work practices on the part of the professional themselves, or through efforts to manage and coordinate the work of others), how the part-time arrangement is perceived by others (is it seen as fair and equitable?), their own position within organisational networks (to avoid being isolated or discounted as a result of their absence), and the boundary between work and non-work (whether it be to facilitate the integration of work and non-work, or to ensure that the boundary between the two remains clear). Lawrence and Corwin (2003) argue that organisational culture is enacted through the ongoing rituals of its members, and that membership is in turn negotiated through participation in these cultural rituals. Moving to a reduced work schedule will, of necessity, mean that the part-time professional is excluded from interaction rituals (in the form of, for example, meetings, social gatherings, or casual conversation in the hallways). The extent to which the part time professional (or their manager or work group) is able to compensate for their absence, strategically participate in key events, or enact new rituals through which to recognize and celebrate organisational membership, will go a long way to determining the success of the part-time professional arrangement, and the satisfaction of affected others (Lawrence and Corwin, 2003). Van Dyne et al. (2007) pick up on this work, suggesting that successful flexible work arrangements can be facilitated by group-level work practices that focus less on 'face time' and more on 'event time,' and by the part-time professional themselves demonstrating both a proactive availability for work as needed, and an ongoing commitment to the needs and objectives of the work group itself.

It is important to note here that conditions at the work group level may be fundamentally at odds with the policies espoused at the more macro levels of the organisation or the government. In her research into part-time work within the British police force, for example, Dick (2004, 2006) has found that legislative-level commitment to increased flexibility within the police does not translate automatically into more flexible work practices (or the adoption of more flexible work schedules) at the local level. Despite efforts from the Home Office to increase the adoption of part-time work within policing, Dick found confusion at the operational level about how (and whether) part-time policing could be implemented. A major challenge was that policing has traditionally demanded a different kind of flexibility from its members, namely 'being prepared to stay behind after a shift has finished so as to complete a task; being prepared to come back to work at short notice or work extra shifts; and being on-call for 24 hours… Police managers resource what is essentially a "demand-led" job' (Dick, 2004: 312). Dick found that managers of part-time officers were confused about the extent to which they could demand this kind of traditional flexibility from their part-time workers, without violating Home Office directives. Police managers also spoke of being frustrated about having to adopt a 'kid glove' approach with part-time officers, where they were used to a more command-and-control type style (Dick, 2004).

The concerns of these police managers echo those found in Callan's (2007) research on the extent to which an organisation's culture results from or hinders the implementation of family-friendly policies. Like Dick, Callan found that, while an organisation might have developed company-wide policies, their effectiveness ultimately came 'down to the managers' and how they used them. Managers in turn felt somewhat constrained by the policies, usually in the sense that policy provision was too generous if fully implemented and that it could hinder their ability to deliver against demanding targets' (Callan, 2007: 679). And in their study of part-time policing within the Australian police force, Charlesworth and Whittenbury (2007) argue that the challenge in police service is to address both institutional and cultural barriers to the use of a part-time police force.

Dick (2004) explains the gulf between organisational-level policies, managerial interpretations of and reactions to those policies, and the part-time professional's *own* reading of flexibility as an example of competing discourses. She argues that 'managers' perspectives on part-time working are frequently produced through a discourse in which flexibility is defined in terms of the organization's needs and wants, whereas part-timers' perspectives are produced through a discourse in which flexibility is defined as meeting the individual's needs and wants' (Dick, 2004: 315). The part-timers' interpretation, she suggests, is reinforced by institutional-level dynamics, such as the increased attention to work-family balance in organisational discourses, and the increased availability of programmes which offer the possibility (even if it is only a possibility) of working to a schedule which offers increased flexibility.

Perceptions about the 'usability' of part-time work arrangements

Another key theme in the part-time literature is the perceived usability of part-time work arrangements. Following Hochschild (1997) and Bailyn (1993), Eaton (2003) argues that flexible work practices *can* lead to increased productivity and commitment, but only if professionals feel that they can adopt these flexible work schedules without facing stigmatisation or suffering adverse organisational consequences. Similarly, Johnson et al. (2006) reference a 2006 American Institute of Certified Public Accountants (AICPA) survey which found that '47% of females and 34% of males working at the staff level in large national and international firms believed that adopting an AWA [alternative work arrangement] after parental leave would have a negative career impact' (Johnson et al., 2006: 49). Johnson and his colleagues developed an experimental design aimed at assessing the extent to which experienced accounting firm managers and partners were predisposed to negatively assess the performance and potential of professionals adopting alternative work arrangements, and found that both part-time work arrangements *and* flexible work arrangements were associated with more negative attributions about the professional's prospects, with a 'reduction in working hours to accommodate other responsibilities...viewed more negatively than a flexible work arrangement with no reduction in work hours' (Johnson et al., 2006: 65).

Making the job and the role part-time

Successful part-time professional work arrangements are, of course, possible, but the above research indicates that they are not a given, even in a broader organisational or institutional environment which appears sympathetic to part-time professional work schedules. The argument to this point has been that the local work context matters: that the predispositions of managers, the perceptions of coworkers, and the nature and sheer amount of the work to be performed all need to be taken into consideration when constructing a part-time professional work arrangement. Beyond these factors, however, is a parallel necessity: to come to terms with questions about one's identity as a part-time professional. The first set of concerns can be broadly classified as issues of making the job part-time; questions of identity invite discussion about what it means to make the *role* part-time. Both issues have been considered in the literature, and will be reviewed here.

In a recent Harvard Management Update entitled 'Making Flexible Schedules Work – For Everyone,' Kossek et al. (2007) offer the following advice to managers: 'You know your employee. Has he demonstrated the drive, adaptability, and commitment that suggest he will be able to perform effectively on a reduced-load schedule?' (p. 1). The authors go on to suggest that, before giving the go-ahead to a professional wanting to drop down to a part-time schedule, managers consider whether some of the duties of the job can be shared (or eliminated), and ways in which the part-time arrangement might be advantageous for the work group (by, for example, affording opportunities for cross-training or more collaborative work) (Kossek et al., 2007). These recommendations echo tactics employed by the successful part-time professionals in Corwin et al.'s (2001) study, who spoke of taking an active role in managing how others worked so as to use their time at work as efficiently as possible, and framing their move to a part-time schedule as an opportunity to develop the leadership capacity of their subordinates. In their interviews with part-time professionals and managers, Lee and Kossek (2004) found that part-timers stressed the importance of maintaining a manageable workload, while at the same time being sure to have some key clients. And Eaton (2003) found that control over time, flexibility, and the pace of work were important prerequisites for the successful use of flexible work arrangements. This can be challenging for professional work, which is typically characterised by task ambiguity, control over critical information, and organisational uncertainty (Abbot, 1991; Lawrence and Corwin, 2003). However, when conditions allow it, making the *job* part-time can be done without significant impact on productivity: Corwin et al. quote a manager of two part-time engineers as saying 'We probably get as much productivity out of our part-time professionals as we do from some of the employees who are here five days a week' (Corwin et al., 2001: 124).

Making the professional *role* part-time can pose more of a challenge. Lawrence and Corwin (2003) review the literature on work time and the professional employee to make the argument that the autonomy that professionals have over their working time comes at a price: the line between work and home becomes increasingly blurred, as professionals are expected to be 'ever-available' for work (cf. Perlow, 1997, 1999). These expectations are reinforced through the formal education associated with obtaining professional status, and strengthened further through performance evaluation systems and bonus schemes which tend to equate commitment to one's job with time spent at work. In her research into the implications of organisational culture on work-life balance programmes (and the effects of those programmes on culture), Callan (2007) explains the ongoing power of the 'ideal worker type': a shared perception that the ideal worker is one who is always available for work, and who demonstrates their commitment through time spent at work in the organisation. Adopting a reduced work schedule, she argues, is often seen as going against this ideal.

The decision to shift to part-time status, then, marks a dramatic break from professional and (sometimes tacit) organisational expectations, which helps to explain why, for example, research has found that professionals were more likely to take advantage of policies which made it easier for them to spend time and energy at work than they were to take up policies which allowed them to work less or to work from a distance (cf. Bailyn, 1993; Callan, 2007; Hochschild, 1997). Mason and Ekman (2007) demonstrate the practical implications of this fact in their discussion of the use of part-time work arrangements in U.S. law firms:

> Ninety-five percent of US law firms offer part-time employment but only 3.5 percent of lawyers take advantage of it. Out of that small percentage, 4.8 percent are associates while 2.8 percent are partners. Some studies have observed that lawyers who use part-time programs feel stigmatized, and that full-time attorneys would rather leave their firms than reduce their schedules because of this perception that part-time programs are not effective. One national study indicates that men rarely go part-time, and of the lawyers who do take advantage of part-time lawyering, the majority, if not all, are probably young mothers. (Mason and Ekman, 2007: 80)

Where professionals *do* adopt reduced schedules in larger numbers, it tends to be in professions (or segments of a profession) that have been deemed 'family-friendly' (read 'where there are a disproportionate number of female professionals'). For example, Mason and Ekman quote a Commonwealth Fund survey which 'found that twenty five percent of female doctors reported working fewer than forty hours per week, compared to 12 percent of male doctors. That trend is most pronounced among younger doctors; on average female doctors work 9 percent fewer hours than male doctors, but among those under forty-five, the number surges to 15 percent' (Mason and Ekman, 2007: 72). The female doctors enjoying these more flexible work arrangements are concentrated primarily in family medicine – what Mason and Ekman term the 'second tier' of medicine – rather than in the surgical specialties, which enjoy more prestige but which continue to demand more from their professionals in terms of time spent at work.

The point of the discussion above is not that there cannot or will not be part-time professionals in *most* professional contexts, but rather that part-time work has been institutionalised for professionals in some sectors significantly more than others. This means that part-time professionals often find themselves going it alone in their organisations: the institutional and managerial support that they might expect for their decision to work a reduced load simply isn't there (Corwin et al., 2001). And if they are able to craft an arrangement that works for them and for their managers and coworkers, there is still the broader question of what it *means* to work part-time. For example, Mason and Ekman posit that professionals who 'drop' to the second tier of their profession are likely to *stay* on that second tier, and argue that, while for some women this second tier represents a positive way of achieving work-life balance, for too many others it reflects the fact that organisations are not designed to allow women to navigate a path to the top while still juggling family responsibilities and their own desires for balance. In contrast to this argument, Susan Pinker's recent (2008) book, *The Sexual Paradox*, makes the argument that many women simply choose to define success in other than conventional, hierarchical terms. This argument is summarised nicely in a quotation from a young female doctor (ironically, quoted in Mason and Ekman's book) who positions her decision to work part-time as being a reflection of her desire to define success in her own terms: 'Most choices I made about my career, in terms of part-time and being a family doctor, had less to do with family and more to do with having a life outside of work. I want to do other things with my life' (Mason and Ekman, 2007: 73).

Research into part-time professional workers suggest that the opportunity to have a life outside of work (and outside of family obligations) may be a significant by-product (even if it wasn't the motivating factor) of part-time work arrangements. In their study of data from a subset of the 1996 U.S. IBM Work and Life Issues Survey, Hill et al. found that professionals and managers working part-time reported greater work-life balance than did their full-time counterparts, and that they used their part-time schedule *not* for child care or household chores, but for 'individual activities that might reduce stress, such as additional sleep, recreation, and other renewal activities' (Hill et al., 2004: 131).

Yet while a part-time schedule offers professionals the *opportunity* for increased work-life balance, it also requires wrestling with cultural, organisational and institutional assumptions around what it means to be a professional. For example, Higgins et al. (2000) looked at the implications of part-time work arrangements for two groups of female workers: managers and professionals, and those in 'earner' positions (their classification for technical, clerical, administrative, retail and production jobs). Their study found that part-time schedules had positive benefits for both groups when it came to work-to-family interference, time management, and overall life satisfaction, but that the part-time arrangement did not help career women manage role overload, family-to-work interference, or family time management (Higgins et al., 2000). The authors conclude that women in earner positions benefit more from part-time schedules than do professionals and managers, and suggest that when it comes to professionals, '[i]t may not be enough to simply make part-time work available. *In order to truly make a difference in the quality of life for women with children, part-time work must also be made desirable and rewarding*' (Higgins et al., 2000: 29, emphasis in original).

Dick and Hyde (2006) come to the same conclusion from a more critical perspective, arguing that 'professional women experience greater problems in achieving ontological security than women in lower status roles, primarily because the latter group are not troubled to the same extent by contradictory discourses targeted at their identities ... professional women are motivated to retain their professional identity in a context where their decision to work reduced hours can be constructed as a sign of their lack of commitment, a direct challenge to the ideology of professionalism (Dick and Hyde, 2006: 558). So while part-time work for non-professional workers may constitute a change in when the work is done, part-time schedules for professionals seem to pose a more significant challenge to the very idea of what the professional *is*. If institutionalised expectations are that professionals be ever-available for work, and define themselves in terms of their profession, then what does it mean to put strict limits around one's availability? To what extent does the choice to cut back on one's work signal a general weakening of one's professional identity? Implicit to this discussion is the notion that the choice to work less is also the 'choice' to define one's own professional identity differently, and that this choice opens up questions for both the professional themselves and their coworkers about how commitment and professionalism are to be enacted and negotiated under this new arrangement.

Finally, just as there are competing narratives around what career success does or should look like, and what it does (or should) mean to be a professional, so are there competing narratives around motherhood and family life. Part-time work for professionals is still strongly equated with balancing the desire for ongoing professional work against the competing demands of child or elder care, which come with their own set of institutionalised expectations. Just as a professional who moves to a part-time schedule must wrestle with the question of what it now means to be professional, so must the part-time professional who is balancing work and child care struggle with the question of how they are defining themselves as a mother. So Dick and Hyde (2006: 555–6) make the argument that, 'in positioning themselves within discourses of professionalism and of motherhood, women can be understood as subjectively resisting (as well as consenting to), some of the central norms of each, in the process creating new truths and knowledge, and thereby constituting new relations of power.' They suggest that part-time professionals challenge both the notion that professionals *need to be* available for work at all times, *and* the notion that 'good mothering' should be equated with constant presenteeism.

Conclusion

This brief overview of recent research has brought to the surface a number of issues and themes which lend support to the notion that part-time professional work is, in fact, still nonstandard, from the perspectives of both scholarship and organisational practice. Moving forward, we can look to Ashford et al.'s (2007) recommendations and see parallels for recommendations with regard to the study of part-time work for professionals.

First, Ashford et al. (2007) recommend that future research into nonstandard work should take a longitudinal perspective, and the same recommendation applies here. Past research has positioned the part-time professional work arrangement as idiosyncratic and enacted at local group levels, with the conclusion that successful part-time professionals tend to be grateful to their organisations for the opportunity to work part-time, and prepared to demonstrate their commitment through considerable behind-the-scenes effort to make the arrangement work (Broschak et al., 2008; Lawrence and Corwin, 2003). What's less clear is how these part-time arrangements are viewed over time: does the gratitude last, and how are the arrangements recrafted as time goes on? Research that takes a longitudinal perspective, and is sensitive to the social and cultural contexts influencing the part-time professional work arrangement, could make a valuable contribution here, and could also help to shed light on why it is that different sets of researchers have reached very different conclusions about the ongoing desirability and viability of part-time professional work (cf. Dick, 2004; Lee and Kossek, 2004).

Ashford et al. (2007) also speak to the need for more theory-driven research into nonstandard work arrangements, suggesting that '[h]igh status, high income nonstandard workers, with their higher levels of power, would be an ideal sample to study the concept of "i-deals" (individualized negotiated agreements about work arrangements)' (p. 99). Part-time professionals fall neatly into this category, and while there has already been work done in this area (cf. Lawrence and Corwin, 2003; Van Dyne et al., 2007), it could certainly bear further investigation.

Finally, another fruitful theoretical approach is suggested by Maitlis and Lawrence's (2007) recent work on sensegiving in organisations. Sensegiving represents the efforts by organisational actors to shape the way that others in the organisation interpret, or make sense, of organisational life. Sensegiving is strongly associated with leadership (in the sense that a key responsibility of leaders is to help followers manage meaning within organisations). However, Maitlis and Lawrence argue that sensegiving can be performed by organisational actors at any level of the organisation, *and* that leaders frequently fail to help followers make sense of organisational life, even in cases where the meaning of events or activities is uncertain and equivocal. They suggest that these gaps in organisational sensemaking processes allow opportunities for sensegiving on the part of leaders or other stakeholders. Maitlis and Lawrence argue that these other stakeholders will be motivated to engage in sensegiving to the extent that they perceive an issue to be important to them (or to the organisation more broadly), that they perceive themselves to possess relevant expertise around the issue, and to the extent that they are afforded opportunities to engage in sensegiving (be it through regular or ad hoc meetings, or the solicitation of their views). A reading of the recent research into part-time work suggests that this situation frequently describes the circumstances in which part-time professionals find themselves: while there may be formal policies in place which allow a professional to move to a part time schedule, there is no shared understanding of what this move to part-time status *means* (for the professional themselves, or for their colleagues or work teams). Organisational-level policies may provide general guidance, but it tends to fall to the part-timer and those they work with to negotiate what the particular part-time arrangement will look like, and these negotiations are conducted in a context of mixed institutional and cultural messages about the 'meaning' of part-time professional work. Previous research suggests that successful part-time professionals enact deliberate strategies for managing how and when they do their work, as well as how they frame both their time spent at work and their time spent away from work, to encourage a positive shared interpretation of the sustainability of their work arrangements and their ongoing professional identity (cf. Corwin et al., 2001; Lawrence amd Corwin, 2003). Sensegiving offers a promising lens through which to continue to explore this process in future research.

This chapter began by questioning the notion that professionals who choose to move to a part-time schedule are well positioned to construct for themselves lifestyles which meet their preferences. This scan of the literature suggests that, indeed, professionals are frequently in the enviable position of moving to part-time status voluntarily, with the espoused commitment of their organisations to work with them to produce sustainable part-time arrangements that will allow those involved continued career mobility and interesting work. However, the shift to part-time brings with it also a variety of questions around the implications for professional role identity, ongoing relationships with colleagues, status within the work group, and impact on power and status, which demonstrate the extent to which the part-time professional's 'choices' are clearly embedded within a broader web of local, organisational, and institutional understandings.

References

Abbott, A. (1991) 'The order of professionalization: an empirical analysis', *Work and Occupations,* 18 (4): 355–84.

Ashford, S., George, E. and Blatt, R. (2007) 'Old assumptions, new work: the opportunities and challenges of research on nonstandard employment', *The Academy of Management Annals,* 1 (1): 65–117.

Bailyn, L. (1993) *Breaking the Mold.* New York: Free Press.

Bonney, N. (2005) 'Overworked Britons? Part-time work and work-life balance', *Work, Employment & Society,* 19 (2): 391–401.

Briscoe, F. (2006) 'Temporal flexibility and careers: the role of large-scale organizations for physicians,' *Industrial and Labor Relations Review,* 60 (1): 88–104.

Broschak, J. and Davis-Blake, A. (2006) 'Mixing standard work and nonstandard deals: the consequences of heterogeneity in employment relationships,' *Academy of Management Journal,* 49 (2): 371–93.

Broschak, J., Davis-Blake, A. and Block, E. (2008) 'Nonstandard, not substandard: The relationship among work arrangements, work attitudes, and job performance', *Work and Occupations,* 35 (1): 3–43.

Callan, S. (2007) 'Implications of family-friendly policies for organizational culture: findings from two case studies', *Work, Employment & Society,* 21 (4): 673–91.

Caputo, R., and Cianni, M. (2001) 'Correlates of voluntary versus involuntary part-time employment among U.S. women', *Gender, Work and Organization,* 8 (3): 311–25.

Charlesworth, S., and Whittenbury, K. (2007) '"Part-time and part-committed?": The challenges of part-time work in policing', *Journal of Industrial Relations*, 49 (1): 31–47.

Chreim, S., Williams, B., and Hinings, C.R. (2007) 'Interlevel influences on the reconstruction of professional role identity', *Academy of Management Journal*, 50 (6): 1515–39.

Clinebell, S. and Clinebell, J. (2007) 'Differences between part-time and full-time employees in the financial services industry', *Journal of Leadership and Organizational Studies*, 14 (2): 157–67.

Corwin, V., Lawrence, T. and Frost, P. (2001) 'Five strategies of successful part-time work', *Harvard Business Review*, 79 (7): 121–7.

Cousins, C. and Tang, N. (2004) 'Working time and work and family conflict in the Netherlands, Sweden and the U.K.', *Work, Employment & Society*, 18 (3): 531–49.

Dick, P. (2004) 'Between a rock and a hard place: The dilemmas of managing part-time working in the police service', *Personnel Review*, 33 (3): 302–21.

Dick, P. (2006) 'The psychological contract and the transition from full to part-time police work', *Journal of Organizational Behavior*, 27 (1): 37–58.

Dick, P. and Hyde, R. (2006) 'Consent as resistance, resistance as consent: re-reading part-time professionals' acceptance of their marginal positions', *Gender, Work & Organization*, 13 (6): 543–64.

Eaton, S. (2003) 'If you can use them: flexibility policies, organizational commitment, and perceived performance', *Industrial Relations*, 42 (2): 145–67.

Feldman, D. (1990) 'Reconceptualizing the nature and consequences of part-time work', *Academy of Management Review*, 15 (1), 103–12.

Felstead, A. and Gallie, D. (2004) 'For better or worse? Non-standard jobs and high involvement work systems', *International Journal of Human Resource Management*, 15 (7): 1293–316.

Fleetwood, S. (2007) 'Why work-life balance now?' *International Journal of Human Resource Management*, 18 (3): 387–400.

Hakim, C. (1991) 'Grateful slaves and self-made women: fact and fantasy in women's work orientations', *European Sociological Review*, 7 (3): 101–21.

Hakim, C. (1998) 'Developing a sociology for the twenty-first century: preference theory', *British Journal of Sociology*, 49 (1): 137–43.

Higgins, C., Duxbury, L. and Johnson, K. (2000) 'Part-time work for women: does it really help balance work and family?' *Human Resource Management*, 39 (1): 17–32.

Hill, J., Martinson, V., Ferris, M. and Baker, R. (2004) 'Beyond the mommy track: the influence of new-concept part-time work for professional women on work and family', *Journal of Family and Economic Issues*, 25 (1): 121–36.

Hochschild, A. (1997) *The Time Bind*. New York: Henry Holt.

Hoque, K. and Kirkpatrick, I. (2003) 'Non-standard employment in the management and professional workforce: training, consultation and gender implications', *Work, Employment & Society*, 17 (4): 667–89.

Johnson, E., Lowe, J. and Reckers, P. (2006) 'Alternative work arrangements and perceived career success: current evidence from the big four firms in the U.S.', *Accounting, Organizations and Society*, 33 (1):48–72.

Kahne, H. (1985) *Reconceiving Part-Time Work*. Totawa, NJ: Rowman & Allanheld.

Kossek, E., Lee, M. and Hall, D. (2007) 'Making flexible schedules work – for everyone', *Harvard Management Update*, May 2007.

Lane, N. (2004) 'Women and part-time work: the careers of part-time NHS nurses', *British Journal of Management,* 15 (3): 259–72.
Lawrence, T. (2004) 'Rituals and resistance: membership dynamics in professional fields', *Human Relations,* 57 (2): 115–43.
Lawrence, T. and Corwin, V. (2003) 'Being there: the acceptance and marginalization of part-time professional employees', *Journal of Organizational Behavior,* 24 (8): 923–43.
Lee, M. and Kossek, E. (2004) 'Crafting lives that work: a six year retrospective on reduced-load work in the careers and lives of professionals and managers', *Alfred P. Sloan Foundation Study Feedback Report.*
Maitlis, S. and Lawrence, T. (2007) 'Triggers and enablers of sensegiving in organizations', *Academy of Management Journal,* 50 (1): 57–84.
Mason, M. and Ekman, E. (2007) *Mothers on the Fast Track: How a New Generation can Balance Family and Careers.* Oxford: Oxford University Press.
McGinnity, F. and McManus, P. (2007) 'Paying the price for reconciling work and family life: comparing the wage penalty for women's part-time work in Britain, Germany, and the United States', *Journal of Comparative Policy Analysis,* 9 (2): 115–34.
Nadeem, S. and Hendry, C. (2003) 'Power dynamics in the long-term development of employee-friendly flexible working', *Women in Management Review,* 18 (1/2): 32–49.
Nardone, T. (1995) 'Part-time employment: reasons, demographics and trends', *Journal of Labor Research,* 16 (3): 275–92.
Perlow, L. (1997) *Finding Time: How Corporations, Individuals and Families Can Benefit from New Work Practices.* Ithaca, NY: Cornell University Press.
Perlow, L. (1999) 'The time famine: toward a sociology of work time', *Administrative Science Quarterly,* 44 (1): 57–81.
Pinker, S. (2008) *The Sexual Paradox: Extreme Men, Gifted Women and the Real Gender Gap.* Toronto: Random House Canada.
Rotchford, N. and Roberts, K. (1982) 'Part-time workers as missing persons in organizational research', *Academy of Management Review,* 7 (2): 228–34.
Rousseau, D. (2001) 'The idiosyncratic deal: flexibility versus fairness?' *Organizational Dynamics,* 29 (4): 260–73.
Rousseau, D. (2005) *I-Deals: Idiosyncratic Deals Employees Bargain for Themselves.* NY: M.E. Sharpe.
Rousseau, D., Greenberg, J. and Ho, V. (2006) 'I-deals: idiosyncratic terms in employment relationships', *Academy of Management Review,* 31 (4): 977–94.
Tilly, C. (1991) 'Reasons for the continuing growth of part-time employment', *Monthly Labor Review,* 114: 10–18.
Tilly, C. (1996) *Half a Job: Bad and Good Part-Time Jobs in a Changing Labor Market.* Philadelphia, PA: Temple University Press.
Van Dyne, L., Kossek, E. and Lobel, S. (2007) 'Less need to be there: cross-level effects of work practices that support work-life flexibility and enhance group processes and group-level OCB', *Human Relations,* 60 (8): 1123–54.
Van Echtelt, P., Glebbeek, A. and Lindenberg, S. (2006) 'The new lumpiness of work: explaining the mismatch between actual and preferred working hours', *Work, Employment & Society,* 20 (3): 493–512.
Walters, S. (2005) 'Making the best of a bad job? Female part-timers' orientations and attitudes to work', *Gender, Work & Organization,* 12 (3): 193–216.

11

Work Values Across Cultures: The Role of Affect and Job Outcomes among Young Executives in Canada, Iran and Turkey

Hayat Kabasakal, Pinar Imer and Ali Dastmalchian

Introduction

This volume is intended to shed light on the issues and challenges associated with lifestyle choices. Lifestyles are patterns of daily life, both within work and outside, characterised by the activities that one spends time on and includes other facets of one's behaviour such as interactions and the implications of these for satisfaction, happiness and well being. The choices people make about how to use their time fundamentally affect the basic dimensions of their lifestyle, as increasing time spent on one activity decreases the time available for other activities. Such choices are likely to have profound implications for organisations in their attempt to attract and retain people and in their search for creating organisational contexts to cope with the changes in their environment, but also to develop their intellectual capital. In this sense, people's work values, mood or affect at work, and the cultural norms within the organisation that guide and support such values, are likely to have an influence on the satisfaction they get from work, their work performance and their choices about ways of living. In addition, in today's 'flat world' (Friedman, 2005) with the global and multi-cultural orientation of organisations, our intention in this chapter is to incorporate national culture in the analysis and examine whether work values, affect, and job satisfaction and performance, and their relationships, vary across cultures.

To understand the attitudes and visible behaviours of individuals at work, one needs to look at their more deeply held 'inner-worlds' (Baron, Byrne and Branscombe, 2006; Hyde and Weathington, 2006). Deep-rooted values and affect influence perceptions, attitudes, behaviours and choices that people make, and play a central role in human life (e.g. Meglino and Ravlin, 1998). Among the work-related attitudes and behaviors, job satisfaction and overall performance are shown to be constructs that are closely associated with employee well-being and quality of work life (Royuela, Lopez-Tamayo and Surinach, 2009). Thus, analyses of deeply-held inner factors and emotions that lead to such positive job outcomes would contribute to understanding and promoting quality of work life. Within this framework, the study reported here aims to examine the role of affect and values on job outcomes in three different cultural settings.

Affect is the phenomenological state of feeling (Thoresen, Kaplan, Barsky, Warren and de Chermont, 2003) and can reflect an individual's feelings at any given point in time (state affect) or express the tendency to have specific affective states over time (dispositional affect), or both (state and dispositional) (Vansteenkiste, Neyrinck, Niemiec, Soenens, Witte and Van den Broeck, 2007). Affect has been shown to influence how people perceive stimuli and to have an impact on their job attitudes and behaviours (George, 1991; Penner, Midili and Kegelmeyer, 1997). Values represent basic beliefs about what is good or bad, desirable or undesirable (Kluckhohn, 1951; Rokeach, 1973). Thus, values influence the evaluations that people make, determine their choices and represent the basic roots of attitudes and behaviours in life generally and at work.

Values are also shown to lie at the core of cultural differences at the societal level (Hofstede, 1980; House et al., 2004). Many researchers argue that gaining a better understanding of cultures across societies is critical in today's inter-connected world (Javidan and Dastmalchian, 2009). Thus a better understanding and appreciation of the values and assumptions underlying different cultural practices has become an essential part of the basic knowledge needed for effective organisational management and for management education (Javidan, Hitt and Steers, 2007). Thus, the present study's attempt to shed light on the implication of the cultural differences for job-related values, attitudes and work outcomes is to re-emphasise the importance of societal culture and the role it can play in the dynamics of ways of living and in people's life choices. Although many researchers look at cross-cultural variations in values, surprisingly few studies examine similarities and differences in the influence of values on job attitudes and performance across cultures (eg. Hattrup, Mueller and Joens, 2007). The present study is designed to contribute to our knowledge of cross-cultural variation of the role of affect and work values on employee job attitudes and performance. Specifically, it aims to analyse how affect and work values influence job satisfaction and performance in three culturally different countries, i.e., Canada, Iran and Turkey. It attempts to reveal the similarities and differences in the dynamics of the relationship between the employees' inner-world views and their job attitudes and performance in these three countries as well as focus on the variations in these variables across cultures based on data collected from young executives. The wide differences in the cultural, religious, demographic and institutional characteristics of the three countries makes this inquiry possible.

Cultural context

Canada

Canada is one of the most developed nations of the world with abundant natural resources and land. It has a high GDP per capita (PPP) (38,613 U.S. $ in 2007) and a high world ranking in Human development index (3rd in 2006) (Human Development Reports, 2008; World Economic Outlook Database, 2008). Canada is a parliamentary democracy, and a constitutional monarchy. It is a bilingual and multicultural country, with both English and French as official languages at the federal level. Central to the society is the predominantly Catholic and Protestant Christian values, the sense of secular tolerance, and a strong legal infrastructure (Ashkanasy, Trevor-Roberts and Earnshaw, 2002). Its cultural profile is identified by a relatively high performance and future orientation as well as gender egalitarianism (English speaking Canada scored highest on these cultural dimensions among the Anglo cluster societies, see Ashkanasy et al., 2002: 34–5). Canada also has relatively high scores on humane orientation and one of the lowest scores on assertiveness orientation as cultural dimensions. Thus, Canada can be regarded as a non-assertive and humane-oriented society with strong individual performance orientation, a clear value towards the future, and a keen sense of gender equality.

Iran

Iran is one of the largest and most populous countries in the Middle East. Despite its abundant natural resources, its economic performance has been sluggish in recent decades, with a GDP per capita (PPP) of 10,570 U.S. $ in 2007 and a medium Human development index (84th) in 2006 (Human Development Reports, 2008; World Economic Outlook Database, 2008). Iranian society is not ethnically homogenous and comprises various ethnicities, including Persians, Turks, Turkomans, Lors, Baluchis, Kurds and Arabs. According to the Iranian Constitution, the common language and alphabet of the Iranian people is Farsi (Persian) and the Shiite branch of Islam is the official religion of the country. The 1979 revolution brought an end to over 2000 years of monarchy and transformed the society from a tradition-breaking and West-leaning culture to the world's largest theocracy (Javidan and Dastmalchian, 2003).

While it is located in the Middle East, its culture is similar to that of its eastern neighbours in South Asia. Iran has been known for its rich culture for many centuries. Cultural values of this old civilization are characterised by high in-group collectivism in the form of strong family ties and high humane-orientation (Dastmalchian, Javidan and Alam, 2001; Gupta, Surie, Javidan and Chhokar, 2002). On the other hand, a sense of individualism exists in the society. This is characterised by low trust in the collective system and a culture identified by individual achievers (Javidan and Dastmalchian, 2003).

Turkey

Turkey is situated mainly in Western Asia and partly in Southeastern Europe, and serves as a bridge between east and west culturally, economically and politically. The country has a medium level of economic development, with a 12, 858 U.S. $ GDP per capita (PPP) in 2007 and ranks at medium levels in terms of the Human development index (76th) in 2006 (Human Development Reports, 2008; World Economic Outlook Database, 2008). The population is heterogeneous in terms of ethnic traits, including the dominant groups of mainly Turks and Kurds in addition to many smaller ethnic groups. The official language is Turkish and is spoken by 90 per cent of the population. Islam is the religion of 99 per cent of the population and the Sunni branch of Islam is the more dominant sect in the country. The Republic of Turkey is a parliamentary democracy and is a secular state formed in 1923 upon the demise of the Ottoman Empire. The Turkish legal structure is organised along Western lines. Its most dominant cultural characteristic is high in-group collectivism in the form of strong family ties and high power distance (Kabasakal and Bodur, 2002; 2007).

The clear differences in the cultural, religious and institutional characteristics of the three countries make them interesting and diverse enough to analyze determinants of work outcomes and investigate whether the relationships are consistent in different cultural settings. Given that most people spend on average one- to two-thirds of their lives at work, correlates of job outcomes have important implications for policy makers and researchers who are interested in quality of work life and employee well-being. Findings of this study will shed light on this based on data drawn from these three different countries and test the universality of relationships between specific organisational variables.

Job satisfaction and performance

The importance of improving job quality is at the top of the employment and social agenda of many developed nations. Policy makers and researchers consider job satisfaction and overall performance to be among the major dimensions of quality of work life and well-being (Royuela, Lopez-Tamayo and Surinach, 2009; Vansteenkiste et al., 2007). It is in the broader context of employee well-being that our interest in exploring the associations among work values and outcomes across cultures will show greatest relevance to the theme of this volume. Broader questions such as 'are people's values towards work and its centrality to their lives changing?', 'do different cultural norms play a role in this or is this a culture free phenomenon?' and 'how do the patterns of these associations relate to ways of living and life style choices?'

Motivation theories have focused on the relationship between employee job satisfaction and performance. According to intrinsic motivation theory, increases in perceived performance and competence in turn increases self-confidence and the motivation levels of employees (Mitchell, 1996; Christen, Iyer and Soberman, 2006). Recent research also shows that employees who obtain higher performance, and by implication higher rewards (both monetary and non-monetary), have greater job satisfaction (Cho and Chang, 2008).

On the other hand, the influence of job satisfaction on performance has been found to be rather weak and indirect. Higher job satisfaction was found to influence performance indirectly through lower absenteeism, tardiness and turnover (Bockerman and Ilmakunnas, 2008; Freeman, 1978). Similarly, Zelenski, Murphy and Jenkins (2008), studying the relationship between happiness and productivity, find that job satisfaction is not a significant predictor of productivity. Their findings show that whilst other happiness indicators strongly predict productivity, job satisfaction has only a weak influence on productivity.

Research Question 1: Despite strong evidence in previous research on the predictor role of performance on job satisfaction, a great majority of previous research on this topic was conducted in the U.S. and theories about job attitudes and behaviour were developed based on data collected from this specific culture. The present study attempts to analyze the relationship between performance and job satisfaction with a cross-cultural approach. We seek to answer the question: Does higher employee performance lead to higher job satisfaction in the more collectivist Iranian and Turkish cultures of the Middle East as well as in the more individualistic Canadian culture?

Affect

Researchers distinguish between affect states and affectivity as a personality trait (George, 1991; George and Brief, 1992). Although various traits may be correlated with positive affect, the personality trait of positive affectivity (PA) seems to be a predictor of frequent experiences of positive affect states (Tellegen, 1985). Watson, Clark and Tellegen (1988) measure affect in terms of Positive and Negative Affect Schedule (PANAS) scale. The PANAS allows for measurements of both short-term and long-term affect, with the latter allowing more general trait-like characteristics. In this approach, positive affect (PA) and negative affect (NA) have been treated as different dimensions rather than suggesting opposite scales.

Previous research investigating the relationship between employee affect on performance have had mixed results. Questions of whether positive affect (Staw and Barsade, 1993) or negative affect (Wright, Cropanzano and Meyer, 2004) is a stronger predictor of performance have been contradictory. Others have failed to find a relationship between affect and performance (Wright and Staw, 1999); and yet, other research reports a significant relationship between affect and performance (Fisher, 2003; George, 1991).

Research in social psychology has shown that positive mood fosters prosocial behavior in a variety of contexts, including the more individualistic societies of the West and the more collectivist cultures if the Middle East (e.g. Brown, 1985; Kabasakal, Dastmalchian and İmer, 2008; Rosenhan, Salovey and Hargis, 1981). Positive emotions have a function of broadening and building skills, social bonds and social capital (Fredrickson, 2001). These behaviours are likely to improve productivity in collaborative work settings. People in positive mood states are attracted to other people and perceive stimuli in a more positive light (George, 1991;

Penner, Midili and Kegelmeyer, 1997), which is expected to improve their perceptions of job facets and attitudes and maintain a positive outlook.

Research Question 2: Based on supporting evidence on the role of affect on human attitudes and behaviours, we expect positive affect to be related to positive job outcomes. Within this framework we seek to answer: Is the impact of positive affect on job satisfaction and performance evident across the three countries, i.e., Canada, Iran and Turkey?

Values

As deep-rooted world views of individuals, values play a significant role in the choices that people make. Values can be considered to be rather durable and stable attributes of individuals (Rokeach and Rokeach, 1989) and values influence individual behaviour (Meglino and Ravlin, 1998). Values represent beliefs that a way of doing things or an end-state of existence is desirable compared to other means or ends (Rokeach, 1973). They show an individual's idea as to what is right, or good, or desirable; whether a way of doing things or an end-state is important and how important it is. As well as variation in the values of individuals, cultures and subcultures also differ in terms of their characteristic values which form the basis for societal norms (Smith and Schwartz, 1997). Most of the current models on cultural variation are based upon analyses of value differences (e.g. Smith, Peterson and Schwartz, 2002).

Research on work values identifies three types of work values: 1) intrinsic or self-actualisation values; 2) extrinsic, material, or security values; and 3) social or relational values (Alderfer, 1972, Borg, 1990). Elizur (1984) classified values based on 'modality of outcomes' into cognitive, material and affective groups; these values largely overlap with the intrinsic, extrinsic and social categories, respectively. Based on these categorisations, it can be proposed that people's views or orientations to work can be characterised as: (i) opportunities to exercise their competencies and develop themselves; (ii) to obtain material outcomes; or (iii) to build up social relationships.

In examining work values, various researchers who analyze the relationship between specific work value orientations and job outcomes report mixed results. Some find a positive relationship between an employee's intrinsic work value orientation and job satisfaction (e.g. Amabile, Hill, Hennessey and Tighe, 1994), but other studies do not support this (e.g. Druumond and Stoddard, 1991). Vansteenkiste and associates (2007) found that holding an extrinsic, relative to an intrinsic, value orientation was associated with less positive outcomes (less satisfaction) and more negative outcomes (higher emotional exhaustion or short-lived satisfaction after successful goal-attainment).

Despite some mixed findings, in general, motivation theories suggest that individuals will engage in behaviours that satisfy their needs and goals, and are in accordance with their values (Kanfer and Ackerman, 1989; Vroom, 1964). Once these needs are satisfied at work, individuals develop positive work outcomes, such as positive job attitudes and higher levels of commitment. According to self-determination theory, the predicted relation between work values and job outcomes depends on the degree to which the work values allow satisfaction of the basic needs (Vansteenkiste, et al., 2007). The highest positive outcomes are expected when an individual's intrinsic values are stronger than extrinsic values because intrinsic values allow for greater satisfaction of the basic psychological needs (Kasser and Ahuvia, 2002). Further, individuals who are intrinsically oriented will be more concerned about developing their skills and competencies, and therefore they will take greater initiatives at work and actively participate in organisational decisions.

Research Question 3: Given the fact that values lie at the core of cultural differences, the present study will expect differences in relationships between work values and work outcomes. We will seek to answer: Do intrinsic work values lead to higher job satisfaction and higher performance and, by corollary, do extrinsic values lead to lower levels of performance in all three cultural settings, i.e., Canada, Iran and Turkey.

In summary, we will investigate the following questions:

- Does higher employee performance lead to higher job satisfaction in the more collectivist Iranian and Turkish culture as well as in Canada?
- Is the impact of positive affect on job satisfaction and performance consistent across the three countries?
- Do intrinsic work values lead to higher levels of satisfaction and performance, or by corollary, do extrinsic vales lead to lower performance, in the three cultural settings?

Methodology

Sample

To investigate the research questions a questionnaire was developed and administered to respondents in Canada, Iran and Turkey. Participants in MBA and Executive Business Administration related training programmes in each country replied to the self-administered questionnaires voluntarily during their course of study. The sample consisted of a total of 220 respondents, 62 from Canada, 81 from Iran and 77 from Turkey. The respondent group represented mostly young executives with the median age of 26 with approximately 6 years of full-time work experience on the average. The sample was almost equally distributed in terms of gender with 108 (49 per cent) males versus 112 (51 per cent) females. Of the 220 participants, 50 per cent was single and the rest were either married or divorced.

Measures

Job satisfaction. Twenty items from the short version of the Minnesota Satisfaction Questionnaire were used to measure job satisfaction on a seven point Likert-type scale ranging from 1 = strongly disagree to 7 = strongly agree. The questionnaire included items measuring satisfaction with several aspects of one's job including material and social earnings, career advancement, relationships with co-workers and supervisors and working conditions. The questionnaire attempted to assess the respondent's level of agreement with a sample of scale items like 'The feeling of accomplishment I get from the job', and 'The praise I get for doing a good job'. The reliability score measured with coefficient alpha for the scale was .91.

Performance. Perceptions of the participants' own performance was investigated with the question 'In comparison to others in your organization, how do you rate your overall performance?' Respondents were expected to rate their own performances on a seven-point Likert-type scale ranging from 1 = very low to 7 = very high.

Affective states. Affective state, conceptualised as an individual's evaluations pertaining to their level of happiness and mood, was assessed with three items modified from Veenhoven's Happiness Index (1984) and, as a way of accounting for temporal aspects of well-being (Kahneman and Schwarz, 1999) A question on current mood ('Thinking about today, what kind of a mood would you say you were generally in?'), was included. Respondents' evaluations of their affective states were measured on a seven point Likert-type scale, ranging from 1 = low positive affect to 7 = high positive affect. The reliability score for the three item scale was .82.

Values. Work related values were measured with twenty-four items of Elizur, Borg, Hunt and Beck's (1991) work values questionnaire. The scale asked respondents to indicate the level of importance they give to material, cognitive and affective modes of work. The original six-point scale was modified as a seven-point Likert-type scale ranging from 1 = very unimportant to 7 = very important for consistency with other scales used in the study.

A factor analysis of work values items yielded five factors instead of a widely accepted three factor structure of social/affective, cognitive/intrinsic and material/extrinsic work related values in the literature. The five factors found in this study were conceptualised as: 1) job content; 2) confidence; 3) social influence; 4) prestige and money; and 5) fringe benefits. The two factors that emerged in this study as content and confidence correspond to the cognitive/intrinsic dimension, the social influence factor corresponds to the social/affective dimension, while the two factors of prestige/money and fringe benefits is thought to represent the material/extrinsic dimension. Table 11.1 displays the results for factor analysis of work values items.

Table 11.1 Loadings from factor analysis of items assessing work values

Items	**F1-Job content**	**F2-Social influence**	**F3-Confidence**	**F4-Prestige/ money**	**F5-Fringe benefits**
Job interest	.725				
Job responsibility	.629				
Fair supervisor	.556				
Independence	.560				
Use of abilities	.723				
Meaningful work	.543				
Influence at work		.735			
Coworkers		.619			
Influence in the organization		.746			
Interaction with people		.578			
Contribution to society		.615			
Personal growth			.574		
Job achievement			.507		
Work conditions			.422		

Continued

Table 11.1 Continued

Items	F1-Job content	F2-Social influence	F3-Confidence	F4-Prestige/ money	F5-Fringe benefits
Advancement			.532		
Work feedback			.586		
Esteem as a person			.586		
Recognition for performance			.586		
Job security			.640		
Good company to work for				.794	
Job status				.611	
Pay				.658	
Benefits					.531
Convenient hours					.832

Note: Extraction Method: Principal Component Analysis. Rotation Method: Varimax with Kaiser Normalization.

The items loading on the job content factor included job interest, job responsibility, fair supervisor, independence, use of abilities and meaningful work. The reliability score represented by Cronbach's alpha for these six items was .77. The eight items that loaded on the confidence factor consisted of personal growth, job achievement, advancement, work feedback, esteem as a person, recognition for performance, job security and work conditions with a Cronbach's alpha of .86. The five items of influence at work, influence in the organization, co-workers, interaction with people and contribution to society loaded on the social influence factor, with a reliability score of .80. Job status, pay and good company to work for were the three items which loaded on the factor of prestige and money with Cronbach's alpha of .68, while the two items of benefits and convenient hours loaded on the factor fringe benefits with a reliability score of .61.

Results

The means, standard deviations, reliabilities and inter-correlations for the study variables and demographics are presented in Table 11.2 for the total sample from the three countries. Results showed acceptable levels of reliabilities for the research variables, represented by the bold numbers in the diagonal. Table 11.2 illustrates above average (4.00) levels for all study variables. General level of job satisfaction, performance and affect, having the mean scores of 5.01, 5.79 and 5.38 respectively, lets us conclude that the participants of the study were somewhat satisfied with their jobs, perceived themselves to be performing above the average and were inclined to be in a rather positive mood. Content related work values had the highest score of 6.19, displaying the participants' level of importance attributed to job interest, responsibility, meaningful work, use of abilities and independence. The second most important factor for the participants appeared as work values related to confidence (6.06), which leads us to conclude that personal development was valued as an essential part of the job. The factor of confidence related work values was followed by the factors of prestige and money (5.90), social influence (5.85) and fringe benefits (5.64) respectively. In general, respondents from the three countries placed less value on monetary and extrinsic work dimensions of prestige/money and the dimension of social influence as compared to the dimensions of job interest and confidence.

Excluding demographics, job satisfaction displayed significant positive correlations with almost all of the study variables, including performance ($r=.263$, $p \leq .01$), affect ($r=.375$, $p \leq .01$), work values of content ($r=.233$, $p \leq .01$), social influence ($r=.285$, $p \leq .01$), confidence ($r=.238$, $p \leq .01$) and prestige/money ($r=.195$, $p \leq .01$), while it did not have a significant relationship with the work values of fringe benefits. These findings indicate that people who are satisfied with their jobs also tend to report that they perform well. They are more likely to report higher interest in their jobs and the desire to take job-related responsibilities. They are also more likely to report feeling positive and they attribute importance to personal growth and advancement. People's higher satisfaction with their jobs does not appear to have any relationship to benefits they receive in their jobs.

In addition, performance perceptions of the participants were also significantly positively correlated with affect ($r=.284$, $p \leq .01$), content-related work values ($r=.339$, $p \leq .01$), social influence values ($r=.283$, $p \leq .01$), confidence values ($r=.252$, $p \leq .01$) and prestige/money ($r=.242$, $p \leq .01$), but uncorrelated with fringe benefits values. These correlations indicate that people who report high performance are mostly those who (1) report that they use their abilities; (2) feel independent in their jobs; (3) say they receive recognition for their performance; (4) value their co-workers; and (5) value reward – their pay. Pearson correlations indicate that perceived performance is not related to fringe benefits.

Table 11.2 Means, standard deviations, Cronbach alphas and intercorrelations among study variables* (n=220)

	Mean	SD	js	p	a	cv	siv	cov	pmv	fbv
Age	22.540	13.395								
gender**	1.509	0.501								
marital status***	1.532	0.568								
number of dependents	0.827	1.196								
full time work experience****	2.116	1.238								
js – job satisfaction	5.008	0.947	**0.907**							
p – performance	5.790	0.860	0.263^	**NA**						
a – affect	5.379	0.999	0.375^	0.284^	**0.820**					
cv – content value	6.186	0.586	0.233^	0.339^	0.151^^	**0.771**				
siv – social influence value	5.854	0.752	0.285^	0.283^	0.095	0.528^	**0.801**			
cov – confidence value	6.059	0.687	0.238^	0.252^	0.099	0.645^	0.665^	**0.860**		
pmv – prestige & money value	5.900	0.791	0.195^	0.242^	0.110	0.365^	0.480^	0.579^	**0.684**	
fbv – fringe benefits value	5.640	1.049	0.063	0.100	0.044	0.191^	0.394^	0.394^	0.450^	**0.614**

Notes: ^ Correlation is significant at the 0.01 level (2-tailed).
^^ Correlation is significant at the 0.05 level (2-tailed).
* Coefficient alphas are reported along the diagonal (no reliability score for performance measured with 1 item).
** 1=Male, 2=Female
*** 1=Single, 2=Married, 3=Divorced, 4=Other
**** 1=0–5years, 2=6–10 years, 3=11–15 years, 4=16–20 years, 5=21–25 years, 6=26–30years, 7=30+ years

If one looks at the inter-correlations among the work values dimensions, it can be stated that work values of content, social influence and confidence have strong positive intercorrelations among themselves. This could point out that intrinsic and social related work values have stronger relationships within themselves rather than the material ones. On the other hand, prestige/money and fringe benefits conceptualised as material dimensions of work values, have strong positive correlations with each other (r=.450, p≤.01), compared to these two dimensions' rather weaker positive correlations with intrinsic or social dimensions of work values.

Two sets of multiple regression analyses were conducted to investigate the research questions developed in this study. The dependent variable in the first set of regression analyses was job satisfaction and in the second one was job performance run separately for the three countries. Table 11.3 presents the standardised beta coefficients with the R-squared and F values for the first regression model.

Table 11.3 Regression analyses results for job satisfaction as the dependent variable

	Countries		
	Canada (n=62)	**Iran (n=81)**	**Turkey (n=77)**
Performance	−.307**	.231**	–
Affect	.421*	.244**	.372*
Content values	–	–	–
Social influence values	.489*	.275**	–
Confidence values	–	–	–
Prestige/money values	−.439**	–	–
Fringe benefits values	–	–	–
R^2	.461	.232	.272
Adjusted R^2	.391	.158	.198
Durbin-Watson value	1.990	2.369	1.860
F	6.598*	3.142*	3.683*
df	7	7	7

Note: Values in the table are standardized beta weights for each predictor construct, unless otherwise indicated.
The items with no value did not enter stepwise regression analyses.
* p<.01, ** p<.05

The regression results shown in Table 11.3 clearly indicate that the predictors of satisfaction are different in the three countries studied. In Canada, perceived performance – negatively – (β=−.307, p<.05), affect (β=.421, p<.01), work values of social influence (β=.489, p<.01) as well as work values of prestige/money – negatively – (β=−.439, p<.05) contributed to a significant model (R^2=.471, F=6.598, p<.01) to predict job satisfaction. For Iran, regression analysis yielded perceived performance (β=.231, p<.05), affect (β=.244, p<.05) and social influence values (β=.275, p<.05) as statistically significant predictors of job satisfaction (R^2=.232, F=3.142, p<.01). Finally for Turkey, affect (β=.372, p<.01) appeared in the model as the only predictor of job satisfaction.

These findings provide a number of explanations regarding our research questions. Concerning our first research question, (Does higher perceived performance lead to higher satisfaction?) it was interesting to see job performance as a negative predictor of job satisfaction in Canada, with high income levels and a rather individualistic orientation, implying that those who rate their own performance as high report lower levels of job satisfaction. For Iran and Turkey, which are lower income counties with relatively collectivistic orientations, the situation is reversed and perceived performance was related to higher reported levels of satisfaction for Iran, while it had no significant impact for the sample from Turkey.

Regarding our second research question, (Is the impact of positive affect on job satisfaction and performance consistent across the three countries?) affect appeared as a significant predictor of job satisfaction, as a positive job outcome, in all three countries: Canada (β=.421, p<.01), Iran (β=.244, p<.05) and Turkey (β=.372, p<.01). This finding is consistent with previous research that has found that maintaining a positive outlook fosters satisfaction with one's job. This is also consistent with the idea that positive, happier people are more positive and 'upbeat' about many aspects of their lives.

For our third research question, (Do intrinsic work values lead to higher levels of satisfaction and performance?) the findings yield mixed results. For the Canadian sample, social values (intrinsic, work values of social influence) was of significant importance (β=.489, p<.01) while material values or work values of prestige/money (extrinsic) influenced job satisfaction levels in a negative way (β=−.439, p<.05). Social values also came out as important predictors of satisfaction with one's job in the Iranian sample (β=.275, p<.05), whereas none of the work related values appeared as significant predictors of job satisfaction in the Turkish sample.

In order to test the effects of work values on self-reports of job performance we conducted a second regression analysis with perceived job performance as the dependent variable. Table 11.4 displays the results for the second regression analyses for the three countries.

In the second set of regression analyses, job satisfaction – negatively – (β=-.261, p<.05), affect (β=.419, p<.01), work values of content (β=.676, p<.01), confidence –negatively – (β=-.441, p<.05) and social influence (β=.382, p<.05) entered the model as significant variables to predict perceived job performance (R^2=.542, F=9.147, p<.01) for the Canadian sample. The regression analyses conducted for Iran and Turkey to investigate the possible predictors of perceived job performance came out as non-significant. These findings verify the earlier reverse relationship between job satisfaction and perceived job performance in Canada. Higher self-reports of performance are accompanied by lower levels of satisfaction with one's job in the sample from Canada. In addition to positive outlook toward life (affect) and social values (social influence), intrinsic work values of content and confidence (negatively) appeared as predicting job performance for Canada. This implies that perceived

Table 11.4 Regression analyses results for performance as the dependent variable

	Countries		
	Canada (n=62)	**Iran (n=81)**	**Turkey (n=77)**
Job satisfaction	−.261**	.261**	–
Affect	.419*	–	–
Content values	.676*	–	–
Social influence values	.382**	–	–
Confidence values	−.441**	–	–
Prestige/money values	–	–	–
Fringe benefits values	–	–	–
R^2	.542	.131	.144
Adjusted R^2	.483	.047	.058
Durbin-Watson value	2.100	2.084	2.329
F	9.147*	1.570	1.664
df	7	7	7

Note: Values in the table are standardized beta weights for each predictor construct, unless otherwise indicated.
The items with no value did not enter stepwise regression analyses.
* p<.01, ** p<.05

performance is fostered in the presence of higher importance attributed to interesting jobs, job responsibilities and meaningful work as well as influence in the organisation and interactions with people, while it is lessened with higher esteem and recognition values in the Canadian sample.

Country differences

In order to test statistically significant inter-country differences to explain the above results, data from the three countries, was subjected to an ANOVA. The results for ANOVA are displayed in Table 11.5.

As displayed in Table 11.5, the three countries did not have a statistically significantly difference in the job satisfaction variable based on ANOVA results. On the other hand, the three countries differed significantly in terms of the job performance variable (F=5.13, p<.01), and Scheffe tests pointed out significant differences between Turkey (6.00) and Canada (5.55), with Iran (5.77) standing in the middle. The three countries also differed in three of the five work values dimensions. For intrinsic work values of content (F=7.50, p<.001), Canada (5.95) and

Table 11.5 Means comparisons (analysis of variance) and multiple comparisons (Scheffé tests) between Turkey, Iran and Canada

Variables	1 Turkey (N=77)	2 Iran (N=81)	3 Canada (N=62)	F	Multiple comparisons
Job satisfaction	5.07 (.95)	4.90 (.87)	5.07 (1.04)	0.89	
Performance	6.00 (.68)	5.77 (.84)	5.55 (.99)	5.13**	1–3
Affect	5.49 (1.03)	5.24 (1.01)	5.43 (.95)	1.25	
Values-content	6.28 (.36)	6.28 (.55)	5.95 (.77)	7.50***	1–3, 2–3
Values-social influence	5.91 (.50)	6.09 (.61)	5.47 (1.00)	13.56***	1–3, 2–3
Values-confidence	6.16 (.48)	6.20 (.57)	5.75 (.92)	9.62***	1–3, 2–3
Values-prestige & money	5.98 (.57)	5.89 (.90)	5.81 (.87)	0.85	
Values-fringe benefits	5.53 (.88)	5.68 (1.21)	5.72 (1.02)	0.64	

Note: Numbers in paratheses indicate standard deviations.
* p<.05, ** p<.01, ***p<.001

Turkey (6.28) were significantly different and Iran (6.28) stayed close to both countries. Iran (6.20, 6.09) and Turkey (6.16, 5.91) were also similar to each other in terms of the other set of intrinsic work values of confidence ($F=9.62$, $p<.001$) and social work values of social influence ($F=13.55$, $p<.001$) and different from Canada (5.75, 5.47). The three countries were not statistically different from one another in terms of material work values of prestige/money and fringe benefits.

Thus, according to ANOVA and Scheffe tests results, Iran and Turkey seemed to be rather similar, whereas Canada stood out as different in terms of the work values dimensions. On the other hand, there were no statistically significant inter-country differences for job satisfaction.

Discussion

This study sought to explore the associations among employee work values, positive mood or affect, and work related outcomes in three different cultures. We argue that values and the ways in which such values influence people's behaviours at work, their choices about life, work and how they spend their time are also influenced by societal culture. We further suggest that work values and the inner life-worlds of individuals are influenced by their cultural contexts. Work related aspects of life – work values, satisfaction with work and how one feels one is doing at work – are significant parts of one's lifestyle preferences and choices (Hakim, 2000) which are not uniformly shared across cultures. We have used similar samples of young executives in three different cultural contexts to explore these questions and to relate them to the higher level issue of ways of living and lifestyle choice and preferences.

In general, work outcomes such as job satisfaction and performance are central concepts that are associated with employee well-being and quality of work life. Policies which promote employees who are satisfied with their jobs and consider themselves to be successful are of value for their own sake (Wright, Cropanzano, Denney and Moline, 2002) as well as for purposes of organisational productivity. The dynamics of the relationship between job satisfaction and performance, as well as the mechanisms that lead to these positive work outcomes, have been attracting the attention of researchers for many years and continue to be on the agenda of researchers. Previous research in organisational behavior has shown that work attitudes and behaviors are likely to be associated with the inner worlds of employees which in turn may be affected by the context. Affective characteristics of individuals together with their values constitute a core part of the inner world that influence work outcomes. However, most of these previous studies were conducted in the western world, particularly in the U.S. The present study investigates how affect and work values influence job satisfaction and performance in different cultural settings and the dynamics of the relationship for these work outcomes.

Findings of the study show both similarities and differences between the three countries in relation to the research questions. In general results from Iran and Turkey were found to be similar to each other and displayed differences from the Canadian sample. Respondents from Iran and Turkey had significantly higher intrinsic work values (job content and confidence) and social domains compared to Canadian respondents. It is interesting to note that Canada, representing the modern capitalistic western world, had significantly lower intrinsic and social work aspirations. In addition, Turkish respondents perceived themselves to be higher performers compared to the perceptions of the Canadian sample, while Iran stood somewhat in the middle. Findings show that the three countries display no significant differences in job satisfaction, affective states and extrinsic work values (prestige/money and fringe benefits).

The regression models were significant in predicting job satisfaction in all three countries, indicating that affect and work values together with performance explain a significant portion of the variance in job satisfaction. On the other hand, the regression model for performance was only significant for the Canadian sample and did not explain the variance in performance for the Iranian and Turkish samples.

Based on the first set of regression analyses, positive mood, or affect, seems to be a significant predictor of job satisfaction in a culture-free manner. That is, positive mood, or affect, was found to be associated with higher job performance in all three countries. It can be proposed that happiness causes a positive outlook which leads to positive evaluations of one's job regardless of the characteristics of the setting or cultural context of the society. In Turkey, no other variable than affect was a significant predictor of job satisfaction whereas performance and work values contributed significantly to the model in Canada and Iran.

Contrary to previous research, performance was found to be negatively associated with job satisfaction in Canada and displayed a positive association for the Iranian sample in line with conceptual and empirical literature on the topic. The differences in the dynamics of the relationship in the three countries suggest that the long-lasting debate on the relationship between job satisfaction and performance needs to take into account the characteristics of the setting. Cultural, socio-economic and institutional attributes of the countries may play a role in explaining these different findings. While the large body of research conducted mainly in the U.S. indicates a positive relationship between job satisfaction and performance, the Canadian sample in the present study displays a negative association between these two constructs. One possible explanation for this may be that the characteristics of executive positions and professional jobs for young people at the early stages of their careers in the highly competitive, capitalistic world. Canadian culture is identified by a high performance orientation (Ashkanasy et al., 2002) and executive/managerial positions are one of the occupations where these norms are strongest. Young professionals in organisations may face greater pressure for performance and the respondents in this study have all attended executive training programmes. Thus, those respondents in Canada who rate themselves as high performers may be experiencing high workload and career pressure lowering their reported levels of job satisfaction. Research on Canadian organisations has shown that the relationship between satisfaction and performance is strongly influenced by the extent of decentralisation and perceived autonomy among the Canadian managers in the health sector (e.g. Acorn, Patner and Crowford, 1997) and in state-owned enterprises (Dastmalchian and Javidan, 1987). Another study, concentrating on entrepreneurial firms in Canada and the U.S., found that the levels of job satisfaction among Canadian managers were lower than their U.S. counterparts (Hornsby, Kuratko and Montagno, 1999).

Another possible explanation for this is that while both U.S. and Canadian cultures are identified by a high performance orientation (Ashkanasy et al., 2002), Canada ranks high in the GLOBE study on humane orientation and low on assertiveness orientation (House et al., 2004). This evidence from the GLOBE project is confirmed when one considers Canada's higher scores in terms of human development index, its lower unemployment rate, and its higher government expenditure on social welfare (Welfare Expenditure Report, OECD, 2001; Human Development Indicators, UNDP, 2003). The Canadian context characterised by the existence of a stronger social net coupled with lower unemployment rates could create less pressure for high performance. The ANOVA findings are in line with this argument, pointing to the significantly lower levels of perceived performance for the Canadian sample as compared to the other two samples.

On the other hand, the Canadian cultural norms favour excellence in performance as well as in future orientation cultural dimensions

(House et al., 2004; Ashkanasy et al., 2002) and push the individuals to perform at higher levels. The individuals who comply with aspirations of higher individualistic performance in a lenient institutional setting may be facing a duality and dissonance. Thus, respondents in Canada, who perceive themselves as high performers, may be more dissatisfied with their jobs. The enigma in the Canadian context, which is created by the opposing forces between the institutional and cultural elements, may be creating an environment where self-reports of performance and satisfaction are negatively related.

In terms of the relationship between job satisfaction and work values, both the Canadian and Iranian findings are in line with previous research (Amabile et al., 1994; Vansteenkiste et al., 2007). In both countries, higher intrinsic work values (social influence) positively predicted job satisfaction, meaning that individuals who aspire to have more social influence at work report being more satisfied. Further, in the Canadian sample higher extrinsic values (prestige/money) were negatively associated with job satisfaction. In line with previous conceptual and empirical studies, findings here suggest that intrinsic values may be aligned with basic human needs and this is more satisfying.

In terms of the tests related to performance, results were significant only for Canada. The negative relationship between performance and job satisfaction prevailed, meaning that individuals who were more satisfied with their jobs had lower perceived performance. Affect was a significant positive predictor of performance, indicating that happier individuals rated themselves as being higher performers. This finding is in line with the happier-productive worker argument (Fisher, 2003; Staw and Barsade, 1993) and can be explained with the expectancy theory of motivation. It can be proposed that positive affect facilitates not only the expectancy that one's effort leads to performance, but also the belief that performance leads to positive outcomes (Wright et al., 2002).

The fact that affect did not predict performance in Iran and Turkey might be related to both the macro economic conditions of the countries as well as cultural values and norms. Both Iran and Turkey are countries with very high unemployment rates and individuals might feel obliged to perform at sufficient levels independent of their feelings and values. Further both countries are characterised by high in-group collectivism, where family lies at the centre of lives. Individuals in these cultures may perceive work as a mechanism for supporting and taking care of their families rather than for individual gains and aspirations (Singelis, Triandis, Bhawuk and Gelfand, 1995). Thus, how one feels and what one values at work may be a insignificant influence on work output.

The results from three culturally diverse settings provide insights for policy makers, human resource practitioners and researchers. One of the important findings is that happiness enhances self-reports of job outcomes and may be valuable as an indicator of employee well-being (Wright et al., 2002). Positive affect shapes how one looks and interprets the surrounding world in general including the work environment.

In shaping their human resource practices and policies, organisations can take into account this relationship between general affect and feelings about general organisational outcomes. Further, the present study highlights the importance of intrinsic work values as antecedents of positive self-reports of job outcomes in two of the cultural settings, Canada and Iran. It can be proposed that as aspirations related to job content and social influence bring higher satisfaction and perceived performance, organisations can promote human resource practices that target satisfaction of these goals, such as opportunities for participation in decision making, contribution to developmental projects, and attending social gatherings as organisational activities.

It should also be noted that the data and the results reported here have many limitations and the findings and our interpretations of them should be viewed in light of such limitations. The data is cross-sectional and many observations we have and interpretations we make assume causality which needs to be considered with caution. The young executive students in each culture live in different contexts. Given the limitations imposed on us by the nature of the cross-cultural study, we did not have the opportunity to qualitatively assess their workplaces and the contexts that they were using as reference points. A richer understanding of those contexts would have enriched our quantitative analyses. In more politically unstable societies, freedom to express views even in a purely work-related and small scale study like ours is also a significant issue and given that we have such countries in our study, again the results have to be looked at with caution.

Despite the above limitations, it can be proposed that both institutional and socio-cultural characteristics of society play a role in understanding values and work outcomes. The on-going question of whether a happy worker is a more productive worker needs to be further investigated with a cross-cultural focus and data collected from a wide range of demographic and occupational groups. On-going research in this will enrich theory development and policy making, while assisting in the development of organisational practices that enhance employee well-being.

References

Acorn, S., Patner, P.A. and Crowford, M. (1997) 'Decentralization as a determinant of autonomy, job satisfaction and organizational commitment among nurse managers', *Nursing Research*, 46 (1): 52–58.

Alderfer, C.P. (1972) *Existence, Relatedness, and Growth: Human Needs in Organizational Settings*. New York: Free Press.

Amabile, T.M., Hill, K.G., Hennessey, B.A., and Tighe, E.M. (1994) 'The work preference inventory: assessing intrinsic and extrinsic motivational orientations', *Journal of Personality and Social Psychology*, 66: 950–967.

Ashkanasy, N.M., Trevor-Roberts, E., and Earnshaw, L. (2002) 'The Anglo-cluster: legacy of the British Empire', *Journal of World Business*, 37: 28–39.

Baron, B.A., Byrne, D., and Branscombe, N.R. (2006) *Social Psychology*, 11th edition. Boston: Pearson.

Borg, I. (1990) 'Multiple facetisations of work values', *Applied Psychology: An International Review*, 39: 401–412.

Böckerman, P. and Ilmakunnas, P. (2008) 'Interaction of working conditions, job satisfaction, and sickness absences: evidence from a representative sample of employees', *Social Science & Medicine*, 67 (4): 520–528.

Brown, R. (1985) *Social Psychology*. New York: Free Press.

Cho, S.D. and Chang, D.R. (2008) 'Salesperson's innovation resistance and job satisfaction in intra-organizational diffusion of sales force automation technologies: the case of South Korea', *Industrial Marketing Management*, 37: 841–847.

Christen, M., Iyer, C., and Soberman, D. (2006) 'Job satisfaction, job performance, and effort: a re-examination using agency theory', *Journal of Marketing*, 70 (1): 137–150.

Dastmalchian, A., Javidan, M., and Alam, K. (2001) 'Effective leadership and culture in Iran: an empirical study', *Applied Psychology: An International Review*, 50 (4): 532–558.

Dastmalchian, A. and Javidan, M. (1987) 'Centralization and organizational context: an analysis of Canadian public enterprises', *Canadian Journal of Administrative Sciences*, 4 (3): 302–19.

Drummond, R.J., and Stoddard, A. (1991) 'Job satisfaction and work values', *Psychological Reports*, 69: 116–18.

Elizur, D. (1984) 'Facets of work values: A structural analysis of work outcomes', *Journal of Applied Psychology*, 69: 379–89.

Elizur, D., Borg, I., Hunt, R., and Beck, I.M. (1991) 'The structure of work values: a cross-cultural comparison', *Journal of Organizational Behavior*, 12: 21–38.

Fisher, C.D. (2003) 'Why do lay people believe that satisfaction and performance are correlated? Possible sources of a commonsense theory', *Journal of Organizational Behavior*, 24: 753–77.

Fredrickson, B.L. (2001) 'The role of positive emotions in positive psychology: the broaden-and-build theory of positive emotions', *American Psychologist*, 56: 218–26.

Freeman, R.B. (1978) 'Job satisfaction as an economic variable', *American Economic Review*, 68 (2): 135–41.

Friedman, T.L. (2005) *The World is Flat: A Brief History of the 20th Century*. New York: Farrar, Straus and Giroux.

George, J.M. (1991) 'State of trait: effects of positive mood on prosocial behaviors at work', *Journal of Applied Psychology*, 76 (2): 299–307.

George, J.M. and Brief, A.P. (1992) 'Feeling good-doing good: a conceptual analysis of the mood at work-organizational spontaneity relationship', *Psychological Bulletin*, 112 (2): 310–29.

Gupta, V., Surie, G., Javidan, M. and Chokar, J. (2002) 'Southern Asia cluster: where the old meets the new?' *Journal of World Business*, 37: 16–27.

Hakim, C. (2002) 'Lifestyle preferences as determinants of women's differentiated labor market careers', *Work and Occupations*, 29 (4): 428–59.

Hattrup, K., Mueller, K., and Joens, I. (2007) 'The effects of nations and organizations on work value importance: a cross-cultural investigation', *Applied Psychology: An International Review*, 56 (3): 479–99.

Hofstede, G. (1980) *Culture's Consequences: International Differences in Work-Related Values*. Beverly Hills: Sage.

Hornsby, J.S., Kuratko, D.F. and Montagno, R.V. (1999) 'Perception of internal factors for entrepreneurship: a comparison of Canadian and U.S. mangers', *Entrepreneurship Theory and Practice*, 24 (2): 9–24.

House, R. Hanges, P.J., Javidan, M., Dorfman, P.J., and Gupta, V. and GLOBE Associates (Eds.) (2004) *Culture, Leadership, and Organizations: The GLOBE Study of 62 Societies*. Thousand Oaks, CA: Sage.

Human Development Reports (2008) *Human Development Report 2008*, Geneva: United Nations Development Programme.

Hyde, R.E. and Weathington, B.L. (2006) 'The congruence of personal life values and work attitudes', *Genetic, Social, and General Psychology Monographs*, 132 (2): 151–190.

Javidan, M. and Dastmalchian, A. (2003) 'Culture and leadership in Iran: the land of individual achievers, strong family ties, and powerful elite', *The Academy of Management Executive*, 17 (4): 127–142.

Javidan, M. and Dastmalchian, A. (2009) 'Managerial implications of the GLOBE project: a study of 62 societies', *Asia Pacific Journal of Human Resources*, 47(1): 41–58.

Javidan, M., Hitt, M. and Steers, R.M. (eds) (2007) *The Global Mindset. Advances in International Management, 19,* New York: JAI Press.

Kabasakal, H. and Bodur, M. (2002) 'Arabic cluster: a bridge between East and West', *Journal of World Business*, 37: 40–54.

Kabasakal, H. and Bodur, M. (2007) 'Leadership and culture in Turkey: a multifaceted phenomenon', In J.S. Chhokar, F. C. Brodbeck, and R.J. House (eds) *Culture and Leadership Across the World: The GLOBE Book of In-Depth Studies of 25 Societies*. Mahwah, NJ: Lawrence Erlbaum Associates: 835–874.

Kabasakal, H., Dastmalchian, A. and İmer, P. (2008) 'Cultural influences on life choices: a study of organizational citizenship behavior in Turkey, Iran, & Canada', International Colloquium on Ways of Living: Work, Organizations, Communities and Lifestyle Choice, Melbourne, December.

Kahneman, D. and Diener, E. Schwarz, N. (1999). *Well-Being: The Foundations of Hedonic Psychology*. NY: Russell Sage Foundation.

Kanfer, R. and Ackerman, P.L. (1996) 'A self-regulatory skills perspective to reducing cognitive interference', in I.G. Sarason, B.R. Sarason, and G.R. Pierce (eds) *Cognitive Interference: Theories, Methods, and Findings*. Mahwah, NJ: Erlbaum: 153–171.

Kasser, T. and Ahuvia, A. (2002) 'Materialistic values and well-being in business students', *European Journal of Social Psychology*, 32: 137–146.

Kluckhohn, C. (1951) 'Value and value orientations in the theory of action', in T. Parsons and E. Shils (eds) *Toward a General Theory of Action*, Cambridge, MA: Harvard University Press: 388–433.

Meglino, B.M. and Ravlin, E.C. (1998) 'Individual values in organizations: concepts, controversies, and research', *Journal of Management*, 24 (3): 351–389.

Mitchell, T. (1996) 'Participation in decision making: effects of using one's preferred strategy on task performance and attitudes', *Journal of Social Behavior and Personality*, 11 (3): 531–46.

Organisation for Economic Co-operation and Development (OECD) (2001) *Welfare Expenditure Report* (Microsoft Excel Workbook). Paris: OECD.

Penner, L.A., Midili, A.R. and Kegelmeyer, J. (1997) 'Beyond job attitudes: a personality and social psychology perspective on the causes of organizational citizenship behavior', *Human Performance*, 10 (2): 111–31.

Rokeach, M. (1973) *The Nature of Human Values*. New York: The Free Press.

Rokeach, M., and Rokeach, S.J.B. (1989) 'Stability and change in American value priorities, 1968–1981', *American Psychologist*, 44 (5): 775–84.

Rosenhan, D.L., Salovey, P., and Hargis, K. (1981) 'The joys of helping: focus of attention mediates the impact of positive affect on altruism', *Journal of Personality and Social Psychology*, 40: 899–905.

Royuela, V., Lopez-Tamayo, and Surinach (2009) 'Results of a quality of work life index in Spain. A comparison of survey results and aggregate social indicators', *Social Indices Research*, 90: 225–41.

Schwartz, S.H. (1994) 'Are there universal aspects in the structure and contents of human values?', *Journal of Social Issues*, 50: 19–45.

Singelis, T.M., Triandis, H.C., Bhawuk, D.S., and Gelfand, M. (1995) 'Horizontal and vertical dimensions of individualism and collectivism: a theoretical and measurement refinement', *Cross-Cultural Research*, 29: 240–75.

Smith, P.B., Peterson, M.F. and Schwartz, S.H. (2002) 'Cultural values, sources and guidance, and their relevance to managerial behavior', *Journal of Cross-Cultural Psychology*, 33 (2): 188–208.

Smith, P.B., and Schwartz, S.H. (1997) 'Values', in J.W. Berry, M.H. Segall, and C. Kagitçibasi (Eds.) *Handbook of Cross-Cultural Psychology*. Needham Heights, MA: Allyn & Bacon: 77–118.

Staw, B.M., and Barsade, S.G. (1993) 'Affect and managerial performance: a test of the sadder-but-wiser vs. happier-and-smarter hypotheses', *Administrative Science Quarterly*, 38: 304–31.

Tellegen, A. (1985) 'Structures of mood and personality and their relevance to assessing anxiety, with an emphasis on self-report', in A.H. Turna and J.D. Maser (eds), *Anxiety and the Anxiety Disorders*. Hillsdale, NJ: Erlbaum: 681–706.

Thoresen, C.J., Kaplan, S.A., Barsky, A.P., Warren, C.R. and de Chermont, K. (2003) 'The affective underpinnings of job perceptions and attitudes: a meta-analytic review and integration', *Psychological Bulletin*, 129: 914–45.

United Nations Development Programme (UNDP) (2003). 'Human development indicators', *Human Development Report 2003*. New York: Oxford University Press for the UNDP. http://hdr.undp.org/reports/global/2003/pdf/hdr03_HDI.pdf.

Vansteenkiste, M., Neyrinck, B., Niemiec, C.P., Soenens, B., De Witte, H. and Van den Broeck, A. (2007) 'On the relations among work value orientations, psychological need satisfaction and job outcomes: a self-determination theory approach', *Journal of Occupational and Organizational Psychology*, 80: 251–77.

Veenhoven, R. (1984) *Conditions of Happiness*. Rotterdam: Eramus Universiteit.

Vroom, V.H. (1964) *Work and Motivation*. New York: Wiley.

Watson, D., Clark, L.A., and Tellegen, A. (1988) 'Development and validation of brief measures of positive and negative affect: the Panas scales', *Journal of Personality and Social Psychology*, 54: 1063–70.

Weiss, D.J., Dawis, R.V., England, G.W. and Lofquist, L.H. (1967) *Manual for the Minnesota Satisfaction Questionnaire*. Industrial Relations Centre, University of Minnesota, Minneapolis.

Wright, T.A., and Staw, B.M. (1999) 'Further thoughts on the happy-productive worker', *Journal of Organizational Behavior*, 20: 31–34.

Wright, T.A., Cropanzano, R., and Meyer, D.G. (2004) 'State and trait correlates of job performance: a tale of two perspectives', *Journal of Business and Psychology*, 18: 365–83.

Wright, T.A., Cropanzano, R., Denney, P.J. and Moline, G.L. (2002) 'When a happy worker is a productive worker: a preliminary examination of three models', *Canadian Journal of Behavioural Science*, 34 (3): 146–50.

World Economic Outlook Database (2008). New York: International Monetary Fund.

Zelenski, J.M., Murphy, S.A. and Jenkins, D.A. (2008) 'The happy-productive worker thesis revisited', *Journal of Happiness Studies*, 9: 521–37.

12

Designing for Well-Being: The Role of the Physical Work Environment

Claudia Steinke, Rei Kurosawa and Ali Dastmalchian

Introduction

The physical work environment has a significant and often unrealised impact on the experience of work and on employee/personal well-being, which in turn has implications for organisations, including the recruitment and retention of staff. With staff absenteeism and turnover representing leading challenges among today's healthcare organisations, this chapter argues that the design of the physical work environment needs to be considered in attempts to address some of the human resource issues in healthcare.

How people experience work is important to their feelings about work and the quality of life. As many people spend the majority of their waking hours at work, and invest in their work as in a vocation, the physical work environment can impact on lifestyle decisions such as where to work, how to work, whether to stay working in an organisation, and even attend work on any given day. Organisational effectiveness is optimized when dimensions of organisational design such as the physical work environment support organisational strategies. For example, if the objective is to increase the recruitment and retention of nurses, the physical work environment should be designed in a way that best supports the needs and wants of nurses. Organisational effectiveness is compromised when the physical work environment interferes with or neglects the needs and wants of the people. This in turn impacts on the experience of work and personal well-being. The question stands however as to how to design the physical work environment in a way that enhances the experience of work and well-being.

This chapter focuses on attributes of the physical work environment that influence the experience of work and personal well-being. Many studies on work and well-being overlook the physical component of the work environment in favour of discussing workplace policies and procedures that promote well-being. Yet the physical environment is constant and ubiquitous. In organisations, all people experience the physical environment and that experience is rarely neutral. As such, changes in the physical work environment provide a potentially powerful tool for enhancing the experience of work and personal well-being.

The physical work environment in healthcare is the focus of investigation due to the growing shortage of healthcare providers and the need to focus on developing healthy workplaces that support recruitment and retention strategies (O'Brien-Pallas et al., 2006). The authors suggest that recruitment and retention strategies could benefit by placing greater emphasis on improving the experience of work for nurses through the design of the physical setting. In this chapter, architecture is not being promoted as the end all and be all to challenges facing organisations. However, this school of thought presents a valuable perspective for organisations in that it affects the experience of work which has implications for the recruitment and retention of staff.

Although this chapter addresses the physical work environment in the industry of healthcare, the concept is relevant across different sectors. Literature from the fields of organisation theory, environmental psychology, architecture and healthcare provide evidence of the role and impact of the physical work environment. Findings from an empirical study that assessed nurse perceptions of the physical work environment in emergency rooms underscores the need to attend to the physical work environment in hospitals.

The chapter is organised in five parts. First, we define *experiential design* and *well-being*. Second, we discuss the situation facing human resources in healthcare in Canada and the need to improve the experience of work for nurses. We then illustrate the link between experiential design and well-being through a discussion on attributes of the physical work environment that influence well-being. The fourth section presents a study that assessed the perceptions of emergency nurses with regard to their physical work environment. Finally, we conclude with a discussion and call for a theoretical development that incorporates a more service-oriented perspective to the physical design of work environments.

Experiential design and well-being

An experiential design creates an environment that is intentionally crafted as a platform to engage the individual (Huelat, 2009; Pine and

Gilmore, 1999). Like the theatre experience, it may use services as a stage and goods as props to engage the person. The more memorable the experience the higher value people place on the experience. Healthcare environments are experiential whether intentionally or unintentionally designed. Healthcare commodities such as medications, diagnostics, and caregiving are provided but how much attention is actually placed on creating a positive and memorable 'experience' for patients and staff? Between emergency rooms, intensive care units, cancer centres and others, medical facilities treat some of the most negative experiences of life. How can we reduce the negative experiences from these environments and better promote the positive and well-being? The design of physical facilities cannot eliminate injury or disease, but it can alter the experience of people as they journey through the facility.

Experiential design that promotes well-being involves capturing the beauty of an experience and engaging the person into the experience. The experience needs to be inviting and the image and atmosphere attractive to the senses (e.g. a waterfall/elements of nature placed at a front entrance). Once the beauty attracts the person into the experience, the design then needs to provide some 'escape' or 'positive distraction'. This allows the person to focus on a pleasurable diversion rather than on the medical component of the healthcare experience. For example, a fish aquarium may provide a positive distraction for patients and staff.

Learning, playful, and restorative elements of design are also important in creating experiential design (Huelat, 2009). Learning elements can take the form of educational media that describe recommended medical procedures or lifestyle activities. Playful elements add pleasure and enjoyment to the experience (e.g. decorative, themed spaces). Restorative elements involve such things as atriums, gardens or small quiet reading spaces designed throughout the facility. Restorative elements involve spaces that are restorative in nature, promote healing and well-being.

In addition, the more effective designs are at engaging the senses, the richer the memory of the experience will be. The sound of music playing on the piano or the smell of fresh flowers in a lobby; the visual delights of artwork and nature; comfortable furnishings; and access to comfort foods provide simple cues to heighten the experience. The five sense design can provide both animate and inanimate cues to the experience, supporting the positive and reducing the negative sensual elements of the environment.

The physical environment, as powerful a place as it is, cannot create health but can promote well-being. An experiential design that promotes well-being is an environment intentionally crafted as a platform to engage the individual in lifestyle choices that promote wellness to body, mind and spirit (Huelat, 2009; Pine and Gilmore, 1999). These lifestyle choices are not so much about choosing to do certain things (e.g. run ten miles a day) as they are about becoming more aware of the influences of the physical environment on well-being and engaging ourselves in spaces that are healthful, restorative and promote well-being.

The experience of work in healthcare in Canada

The experience of work in healthcare is stressful and across the globe many nurses have left the system or retired early due to injury, illness, burnout or disability (O'Brien-Pallas et al., 2006). These result in important part from spending too much time in an overworked and overstressed system where supply cannot keep up with demand. It has been reported (O'Brien-Pallas et al., 2006) that in any given week, more than 13,700 registered nurses in Canada or 7.4 per cent of the workforce are absent from work because of injury, illness, burnout or disability. It is estimated that by 2012 in the Canadian province of Alberta alone, there will be a shortage of 6,400 registered nurses if the government does not intensify efforts to recruit and retain more nurses.

There are a variety of reasons for the intense and ongoing shortage of nurses in Canada. As mentioned above, many are leaving the system altogether, choosing to retire early, or moving out of country to work elsewhere under different models of care. Another factor is the low number of nurses being trained in the educational setting where the supply of nurses is not meeting the demand. The Canadian Labour and Business Centre (CLBC, 2002) reports that nurses working full-time have a rate of absence that is 80 per cent higher than the rate found among the overall full-time labour force (8.1 per cent compared with 4.5 per cent). Lost hours due to illness and injury are estimated to total 311,364 hours per week (22.7 hours per absent nurse). It is further estimated that during 2001, a total of 16.2 million hours, the equivalent of almost 9,000 full-time nursing positions were lost to illness and injury. In addition, Canadian nurses work almost a quarter of a million hours of overtime each week, the equivalent of 7,000 full-time jobs per year. The cost of overtime, absentee wages and replacement for registered nurse absentees is between $962 million and $1.5 billion annually (CLBC, 2002).

Delving deeper into the problem of recruitment and retention, it is well known that nurses experience a high level of work stress. Several studies indicate that high workplace stress contributes to employee burnout and an intention to leave the job (Barrett and Yates, 2002; Topf and Dillon, 1988). This is supported by the annual turnover rate of nurses which averages 20 per cent (Joint Commission, 2002) and is largely claimed to be the result of an insufficient renewal of the workforce. Factors in the work environment make it impossible to restore and maximize the productivity of nurses, and insufficient funds act as barriers to hiring and educating the number of nurses needed.

In addition, healthcare providers are exposed to various occupational hazards on a daily basis that negatively impact on the experience of work and well-being (e.g. contaminants and airborne infections, the manual lifting of patients, needle stick injuries, physical and verbal assaults, and poorly entrained circadian rhythms and lack of sleep). Such factors contribute to ongoing stress, fatigue, and health deterioration. In addition, other environmental stressors such as high noise levels, inadequate light and poorly designed workspaces impact on the health and safety of nurses.

The implications of the nurse shortage in Canada demands a renewed interest in the work environment in efforts to improve the work experience for nurses. Although an understanding of the relationship between nurse staffing and nurse outcomes (e.g. job satisfaction, well-being) is beginning to emerge in the literature, little is actually known about the impact of the physical work environment on similar staff outcomes. Numerous studies (e.g. Ulrich et al., 2004) have illustrated the impact of the physical environment on patient outcomes (e.g. patient satisfaction, clinical outcomes, and well-being); however, less attention has been placed on its effects on staff.

The next section illustrates the link between attributes of the physical work environment in healthcare that can have positive or negative implications for well-being.

Attributes of the physical work environment and well-being

Recently there has been a renewed interest in the design of the physical work environment stimulated by sources from the fields of service management (Bitner, 1992), healthcare (Ulrich and Zimring, 2004), architecture (Hamilton and Sherman, 2005) and marketing (Berry, Parker,

Coile, Hamilton, O'Neil and Sadler, 2004). Several studies have been conducted that explore the impact of natural daylight, views of nature, multiple versus single patient rooms, ventilation systems, and the design and layout of nursing units on patient outcomes such as rate of adverse events (fall, medical errors), length of stay, analgesic use, and patient satisfaction (Devlin and Arneil, 2003). Although studies have been conducted on the design of the physical environment and its impact on patients, few studies have focused on staff. Despite convincing statistics on the negative impact of workplace stress on the absenteeism and retention of nurses, few studies have actually examined the impact of physical work environment on these same measures (Marberry, 2006; Ulrich et al., 2004, 2008).

In a landmark review of the literature on what is termed 'evidence-based design', researchers at Texas A & M and Georgia Institute of Technology (Ulrich and Zimring, 2004) identified more than 600 studies demonstrating the impact of hospital design on outcomes. These measures largely focused on patient outcomes but some did include evidence of reductions in staff errors and stress. Their conclusion was two-fold: first, there is more than sufficient evidence from the scientific literature to guide current hospital design from the patient perspective; and second, utilising that information to improve hospital design can have a significant impact not only on patients, but also on staff (Ulrich et al., 2004). In no other type of facility has design been shown through systematic research to have such a significant effect on outcomes considered essential to the long-term survival and performance of people and organisation. For that reason, many in the healthcare industry are turning to 'evidence-based design' as a means of making more informed choices about hospital facility design that not only helps to improve outcomes for patients (e.g. clinical outcomes, health status) but also improve outcomes for staff (e.g. improved health, well-being and experience of work, reduced turnover and absenteeism, reduced workplace injuries).

The following section describes attributes of the physical environment that are discussed largely in the literature as having an influence on patient outcomes. However, it is felt the findings are relevant to both user groups (patients and nurses) and are important to consider in designing the physical environment in ways that positively impact on experience and well-being. The attributes discussed are acoustics, air quality, colour, lighting, views of nature, and culture.

Acoustics

Noise is the most frequently studied environmental factor related to stress in hospitals. However, much of the research has examined the effects of noise on patients with few studies on staff. In the research reported, staff perceived higher sound levels as stressful and interfering with their work (Ulrich et al., 2008). More importantly, Topf and Dillon (1988) found that noise-induced stress correlates with reported emotional exhaustion or burnout among critical care nurses. A quasi-experimental study by Blomkvist et al. (2005) in Sweden demonstrated the positive impact of a single environmental factor – sound-absorbing ceiling tiles (versus sound-reflecting ones) on the perceived reduction of stress by the same group of coronary intensive care nurses over a period of months. Nurses perceived significantly lower work demands and reported less pressure and strain when the sound-absorbing tiles were in place. A survey by Hamilton, Orr and Raboin (2008) in neonatal intensive care units found that staff perceived a unit with single-patient rooms to be less stressful for both family and staff than an open-bay unit, owing to better privacy and control over the environment with respect to noise, lighting, temperature, and traffic.

As far as measurement, sound is typically measured using a meter with an A-weighted scale in decibels (dB(A)). Hearing loss usually occurs at 90 dB(A) (Baker, 1984). The World Health Organisation (WHO) guideline values for continuous background noise in hospital patient rooms are 35 dB(A) during the day and 30 dB(A) at night, with nighttime peaks in wards not to exceed 40 dB(A) (Berglund et al., 1999). Busch-Vishniac and colleagues (2005) examined hospital noise levels reported in 35 published research studies over the last 45 years. They found that not one published study reported noise levels that complied with the WHO guidelines for noise levels in hospitals. Further, hospital noise levels have been rising consistently since the 1960s. The background noise levels in hospitals rose from 57 dB(A) in 1960 to 72 dB(A) in 2005 during daytime hours, and from 42 dB(A) in 1960 to 60 dB(A) in 2005 during nighttime hours (Busch-Vishniac et al., 2005; Ulrich et al., 2008). Further, many studies indicate that peak hospital noise levels often exceed 85 dB(A) to 90 dB(A) (Blomkvist et al., 2005; Kent et al., 2002; Ulrich et al., 2008). Noises from alarms and certain equipment that exceed 90 dB(A) (e.g. portable x-ray machines) are comparable to walking next to a busy highway when a motorcycle or large truck passes. Federal workplace safety standards list 85 dB(A) as the safe maximum level of noise exposure for an eight-hour shift without ear protection (Ulrich et al., 2008).

Laboratory studies (Parsons and Hartig, 2000) of non-healthcare groups have found that noise often does not impair task performance when there is incentive to increase effort or pressure to maintain exacting standards. The laboratory findings suggest that adequate performance during noise is maintained by increasing effort, as evidenced by heightened cardiovascular response and other physiological mobilisation. The research implies the possibility that healthcare staff may be able to maintain exacting performance during some noisy situations, but at the cost of exerting greater effort and becoming more fatigued.

Overall, the findings from the research suggest that acoustics and the experience of heightened noise levels in the hospital work environment impacts on the experience of work and personal well-being.

Air quality

Air quality is another important attribute of the physical work environment that can enhance the experience of work and promote well-being in organisations. For example, poor air quality due to factors such as poor ventilation and fungal contamination of the ventilation system have been linked to the spread of hospital acquired infections among patients, which can also affect staff. Healthcare providers are at serious risk of contracting infectious diseases from patients due to airborne and surface contamination (Clarke, Sloane and Aiken, 2002; Jiang et al., 2003; Kromhout et al. 2000; Kumari et al., 1998; Smedbold et al., 2002). For example, one study that examined the relationship between indoor environmental factors and nasal inflammation among nursing personnel found the contamination of air ducts with *Aspergillus Fumigatus* to be the source of infection (Smedbold et al., 2002). A study conducted in the wake of the severe acute respiratory syndrome (SARS) epidemic found that isolating SARS cases in wards with good ventilation could reduce the viral load of the ward and might be the key to preventing outbreaks of SARS among healthcare workers, along with strict personal protection measures in isolation units (Jiang et al., 2003). While ventilation-system design and maintenance are critical to controlling the spread of airborne infections, infections are often spread through direct and indirect contact with patients. Ulrich and colleagues (2004) in their extensive literature review, concluded that poor hand washing compliance among staff is the primary cause of contact transmission of infections. They suggest that providing environmental supports to increase hand washing including visible, conveniently placed sinks; hand washing liquid dispensers; and alcohol rubs might be more successful in improving and sustaining hand washing compliance than education programs alone (Ulrich et al., 2004). They also document several studies that clearly show that hospital acquired infection rates are lower in single patient rooms as compared to semi-private rooms.

Environmental measures that are linked to increased patient safety also protect staff from acquiring hospital related infections.

Colour

Colour is a fundamental element of physical design that has been found to contribute to well-being (Joseph, 2006). It is linked to psychological, physiological, and social reactions of human beings, as well as aesthetic and technical aspects of building or facility design. Choosing a colour palette for a specific setting may depend on several factors including geographical location, characteristics of potential users (e.g. culture, age), type of activities to be performed in the facility or workspace, the nature and character of the light sources, and the size and shape of the space. Striving to better understand the influence of colour on human behaviour, researchers have looked at the physiological and psychological responses to colours. Building on these studies, various authors have claimed that specific colours have experiential effects such as the capacity to arouse and excite people while other colours possess qualities that may calm or relax individuals (Tofle et al., 2004).

Wilson (1966) speculated that red induces higher levels of arousal than green. He showed highly saturated red and green slides to twenty subjects by alternating the slides every minute for a total of 10 minutes and concluded that there was support for the hypothesis that red is more arousing, more stimulating, more exciting. Wexner (1954) hypothesized that certain colours are associated with particular moods. Accordingly, he claimed that yellow and red are perceived as 'exciting' and 'stimulating', while blue and green are considered as 'secure' and 'soothing.' Mehrabian and Russell (1974) also theorized that colour might affect people's mood and level of arousal, and that these differences in mood, arousal, and attitudes might affect task performance. In healthcare, colour and lighting have an impact on peoples' perceptions and responses to the environment and have been shown to affect patient recovery rates (Ulrich et al., 2004, 2008). Colour and appropriate lighting are also powerful tools for coding, navigation and wayfinding. Colour can also promote a sense of well-being and independence. The visual environment, including the colour and quality of daylight and electric light, is a vital element that influences the hospital experience, including staff morale and productivity.

Lighting

Lighting is another attribute of physical design that is important to creating experiential well-being. A study by Partonen and Lonnqvist (1998) found that bright light exposure has a positive effect on mood even in healthy people. Several studies have documented the importance of light and lighting in reducing depression, seasonal affective disorder (Partonen and Lonnqvist, 1998), modulating circadian rhythms, and improving sleep quality. By controlling the body's circadian system, appropriate exposure to intermittent bright light also aids the adjustment to nightshift work among staff, as demonstrated by several studies (Baehr, Fogg and Eastman, 1999; Boivin and James, 2002; Crowley, Lee, Tseng, Fogg and Eastman, 2003). One study with 87 female night-shift nurses examined whether repeated, brief exposure (4 x 20 minutes) to bright light (over 5,000 lux) during night shifts improved subjective well-being during and after night work (Leppamaki et al., 2003). Results showed that light significantly alleviated the subjective distress associated with nightshift work, in both summer and winter.

Another study found that staff with more than three hours of daylight exposure during their shift had higher job satisfaction and less stress than staff with less daylight exposure (Alimoglu and Donmez, 2005; Joseph, 2006). However, the findings are complicated by the factor of types of nursing activities. Nurses from intensive care units, emergency departments or operating rooms were mostly exposed to daylight for less than three hours, while nurses from inpatient units mostly had an exposure of more than three hours (Alimoglu and Donmez, 2005). It is clear that light and lighting impacts on personal well-being; however, more research is needed to understand the impact of natural light on stress levels and the well-being of healthcare providers.

Nature

Numerous studies have generated strong evidence that real or simulated views of nature can produce substantial relief from stress (Joseph, 2006; Ulrich et al., 2004, 2008). The strength of these findings is enhanced by the fact that some studies have used randomized controlled samples and obtained physiological as well as self-reported measurements of stress. Researchers have reported consistently that stress-reducing or restorative benefits of viewing nature are manifested as positive emotional, psychological, and physiological changes. Positive feelings such as pleasantness and calm increase, while anxiety, anger, or other negative emotions decrease (Ulrich, 1979; Ulrich, 1991; Van den Berg, Koole and Van der Wulp, 2003). Also, many nature scenes sustain positive interest and thus function as pleasant distractions that may block worrisome, stressful thoughts which are important in settings such as healthcare (Ulrich, 1981).

Regarding the physiological effects of exposure to nature, restoration is apparent when changes in bodily systems indicate reduced stress levels, for instance, reduced sympathetic nervous system activity. Physiological restoration is manifested within three minutes at most, or as fast as a few seconds in certain systems (Hartig, Book, Garvill, Olsson and Gärling, 1995; Joye, 2007; Parsons and Hartig, 2000; Ulrich, 1981). In contrast to viewing nature-dominated settings, there is convincing evidence that looking at built environments that lack nature (e.g. parking lots) is significantly less effective in fostering restoration and may actually increase stress (e.g. Ulrich, 1979, 1991; Van den Berg et al., 2003).

Culture

Lastly, culture is an important topic to be addressed in discussions pertaining to the design of the physical work environment and experiential well-being. For the physical environment to assist in addressing any of the organisational challenges in healthcare (e.g. nursing shortage) there must be a corresponding change in organisational culture (Hamilton, Orr and Raboin, 2008; Pfeffer, 1982). An example of this is with the Planetree model for healthcare that was developed in the 1980s (Planetree, 2008). Planetree has grown over the years to become a non-profit organisation that challenges the healthcare system to move from the prevailing physician-centric approach to a patient centered model for well-being and care delivery. With this model, patients are empowered to play a role in directing their course of care, have access to clinical information about their condition, are encouraged to read their medical record and make their own notes, and have family participate in the care giving process. In addition to these practices, facility design reflects this culture by including such things as pleasant, homelike surroundings that incorporate natural elements such as the warmth of wood, stone décor, and carpeting. The inclusion of warm, natural elements and views of nature are important to this design. Positive distractions such as music and patient choice of artwork in the rooms are considered part of the treatment process. Spaces for resource centres and family accommodations have been added, including kitchens where family members can prepare a meal or learn to cook healthy post-discharge diets. This new model of care delivery also includes private rooms, technology investments, and decentralised staff locations.

The coordinated efforts of organisational restructuring that initially occurred with this new model of care required a facility change and an inevitable culture change. An overarching culture of efficiency and well-being was required to deliver the updated model of care in the new setting. Planetree claims this produced dramatic results that transformed a losing operation into a successful financial performer in the healthcare system based on operating margin. This organisation was rewarded by a 13.8 per cent improvement in the ratio of full-time equivalent staff to adjusted occupied beds. Planetree has since evolved into an international alliance of more than 90 affiliates dedicated to the delivery of holistic patient-centered care based on the Planetree philosophy (Hamilton, Orr and Raboin, 2008).

Summary of the attributes

In no other type of facility (i.e. hospitals), has design been shown through systematic research to have such a significant effect on outcomes considered essential to well-being and performance. The literature above describes numerous studies that illustrate the influence of the physical environment on patient and staff outcomes. The attributes highlighted were acoustics, air quality, colour, lighting, views of nature, and culture.

The following section describes an empirical study that assessed nurse perceptions of the physical work environment in emergency rooms in Canada. The findings provide empirical support for the importance of physical design, and the need to attend to attributes of the physical work environment in ways that enhance the experience of work for nurses.

The study

Sample and methodology

A paper, mail-out survey was used as the means for data collection to assess emergency nurses' perceptions of their physical work environment. The target population and sample were emergency nurses within one province in Canada. Out of a sample of 600, 180 responded (a response rate of 30 per cent). Eighty seven per cent of respondents were female and the mean age of nurses was 45 years (birth year mean: $M = 1963$; $SD = 9.40$). This figure provides support for the literature that identifies nursing as an ageing profession (Clarke et al., 2002). Fifty-three per cent of respondents were full-time, regular employees; 30 per cent were part-time, regular employees; and 17 per cent were employed on a casual basis. Ninety one per cent of respondents were employed as a staff nurse. Half (51 per cent) were educated at the college level, just over a quarter (27 per cent) at the university undergraduate level, and just over a fifth (22 per cent) at the graduate level. On average, respondents had been working in the ER setting for a period of 121.12 months or 10.09 years. The mean time respondents had been working in their current ER was 85.19 months or 7.10 years. Respondents claim to have been working in their current capacity, the majority working as a staff nurse, on average for a period of 82.43 months or 6.87 years.

Instrument and measures

Twenty-four items measured perceptions of the physical work environment. The items were scored on a five-point Likert Scale where 1 was Strongly Disagree and 5 Strongly Agree. An example of items used to measure the 'ambience' of the physical setting where colour and lighting are discussed are as follows:

- The physical appearance and layout of the department supports intuitive way-finding.
- The quantity of space with natural daylight is optimized.
- Artificial light levels are controllable by staff.
- The colour scheme of the department creates a warm and comfortable ambience.
- The physical interior (e.g. furnishings, finishes) offers variety and contrast.
- The physical internal appearance of the department is calming and non-intimidating.

These items were taken from an instrument used by the NHS Estates and Department of Health in the United Kingdom, available for public use. The instrument is entitled the *OnDesign Healthcare Portal: ASPECT Toolkit.* ASPECT is the acronym for 'A Staff and Patient Environment Calibration Tool,' which is based on a database of over 600 pieces of research (DH, 2006) and deals with the way the healthcare environment can impact on the levels of satisfaction shown by staff and patients and on the health outcomes of patients and the performance of staff.

The dimensions of the physical work environment that were assessed in this study are as follows: *Ambience* – factors that affect perceptions of and responses to the physical environment (six items, Cronbach's alpha 0.86); *User-friendly* – the extent to which the physical environment provides comfort to users (six items, Cronbach's alpha 0.76); *Layout* – the way the department is laid out, enabling users to perform their duties and operate as a system (four items, Cronbach's alpha 0.71); *Amenities* – access to amenities such as shopping for essentials, food services, banking, the outdoors, and media/technology (three items, Cronbach's alpha 0.62); *Cleanliness* – the internal and external cleanliness of the department (two items, Cronbach's alpha 0.76); and *Adaptability* – how accommodating and adaptable the space is in relation to purpose (three items, Cronbach's alpha 0.61). Factor analysis with varimax rotation (Table 12.1) produced six components with eigenvalues over 1.00 explaining 62.4 per cent of the variance; the rotation converged in 13 iterations. Items were scored on a five-point rating scale ranging from one (strongly disagree) to five (strongly agree). Higher scores were indicative of higher levels of each item.

Descriptive analyses

General statistical analysis of the survey data was conducted using Statistical Package for the Social Sciences (SPSS). Table 12.2 shows the mean values, standard deviations, final internal consistencies, and intercorrelations of scales. With regard to the descriptive statistics, there were low ratings of all the variables that assessed the physical work environment, particularly for flexibility/adaptability ($M = 2.14$, $SD = .82$), user-friendliness ($M = 2.36$, $SD = .75$), and ambience ($M = 2.48$, $SD = .89$). In contrast, emergency nurses gave an average rating to amenities ($M = 3.19$, $SD = .83$).

As expected, there were significant and positive correlations between the six attributes of the physical work environment. There were strong and significant correlations between ambience and user-friendliness ($r = .59$), ambience and layout ($r = .59$), ambience and cleanliness ($r = .56$), and ambience and flexibility ($r = .54$), User-friendliness and layout were also strongly and positively correlated ($r = .57$) as was user-friendliness and flexibility ($r = .51$). These findings illustrate that emergency nurses perceive a clean, user-friendly and well-laid out department to be important to the design of the physical work environment in emergency rooms. In addition, the 'ambience' of the physical work environment was found to be important to nurses and had strong correlations with the majority of the attributes. The findings highlight the importance of the physical work environment to the work experience of nurses and identify attributes of physical design (e.g. ambience, flexibility) that need to be considered more in the design of the physical setting.

Discussion

This chapter has explored attributes of the physical work environment that influence the experience of work and personal well-being. Many studies on work and well-being overlook the physical component of the

Table 12.1 Results of the principal components analysis (n = 180)

Items: Physical Design	**Component 1 Ambience**	**Component 2 User-friendly**	**Component 3 Layout**	**Component 4 Amenities**	**Component 5 Cleanliness**	**Component 6 Adaptability**
PD Variety	0.83					
PD Interesting	0.79					
PD Colour	0.79					
PD Calming	0.72					
PD Nat. Light	0.67					
PD Art. Light	0.54					
PD Suff. Furnish		0.68				
PD Comfor. Furn		0.60				
PD Relax		0.58				
PD Technology		0.57				
PD Spacious		0.54				
PD Privacy		0.45				
PD Layout			0.70			
PD Proximity			0.63			
PD Security			0.50			
PD Wayfinding			0.42			
PD Amenities				0.83		
PD Outdoors				0.65		

Continued

Table 12.1 Continued

Items: Physical Design	**Component 1 Ambience**	**Component 2 User-friendly**	**Component 3 Layout**	**Component 4 Amenities**	**Component 5 Cleanliness**	**Component 6 Adaptability**
PD Media				0.54		
PD Ext. Tidy					0.83	
PD Int. Tidy					0.67	
PD Storage						0.72
PD Flexible						0.51
PD Isolation						0.46
Alpha	0.86	0.76	0.71	0.62	0.76	0.61
Eigenvalues	8.37	1.84	1.43	1.23	1.08	1.03
% Variance	34.89	7.65	5.94	5.11	4.52	4.29

Table 12.2 Descriptive statistics (aggregated measures; n = 180)

	Variable	M	SD	n	α	*1*	*2*	*3*	*4*	*5*	*6*	*7*
1	*PD Ambience*	*2.48*	*.89*	*176*	*.86*	*1.00*						
2	*PD User-Friendly*	*2.36*	*.75*	*179*	*.76*	*.59***	*1.00*					
3	*PD Layout*	*2.57*	*.79*	*178*	*.71*	*.59***	*.57***	*1.00*				
4	*PD Amenities*	*3.19*	*.83*	*180*	*.62*	*.30***	*.45***	*.32***	*1.00*			
5	*PD Cleanliness*	*2.81*	*.98*	*179*	*.76*	*.56***	*.47***	*.45***	*.27***	*1.00*		
6	*PD Flexibility*	*2.14*	*.82*	*178*	*.61*	*.54***	*.51***	*.53***	*.32***	*.44***	*1.00*	

Note: ** Correlation is significant at the 0.01 level (2-tailed).

work environment in favour of discussing workplace policies, practices and procedures that promote well-being. The physical work environment is often minimised in discussions of organisational design and change management strategies geared towards human resources; however, design offers a powerful tool for enhancing the experience of work and personal well-being.

Elements of physical design that are important in creating experiential design are beauty, invitation, positive diversion, learning, playfulness, and restoration. Attributes of the physical environment that are found to be important in promoting well-being are acoustics, air quality, colour, lighting, views of nature, and culture. The combination of these elements and attributes has important implications for the experience of work and well-being.

The industry of healthcare was the focus of investigation due to the growing shortage of healthcare providers and the need to focus on developing healthier work environments that support recruitment and retention efforts. With staff absenteeism and turnover representing leading challenges among today's healthcare organisations, this chapter supports the notion that physical design should be applied more readily as a strategic tool for addressing some of the human resource issues in healthcare.

The ongoing shortage of nurses may be largely attributed to the demanding and stressful experience of work. It is well documented that high workplace stress contributes to employee burnout and intention to leave the job. Nurses especially face obstacles with decreasing rates of retention, high levels of turnover, an ageing workforce, and the highest rates of workplace injury in all of the healthcare related professions. The importance of the physical work environment on the well being of nurses becomes apparent through the growing body of research, whether it is by improving acoustics or creating environments with ample natural lighting. Thus, a well designed physical work environment may not only have benefits for physical well being in terms of reducing injuries and decreasing stress, it can also have positive effects on perceptions of the organisation and the value placed on staff. This can affect attitudes about work, quality of work life, and lifestyle decisions such as where to work and whether to stay working for a particular organisation.

Findings from an empirical study that assessed the perceptions of emergency nurses with regard to the physical work environment underscored the need to attend to the physical design of emergency departments in a way that enhances the experience of work for nurses and promotes well-being. For example, the study found that the physical appearance and layout of emergency departments did not well support intuitive way-finding; the quantity of space with natural daylight was not optimized; artificial light levels were not well controlled by staff; the colour scheme of the department did not create a warm, comfortable, inviting ambience; and the physical appearance of the department was not calming and non-intimidating.

The implications of the research call for greater attention to be placed on the physical work environment in organisations that enhance the experience of work and promote well-being. A theoretical development of experiential design that incorporates a more ecological and service oriented perspective to the design of the physical work environments would be of value. The development of an integrated (cross-sector), theoretical model for experiential design has the potential of engaging organisations in strategically applying physical design in ways that enhance organisational performance and success. Such a model would emphasise creating a positive experience at work that contributes to well-being.

References

Alimoglu, M.K. and Donmez, L. (2005) 'Daylight exposure and the other predictors of burnout among nurses in a university hospital', *International Journal of Nursing Studies*, 42 (5): 549–55.

Baehr, E., Fogg, L.F. and Eastman, C.I. (1999) 'Intermittent bright light and exercise to entrain human circadian rhythms to night work', *American Journal of Physiology*, 277: 1598–604.

Baker, C.F. (1993) 'Annoyance to ICU noise: A model of patient discomfort', *Critical Care Nursing Quarterly*, 16: 83–90.

Barrett, L. and Yates, P. (2002) 'Oncology/haematology nurses: A study of job satisfaction, burnout, and intention to leave the specialty', *Australian Health Review: A Publication of The Australian Hospital Association*, 25 (3): 109–21.

Berglund, B., Lindvall, T. and Schwela, D.H. (1999) *Guidelines for Community Noise*. World Health Organization: Protection of the Human Environment.

Berry, L., Parker, D., Coile, R., Hamilton, D., O'Neill, D. and Sadler, B. (2004) 'The business case for better buildings', *Frontiers of Health Services Management*, 21 (1): 3–24.

Bitner, M. (1992). 'Servicescapes: The impact of physical surroundings on customers and Employees', *Journal of Marketing*, 56: 57–71.

Blomkvist, V., Eriksen, C.A., Theorell, T., Ulrich, R.S. and Rasmanis, G. (2005) 'Acoustics and psychosocial environment in intensive coronary care', *Occupational and Environmental Medicine*, 62: 132–9.

Boivin, D. and James, F. (2002) 'Circadian adaptation to night-shift work by judicious light and darkness exposure', *Journal of Biological Rhythms*, 17 (6): 556–67.

Busch-Vishniac, I., West, J., Barnhill, C., Hunter, T., Orellana, D. and Chivukula, R. (2005) 'Noise levels in Johns Hopkins Hospital', *Journal of the Acoustical Society of America*, 118 (6): 3629–45.

Canadian Labour and Business Centre (2002) *Full-Time Equivalents and Financial Costs Associated with Absenteeism, Overtime and Involuntary Part-Time Employment in the Nursing Profession*. A report prepared for the Canadian Nursing Advisory Committee.

Clarke, S., Sloane, D. and Aiken, L. (2002) 'Hospital nurse staffing and patient mortality, nurse burnout, and job dissatisfaction', *Journal of the American Medical Association*, 288: 1987–93.

Crone, R.A. (1999) *A History of Colour: The Evolution of Theories of Lights and Colour*. Boston, MA: Kluwer Academic Publishers.

Crowley, S.J., Lee, C., Tseng, C.Y., Fogg, L.F. and Eastman, C.I. (2003) 'Combinations of bright light, scheduled dark, sunglasses, and melatonin to facilitate circadian entrainment to night shift work', *Journal of Biological Rhythms*, 18 (6): 513–23.

Department of Health (2006) *OnDesign Healthcare Portal: ASPECT Toolkit*. NHS Estates. Retrieved on 18 March 2006 from http://www.design.dh.gov.uk.

Devlin, A. and Arneil, A. (2003) 'Healthcare environments and patient outcomes: a review of the Literature', *Environment and Behaviour*, 35: 665–94.

Hamilton, K., Orr, D. and Raboin, E. (2008) 'Culture change and facility design: a model for joint optimization.' *Healthcare Leadership White Paper Series*. The Center for Health Design, 5 (5): 1–75.

Hamilton, K. and Sherman, S. (2005, August) *Architecture as an Organization Development Intervention*. Paper presented at the Academy of Management Annual Meeting, Honolulu, HI.

Hamilton. K., Orr, R. and Raboln, W. (2008) 'Culture change and facility design: A model for joint optimization', *Healthcare Leadership*, 2 (5): 1–14.

Hartig, T., Book, A., Garvill, J. Olsson, T. and Gärling, T. (1995) 'Environmental influences on psychological restoration', *Scandinavian Journal of Psychology*, 37: 378–93.

Heerwagen, J. (2002) 'A balanced scorecard approach to post-occupancy evaluation: using the tools of business to evaluate facilities', *Learning from Our*

Buildings: A State of the Art Practice Summary of Post-Occupancy Evaluation: 79–87.

Jiang, S., L. Huang, X. Chen, J. Wang, W. Wu, S. Yin et al. (2003) 'Ventilation of wards and nosocomial outbreak of severe acute respiratory syndrome among healthcare workers', *Chinese Medical Journal*, 116 (9): 1293–7.

Joint Commission. (2002) *Healthcare at the Crossroad: Strategies for Addressing the Evolving Nursing Crisis.* Oakbrook Terrace, IL: Joint Commission.

Joseph, A. (2006) *The Role of the Physical and Social Environment in Promoting Health, Safety and Effectiveness in the Healthcare Workplace.* Concord, CA: Center for Health Design.

Joye, Y. (2007) 'Architectural lessons from environmental psychology: The case of biophilic Architecture', *Review of General Psychology,* 11 (4): 305–28.

Kent, W.D., Tan, A.K., Clarke, M.C. and Bardell, T. (2002) 'Excessive noise levels in the neonatal ICU: Potential effects on auditory system development', *Journal of Otolaryngology,* 31 (6): 355–60.

Kromhout, H., F. Hoek, R. Uitterhoeve, R. Huijbers, R.F. Overmars, R. Anzion, et al. (2000) 'Postulating a dermal pathway for exposure to anti-neoplastic drugs among hospital workers: applying a conceptual model to the results of three workplace surveys', *The Annals of Occupational Hygiene*, 44 (7): 551–60.

Kumari, D.N., Haji, T.C., Keer, V., Hawkey, V., Duncanson, V. and Flower, E. (1998) 'Ventilation grilles as a potential source of methicillin-resistant Staphylococcus aureus causing an outbreak in an orthopaedic ward at a district general hospital', *Journal of Hospital Infection*, 39 (2): 127–33.

Leppamaki, S., Partonen, T., Piiroinen, P., Haukka, J. and Lonnqvist, J. (2003) 'Timed brightlight exposure and complaints related to shift work among women', *Scandinavian Journal of Environmental Health,* 29 (1), 22–6.

Marberry, S. (2006) *Improving Healthcare with Better Facility Design.* Chicago, IL: Health Administration Press.

McCoy, J. and Evans, G. (2005) 'The physical environment', in J. Barling, E. Kelloway and M. Frone (eds) *Handbook of Work Stress.* Thousand Oaks, CA: Sage.

Mehrabian, A. and Russell, J.A. (1974) *An Approach to Environmental Psychology.* Cambridge, MA: MIT Press.

O'Brien, L., Griffin, P., Shamian, J., Buchan, J., Duffield, C., Hughes, F., Laschinger, S. North, N. and Stone, P. (2006) 'The impact of nurse turnover on patient, nurse and system outcomes: a pilot study and focus for a multicenter international study', *Policy, Politics, & Nursing Practice,* 7 (3): 169–79.

Parsons, R. and Hartig, T. (2000) 'Environmental psychophysiology', in J.T. Caccioppo, Tassinary, L.G. and G. Berntson (eds) *Handbook of Psychophysiology.* New York: Cambridge University Press.

Partonen, T. and Lonnqvist, J. (1998) 'Seasonal affective disorder', *Lancet,* 352 (9137): 1369–74.

Pfeffer, J. (1982) *Organization and Organization Theory.* Marshfield, MA: Pitman Publishing.

Pine, J. and Gilmore, J. (1999) *The Experience Economy.* Boston, MA: Harvard Business School Press.

Planetree. (2008) *About Planetree.* Retrieved from http://www.plantree.org on 28 March 2009.

Smedbold, H.T., Ahlen, C., Unimed, S., Nilsen, A.M., Norbaeck D. and B. Hilt. (2002) 'Relationships between indoor environments and nasal inflammation in nursing personnel', *Archives of Environmental Health*, 57 (2): 155–61.

Tofle, R., Schwarz, B., Yoon, S. and Max-Royale, A. (2004) *Colour in Healthcare Environments. Coalition for Health Environments Research.* Retrieved on 1 December 2008 from http://www.cheresearch.org

Topf, M. (1988) 'Noise-induced occupational stress and health in critical care nurses', *Hospital Topics*, 66: 30–4.

Topf, M. and Dillon, E. (1988) 'Noise-induced stress as a predictor of burnout in critical care Nurses', *Heart & Lung*, 17: 567–74.

Ulrich, R. (1979) 'Visual landscapes and psychological well-being', *Landscape Research*, 4 (1): 17–23.

Ulrich, R. (1981) 'Natural versus urban scenes: some psychophysiological effects', *Environment and Behavior*, 13: 523–56.

Ulrich, R. (1991) 'Effects of interior design on wellness: theory and recent scientific research', *Journal of Healthcare Interior Design*, 3 (1): 97–109.

Ulrich, R. and Zimring, C. (2004) *The Role of the Physical Environment in the Hospital of the 21st Century: A Once in a Lifetime Opportunity.* Report for the Center for Health Design. Concord, CA: Robert Wood Johnson Foundation.

Ulrich, R., Zimring, C., Zhu, X., DuBose, J., Seo, H., Choi, Y., Quan, X. and Joseph, A. (2008) 'Evidence based design resources for healthcare executives', *Healthcare Leadership White Paper Series.* The Center for Health Design, 5 (5): 1–75.

Van den Berg, A., Koole, S.L. and Van der Wulp, N.Y. (2003) 'Environmental preference and restoration: how are they related?' *Journal of Environmental Psychology*, 23: 135–46.

Wexner, L.B. (1954) 'The degree to which colours (hues) are associated with mood-tones', *Journal of Applied Psychology*, 38: 432–35.

Wilson, G.D. (1966) 'Arousal properties of red versus green', *Perceptual and Motor Skills*, 23: 947–9.

13

Shifting Responsibility for Health and Healthy Lifestyles: Exploring Canadian Trends

Angela Downey, Ali Dastmalchian, Helen M. Kelley, David Sharp and Kristene D'Agnone

Canadians are extremely proud of their universal healthcare system. However, today this system is in trouble. Skyrocketing costs caused by multiple factors including an ageing-population (Baxter, 2002), expensive health technologies (Downey et al., 2007), pressures from a shortage of workers in the healthcare field (Dirnfeld, 2002), and escalation of chronic diseases such as diabetes (Canadian Diabetes Association and Diabète Québec, 2005) are combining with individual demands for services and pharmaceuticals. This phenomenon is being accelerated by increasing amounts of health information and enormous advertising campaigns aimed at influencing individual demand for pharmaceuticals. But at this unique time in the history of healthcare in Canada, there are three growing trends that may curb the cost crisis and reduce demand for healthcare services: a movement in the healthcare system towards prevention of morbidity rather than treatment after onset; the increase in both societal and individual interest in healthier living; and an increasing movement towards employee health promotion in the workplace.

This chapter will summarise how these three trends have evolved and how our notions of who is responsible for an individual's health and well-being are being shaped by these trends. We also advocate that it is the last trend, the growth in worksite health promotion (WHP), that may, as part of a multi-pronged approach to the health-care crisis, provide the missing link to effective strategies based on prevention and health promotion which will result in a healthier population and lead to a viable healthcare system in Canada.

Trend one: the movement toward prevention in the Canadian healthcare system

In Canada, the notion of determinants of health was derived from the work of Thomas McKeown, a professor of social medicine at the University of Birmingham during the establishment of Britain's National Health Service. McKeown influenced two somewhat different movements that together are now referred to as 'population health.' Health promotion, the earlier of these movements, was first articulated by Hubert Laframboise in the widely circulated Lalonde report of 1974 (Lalonde, 1974). The second, research focusing on inequalities in health, grew out of the efforts of Fraser Mustard and the Canadian Institute for Advanced Research (Evans et al., 1994). Both have had a strong effect on how health is viewed, and how health information is gathered and disseminated in Canada, although they have had a more limited influence on health policy. Glouberman's work (2001) on determinants of health and health policy has had a significant impact on the field which we use to describe the evolution of the concept of 'health' in Canada.[1]

The Lalonde (1974) report marked the first stage of health promotion in Canada. It used McKeown's ideas to develop a framework labelled 'the health field concept' and applied this to an analysis of the then current state of health among Canadians. The report made a number of policy recommendations.

Determinants of health

Although McKeown is credited as the first author to use the term 'determinants of health' (Glouberman and Millar, 2003; McKeown, 1979) it is the Lalonde (1974) report that identifies the four major components of the health field concept: *human biology, healthcare systems, environment*, and *lifestyle*. *Human biology* includes all those aspects which are developed within the human body as a consequence of the basic biology of man and the organic make-up of the individual, e.g. the genetic inheritance of the individual, ageing, and the internal systems such as skeletal, nervous, muscular, cardio-vascular, endocrine, digestive and so on (Lalonde, 1974: 31). *Healthcare system* 'consists of the quantity, quality, arrangement, nature and relationships of people and resources in the provision of healthcare. It includes medical practice, nursing, hospitals, nursing homes, medical drugs, public and community healthcare services, ambulances, dental treatment and other health services such as optometry, chiropractics and podiatry' (ibid: 32). *The environment* includes all those matters related to health which are external to the human body and over which the individual has little or no control. Finally, lifestyle consists of the aggregation of decisions by individuals which affect their health and over which they more or less have control (ibid). In addition, it proposed health education and social marketing as the tools to persuade people to adopt healthier lifestyles.

Health promotion advocates recognised that an excessive emphasis on lifestyle could lead to a 'blame the victim' mentality. Smoking, for example, was not merely a matter of personal choice but also a function of one's social environment. As a result, physical and social environments are differentiated, with growing emphasis placed on the latter. By 1996, as more distinctions and additions occurred, the four determinants of health described in the Lalonde (1974) report have expanded to more than twelve determinants (Nickoloff, 1996).

The Lalonde (1974) report calls attention to the existing fragmentation in terms of responsibility for health and, under the 'Health Field Concept', these fragments are brought together into a unified whole which allows everyone to see the importance of all factors including who is responsible for each of the factors. In the 1970s this report was ahead of its time in identifying the need for inter-sectoral collaboration and recognising that multiple interventions – a combination of research, health education, social marketing, community development, and legislative and public health policy approaches – are needed to properly address health and the determinants of health. However, it would be years before these ideas would begin to find their way into mainstream thought.

Public policy response and outcomes

The health promotion movement promised to prevent illness and reduce the ever-increasing demands for and costs of healthcare services. It was believed that if the incidence of sickness could be reduced by prevention then the cost of services would be lessened, or at least the rate of increase would be diminished (Lalonde, 1974: 37). Governments concerned by the escalating costs of healthcare largely adopted the recommendations of the Lalonde report.

Multiple interventions in the area of Canadian health promotion, including public policies and legislation, have had positive outcomes in recent years:

- As a result of health education messages and restrictions on advertising, the national smoking rate dropped from approximately 50 per cent to approximately 25 per cent (Groff and Goldberg, 2000).

- New legislation increased the use of seat belts (Groff and Goldberg, 2000) and bicycle and motorcycle helmets (FPTAC, 1999).
- Impaired driving decreased in response to both education efforts and stricter enforcement of laws prohibiting impaired driving (Groff and Goldberg, 2000).
- Dietary habits changes; people began to consume less red meat, more fish, less fat, and more fruits and vegetables (Groff and Goldberg, 2000).
- Physical exercise increased in response to various health promotion publications (e.g. the Canada Food Guide) and programs (e.g. the 'Participaction' program) established by the government of Canada to support health priorities, particularly the promotion of healthy, active living, in unique and innovative ways (Health Canada, 1989).

During the late 1980s, the health promotion movement adopted a 'settings' approach which focused on improving health in schools, workplaces, and communities. 'Empowerment' became a central concept in the promotion of good health—fostering the notion that each individual has control over many of his or her own life-style choices that impact overall health. This approach emphasises processes more than outcomes, and while it enjoys a certain degree of success (notably in the healthy communities and cities movements, which continue to function in some jurisdictions), the lack of measurable outcomes and means of evaluating program effectiveness has attracted substantial criticism.

During the early 1990s, when increasing healthcare expenditures led governments to seek ways to cut healthcare spending, health promotion came under negative scrutiny. First, health promotion policies did not generate the anticipated savings in healthcare costs because new therapeutic and diagnostic technologies inexorably drove costs up. Second, health promotion messages were better received among the more advantaged sectors of society, and consequently inequities in certain risk behaviours (e.g. tobacco use, obesity) actually worsened (Groff and Goldberg, 2000). Third, other unexpected developments resulted in new problems. Although people exercised more, they also spent more time watching television and driving in vehicles, and while the nature of their diet improved, the quantities consumed increased. Similarly, after an initial decline, smoking rates levelled off at about 25 per cent (Federal Provincial and Territorial Advisory Committee, FPTAC, 1996). Finally, there was a growing perception that health promotion failed to deliver adequate outcomes especially as certain programs (e.g. Participaction), after initial successes, failed to make continued improvements. Price Waterhouse was hired to evaluate the federal health promotion program in 1989. The consulting firm drew the negative conclusion that 'the paradigm which envisages health as the product of anything and everything does not readily lend itself to being actioned' (Health & Welfare Canada, 1992).

Population health and research in health promotion

Health inequities along social class lines have been an ongoing feature of epidemiological studies. Many health outcomes can be seen as gradients when they are plotted against an array of socioeconomic determinants. For example, in the case of cancer and heart disease, better health status has been closely correlated with socioeconomic variables (Glouberman and Millar, 2003; Marmot et al., 1997).

Similar to Laframboise and colleagues, Fraser Mustard and researchers at the Canadian Institute for Advanced Research (CIAR) were influenced by McKeown. McKeown had argued that health gains achieved in the 19th and 20th centuries were largely attributable to reduced family sizes and better nutrition. CIAR and others extended this analysis to identify social and economic factors that have powerful effects on the health of individuals and communities or nations (McKay, 2000).

The authors of *Why Are Some People Healthy and Others Not?* (Evans et al., 1994) used epidemiological evidence to explain how different factors influence health and they concluded that social and economic environments have a far stronger impact on health than individual behaviours. Several other studies reached similar conclusions. For example, the Whitehall study (Marmot et al., 1997) illustrates that the pronounced differences in disease incidence and mortality rates evident across income and social groups are not just caused by lifestyle and genetic makeup. The authors posit that decision making power and control are important mediators of health inequalities. Wilkinson (1996) argues that economic development and the distribution of wealth in a society are important determinants of population health and Marmot et al. (1997) suggest that aspects of the workplace environment, both from a physical perspective and in terms of decision making latitude (control) are important health determinants. In addition, studies have found that early development is extremely important in regards to children's future schooling, employment, as well as their health (Jenkins and Keating, 1999) and is also critical in terms of the development of their future coping skills (Keating and Hertzman, 2000).

The term 'population health', introduced by Mustard and CIAR, was for some time the subject of debate. Eventually, Health Canada and many provincial governments adopted the term for a large part of their health promotion activity, although the main emphasis was not on reducing inequalities in health. Recently, researchers focusing on health inequalities have attempted to incorporate many of the principles of health promotion, and 'population health' is increasingly being used to refer to this more unified approach. Researchers argue that not all determinants of health are of equal importance; for instance, Marmot and others emphasise a subset of determinants that link health status with such areas as control over work (Marmot et al., 1997).

Societal and policy impacts

The health promotion movement stressed that inter-sectoral collaboration is necessary if policies are to deal with the many determinants of health. In Canada, there are initiatives that can be traced to these combined ideas regarding population health and many of these have been initiated through the Canadian system of joint federal provincial/territorial committees.

- All of the Canadian provinces have set health goals that encompass the varied determinants of health (Federal Provincial and Territorial Advisory Committee, 1999). Their objectives include improvements in working and living conditions, health behaviours, early child development, access to effective healthcare services, and aboriginal health.
- All provinces have regionalised the delivery of health services (a policy recommended in the Lalonde report) and have focussed more on addressing the broad determinants of health (Health Canada, 1996). Regional healthcare managers are engaging in inter-sectoral activities designed to address these determinants. For example, Capital Health in Edmonton, Alberta is working with the board of education to address obesity (Capital Health, 2001). In addition, funding for research on population health has increased considerably. In 1999, the Canadian Population Health Initiative received $20 million to fund further research over a four year period. More recently, the Canadian Institutes for Health Research (CIHR) included population health as one of its four pillars in addition to biomedical, clinical, and health services research. Of the 13 institutes funded under this scheme, five are clearly focused on population-related areas such as

population and public health, aboriginal health, gender and health, ageing and health, and child development.

- The child tax benefit illustrates the government's recognition of the effects of poverty on children and families (Canadian Council on Social Development, 2001). The importance of early child development has been addressed through the Children's Agenda, which attracted $2 billion in federal funding in 2000 (National Children's Alliance, 1998). Several jurisdictions are monitoring the adequacy of children's early development designing indicators to capture standardised data (Human Resources Development Canada, 1999).
- Another federal government tax policy appears to be linking the benefits of physical activity to health-related issues such as childhood obesity. In 2007, a $500 tax credit for physically active children was introduced by the federal government and appears to be a trend that the provinces will adopt. For example, a private member's bill for a physical activity tax credit for all Albertans (children and adults) was introduced and passed first reading in the Legislative Assembly in November 2008.
- Programs that have broadened their strategies to accommodate a population-based approach have experienced some success.[2] A good example is tobacco use reduction programs which incorporate restrictions on advertising, package warnings, restrictions on sales to minors, and increased restrictions on smoking in public places. The Canadian smoking rate has dropped to 20 per cent, and rates are even lower in British Columbia and Ontario (Statistics Canada, 2001).

Several academic institutions have responded to these positive changes by establishing institutes or centres for population health research (e.g. University of Ottawa, University of British Columbia).

Regular reports on population health and the determinants of health are now published at the regional, provincial, and national levels, for example the Annual Report on the Health of British Columbians (British Columbia Ministry of Health, 1999) and the Maclean Health Reports (Maclean Health Reports, 1999). In addition, several large, linked (and, in some cases, longitudinal) databases have been established nationally as well as in British Columbia, Alberta, Manitoba, and Quebec, providing powerful resources for population health research. The Canadian Community Health Survey (formerly the National Population Health Survey) has been enhanced to provide more locally relevant data. The National Longitudinal Study on Children and Youth, funded by Human

Resources Development Canada, is another important source of data for understanding population health and developing new policies. Finally, the Canadian Institute for Health Information, in partnership with Statistics Canada, has developed a population health indicators framework. Data are now available to support some 80 to 90 indicators across the four domains of this framework (Health Status, Determinants of Health, Health System Performance and Community and Health System Characteristics) and have been included in the 'Report on the Health of Canadians' (Federal Provincial and Territorial Advisory Committee, 1996) and in 'Healthcare in Canada' (Federal Provincial and Territorial Advisory Committee, 1999). These data, because they are standardised, support the development of reports on population health and the healthcare system across Canada at both the regional and provincial levels. They also allow for international comparisons of the health of the Canadian population and the performance of the Canadian healthcare system.

This discussion reveals that there is a great deal of interest, activity, and resources being deployed in pursuit of conceptualising and understanding population health concepts. To some extent, this is due to the bandwagon effect that has surrounded the term 'population health.' Despite several modest successes (e.g. in the areas of tobacco use and child development), however, the population health approach, while providing a deeper understanding of socioeconomic gradients in health status, has not yet resulted in adequate corresponding policy development to effectively reduce inequalities in health (Glouberman and Millar, 2003).

In the mid-1970s to mid-1980s, during the period of the Lalonde (1974) report and the Ottawa Charter (1986),[3] Canada was among the countries leading the world in health promotion. Over the past decade, as the public dialogue has been dominated by concerns about the costs and delivery of healthcare services, inadequate attention has been paid to important emerging health issues, especially those that relate to inequalities. For example, family poverty, epidemic obesity, early childhood development, and aboriginal health are major health issues for which there is no coordinated national plan. In the meantime, countries such as the United Kingdom and Sweden have developed plans to address many of these issues and others such as teenage pregnancy, education, unemployment, access to healthcare, housing, and crime. These plans have been achieved through the involvement of other government departments such as education, justice, economic development, finance, housing, and social security.

Several Canadian health commissions (e.g. Fyke, 2001; Romanow, 2002) have emphasised the importance of addressing the determinants of health and incorporating population health concepts and approaches into the healthcare system so as to improve the health of individuals and communities and reduce inequities. The Commission on the Future of Healthcare (Romanow, 2002) released its recommendations for improving the public healthcare system, helping to clear the way for policymakers and the public to turn their attention toward some of the neglected health issues mentioned above. With effective political leadership, collaborative efforts between different sectors (government, the private sector, voluntary organisations), and the development of policies based on the best available evidence, Canada may once again join the countries leading the way in health promotion and population health.

Creating a comprehensive policy framework that supports the necessary shift in the way we think about health and engaging credible healthcare champions of change are critical first steps. However, creating change in individuals' attitudes towards their health and their role in determining their own health and well-being will also play an important part in developing improved population health. The next section outlines the second trend that is helping the movement towards this goal.

Trend two: the increase in societal and individual interest in healthier living

Institutional and professional roles in prevention

With increasing emphasis on prevention, greater emphasis has been placed on community resources to provide education to organisations and individuals looking to adopt healthier lifestyle choice (Denis et al., 1999). Healthcare institutions are capitalising on society's general interest in health promotion through aggressive marketing campaigns. These include campaigns directed at the growing epidemic of obesity across North America (Pratt, 2008), at support and encouragement of breastfeeding (McIntyre et al., 2002), and at immunisation programs for influenza and childhood diseases.

One example of marketing having an impact on changes in values and beliefs within healthcare is attitudes and policy changes towards breast feeding. Breastfeeding is widely recognised for its benefits to both mother and infant (McIntyre et al., 2002). Research has demonstrated that infants who are breastfed are less likely to have allergies and have a reduced likelihood of the onset of a number of chronic conditions such as diabetes, while the mother is able to reduce her personal risk of breast and ovarian cancer (McIntyre et al., 2002). To promote the benefits of breastfeeding and support a mother's choice to breastfeed, many organisations have made changes to policies to provide women with the opportunity and resources to breastfeed while returning to work. Healthcare resources offer education programs, consultations, and free assessments to encourage women to continue breastfeeding and actively pursue information to support their choice.

In addition to organisational changes to policy, federal and provincial bodies also act to encourage specific behaviours through legislation. Smoking cessation programs are prominent throughout North America and are supported by changes limiting the opportunity to smoke in public places. As a result, an entire industry has been established to support individuals seeking to modify their smoking behaviour (Anonymous, 2006).

While health is generally seen as being an individual issue, organisations and legislative bodies recognise the need to support these initiatives (Pratt, 2008). It has been essential for attitudes to change on a societal and professional level (Horton, 2008) in order for health promotion to gain momentum and support. Powell et al. (1999) indicate that while external pressures can create a demand for change to occur, internal pressures must also demonstrate a commitment towards challenging the existing approaches and structures. Recognition of the need for health promotion by health authorities, organisations, individuals and professionals has acted to facilitate the shift in values and beliefs but requires continued momentum to institutionalise the change (Powell et al., 1999).

Doctors, nurses, and other healthcare practitioners, as a profession, have to redefine their role in the treatment of patients to a more preventative approach including educational elements (Mellor and St. John, 2007). While physicians have traditionally been seen as the dominant group (Denis et al., 1999), they may be more willing to change their traditional roles as the population continues to age (Baxter, 2002) and demands for healthcare subsequently increase. That is, prevention education in the past has not been a priority for physicians as their focus has been on treating the symptoms rather than on educating the individual on how to prevent chronic illnesses such as diabetes or heart disease. As a result of this movement from a curative to a preventive system, physicians are having to redefine their approach to dealing with patients. Physicians may also recognise the need to adopt a wellness mindset to maintain their power and dominance within the health field (Abbott, 1988) and to define the boundaries of work to be done (Scott and Backman, 1990) within a new paradigm. The willingness of physicians to cooperate and make a substantial change to their profession as a whole may explain why there has been little resistance towards WHP and its goals and objectives (Greenwood and Hinings, 1996). In addition, the recent acceptance of nurse practitioners in Ontario to offer some of the traditional services normally reserved for physicians, coupled with the release of a best practice guideline (Registered Nurses Association of Ontario, 2008) for a healthy workplace for nursing professionals, may indicate that the nursing profession is poised to play an even larger role in prevention initiatives.

Individual choice of better lifestyle

Never has a population made a more purposeful choice to adopt lifestyle choices that will improve their well-being (Maurx, 2004). In Canada, we see increased awareness of the links between life-style choices and overall health. For example, the role that physical activity can play in personal well-being is seen throughout the streets of the nation as more and more people walk and run for health. The role that healthy eating plays in health is also well established. With individuals actively becoming involved in their own health, they have increased expectations and are demanding increased access and integration of health services (Mason, 1998). Maurx (2004: 4) states 'with increased awareness and knowledge about the importance of lifestyle and/or behaviour modification, individuals tend to take more responsibility for their health.'

Individuals are motivated to play a more active role in their health due to the abundance of information available through technological advancements like the internet (Mason, 1998) coupled with a willingness to educate themselves about health and wellness. Educated individuals are seeking alternatives to medicine and are more interested in taking care of minor health issues in the hope of avoiding major complications later in life (Maurx, 2004).

However, with all the knowledge and information available that link improved lifestyle choices to improved health, the evidence also suggests that it is difficult to develop good habits that allow us to deny ourselves all the pleasures that we are bombarded with via the advertising media. High fat foods tempt us every day. 'Super-sizing' encourages us to eat more than we need. Increased passive activity like television in home-movie settings and video games encourage us to do less and eat more. The obesity crisis continues to grow. So why is it that with such an educated population and the availability of information that points to better life-style choices as the key to improved wellness, many continue to make poor choices in their life? It is likely to be our fundamental desire to seek gratification even if it is bad for us (encouraged by media and advertising).

It appears that government systems that encourage health promotion and prevention coupled with increased information on the benefits of making better individual choices is not achieving the overarching goals for the society. There is a need to better reach people and connect with them regarding their everyday lives and ways of living. The following section suggests that work-site health promotion may be the approach to encourage individuals to internalise improved lifestyle choices as a way of life.

Trend three: increased worksite health promotion

While the Canadian healthcare system is shifting from a philosophy of treatment to one of prevention of acute and chronic illnesses to curb its cost crisis, worksite organisations are developing programs to address similar concerns. Health promotion programs were initially implemented to address job satisfaction, productivity, rising healthcare costs, short-term and long-term disability and absenteeism (Maurx, 2004; Downey, 2000). Originally, organisations focused on programs that emphasised occupational health and safety programs; however, as employees begin to take a more pro-active approach to their health (Mason, 1998), and Health Canada's vision expanded to promote healthier lifestyles (see Health Canada's website at www.hc-sc.gc.ca) organisations as employers have begun to implement a growing number of work-site health promotion (WHP) activities (Pratt, 2008).

In the United States, WHP programs are reported to presently be as high as 90 per cent of large companies, 61 per cent of companies with less than 250 employees (Haines et al., 2007; Kossek et al., 2001; Milano, 2007) and this number is increasing (Madsen, 2003). Many WHP programs have activities that are linked to multiple dimensions of well-being (Milano, 2007) such as physical well-being (noon-time walking clubs and membership subsidies in fitness facilities), intellectual well-being (general education and training opportunities for employees), mental well-being (activities that relieve stress such as participation in company sports activities), emotional well-being (such as programs that teach cross-cultural respect and the value of each individual) and spiritual well-being (such as recognising and accepting everyone's religious choices). Evidence suggests that the incidence of WHP in Canada is more limited than that of the United States as the motivation to implement WHP is not as strong in countries with national healthcare systems as in those without (Downey and Sharp, 2007).

Worksite health promotion (WHP) research provides evidence to convince many employers that employees who adopt healthier lifestyle choices tend to miss less work due to illness, are more productive when at work, have a better attitude toward work, and are more likely to stay with an organisation (Maurx, 2004; Downey, 2000). Despite strong advocates for organisational benefits, a lack of evidence based research in the 1990s (Leeuw, 2006) along with a lack of directive strategies guiding development and implementation of activities designed to modify behaviour (Weiner et al., 2000) have limited the scope of health promotion programs within many organisations. There are still significant gaps regarding the evaluation of the quality and processes associated with WHP programs (Mittelmark, 2007) and its impact on the community as a whole.

Although there tends to be a lack of intuitive models[4] to guide health promotion implementation (Pluye et al., 2004), organisations are the ideal venue to facilitate the development of innovative activities designed to promote healthy living. Kegler et al. (2008) states 'much of community health improvement occurs through organizations; organizations develop programs, obtain and allocate resources and implement policies that directly affect the quality of life for community residents' (p. 109). Kegler et al. (2008) then states that 'organizational change can also be a catalyst for broader-scale community change; in other words, a change in organizations and their interrelationships can impact the system as a whole' (p. 109).

Identifying how to sustain health promotion activities (Pluye et al., 2004) through programs that have been haphazardly introduced into the organisation is increasingly becoming a concern. Mittelmark (2007) identifies that the lack of communication about resource requirement, of infrastructure and of the skills needed to effectively deliver on the goals of WHP initiatives are key difficulties for organisations during implementation.

Motivating organisations to maintain and expand health promotion activities can be challenging when it takes between three to five years for organisations to benefit from initial costs associated with implementing wellness programs (Milano, 2007). While the returns on initial investments take time to be realised within the organisation, the shift in organisational values to support health promotion facilitates the development of relationships with community resources and a shift to a preventative approach to healthcare.

With increased individual responsibility, employees have played an integral role in determining the type of activities implemented by organisations. Popular WHP activities include employee fitness (Adams, 2007; Haines et al., 2007; Kossek et al., 2001; Pratt, 2008; Riley et al., 2008), diet choices (Adams, 2007; Ellis et al., 2008; Pratt, 2008), physical, walking/running programs (Haines et al., 2007), substance abuse and stress levels (Deitz et al., 2005), flexibility and repetitive motion analysis, cholesterol screening (Devaney, 2008), tobacco reduction (Ellis et al., 2008; Pratt, 2008; White and Jacques, 2007), chronic disease prevention (Ellis et al., 2008; Riley et al., 2008), mental health (Deitz et al., 2005; Horton, 2008), aids awareness (Downey, 2000), health education, screening programs, and wellness assessment components (Kossek et al., 2001). Participation levels in these programs should not be the sole criteria in determining the effectiveness of WHP and employee interest. Wolf and Parker (1994) suggest that peer pressure influences the decisions made by other members of the organisation about health behaviours. So, for example, an employee may not participate in a 'fitness at work program' but their co-workers' involvement and the benefits that have flowed from this, have encouraged him or her to join a community fitness program or join a gym near home. So, there are more than likely indirect effects to workplace health program that are more difficult to measure than just participation in the programs.

With organisations and employees adopting healthier lifestyles through participation in an increasing number of programs, a growing number of organisations in Canada are expanding existing WHP programs. The next section outlines changes in WHP in Canada between 1996 and 2006.

Highlighting a decade of change

The Canadian organisational environment has lagged the US in developing worksite health promotion programs and this is more than likely due to the very different motivations for undertaking these endeavours. US employers experience fluctuating health insurance ratings and associated costs based on the interactions between employees and the healthcare system. In Canada, with a National healthcare system, the motivation for employers to create environments that encourage improved employee lifestyle choices which would reduce use of the healthcare system is very different (Downey and Sharp 2007). However, a recent study by Downey et al. (2008) illustrates WHP is alive and growing in Canada. The results of this study illustrate some interesting differences compared with a similar study undertaken a decade previously (Downey 2000) and reveals changes occurring in organisational environments with regards to organisational commitment to employee wellbeing.

The Downey et al. (2008) study[5] reveals that even among 74 Canadian organisations considered to have exemplary health promotion programming there are differences in the nature and type of WHP and the organisational commitment to them. Using non-probability sampling (snowball method) firms were identified that had received awards for their WHP programs, had been reported via media reports to have exemplary WHP, or were suggested by Canadian WHP experts to have exemplary programs. The 74 organisations were pre-interviewed by telephone to confirm the comprehensiveness of their WHP prior to receiving access to a web-based survey. The survey included both open-ended and closed-ended questions aimed at determining the 'current state' of their WHP including the extent of activities (number, type, and participation levels), the length of time the organisation had been involved in WHP, the organisational infrastructures established to support WHP, and a description of how exemplary WHP programs evolved.

Downey (2000) found that firms in 1996 (a sample of 102 firms from one industry, auto parts manufacturing) were relatively new to the notions of WHP with less than 3 per cent of the organisations offering comprehensive programs that included a range of activities (education, intervention, and monitoring) coupled with strong supporting organisational infrastructures (budgets, wellness committees, top management commitment, linkage to firm strategies). By 2006, nearly 75 per cent of organisations had made extensive or moderate changes to their policies, processes, structures, beliefs and awareness to implement and support WHP. In addition, over 80 per cent of these organisations had linked WHP to their organisational strategies (Downey et al., 2008).

Over time there has been a change in the type of WHP activities offered as well as changes in the dimensions of well-being addressed in current programming. In the early 1990s, Wolfe and Parker (1994) suggested that comprehensive WHP programming should address the psychological, mental, and social well-being of individuals. However, the most prevalent activities in Canada in 1996 were almost exclusively linked to physiological well-being, either screening or preventing physiological problems. By comparison, a decade later, organisations offered activities that were focused on five dimensions of WHP; physiological (72 per cent), social (42 per cent), emotional/mental (40 per cent), intellectual (22 per cent) and spiritual (22 per cent). Although WHP focus still centres on employees physical health, where extensive prior evidence suggests that improvement leads to solid economic returns, we see a growth in activities that address the needs of the whole person.[6] Table 13.1 below compares specific activities and the changes that occurred within organisations between 1996 and 2006.

The comparison between 1996 and 2006 is limited to the activities that were reported as most important in the earlier study (many of which are linked to the traditional occupational safety and health programs mandated by government). But even with this limitation, it is obvious the percentage of organisations involved in this limited list of activities has increased significantly over the ten-year period.

Another interesting difference between the two studies centres on the individual charged with the responsibility of overseeing the WHP programs at organisations. In 1996, WHP was found under the rubric of either the Human Resource function or Health and Safety. By 2006, WHP was most often not the responsibility of the traditional Health and Safety function but was overseen by the Human Resource function often under the direction of an individual with the title of 'Wellness Director' (60 per cent of organisations).

These two studies also examine the motivation to implement and maintain WHP. In 1996, managements' motivation was linked to

Table 13.1 The incidence of workplace health activities, 1996 and 2006

Component	% Involved in 1996	% Involved in 2006
Work Injury Prevention	33 %	91%
Stress Management Training	13 %	84 %
Proper Nutrition	14 %	87 %
Blood Pressure Monitoring	27 %	71 %
Breast Cancer Screening	1 %	71 %
Cholesterol Testing	6 %	54 %
Diet Club	14 %	55 %
Back Programs	33 %	65 %
Individual Counseling	50 %	87 %
Smoking Cessation	33 %	78 %
Stress Management	13 %	79 %
Substance Abuse Support	57 %	69 %

improved morale and productivity as well as decreased absenteeism and turnover. Although these motivations are still present in 2006, there are new motivations emerging that are directly linked to the core of WHP – promoting employee health and well-being and reducing health benefit costs (e.g. pharmaceutical expenses).

The comparison of these two studies, a decade apart, provides evidence of the commitment of organisations to providing an environment that supports improved life-style choices that should in turn prevent health failure is increasing in Canada. Even with employer cost for employee healthcare driven by flat rates as determined by the National healthcare system, Canadian organisations are creating environments that encourage employees to take responsibility for their own well-being and are providing programs and support to assist. This trend is likely to reduce the demand for healthcare services in the future.

Conclusion

It was suggested in the opening paragraphs of this chapter that encouraging healthier individual life-style choices requires a multi-pronged approach. The first approach highlighted was the movement in Canada to build prevention and promotion of improved individual choices into the healthcare system. Today, there is ample evidence that Canada's healthcare system has undergone a shift in its approach to providing healthcare. No longer is the system just focused on providing service after the onset of morbidities but has changed its vision and mission to prevent and reduce the risks to individual health and to promote healthier lifestyles. We have illustrated changes in structures, funding, collaborations, and goals that have moved the system along the continuum of prevention. In addition we have outlined some fundamental changes in both individual and societal attitudes towards their own role in their health via life-style choices. Finally we have shown that there is a growing trend towards work-site health promotion programs as organisations recognize the 'win-win' of playing a role in creating an environment at work that encourages employees to make better life-style choices.

It is our assertion in this chapter that the final of the multi-pronged approaches is contained in the workplace. By establishing an integrated approach to wellness that links the healthcare system, society and individual roles and beliefs with an environment in the workplaces of Canada that encourages and reinforces prevention and health promotion, we may see a lasting improvement in individual life-styles that will reduce demand for healthcare services and relieve the cost crisis that currently exists in our national healthcare system. As a result of changes in healthcare philosophies, society as a whole, institutions, governing bodies, organisations and individuals are beginning to make changes to their values and belief systems to support a preventative approach to health which is likely to support healthier lifestyle choices and reduce healthcare costs.

Notes

1. We have emphasised that the idea of prevention emanated out of the development of the notion of population health in the UK which indeed is a valuable lens through which to look at and to understand how prevention has become part of the fabric of the Canadian healthcare system. However, we tend to think that 'prevention' spreads from the healthcare system to the work environment (see Downey et al., 2007). In fact, it could be argued that the notion of prevention as it is conceived in the worksite health promotion programs has found its way to the Canadian context from the US (clearly with some influences from the UK developments of worksite Health Promotion platforms). We would like to point out that the American business environment has historically had very different drivers and incentives for controlling the healthcare spending at the workplace level. Without national healthcare, US businesses offering employee health benefits undergo a similar rating and insurance charge as the Canadian's worker's compensation processes. In this context increasing claims will have a direct impact on the insurance costs. Thus typical US employers have been considerably more concerned about the employees' frequency and extent of access to the healthcare system compared with the Canadian counterparts. As the respective costs in Canada have been increasing in recent years, more Canadian employers are getting involved in implementing WHP. Thus WHP in Canada has been growing alongside the prevention notion in the healthcare system but the system growth has not been solely responsible for the worksite growth. Rather the cost and the worksite developments in the US have had a partial impact on the growth of WPH in Canada.
2. Of interest, the province of Alberta started to de-regionalise and move toward a centralised healthcare model called Alberta Health Services in 2008. The action suggests that regionalisation was not achieving the anticipated benefits. Whether the other provinces follow the same trend is a salient question worth tracking in the future.
3. The Ottawa charter of 1986 (WHO Conference on health promotion) has laid the foundation for global HP recognition. Although the Ottawa charter is now 20 years old, many researchers still reference it and use it as the standard for HP.
4. Green and Krueter's PRECEDE-PROCEED (Green and Kreuter, 1999) model provides a comprehensive structure for assessing health and quality-of-life needs and for designing, implementing, and evaluating health promotion

and other public health programs to meet those needs. Unfortunately this model is complex and has not been used widely in practice.
5. The 2006 study was funded by The Change Foundation of Ontario.
6. There may be an emerging dimension to WHP that focuses on the physical work environment. See the chapter in this book entitled 'Designing for Well-Being: The Role and Influence of the Physical Work Environment.'

References

Abbott, A. (1988) *The System of Professions: An Essay on the Division of Expert Labor.* Chicago, IL: The University of Chicago Press.
Adams, S. (2007) 'Green light for drivers', *Occupational Health*, 59 (11): 29–31.
Anonymous. (2006) 'Use of cessation methods among smokers aged 16–24 years–United States, 2003', *Morbidity and Mortality Weekly Report,* 55 (50): 1351–54.
Baxter, D. (2002) 'Population matters: demographics and healthcare in Canada', in D. Gratzer (ed.), *Better Medicine: Reforming Canadian Healthcare.* Toronto, ON: ECW Press: 135–72.
British Columbia Ministry of Health (1999) *A Report on the Health of British Columbians.* Victoria, British Columbia, Canada: British Columbia Ministry of Health.
Canadian Diabetes Association and Diabète Québec (2005). *Diabetes Progress Report 2005* Ottawa, ON: Canadian Diabetes Association and Diabète Québec.
Capital Health (2001) 'The supersize generation: responding to the obesity epidemic'. Paper presented at: Strategic Planning Workshop, June 2001, Edmonton, Alberta, Canada.
Canadian Council on Social Development (2001) *Equality, Inclusion and the Health of Canadians.* Ottawa, Ontario, Canada: Canadian Council on Social Development.
Deitz, D., Cook, R. and Hersch, R. (2005) 'Workplace health promotion and utilization of health services', *The Journal of Behavioural Health Services and Research,* 32 (3): 306–19.
Denis, J., Lamothe, L., Langley, A. and Valette, A. (1999) 'The struggle to redefine boundaries in healthcare systems', in Brock, D., Powell, M. and Hinings, C.R. (eds), *Restructuring the Professional Organization: Accounting, Healthcare and Law.* New York: Routledge: 105–130.
Devaney, M. and Noone, P. (2008) 'Is lifestyle screening worth it?', *Occupational Health*, January: 27–29.
Dirnfeld, V. (2002) 'Foreword', in D. Gratzer (ed.), *Better Medicine: Reforming Canadian Healthcare.* ,Toronto, ON: ECW Press: 135–72.
Downey, A. (2000) 'The status of worksite health promotion in a Canadian environment: an examination of the motives of different management groups', Doctoral Dissertation, The University of Western Ontario, 1990.
Downey, A. and Sharp D. (2007) 'Why managers allocate resources to workplace health promotion programmes in countries with national health coverage', *Health Promotion International,* 22 (2): 102–11.
Downey, A., Kelly, H., D'Agnone, K., Sharpe, D. and Dastmalchian, A. (2008) 'Growth of worksite health promotion in Canada', Paper presented at the

Administrative Science Association of Canada Annual Conference (Healthcare Management Division), Halifax, NS, (June).

Ellis, N., Mackenzie, A.and Mobbs, R. (2008) 'Compensation and wellness: a conflict for veterans' health', *Australian Health Review,* 32 (2): 308–12.

Evans R., Barer M. and Marmor T. (eds) (1994) *Why Are Some People Healthy and Others Not?: The Determinants of Health of Populations.* New York, NY: Aldine de Gruyter.

Federal Provincial and Territorial Advisory Committee (FPTAC) (1996) *Report on the Health of Canadians.* Toronto, ON: Federal Provincial and Territorial Advisory Committee on Population Health.

Federal Provincial and Territorial Advisory Committee (FPTAC) (1999)*Toward a Healthy Future: Second Report on the Health of Canadians.* Ottawa, ON: Federal, Provincial and Territorial Advisory Committee on Population Health.

Fyke K. (2001) *Caring for Medicare: Sustaining a Quality System.* Regina, Saskatchewan, Canada: Commission on Medicare.

Glouberman S. (2001) *Towards a New Perspective on Health Policy.* Ottawa, ON: Canadian Policy Research Networks.

Glouberman S. and J. Millar (2003) 'Evolution of the determinants of health policy and human information systems in Canada', *American Journal of Public Health,* 93 (3): 388–72.

Green, L.W. and Kreuter, M.W. (1999) *Health Promotion Planning: An Educational and Ecological Approach,* 3rd edition. Mountain View, CA: Mayfield.

Greenwood, R. and Hinings, C.R. (1996) 'Understanding radical organizational change: Bringing together the old and the new institutionalism', *Academy of Management Review,* 21 (4): 1022–54.

Groff, P. and Goldberg S. (2000) *The Health Field Concept Then and Now: Snapshots of Canada.* Ottawa: Canadian Policy Research Networks.

Haines, D.J., Davis, L., Rancour, P., Robinson, M., Neel-Wilson, T. and Wagner, S. (2007) 'A pilot intervention to promote walking and wellness and to improve the health of college faculty and staff', *Journal of American College Health,* 55 (4): 219–25.

Health & Welfare Canada (HWC) (1992) *Discussion Paper on Phase I of a Study of Healthy Public Policy at Health & Welfare Canada.* Ottawa, ON: Policy, Planning and Information Branch, Program Evaluation Division.

Health Canada (1989) *Participaction: Our History and Evolution; 1971–.* Ottawa, ON: Health Canada.

Health Canada (1996) *Key Determinants of Health.* Ottawa, ON: Health Canada.

Horton, R. (2008) 'Danger: people at work', *The Lancet,* 371 (March 22): 971–2.

Human Resources Development Canada (1999) Helping Communities Give Children the Best Possible Start. Ottawa, Ontario, Canada.

Jenkins J. and Keating D. (1999) *Risk and Resilience in Six and Ten Year-Old Children.* Toronto, ON: University of Toronto.

Keating D. and C. Hertzman (2000) *Developing Health and the Wealth of Nations: Social, Biological, and Educational Dynamics.* NY: Guilford Press.

Kegler, M.C., Norton, B.L. and Aronson, R. (2008) 'Achieving organizational change: findings from case studies of 20 California health cities and communities coalitions', *Health Promotion International,* 23 (2): 109–18.

Kossek, E., Ozeki, C. and Kosier, D. (2001) 'Wellness incentives: lessons learned about organizational change', *Human Resource Planning,* 24 (4): 24–35.

Lalonde M. (1974) *A New Perspective on the Health of Canadians*, Ottawa: Government of Canada.

Leatt, P., Pink, G. and Naylor, C.D. (1996) 'Integrated delivery systems: Time to experiment in Canada?', *Journal of the American Society of CLU and CHFC*, September: 54–9.

Leeuw, E. (2006) 'Health promotion impact factor: join up, no translation', *Health Promotion International*, 21 (4): 257–8.

LeTourneau, B. and Fleischauer, A. (1999) 'What physicians want', *Healthcare Executive*, 14 (3): 10–15.

The Maclean's Health Reports (1999) Toronto, ON: Maclean Hunter Publishing Ltd.

Madsen, S. (2003) 'Wellness in the workplace: preparing employees for change', *Organization Development Journal*, 21 (1): 46–54.

Mason, S.A. (1998) 'Service reconfiguration: preparing for clinical integration', *Healthcare Executive*, 7/8: 13–16.

Maurx, J.C. (2004) 'The financial impact of worksite comprehensive health promotion disease prevention interventions on modifiable risk factors and absenteeism'. (UMI No. 3129652).

McIntyre, E., Pisaniello, D., Gun, R., Sanders, C. and Frith, D. (2002) 'Balancing breastfeeding and paid employment: a project targeting employees, women and workplaces', *Health Promotion International*, 17 (3): 215–22.

McKay L. (2000) *Health Beyond Healthcare: Twenty-Five Years of Federal Health Policy Development*. Ottawa, ON: Canadian Policy Research Networks.

McKeown T. (1979) *The Role of Medicine: Dream, Mirage or Nemesis?* Oxford, England: Basil Blackwell.

Mellor, G. and St. John, W. (2007) 'Occupational health nurses' perceptions of their current and future roles', *Journal of Advanced Nursing*, 58 (6): 585–93.

Milano, C. (2007) 'What ails workplace wellness programs?', *Risk Management*, 54 (6): 30–6.

Mittelmark, M. (2007) 'Shaping the future of health promotion: priorities for action', *Health Promotion International*, 23 (1): 98–102.

Marmot, M., Bosma, H., Hemingway, H., Brunner, E. and Stansfeld, S. (1997) 'Contribution of job control and other risk factors to social variations in coronary heart disease incidence', *The Lancet*, 350: 235–9.

Nickoloff, B. (1996) *Towards a Common Understanding: Clarifying the Core Concepts of Population Health: A Discussion Paper.* Ottawa, ON: Health Canada.

National Children's Alliance (1998) *Investing in Children and Youth: A National Children's Agenda*. Ottawa, Ontario, Canada: National Children's Alliance.

O'Reilly, N. (2008) 'The black report', *Occupational Health*, 60 (5): 22–4.

Pluye, P., Potvin, L., Denis, J.L. and Pelletier, J. (2004) 'Program sustainability: focus on organizational routines', *Health Promotion International*, 19 (4): 489–500.

Powell, M.J., Brock, D.M. and Hinings, C.R. (1999) 'The changing professional organization', in Brock, D., Powell, M. and Hinings, C.R. (eds), *Restructuring the Professional Organization: Accounting, Healthcare and Law*. New York: Routledge: 1–19.

Pratt, C.B. (2008) 'Crafting campaign themes (and slogans) for preventing overweight and obesity', *Public Relations Quarterly*, 52 (2): 2–8.

Registered Nurses Association of Ontario (2008) *Workplace Health, Safety and Well-being of the Nurse*. Toronto, ON: Registered Nurses Association of Ontario.

Riley, B., Edwards, N. and d'Avernas, J. (2008) 'People and Money Matter: Investment Lessons from the Ontario Heart Health Program', *Health Promotion International*, 23(1), pp. 24–34.

Romanow, R. (2002) *Building on Values: The Future of Healthcare in Canada*. Ottawa, Ontario, Canada: Commission on the Future of Healthcare in Canada.

Scott, W.R. and Backman, E.V. (1990) 'Institutional theory and the medical care sector', in Stephen M.S. and Associates (ed.), *Innovations in Healthcare Delivery: Insights for Organization Theory*. Oxford: Jossey-Bass: 20–52.

Statistics Canada (2001). *Tracking Tobacco Use Monitoring Survey (CTUMS)*. Ottawa, ON: Statistics Canada.

Wall, R. and Nicholas, I.D. (1985) 'Healthcare costs: getting to the heart of the problem', *Risk Management*, 32 (7): 20–3.

Weiner, B.J., Alexander, J.A. and Zuckerman, H.S. (2000) 'Strategies for effective management participation in community health partnerships', *Healthcare Management Review*, 25 (3): 48–66.

Wilkinson R.G. (1996) *Unhealthy Societies: The Afflictions of Inequality*. London: Routledge.

White, K. and Jacques, P. (2007) 'Combined diet and exercise intervention in the workplace', *AAOHN Journal*, 55 (3): 109–14.

Wolfe, R.A. and Parker, D.F. (1994) 'Employee health management: challenges and opportunities', *The Academy of Management Executive*, 8 (2): 22–31.

Name Index

Aarts, H. 154
Abbott, A. 227, 238, 298
Abrahamse, W. 42
Ackerman, P. 248
Ackroyd, S. 204
Acorn, S. 260
Adams, S. 301
Ahuvia, A. 248
Aiken, L. 274
Alam, K. 244
Alderfer, C. 247
Alimoglu, M. 276
Allahar, A. 82, 85
Allan 177
Amabile, T. 247, 261
Andorka, R. 23
Anisef, P. 77
Arneil, A. 272
Arnett, J. 77, 78, 79
Arthur, M. 101, 118
Ashford, S. 223, 236, 237
Ashkanasy, N. 243, 260, 261
Axelrod, P. 77

Backman, E. 298
Baehr, E. 276
Bailyn, L. 231, 233
Baker, C. 273
Bardwick, J. 81
Barg, J. 154
Baron, B. 242
Barratt, F. 101
Barratt, L. 271
Barsade, S. 246, 261
Barsky, A. 242
Bauman, Z. 3, 7, 19, 148
Baxter, D. 288, 297
Beaujot, R. 76, 78, 80, 83, 86, 90, 91, 92, 93
Beck-Gernsheim, E. 147, 149
Beck, I. 249
Beck, U. 6, 18, 147, 148, 149, 173
Becker, G. 35
Becker, H. 178
Bennett, A. 82
Berger, S. 207
Bergland, B. 273
Berry, L. 271
Betcheman, G. 80, 94
Bhawuk, D. 261
Binkley, S. 2, 7
Bitner, M. 271
Bittman, M. 33
Blomkvist, V. 273
Blunsdon, B. 2, 5, 6, 11, 178
Blyton, P. 1, 6, 11, 203, 207
Bockerman, P. 245
Bodur, M. 244
Boivin, D. 276
Bonney, N. 224
Bonss, W. 6, 149
Borg, I. 247, 249
Borghesi, S. 185
Borstorff, P. 127
Bourdieu, P. 19, 21, 155
Boyd, M. 75, 85
Branscombe, N. 242
Brisbois, R. 92
Briscoe, F. 227
Brohmann, B. 34
Broschak, J. 225, 226, 228, 236
Brown, B. 83
Brown, R. 246
Budgeon, S. 176
Busch-Vishniac, I. 273
Byrne, D. 242

Callan, S. 137, 225, 230, 232, 233
Camstra, R. 154
Cappelli, P. 81, 82
Caputo, R. 224
Casey, C. 102
Castleman, T. 10
Chan, T. 20, 21
Chang, D. 245
Charlesworth, S. 230

Chen, B. 41, 42
Chhokar, J. 244
Cho, S. 245
Chreim, S. 227
Christakis, N. 4
Christen, M. 245
Cialdini, R. 6, 154
Cianni, M. 224
Clark, L. 246
Clark, W. 85
Clarke, S. 274, 278
Clinebell, J. 225
Clinebell, S. 225
Cobble, D. 206
Cockburn, C. 101
Coile, R. 272
Coontz, S. 80, 88
Corwin, V. 11, 117, 137, 224, 228, 229, 232, 234, 236
Cote, J. 82, 85
Cousins, C. 224, 225
Craig-Lees, M. 180
Craig, T. 10
Crompton, R. 1
Cropanzano, R. 246, 258
Crowford, M. 260
Crowley, S. 276
Cucumel, G. 4, 10
Cully, M. 204

D'Amico, C. 91
Damon, W. 94
Daniel, W. 205
Dastmalchian, A. 11, 12, 207, 242, 244, 246
Devadason, R. 104
Davis 277
Davis-Blake, A. 228
de Chermont, K. 242
De Witte, H. 242
Deitz, D. 301
Denis, J. 296, 297
Denney, P. 258
Dent, M. 101, 102, 109
Deresky, H. 139
Devaney, M. 301
Devlin, A. 272
Dick, P. 137, 224, 226, 229, 230, 235, 236
Dijksterhuis, A. 154
Dillon, E. 271, 273
Dirnfeld, V. 288
Donavan, C. 5
Donmez, L. 276
Donovan, C. 147
Dowlatabadi, H. 42
Downey, A. 9, 12, 288, 299, 300, 301, 302
Driver, M. 81
Druumond, R. 247
Duchin, F. 33
Durkheim, E. 178
Duxbury, L. 91

Earnshaw, L. 243
Eastman, C. 276
Eaton, S. 231, 232
Ekman, E. 233, 234
Elder-Vass, D. 3, 4
Elizur, D. 247
Elizur, D. 249
Esping-Anderson, G. 76
Etzioni, J. 179, 180
Evans, G. 277
Evans, R. 289
Featherstone, M. 22

Feldman, D. 92, 224
Felstead, A. 225
Fevre, R. 202
Finch, J. 150, 169, 170
Fisher, C. 246, 261
Fleetwood, S. 224, 225, 226
Fogerty, M. 207
Fogg, L. 276
Foot, D. 75, 81, 92
Fowler, J. 4
Francis, H. 207
Fredrickson, B. 246
Freeman, R. 245
Friedman, T. 241
Frijters 196
Fujimori, K. 132
Fyke, K. 296

Gallie, D. 225
Ganzeboom, H. 21
Gardiner, J. 216

Garling, T. 277
Gatersleben, B. 41, 42
Gaudet, S. 76, 78, 82, 83, 87, 92, 95
Gayo-Cal, M. 19, 20
Gee, E. 92
Gelfand, M. 261
Genda 133
George, J. 242, 246
Gershuny, J. 34, 35, 39, 40, 60
Gerson, K. 33
Gerth, H. 100
Giddens, A. 5, 6, 7, 18, 22, 147, 148, 149, 151, 179
Gilmore, J. 269, 270
Glouberman, S. 289, 292, 295
Goldberg, S. 290, 291
Goldthorpe, J. 20, 21
Goss, R. 147, 150
Gossmann, H. 126, 127
Goulding, C. 6, 11, 181
Greening, L. 43
Greenwood, R. 298
Gribsy, M. 180
Groff, P. 290, 291
Gupta, V. 244

Haines, D. 299, 300
Hakim, C. 1, 214, 225, 258
Hamilton, C. 175, 180
Hamilton, K. 271, 272
Hamilton, K. 278
Hargis, K. 246
Harris, C. 202
Harris, D. 273, 277
Harris, F. 1
Hartig, T. 273, 277
Hattrup, K. 243
Haub, C. 90
Heaphy, B. 5, 147
Heery, E. 205
Heinzle, S. 34
Hendry, C. 225
Hennessey, B. 247
Herbig, P. 127
Hertzman, C. 292
Higgins, C. 91, 234, 235
Hill, C. 180
Hill, J. 234
Hill, K. 247
Hinings, C. 298
Hitt, M. 242
Hochschild, A. 224, 231, 233
Hofstede, G. 242
Hornsby, J. 260
Horton, R. 301
Hosokyoku, N. 127
House, R. 242, 261
Huberman, M. 183
Hudson, M. 207
Huelat 268, 269, 270
Huneke, M. 180
Hunt, R. 249
Hyde, R. 229, 235, 236, 242

Ilmakunnas, P. 245
Imer, P. 11, 246
Ironmonger, D. 24
Ito, K. 132
Ito, M. 130, 131
Iyer, C. 245

Jackson, T. 3, 4, 179
Jacobs, J. 33
Jacques, P. 301
Jalas, M. 43
James, F. 276
Javidan, M. 242, 244, 260
Jekeliuk, S. 83
Jenkins, D. 245
Jenkins, J. 6, 11, 203, 292
Jiang, S. 274
Jisho, K. 132
Joens, I. 243
Johnson, E. 231
Jones, L. 85
Joseph, A. 275, 276
Joye, Y. 277
Judy, R. 91

Kabasakal, H. 9, 11, 244, 246
Kahne, H. 224, 225, 226
Kahneman, D. 249
Kalbach, W. 90
Kallgren, C. 6, 154
Kamiya, S. 129, 138
Kanfer, R. 248
Kanno, E. 138
Kaplan, H. 77

Kaplan, S. 242
Kasser, T. 248
Kawakami 133
Keating, D. 292
Kegelmeyer, J. 242, 247
Kegler, M. 300
Kelaher, M. 4
Kenkyusho, T. 131
Kerfoot, D. 101
Kern, R. 20
Kerr, D. 76, 80, 83, 86, 90, 92, 93
Kersley, B. 204
Kihara, K. 140
Klein, H. 4
Kluckhohn, C. 242
Koole, S. 276
Korosawa, R. 12
Kossek, E. 226, 231, 232, 236, 299, 300
Kromhout, H. 274
Kumari, D. 274
Kuratko, D. 260
Kyale, S. 103

Lalonde, M. 289, 290
Lancaster, L. 79, 93
Landeweerd 271
Lane, N. 225
Larson, R. 79
Lash, S. 148
Lau, C. 6, 147, 148, 149, 173
Lausch, B. 203
Lawrence, T. 227, 228, 229, 232, 236, 237, 238
Leana, C. 81, 82
Lee, C. 276
Lee, M. 226, 232, 236
Leeuw, E. 300
Leppamaki, S. 276
Levine, M. 79, 92
Little, B. 83
Lobron, A. 92
Lonngvist, J. 275
Lopez, J. 3, 4, 6
Lopez-Tamayo 242, 245
Lovering, J. 207
Lowe, G. 81
Lozano, E. 126
Lutzenheiser, L. 33, 40, 41

McCrae, S. 1, 2
McEachern, S. 10
McGinnity, F. 225
McIntyre, E. 296, 297
McKay, L. 292
McKeown, T. 288, 290, 292
McManus, P. 225
McNeil, N. 5, 6, 11, 178
McVey, W. 90
Madsen, S. 299
Mail, E. 175
Maitlis, S. 237
Marberry, S. 272
Marmot, M. 292, 293
Mason, M. 233, 234
Mason, S. 298, 299
Maurx, J. 298, 299, 300
Meglino, B. 242
Mehrabian, A. 275
Mellor, G. 297
Meyer, D. 246
Midili, A. 242, 247
Milano, C. 299, 300
Miles, M. 183
Millar, J. 289, 292, 295
Mills, C. Wright 100
Minchington, W. 207
Mitchell, B. 75, 77, 79, 80, 81, 82, 85, 86, 87, 88, 94
Mitchell, T. 245
Mittelmark, M. 300
Moline, G. 258
Montagno, R. 260
Morisette, R. 91
Morrison, E. 93
Moses, B. 93
Mueller, K. 243
Munck, R. 206
Munday, M. 208
Murphy, J. 1
Murphy, S. 245
Mustard, F. 289, 292
Myles, J. 91

Nadeem, S. 225
Nardone, T. 224
Neumark, D. 83
Newholm, T. 180
Neyrinck, B. 242

Nickoloff, B. 290
Niemiec, C. 242
Noon, M. 203
Norris, D. 75, 85
North, S. 120

O'Brien, L. 268, 270
O'Connor, W. 183
Oliphant, M. 33, 42
O'Neil, D. 272
O'Neill, B. 41, 42
Orr, D. 278
Osawa, M. 126
Otake, T. 129
Owram, D. 85

Pahl, R. 5, 150, 151, 152, 160, 176
Parker, D. 271
Parkin, F. 100
Parsons, R. 273, 277
Partonen, T. 275
Patner, P. 260
Penner, L. 242, 247
Perlow, L. 232
Peterson, M. 247
Peterson, R. 19, 20
Pevalin, D. 5, 151, 176
Pfeffer, J. 277
Phizacklea, A. 211
Pine, I. 269, 270
Pinker, S. 234
Pluye, P. 300
Powell, M. 297
Pratt, C. 296, 297, 299, 301
Pringle, R. 101
Probert, B. 1
Procter, S. 204
Pudelko, M. 126
Putnam, R. 149, 150, 151, 173

Quintini, G. 84

Raboin, E. 278
Raudenbush, S. 4
Ravlin, E. 242
Reed, K. 2, 4, 6, 10, 11, 181
Reed, R. 10
Reidpath, D. 4
Reischauer, E. 127, 138, 140
Reno, R. 6
Reno, R. 154
Ricard, F. 78, 80
Rice, J. 33
Riley, B. 301
Ritchie, J. 183
Robbins, A. 78, 79
Roberts, K. 224
Robinson, J. 35
Rokeach, M. 242, 247
Rokeach, S. 247
Romanow, R. 296
Roseneil, S. 176
Rosenhan, D. 246
Rotchford, N. 224
Rousseau, D. 228
Royuela,V. 242, 245
Rusbult, C. 178
Russell, J. 275

Sadler, B. 272
Salazar, M. 78
Salmon, J. 205
Salovey, P. 246
Sampson, R. 4
Savage, M. 19
Schipper, L. 38, 39, 43
Schor, J. 7, 39
Schwartz, B. 93
Schwartz, S. 247, 249
Scott, J. 3, 4, 6
Scott, W. 298
Scully, M. 203
Shanahan, M. 79, 93
Sharp, D. 300
Shaw, D. 180
Sherman, S. 271
Simkus, A. 19, 20
Singelis, T. 261
Singhai, A. 126
Sloane, D. 274
Smedbold, H. 274
Smith, D. 207
Smith, P. 247
Soberman, D. 245
Soenens, B. 242
Spencer, L. 5, 150, 151, 152, 160, 176, 183
St. John, W. 297

Staw, B. 246, 261
Steers, R. 242
Steg, L. 41, 42
Steinke, C. 9, 12
Stern, P. 42
Stillman, D. 79, 93
Stoddard, A. 247
Stritof, B. 133
Stritof, S. 133
Sullivan, O. 34, 39, 40, 60
Sunter, D. 91
Surie, G. 244
Surinach 242, 245

Tacitos, T. 4
Tang, N. 224, 225
Tellegen, A. 246
Thomas, M. 91, 92
Thoresen, C. 242
Tighe, E. 247
Tilly, C. 224, 225
Tofle, R. 275
Topf, M. 271, 273
Trevor-Roberts, E. 243
Triandis, H. 261
Trunk, P. 94
Tseng, C. 276
Tsukuda, H. 126
Turnbull, P. 205
Twenge, J. 78, 79, 93

Ulrich, R. 271, 272, 273,
274, 275, 276, 277

Van den Berg, A. 276, 277
Van den Broeck, A. 242
Van der Wulp, N. 276
Van Dyne, L. 228,
229, 237
Van Echtelt, P. 137, 227, 228
Vansteenkiste, M. 242, 245,
247, 248, 261
Veblen, T. 19
Veenhoven, R. 249
Venne, R. 10, 81, 91, 92
Vercelli, A. 185

Subject Index

Absenteeism 9
Addiction 4 *see also* Habits
Adolescence 78–9
Agency versus structure debate 1
Australia 24–31, 181–3
Authorities 9–10 *see also* Knowledge, Expert

Baby boomers 81
Beliefs 4, 6
'Boomerang kids' 77
Burberry 202
  Plant/Factory closure 207–9, 214

Canada 24–31, 243–63, 267–84
  Health promotion 288–305
Career 101
  Choices 104
  Dual 115
  Patterns 81–2
  Professional 99, 102–3
CATI 155
Change
  Behavioural 175
  Circumstantial 6
  Economic 81
  Institutional 117–18
  Labour force participation 81
  Social 18–21
  Structural 4–6
  Taste 26–7
  Value 79
Childrearing 91
Children 52
Choice 1–3, 7–8, 10, 17
  Adaptive 6, 154
  Consumption 17–19
  Economic models 2
  and happiness 175
  Identity 7
  Individual 2, 9, 172 *see also* Individualisation
  Lifestyle *see* Lifestyle, Choice
  and lifestyle change 175–82
  Moral values 4
  Part-time working 225
  Rational choice theory *see* Rational choice theory
  Social relationships 178
  Unsustainable 4
  Utilitarian values 4
  Work–life 120–2 *see also* Work–life balance, model of
Church 9
Class 2 *see* also Social, Class
Climate change 33
  Policy 61
Clothing
  Manufacturing 203–16 *see also* Burberry
'Cluttered nest' 75 *see also* Youth, Living at home
Commitment 178
  Professional 103 *see also* Professional, Professionals
Commodification 4
Community 176
  Activities 167
  Change 209
  Configurations 164
  Geographic 9
  Imagined 7
  Personal *see* Personal communities
Constraints 7, 16
  Normative 2, 5
  Social 1
  Structural 2
Consumption
  Activities 25
  Cultural 18, 20 *see also* Cultural consumption
  Dual earner households 40 *see also* Household, dual working
  Energy 33–74
  Household 33–74

Consumption (*cont.*)
Macro level change 43
Mass 7
Over 7
Correspondence analysis 26–32
Credentialism 79, 82
Cultural consumption 18, 20
Culture 6
Class 19
Consumer 6–10
High 30–1
Highbrow 20
National 241–63
Organisation 277–8
Pop, popular 20–1
and work–life balance 120–41
see also Work–life balance, and culture

Data
Census 17, 76
Household Income and Labour Dynamics in Australia (HILDA) 33–74
Household level 45
Time use 17–31, 33–74
Decision making 5–11
Life-style choice 191
Demography
Of labour force supply 81
Downshifting 175–99 *see also* Lifestyle change

Economic capital 19
Education
Levels 84
Time in 85
and wages 83
Electricity
Expenditure 49 *see also* Consumption, Energy
'Emerging adulthood' 78
Employee
Affect 243
Turnover 9
Well-being 242, 267
Employees
Managerial 223–4
Professional 99–119, 223–40
see also, Professionals
Employment 33
Choices 2
Flexible 204
Lifetime 81
Mobility 82
Paid 165
Related travel 53
Environment
Global 9
Physical *see* Physical work environment
Social 4
Expenditure
Auto fuel 54
Electricity 52

Family 156–8
Arrangements 169
Blood 5, 9, 147, 149–50 *see also* 'Families of fate', nuclear family
Changing 150 *see also* Kinship networks
Chosen 147 *see also* Friends
'Families of fate' 149–50, 168–9
Geographic proximity 170
Impact on consumption 166
Importance of 168–9
Influence of 149, 164
Nuclear 5–6, 149–50
Occasions 159
Roles 170
Social support 160, 165–6
Traditions 159–60
Travel 158
Fertility
Decline 90
Patterns 90
Fitness 8
'Fledgling adults' 78 *see also* 'Emerging adulthood', Quarter life crisis
Frame analytic approach 183
France 24–31
Friends 147
Leisure 167 *see also* Time Use, Leisure
School 5

and work 211
Friendship 5, 17, 151–3, 160–1, 177
Careers 152
Mode 153
Nature of 151–2
Repertoires 152, 161
Trajectories 161
Types 152, 160–1, 171–2

Gender identity 2
Globalisation 6
Competitive pressure 137–8
Supply chains 207

Habits 4 *see also* Routines
Happiness 2
Choice 175
and health 185–6
and job performance 245
Search for 191
Health 9, 18
Inequalities 293
Job loss 212 *see also* Redundancy, Health
Legislative change to promote 297
Physical 4
Preventative approach 305
Promotion *see* Health promotion
Psychological 4
Healthcare 267–87
Health promotion 9, 288–309 *see also* Workplace Health Promotion (WHP)
and advertising 299
and cost savings 292
Determinants of health 289
Education 297
Implementation in organisations 300
Institutional 296–7
Lalonde Report 290
and lifestyle 290
Movement 292
National system 300
Policy 288–96
Population health approach 289
and professionals 297
Settings approach 292
and work organisations 288–302
Workplace *see* Workplace Health Promotion (WHP)
Holidays 163
Home
Returning 86 *see also* 'Boomerang generation'
Homeworking 41 *see also* Work, Flexible
Hospitals 268–87
Household
Couple 52
Dual working 34, 52
Energy demand 42–3
Income 49
One person 54
Single parent 50, 52
Human resource management
and health promotion 303
Issues 262, 267

'Idealised lifestyle' 181
Identity 7
Change 190
Construction 147–8
Formation 9
and part-time employment 231 *see also* Professional, Identity
Professional 112–13, 176, 235 *see also* Professionals, Professions
Seeking 8
Income 34, 60
Individual
Affect 246–7, 259, 262
Affect measure 249
Decision making 77
Individualisation 148–9, 172, 176 *see also* Post modernity
Individualism 18
Industrial campaign
Burberry 207–9
Community 212–14
Information
Dissemination 10
Institutions
Traditional 9, 18
Iran 243–63

Japan 120–44
  Cultural difference 138–9
  Divorce 134
  Economic change 125–6
  'Freeters' 130 *see* Work, Arrangements
  Gender roles 126–7, 138–9
  Government work–life initiatives 135–6
  Health and work 130–2 *see also* Work–life balance, Health
  HR Policies 128 *see also* Human resource management
  Job satisfaction/dissatisfaction 130 *see also*, Job, Satisfaction
  Labour productivity 138
  Male breadwinner model 138 *see also* Work, Male breadwinner model
  Marriage, changes in 127
  Meaning of work 139–40
  Population change 132–3
  Post WWII 123–4
  Social change 120–8
  Social problems 133
  Work ethic 127–8
  Work–family balance policy 129 *see also* Work–life balance
  Working hours 135 *see also* Work, Hours
  Work–life balance from 1990 124–30
Job
  Attitudes 243
  Growth 82
  Performance 242, 245
  Performance measure 249
  Plans 106
  Satisfaction 106, 130, 241, 245–6, 249
  Shopping 84
  Stress 107
  Turnover 84
Jobs
  Middle-management 81
  Temporary 85
  White collar 81, 99–119, 223–40
Job satisfaction–performance relationship 245–6, 252–7, 260–1
  Country differences 245, 252–8

Kinship networks 150 *see also* Family, Blood
Knowledge
  Expert 9
  Rational 9
  Scientific 6–8

Labour
  Domestic 36, 49
  Market 36, 49, 55, 66, 82, 204
Leisure 5, 36, 39
Life
  Choices 1–3
  Cycle 76
  Expectancy 75
  Meaning of 191
  Patterns of daily 1
  Satisfaction 116, 148, 180
  Situation 10
  Span 77–8
Lifecourse 31, 75, 77
  Change 75–98
  Home leaving 76
  Transition education to work 76
  Transition to adulthood 75
Lifestyle 2, 7, 22, 154–5, 164–8
  Balanced 9
  Brands 7
  Choice 1–4, 8, 179, 241, 298–300
  Configurations 6
  Construction 4
  Consumer 17
  Decision making 9
  Definitions of 2, 17–18, 20–1, 154
  Desirable 181 *see also* Lifestyle, Ideal
  Formation 10
  Goods 7
  Health promotion 290
  Household influence on 165
  Ideal 7
  Image 7
  Imagined 7
  Low consumption 179 *see also* Voluntary simplicity
  Outcomes 4
  Patterns 24–41
  Preferences 1–3
  Routines 17
  Self sufficient 189

Simplicity 176 *see also* Downshifting
Simplification 201
Space 19
Sustainable 9, 180, 189
Lifestyle change 6, 175–99
Health 185–6
Influences on 191
Life events 184
and life history 192–4
and personal networks 194–5
Process of 184
Radical 175
and risk 192
Stress 186
Longevity 8

Manufacturing supply chains 207
Marketing to youth 7
Marketisation 7–8 *see also* Culture, Consumer
Markets 9, 17
Marriage 85
Age of first 87
Japan 127 *see also* Japan, Marriage changes in
Mass production 7
Media 17
Modernity 10
Early 5, 148
Reflexive 6 *see also* Reflexive modernity
Motivation 245–8

Nation-state 6
National differences
Affect, satisfaction, performance 241–66
Lifestyle patterns 24–30
Time use 24–41
Neighbourhoods 167–8 *see also* Physical space
Neighbours 162–4
Geographic proximity 181
and lifestyle 167
Norms 4–8, 192
Organisational 241 *see also* Organisation, Values
Nurses 278–9
Shortage of 283

Occupations 20
Opportunities 16
Organisation 9–10
Culture 289
Health promotion *see* Health promotion, Workplace Health Promotion (WHP)
Healthy 9
Outcomes 10
Policies and practices 10 *see also* Human resource management
Values 241

Parents 165
Part-time work 209–11, 214–16, 223–40
and career 226
and caring 236
Job types 225
Local organization context 231
Meaning of 234
Stability/Instability 231
Work groups 228–30
Personal communities 4–6, 9, 182, 150–72, 176–7
Commitment to 177–8
Configurations 153
Development of 150–1
Family focused 172
Individual choice 151
Nature of 168–72
and routines 155
and technology 151
Types 168
Personal networks 177
see also Personal communities
Personal relationships 149 *see also* Personal communities, Personal networks
Physical space 167–8
Physical work environment
Attributes of 267, 271–8
Health care 268–84
Measure of 279–80
and well being 267–87
Policy
and demographic change 106
Family friendly 91, 120, 225
Health promotion 288–305
Organisational 230–1, 262

Population
  Aging 90
  Health 292–3
  Patterns 90
'Post industrial' age 80
Post modernity 148–9
'Post traditional' society 6, 153
Post World War II 20, 76
  'Cult of marriage' 85
  Prosperity 80 *see also* Change, Economic; Social
Power 5
  Social 19
Preference theory 1–2, 225 *see also* Part-time work
Production
  Over 7
Professional
  Collegiality 107
  Commitment to 116–17
  Confidence 113
  Identity 112–13, 231, 235
  Privilege 102
  Recognition 109
  Responsibility 117
  Status 102
Professionals
  Early career 99–119
  Factors for success 110–12
  Gender differences 118
  and life choices 99
  Part-time work 223–38 *see also* Part-time work
  'Reluctant' 105
  As 'strategic' 104
  Young 100 *see also* University graduates
Professions
  As community 100
  'Family friendly' 233
  and gender 100, 110
  Growth in 101

Quarter life Crisis 79

Rational choice theory 181
Rationalisation 4
  Of knowledge 8–9
Redundancy
  Community involvement 212
  Friends 212
  Health 212
  Life after 202–19
  Redundancy Payments Act 205
  Risk of 203–7
  Social networks 212
Reflexive modernity 6, 11
Reflexivity 18 *see also* 'Post traditional' society
Relationships
  Diffuse 178
  Maintenance of 160
  Social 178
Religious affiliation 2
Resources 178
  Economic 8
Roles
  Gender 5
  Management 108

Satisfaction
  Life 180
Smoking 8
Social
  Change 5, 18–21
  Class 19
  Constraints 1–2
  Differentiation 19
  Groups 5
  Landscape 6
  Life 6
  Location 19
  Networks 4–5 *see also* Personal communities, Personal networks
  Norms *see* Norms
  Position 20 *see also* Class
  Rules 8
  Status 19 *see also* Social, Class; Position
  Stratification 18 *see* Social, Class; Position; Status
  Structure 21
  Support 165–6
Socialisation 4 *see also* Norms and Social, Norms
Society
  Aging 132–3 *see also* Population, Aging

Differences 17
Post modern 19 *see also* Post modernity
Post traditional 147–8 *see also* 'Post traditional' society
Stress 186–7
Management 9
Structural change 4–6
Structure 3–6
Class 18
Embodied 3–4, 6
Institutional 5–9
Normative 5
Relational 4, 6
Social 4
Traditional 7

Taste 19–22
Change in 20 *see also* Change, Taste
Time 22
Discretionary 5 *see also* Leisure
Pressure117 *see also* Work–family balance
Spent at work 33 *see also* Work time
Time Use 17–31, 33–74
Activities 36
and age differences 31
Australia 24–31
Canada 24–31
Constraints 35
Country differences in 17–32
Data 22–5
and energy consumption 333–74
France 24–31
Gender differences 37
Household activities 33
Leisure 167
and physical space 35
and socio demographic differences 42
U.K. 24–31
Transition
Demographic 90
Economic prosperity 80
Education to work 79
Individualised 88
Turkey 243–63

U.K. 24–31, 175, 203–16
National Minimum Wage (NMW) 211
University graduates 100

Values 4, 6, 241, 247–8
Cultural 243
and job satisfaction 261
Voluntary simplicity 179
Downshifters 179 *see also* Downshifting
Holistic simplifiers 180

Wales
South industrial district 207–8
Ways of living
Desired *see* Lifestyle
Welfare
Regimes 6
Work
Arrangements 130, 209–11, 223–40
Commitment 9, 188
Dissatisfaction with 188–9
Experience of 9, 267
Flexible 225, 232
Home 52
Hours 104, 120
Male breadwinner model 6, 138
Management 223–4
Meaning of 139–40, 234
Practices 230
Self-employed 53 *see also* Employment, type
Values 241, 248 *see also* Values
Values measure 250
Workers
Female 209
Low income 202–3
Redundant *see* Redundancy
Workforce
Women's participation 2
Working hours 2, 39–40, 227–8
and consumption patterns 35–51
Energy use 39–41

Work–life balance 9, 113–15, 118, 202
  and culture 120–41
  Health 130–2
  Healthy society 130
  Japan 120–41 *see also* Japan
  Long working hours 187–8 *see also* Time, Spent at work, Working hours
  Model of 122
  and part-time work 214–16 *see also* Part-time work
  Professionals 232–3 *see also* Professionals
Workplace
  Design 10, 267–87 *see also* Physical work environment
  Influence 9
  Wellness 9, 300
Workplace Health Promotion (WHP) 288–305
  Motivation for 304

Youth 75–98
  Expansion of 77
  Living at home 86
  Vulnerable 83